First World War
and Army of Occupation
War Diary
France, Belgium and Germany

17 DIVISION
52 Infantry Brigade
Queen's Own (Royal West Kent Regiment)
3/4th Battalion
31 May 1917 - 28 February 1918

WO95/2013/2

The Naval & Military Press Ltd
www.nmarchive.com
Published in association with The National Archives

Published by

The Naval & Military Press Ltd

Unit 10 Ridgewood Industrial Park,

Uckfield, East Sussex,

TN22 5QE England

Tel: +44 (0) 1825 749494

www.naval-military-press.com

www.nmarchive.com

This diary has been reprinted in facsimile from the original. Any imperfections are inevitably reproduced and the quality may fall short of modern type and cartographic standards.

© **Crown Copyright**
Images reproduced by permission of The National Archives, London, England, 2015.

Contents

Document type	Place/Title	Date From	Date To
Heading	WO95/2013/2		
Heading	17th Division 52nd Infy Bde 3-4th Roy. West Kent Regt June 1917-Feb 1918		
Miscellaneous	Colonel i/c No. 2 Record Office.	04/05/1918	04/05/1918
War Diary	Canterbury	31/05/1917	31/05/1917
War Diary	Southampton	31/05/1917	31/05/1917
War Diary	Havre	01/06/1917	02/06/1917
War Diary	Hesdin	03/06/1917	31/07/1917
Miscellaneous	A		
Operation(al) Order(s)	51st. Infantry Brigade Operation Order No. 172	08/07/1916	08/07/1916
Diagram etc			
Miscellaneous	Sheet I "D" Work Report W 9		
Miscellaneous	Sheet I Work Report W 8		
Miscellaneous	Sheet I Work Report W 10	13/07/1917	13/07/1917
Miscellaneous	Sheet I Work Report W 11	14/07/1917	14/07/1917
Miscellaneous	Sheet I Work Report W 12	15/07/1917	15/07/1917
Miscellaneous	Sheet I Work Report W 13	16/07/1917	16/07/1917
Miscellaneous	Sheet I Work Report W 14	17/07/1917	17/07/1917
Miscellaneous	Sheet I Work Report W 15	18/07/1917	18/07/1917
Miscellaneous	Sheet I Work Report W 16	19/07/1917	19/07/1917
Miscellaneous	Sheet I Work Report W 17	20/07/1917	20/07/1917
Miscellaneous	Sheet I Work Report W 19	22/07/1917	22/07/1917
Miscellaneous	Sheet I Work Report W 20	23/07/1917	23/07/1917
Miscellaneous	Sheet I Work Report W 22	24/07/1917	24/07/1917
Miscellaneous	Sheet I Work Report W 23	24/07/1917	24/07/1917
Miscellaneous	Sheet I Work Report W 24	26/07/1917	26/07/1917
Miscellaneous	Sheet I Work Report KF 1	27/07/1917	27/07/1917
Miscellaneous	Sheet I Work Report KF 2	28/07/1917	28/07/1917
Miscellaneous	Sheet I Work Report WM 10	29/07/1917	29/07/1917
Map			
Operation(al) Order(s)	17th. Divisional Order No. 179	28/07/1917	28/07/1917
Operation(al) Order(s)	17th. Divisional Order No.182	31/07/1917	31/07/1917
War Diary		01/08/1917	08/08/1917
War Diary	H.11a 62	09/08/1917	31/08/1917
Operation(al) Order(s)	52nd Infantry Brigade Order No. 176	01/08/1917	01/08/1917
Operation(al) Order(s)	17th. Divisional Order No 183	01/08/1917	01/08/1917
Operation(al) Order(s)	3/4 R. West Kent Regt Order No 1	02/08/1917	02/08/1917
Miscellaneous			
Operation(al) Order(s)	3/4 R. West Kent Order No 3	12/08/1917	12/08/1917
Operation(al) Order(s)	3/4th. Battn. Royal West Kent Regiment. Operation Order No 2	08/08/1917	08/08/1917
Operation(al) Order(s)	52nd Infantry Brigade Order No. 176	08/08/1917	08/08/1917
Miscellaneous	March Table Issued With O.O.176		
Miscellaneous	Lancashire Fusiliers.	06/08/1917	06/08/1917
Map			
Map	Greenland Hill & Chemigal Works Sectors		
Operation(al) Order(s)	52nd Infantry Brigade Order No. 179	11/08/1917	11/08/1917
Operation(al) Order(s)	52nd Infantry Brigade Order No. 181	16/08/1917	16/08/1917
Miscellaneous			
Operation(al) Order(s)	52nd Infantry Brigade Order No. 182	19/08/1917	19/08/1917

Miscellaneous	Lancashire Fusiliers.	20/08/1917	20/08/1917
Operation(al) Order(s)	52nd Infantry Brigade Order No. 184	22/08/1917	22/08/1917
Miscellaneous			
Miscellaneous	3/4th R West Kent Order No	24/08/1917	24/08/1917
War Diary	St. Nicholas	01/09/1917	01/09/1917
War Diary	H.11.b.6.8.	05/09/1917	05/09/1917
War Diary	H.12.b.1.9.	09/09/1917	25/09/1917
War Diary	Wanquetin	26/09/1917	28/09/1917
War Diary	Lucheux	30/09/1917	30/09/1917
Miscellaneous			
Operation(al) Order(s)	3/4th. Battn. Royal West Kent Regt. Operation Order No. 6.	01/09/1917	01/09/1917
Operation(al) Order(s)	52nd Infantry Brigade Order No. 185	31/08/1917	31/08/1917
Miscellaneous	March Table Issued With O.O. 185		
Miscellaneous			
Operation(al) Order(s)	52nd Infantry Brigade Order No. 187	04/09/1917	04/09/1917
Miscellaneous			
Operation(al) Order(s)	3/4 R. West Kent Regt. Order No 9	11/09/1917	11/09/1917
Operation(al) Order(s)	52nd Infantry Brigade Order No. 189	10/09/1917	10/09/1917
Operation(al) Order(s)	52nd Infantry Brigade Order No. 190	11/09/1917	11/09/1917
Miscellaneous			
Operation(al) Order(s)	52nd Infantry Brigade Order No. 191	13/09/1917	13/09/1917
Miscellaneous			
Operation(al) Order(s)	52nd Infantry Brigade Order No. 193	19/09/1917	19/09/1917
Miscellaneous	Table Of Moves Issued With O.O. 193		
Operation(al) Order(s)	3/4 R.W. Kent Regt. Order No 11	17/09/1917	17/09/1917
Miscellaneous			
Miscellaneous	Lancashire Fusiliers.	20/09/1917	20/09/1917
Operation(al) Order(s)	52nd Infantry Brigade Order No. 196	21/09/1917	21/09/1917
Miscellaneous	March Table to Accompany Brigade Order No. 196.		
Miscellaneous	Warning Order.		
Miscellaneous	Reference Administrative Instructions No. 17	21/09/1917	21/09/1917
Miscellaneous			
Operation(al) Order(s)	52nd Infantry Brigade Order No. 197	25/09/1917	25/09/1917
Miscellaneous	March Table to Accompany Brigade Order No. 197.		
Operation(al) Order(s)	3/4 Royal Went Kent Regt. March Order No 1.		
Miscellaneous		22/09/1917	22/09/1917
Heading	War Diary of 3/4th Bn. Royal West Kent October 1917 Vol 4		
Heading	War Diary of A? Section July September October December 1919, January & February 1920		
War Diary	Lucheux	01/10/1917	05/10/1917
War Diary	Proven	10/10/1917	10/10/1917
War Diary	Dublin Camp	14/10/1917	14/10/1917
War Diary	Parroy Camp	16/10/1917	26/10/1917
War Diary	Dragon Camp	27/10/1917	28/10/1917
War Diary	La Panne	31/10/1917	31/10/1917
Miscellaneous			
Miscellaneous	Entraining		
Miscellaneous	Administrative Instructions No.19	01/10/1917	01/10/1917
Miscellaneous	3/4th Battn. Royal West Kent Regiment.	01/10/1917	01/10/1917
Miscellaneous	Move To Proven Area.	02/10/1917	02/10/1917
Miscellaneous	Entraining Table 52nd Infantry Brigade.		
Miscellaneous	Distribution.		
Miscellaneous	Administrative Instructions.	01/10/1917	01/10/1917
Miscellaneous	Strategical Move Of 17th Division	01/10/1917	01/10/1917

Type	Description	Date From	Date To
Miscellaneous	17th Division (Less Artillery).		
Miscellaneous	Lan. Fus.	02/10/1917	02/10/1917
Miscellaneous	Move of 17th Div. Deport Battalion to Fifth Army.	01/10/1917	01/10/1917
Miscellaneous	Lan. Fus.	02/10/1917	02/10/1917
Miscellaneous			
Operation(al) Order(s)	3/4th. Battn. Royal West Kent Regiment. March Orders No. 2	03/10/1917	03/10/1917
Miscellaneous			
Operation(al) Order(s)	3/4th. Battn. Royal West Kent Regiment. March Order No. 3	09/10/1917	09/10/1917
Miscellaneous	Reference Table "B" issued with O.O. 198	09/10/1917	09/10/1917
Miscellaneous	Administrative Instructions No.22	09/09/1917	09/09/1917
Miscellaneous	Lan. Fus.	12/10/1917	12/10/1917
Operation(al) Order(s)	52nd Infantry Brigade Order No. 198	09/10/1917	09/10/1917
Miscellaneous	March Table "A" issued with O.O. No. 198		
Miscellaneous	Administrative Instructions. No.30	08/10/1917	08/10/1917
Miscellaneous	Administrative Instructions No.21		
Miscellaneous	Administrative Instructions No.20	08/10/1917	08/10/1917
Miscellaneous	Table A.		
Miscellaneous			
Operation(al) Order(s)	3/4th. Battn. Royal West Kent Regiment. Warning Order No. 3		
Operation(al) Order(s)	3/4th Battn. Royal West Kent Regt. March Orders No. 4	14/10/1917	14/10/1917
Miscellaneous	March Table.		
Operation(al) Order(s)	52nd Infantry Brigade Order No. 200	13/10/1917	13/10/1917
Miscellaneous	March Table To Accompany 52nd Infantry Brigade Order No. 200.		
Operation(al) Order(s)	52nd Infantry Brigade Order No. 199	11/10/1917	11/10/1917
Operation(al) Order(s)	52nd Infantry Brigade Order No. 201	14/10/1917	14/10/1917
Miscellaneous	Table Of Reliefs.		
Miscellaneous	Administrative Instructions No.25	13/10/1917	13/10/1917
Miscellaneous	Administrative Instructions. No. 42	14/10/1917	14/10/1917
Miscellaneous	Administrative Instructions. No. 41	12/10/1917	12/10/1917
Miscellaneous	Administrative Instructions. No. 25	15/10/1917	15/10/1917
Map			
Miscellaneous	Belgium 20 S.W. Scale 1/20,000		
Miscellaneous	C Form (Quadruplicate). Massages And Signals.		
Miscellaneous			
Operation(al) Order(s)	3/4th. Battn. Royal West Kent Regiment. March Order No. 5	26/10/1917	26/10/1917
Miscellaneous			
Miscellaneous	O.C. 173rd Tunnelling Coy, R.E.	19/10/1917	19/10/1917
Miscellaneous	O.C. 173rd Tunnelling Coy.	19/10/1917	19/10/1917
Heading	War Diary 3/4 Royal West Kents November 1917 Vol 6		
Heading	War Diary of 3/4 Royal West Kent Regt November 1st 1917 To November 30th 1917		
War Diary	La Panne	01/11/1917	06/11/1917
War Diary	Soult Camp	07/11/1917	07/11/1917
War Diary	Marsouin Camp	09/11/1917	09/11/1917
War Diary	Louis Farm U 24.C. 50.95	11/11/1917	11/11/1917
War Diary	Huddleston Camp	13/11/1917	13/11/1917
War Diary	Dublin Camp	19/11/1917	19/11/1917
War Diary	Bridge Camp	25/11/1917	25/11/1917
War Diary	Beacefm	25/11/1917	27/11/1917
War Diary	Recquete Fm	27/11/1917	27/11/1917
War Diary	Louis Fm	28/11/1917	28/11/1917

Type	Description	Date From	Date To
War Diary	Double Cotts	30/11/1917	30/11/1917
Miscellaneous	Lan. Fus.	03/11/1917	03/11/1917
Operation(al) Order(s)	52nd Infantry Brigade O.O. No. 202.	05/11/1917	05/11/1917
Miscellaneous	Table "A"		
Miscellaneous	Table "B"		
Operation(al) Order(s)	3/4th. Battn. Royal West Kent Regiment. March Orders No. 6	05/11/1917	05/11/1917
Miscellaneous	Train Time Table.		
Miscellaneous	3/4th. Battn. Royal. West Kent Regiment. Administrative Instructions No. 4	05/11/1917	05/11/1917
Miscellaneous			
Miscellaneous	A Form. Messages And Signals.		
Miscellaneous	March Table.		
Miscellaneous			
Miscellaneous	A Form. Messages And Signals.	08/11/1917	08/11/1917
Miscellaneous	A Form. Messages And Signals.		
Miscellaneous			
Operation(al) Order(s)	3/4 R West Kent Rgt Order No XI	09/11/1917	09/11/1917
Miscellaneous	Lancs Fus	11/11/1917	11/11/1917
Operation(al) Order(s)	3/4 R West Kent Order No X2	11/11/1917	11/11/1917
Miscellaneous			
Operation(al) Order(s)	3/4 Royal West Kent Regt Order No X3	12/11/1917	12/11/1917
Operation(al) Order(s)	52nd Infantry Brigade O.O. No. 202	12/11/1917	12/11/1917
Miscellaneous	Reference 52nd Inf. Bde. Order No. 202	12/11/1917	12/11/1917
Miscellaneous	Table "C" issued with O.O. No. 202.		
Miscellaneous	Table "A"		
Miscellaneous			
Operation(al) Order(s)	52nd Infantry Brigade O.O. No. 204	18/09/1917	18/09/1917
Map			
Miscellaneous	March Table Issued With O.O. 204		
Operation(al) Order(s)	3/4th Battn. Royal West Kent Regiment. March Order No. 7	18/11/1917	18/11/1917
Miscellaneous			
Miscellaneous	3/4th Battn. Royal West Kent Regiment.	24/11/1917	24/11/1917
Operation(al) Order(s)	3/4th. Battn. Royal West Kent Regiment. Operation Order, No. 9	24/11/1917	24/11/1917
Operation(al) Order(s)	52nd Infantry Brigade O.O. No. 205	23/11/1917	23/11/1917
Miscellaneous	Table "A" (First Stage).		
Miscellaneous	Table "B" (Second Stage).		
Miscellaneous			
Miscellaneous		27/11/1917	27/11/1917
Operation(al) Order(s)	3/4 Bn West Kent Regt Order No 10	28/01/1917	28/01/1917
Operation(al) Order(s)	52nd Infantry Brigade Order No 206	27/11/1917	27/11/1917
Miscellaneous	Relief Table Attached To Brigade Order No 206		
Miscellaneous	A Form. Messages And Signals.		
Miscellaneous	3/4th. Battn. Royal West Kent Regiment.	22/11/1917	22/11/1917
Heading	War Diary of 3/4 Bn. Royal West Kent Regt From 1st December 1917 To 31st December 1917 Vol 7		
War Diary	Double Cotts	01/12/1917	01/12/1917
War Diary	Dublin Camp	05/12/1917	05/12/1917
War Diary	Paddington Camp	08/12/1917	08/12/1917
War Diary	La Panne	12/12/1917	12/12/1917
War Diary	Moulle	14/12/1917	14/12/1917
War Diary	Achiet Le Petit	16/12/1917	16/12/1917
War Diary	Rocquigny	21/12/1917	21/12/1917
War Diary	SW British Front Line	22/12/1917	23/12/1917

Type	Description	Date From	Date To
War Diary	Flesyvieres	27/12/1917	27/12/1917
War Diary	Bertincourt	30/12/1917	30/12/1917
War Diary	K15d 9.1	31/12/1917	31/12/1917
Miscellaneous	A Form Messages And Signals.		
Operation(al) Order(s)	3/4 Bn. Royal West Kent Regt Order No. 11	30/11/1917	30/11/1917
Operation(al) Order(s)	3/4 Bn. Royal West Kent Regt Order No. 16	27/12/1917	27/12/1917
Operation(al) Order(s)	52nd Infantry Brigade O.O. No. 207	30/11/1917	30/11/1917
Miscellaneous	Table issued with 52nd Infantry Brigade O.O. No. 207.		
Miscellaneous	A Form. Messages And Signals.		
Miscellaneous	Administrative Instructions No. 39	20/11/1917	20/11/1917
Miscellaneous	Supply Officer. Q.M. Lan. Fus.	28/11/1917	28/11/1917
Miscellaneous	Brigade Major.	03/12/1917	03/12/1917
Operation(al) Order(s)	52nd Infantry Brigade Order No. 208	04/12/1917	04/12/1917
Miscellaneous	Table "B" to Accompany 52nd Infantry Brigade Order No. 208		
Miscellaneous	Table "A" to Accompany 52nd Infantry Brigade Order No. 208		
Operation(al) Order(s)	3/4th. Battn Royal West Kent Regiment Order No. 12		
Miscellaneous	C Form. Messages And Signals.		
Miscellaneous	Administrative Instructions No. 41		
Miscellaneous	Table A.		
Miscellaneous	Table A. (2).		
Miscellaneous			
Miscellaneous	Table B-Transport March Table.		
Miscellaneous	C Form. Messages And Signals.		
Miscellaneous	Administrative Instructions. No. 47		
Miscellaneous	Langemark Areas. Appendix "A"		
Operation(al) Order(s)	52nd Infantry Brigade O.O. No. 209	06/12/1917	06/12/1917
Miscellaneous	Corrigenda To Administrative Instructions No. 41	07/12/1917	07/12/1917
Operation(al) Order(s)	3/4th. Battn. Royal West Kent Regiment. Order No. 13		
Miscellaneous	Move Of Divisional H.Q. 51st & 52nd Brigades By Rail.	06/12/1917	06/12/1917
Miscellaneous	Supply Arrangements. 50th Brigade. Rations For Consumption 8th		
Operation(al) Order(s)	52nd Infantry Brigade Order No. 210	10/12/1917	10/12/1917
Miscellaneous			
Miscellaneous	March Table to Accompany B.O. 210		
Miscellaneous	A Form. Messages And Signals.		
Miscellaneous	Administrative Instructions No. 48	09/12/1917	09/12/1917
Miscellaneous	Administrative Instructions No. 42	10/12/1917	10/12/1917
Operation(al) Order(s)	3/4th. Battn. Royal West Kent Regiment. Orders No. 14	11/12/1917	11/12/1917
Miscellaneous	H.Q. 52nd Infantry Bde. 52 G 4423		
Miscellaneous	Lancashire Fusiliers.	12/12/1917	12/12/1917
Miscellaneous		13/12/1917	13/12/1917
Miscellaneous	Move Of 17th Division (less Artillery)	13/12/1917	13/12/1917
Miscellaneous	Move Of 17th Division (Less Artillery)		
Miscellaneous	Administrative Instructions No 43	12/12/1917	12/12/1917
Miscellaneous	Table "A"	12/12/1917	12/12/1917
Operation(al) Order(s)	52nd Infantry Brigade O.O. No. 211.	12/12/1917	12/12/1917
Miscellaneous	March Table issued With B.O.I.O.211		
Miscellaneous	Administrative Instructions No 49	11/12/1917	11/12/1917
Miscellaneous	Administrative Instructions, No. 49	12/12/1917	12/12/1917
Operation(al) Order(s)	3/4th Battn. Royal West Kent Regiment. March Order No. 15	13/12/1917	13/12/1917
Miscellaneous	C Form. Messages And Signals.		
Miscellaneous	Administrative Instructions.	15/12/1917	15/12/1917

Operation(al) Order(s)	52nd Infantry Brigade O.O. No. 212	15/12/1917	15/12/1917
Miscellaneous	March Table issued with Order No. 212.		
Miscellaneous	A Form. Messages And Signals.		
Miscellaneous	Administrative Instructions No 46	20/12/1917	20/12/1917
Operation(al) Order(s)	52nd Infantry Brigade O.O. No. 213	20/12/1917	20/12/1917
Miscellaneous	March Table issued with O.O. No. 213		
Miscellaneous	Administrative Instructions No. 46	20/12/1917	20/12/1917
Miscellaneous	Administrative Instructions No. 45		
Miscellaneous	Table A.	20/12/1917	20/12/1917
Miscellaneous	Warning Order.	22/12/1917	22/12/1917
Operation(al) Order(s)	52nd Infantry Brigade O.O. No. 214	21/12/1917	21/12/1917
Miscellaneous	Movement Table issued with O.O. No. 214		
Operation(al) Order(s)	3/4th. Battn. Royal West Kent Regiment. Order No 18.	30/12/1917	30/12/1917
Heading	War Diary January-1918. 46th. Brigade R.F.A. Volume XXXIII. 47th. Brigade R.F.A. Volume XXXIII. 14th Div'l. Ammun. Column. Volume XXXIII. X/14, Y/14, Z/14 & V/14 Trench Mortar Batteries.		
Heading	3/4 R W Kent Rgt Vol 8 Jan 1918		
War Diary		03/01/1918	03/01/1918
War Diary	Graincourt	04/01/1918	20/01/1918
War Diary	NE of Hermies	23/01/1918	26/01/1918
Miscellaneous	Spoil Head J 35 D.	27/01/1918	28/01/1918
War Diary	Phipps Camp	31/01/1918	01/02/1918
Miscellaneous	Orders A		
Operation(al) Order(s)	3/4 Bn. Royal West Kent Regt Order No. 18	04/01/1918	04/01/1918
Miscellaneous			
Operation(al) Order(s)	52nd Infantry Brigade O.O. No.217	02/01/1918	02/01/1918
Miscellaneous			
Miscellaneous	Orders B		
Operation(al) Order(s)	3/4 Royal West Kent Regt Operation Order No. 19	07/01/1918	07/01/1918
Miscellaneous	C Form. Messages And Signals.		
Operation(al) Order(s)	52nd Infantry Brigade O.O. No. 218	07/01/1918	07/01/1918
Miscellaneous			
Miscellaneous	Orders C		
Operation(al) Order(s)	3/4 Royal West Kent Regt Operation Order No. 20	13/01/1919	13/01/1919
Operation(al) Order(s)	52nd Infantry Brigade O.O. No. 220	11/01/1918	11/01/1918
Miscellaneous	March Table issued with 52nd Infantry Brigade O.O. No. 220	11/01/1918	11/01/1918
Miscellaneous	Annexe to 17 Div, Summary No. 20		
Miscellaneous	Annexe To V Corps Summary Of Intelligence		
Miscellaneous	Orders D		
Operation(al) Order(s)	3/4th. Battn. Royal West Kent Regiment. Operation Orders 21	18/01/1918	18/01/1918
Miscellaneous	Orders E		
Operation(al) Order(s)	52nd Infantry Brigade O.O. No. 221	17/01/1918	17/01/1918
Miscellaneous	Movement Table issued with O.O. No. 221		
Operation(al) Order(s)	3/4 Royal West Kent Regt Operation Order No 22	23/01/1918	23/01/1918
Operation(al) Order(s)	52nd Infantry Brigade O.O. No. 222	22/01/1918	22/01/1918
Miscellaneous			
Miscellaneous	Orders F		
Operation(al) Order(s)	Operation Order 23	27/01/1918	27/01/1918
Operation(al) Order(s)	3/4 R.W. Kent Rgt O.O. No. 23		
Operation(al) Order(s)	52nd Infantry Brigade O.O. 223	26/01/1918	26/01/1918
Miscellaneous			
Miscellaneous	Orders G		
Operation(al) Order(s)	3/4 Royal West Kent Regt Operation Orders 24	30/01/1918	30/01/1918

Miscellaneous	Amendment to O.O. No 24	31/01/1918	31/01/1918
Miscellaneous	C Form. Messages And Signals.		
Operation(al) Order(s)	52nd Infantry Brigade Order No. 22	30/01/1918	30/01/1918
Miscellaneous	Table issued with 52nd Infantry Brigade Order No. 224.		
Heading	War Diary of 3/4th Bn. Royal West Kent Regt From 1st February to 28th February Vol 9		
War Diary	Phipps Camp	01/02/1918	10/02/1918
War Diary	Velu Wood	11/02/1918	28/02/1918
Operation(al) Order(s)	3/4th. Battn. Royal West Kent Regiment. Order No. 25.	04/02/1918	04/02/1918
Operation(al) Order(s)	3/4th. Battn. Royal West Kent Regiment. Order No. 26.	05/02/1918	05/02/1918
Operation(al) Order(s)	3/4th. Battn. Royal West Kent Regiment. Order No. 27.	09/02/1918	09/02/1918
Miscellaneous	The Officer Commanding 3/4th. Royal West Kents.	03/02/1918	03/02/1918

WO 2013/2

17TH DIVISION
52ND INFY BDE

3-4TH ROY. WEST KENT REGT
JUNE ~~DEC~~ 1917 - FEB 1918

FROM UK

DISBANDED

R.W.K. 3172/2

From: Colonel i/c No. 2 Record Office,
Staines Road, Hounslow.

To: Committee of Imperial Defence,
(Historical Section),
Military Branch,
m
Public Record Office, Chancery Lane. W.C. 11

Hounslow.
4-9-18.

The accompanying War Diary of the 3/4th Bn. Royal West Kent
Regiment is returned, with many thanks, the desired copy having now
been made.

Major for Lt-Colonel.
i/c Records.

WAR DIARY

Army Form C. 2118.

Transferred to 52 Bn 20.7.17

3/4th Bn. Queen's Regt.

Hour, Date, Place		Summary of Events and Information	Remarks and references to Appendices
1.15 am	31/5/17 CANTERBURY	1st (Railway) echelon for SOUTHAMPTON: includes whole Battalion with 17	Commanding Officer Lt Col A.E.T Simpson was with 1st
3.00 am	"	2nd "	Hospital ship to Havre Seaport	with 2nd
7.00 am	"	1st echelon } arrive SOUTHAMPTON DOCKS	with 3rd
8.40 am	"	2nd " }	
6.00 pm	" SOUTHAMPTON	Battalion embarks mainly for FRANCE - strength 34 officers 962 other ranks	
7.45 am	1/6/17 HAVRE	Battalion land at HAVRE & marches to No 1 B. Rest Camp.	
1.10 pm	2/6/17 HAVRE	Battalion entrains strength 34 officers 967 other ranks. O.R Sgt. to D.A.G 3rd Echelon	
12.15 pm	3/6/17 HESDIN	Battalion detrains at HESDIN & marches to WAMIN & billets	
	4/6/17 HESDIN	time	
	5/6/17 HESDIN	3 to Hospital	
		4 ASC duty incurred	
10 am	6/6/17 HESDIN	Battalion now transferred to home with 2/4 R W Surrey Regt to form 1st H.J. Bat. 13 Aug transferred to St Pol	
		Buisans which is reached at 2 pm: Battalion proceeds by march	
		route to Y Huts EtRUN. Lt Col Simpson takes command of the Battalion together with 3/4 R W Surrey Regt & 3/10 Middlesex	
		Regt Command of Battalion devolves on Major A.E. Jones	

Forms/C. 2118/11.

WAR DIARY
or
INTELLIGENCE SUMMARY

(Erase heading not required.)

Army Form C. 2118.

Hour, Date, Place	Summary of Events and Information	Remarks and references to Appendices
7.30 p.m. 6/6/17	Transport move b/march route from St POL to YPRES ETRUN	W.M.
7/6/17	4 A.S.C lorries lift strength below hrs 8 horses & 4 vehicles. Colonel Sulphen resumes command of Battalion which is included in 1st S. African Brigade (Brig. General Dawson) 9th Division XVIII Corps Third Army.	W.M.
8/6/17	Fiend Intelligtr & trabismen taken on attached strength.	W.M.
9/6/17	Pte Cowlrey stores for hospital - increase Corp MESTON H C Coy (No 200798) accidentally wounded: Decrease.	W.M.
11/6/17	10408 Pte SMITH J B Coy proceeds to have been left behind in England - a deserter. 204427 Pte HANN R D Coy left in Salonica in England. B/Lt at strength proceeds. Decrease	W.M.
12/6/17	Lieut H BARING & 2/Lieut P A COULTER struck off strength to go from 1/6/17 not having proceeded with unit from ENGLAND: Decrease.	W.M.
14/6/17	Pte Cumliffe returns from hospital - increase	E.C.N.

WAR DIARY
or
INTELLIGENCE SUMMARY.
(Erase heading not required.)

Army Form C. 2118.

Hour, Date, Place	Summary of Events and Information	Remarks and references to Appendices
15/6/17	CO: A/Lt(Lt MONCKTON) + RQM (Lt C.T. RUSE) + 3 NCOs per Coy + 31 other ranks attached to 101st Bde for training in the line. 101 Bde consists of 15th & 16th R. Scots, 10th Lincolns & 11th Suffolks.	[Brig Gen GORE - 101 Bde] [Brig Gen C.J Griffin - 103 Bde]
16/6/17	2 O.R. transferred to 9th L.B.D. ETAPLES Decrease.	
18/6/17	Battalion went into the line for instruction with 103 Bde having spent by Platoons over two Bde a[rea]s. A Coy into 24th Northumberland Fusiliers B Coy with 25th N.F. C Coy with 26th N.F. D with 27th. A & B Coys were in the front line & C & D in support. (Ref FRANCE Sheet 51.B. N.W.) The Bde frontage was from M.1.a.77.10 to 10.C.95.35. The O. Ps were with 27th N.F.	
20/6/17	1 O.R. A Coy wounded. 2/Lt. M.R RAINEY wounded slight at duty	
21/6/17	2 O.R A Coy killed 3 OR A Coy wounded. 1 OR A Coy wounded. 1 OR C Coy killed, 1 R C Coy died of wounds, 1 OR C Coy wounded, 1 OR D Coy wounded.	

Army Form C. 2118.

WAR DIARY
or
INTELLIGENCE SUMMARY.
(Erase heading not required.)

Instructions regarding War Diaries and Intelligence Summaries are contained in F.S. Regs., Part II. and the Staff Manual respectively. Title pages will be prepared in manuscript.

Hour, Date, Place	Summary of Events and Information	Remarks and references to Appendices
22/6/17 1am - 3am	1 O.R. B Coy killed	
22/6/17	Battalion (as part of 103 Bde) relieved by the 52 Bde o/tr an uneventful tour of duty & attached to 51 Bde in camp at ST NICHOLAS.	[51 Bde - Brig Gen Bond]
	Battalion Strength 951 (incl. att'd) & 34 Officers. Fighting Strength 935 " & 33 "	6pm.
26/6/17 7.15 pm	150 men & 3 officers from each coy accompany separate Battalion working parties of the 51st Brigade digging a cable trench S of the SCARPE return to camp 5 am	6pm.
	27th : map reference of workings H23 b32.	
27/6/17	2Lt P. Maxey joined for duty	
	Pte Nicholls 64 strength as from 16/6/17.	F. Ch.
	Trench Interpreters batman off attached strength	
29/6/17	Col. Simpson +Adjt [Lt. W. T Moreton] admitted to Hospital command of battalion devolves on Major A. E. Jones.	F. Ch.
11.15 pm - 1am	Battn (as part of 51 Bde) went into the line distributed as follows:-	F. Ch.

Army Form C. 2118.

WAR DIARY
or
INTELLIGENCE SUMMARY.
(Erase heading not required.)

Instructions regarding War Diaries and Intelligence Summaries are contained in F.S. Regs., Part II. and the Staff Manual respectively. Title pages will be prepared in manuscript.

Hour, Date, Place	Summary of Events and Information	Remarks and references to Appendices
29/6/17	Batt. Headquarters, A + B Coys relieved 2 Coys 10th W.Yorks Regt in GANRELLE SWITCH in HURRUM + HELFORD [H.Q in HURRUM] C Coy attd. to 10th Sherwood Foresters who relieved 6th DORSETS in Left Batt. Sector in the front line. D Coy attd. to 8th S. STAFFORDS - right Batt. Sector in front line. Ref FRANCE 51 B NW]	
30/6/17	2 OR. C Coy killed, 2 oR. D Coy killed. Died of wounds: 1 oR. C Coy Wounded:- 1 oR. C Coy, 4 oR. D Coy.	E.C.W

WAR DIARY
or
INTELLIGENCE SUMMARY.
(Erase heading not required.)

Army Form C. 2118.

3/4 R.W. Kent Regt.

Hour, Date, Place	Summary of Events and Information	Remarks and references to Appendices
July 1st	Batn. H.Q. at H.6.c.1552 [Ref 51 13 NW 20000] Working party of 1 officer + 20 O.R. been detailed to be under orders of No 1 New Zealand Tunnelling Coy to work near CINEMA + CHEMICAL WORKS, ROEUX – 2/Lt Brook + 20 O.R. from 'A' Coy detailed – Lt Waite detailed as O.C. detachment from 8th S.Staffs. CAPT ROBERTS M.G. O.C. Bde detachments. – H.Q. at H.14.a.03. Killed 3 O.R. 'C' Coy, 3 O.R. 'D' Coy. Wounded – 1 O.R. 'C' Coy, 3 O.R. 'D' Coy.	E. Nisse E.W.
July 4/5	7th BORDER Regt relieves 10th SHERWOOD FORESTERS in front line. B Coy 3/4 R.W. KENTS relieves 'C' Coy 3/4 R.W.KENTS + comes under orders of O.C. 7th BORDER REGT. A Coy relieves D Coy in front line + is attached to 8th S. STAFFS. C + D Coys take up their positions in HURRON + HELFORD (H.6.c.2291) 1 O.R. 'B' Coy wounded (rejoined on 8th)	E.W.

WAR DIARY
or
INTELLIGENCE SUMMARY.
(Erase heading not required.)

Army Form C. 2118.

Instructions regarding War Diaries and Intelligence Summaries are contained in F. S. Regs., Part II. and the Staff Manual respectively. Title pages will be prepared in manuscript.

Hour, Date, Place	Summary of Events and Information	Remarks and references to Appendices
July 6th	7th LINCOLNS relieves 2th S. STAFFS — A Coy 3/4 R.W Kent remains in front line + comes under orders of O.C. 7th LINCOLNS. 1 O.R. (Coy wounded) per C Coy accidentally wounded.	E. Ch.
July 7th	2 O.R. B Coy killed, 1 O.R. D Coy wounded. The Adjutant (Lt W.T. Monckton) rejoins for duty.	E. Ch.
July 8/9th	10th SHERWOOD FORESTERS relieves 7th BORDER REGT + B Coy 3/4 R.W Kent. 2 Coys of 7th BORDER REGT relieve C+D Coys 3/4 R.W.K. in GAVRELLE SWITCH. A Coy 3/4 RWK withdrawn from front line, whole battn moves back to ST NICHOLAS camp (G.N.A) Strength 35 offrs 920 O.R. (including attd)	vide memo attached "A". Uneventful tour, day spent in consolidating lines of defence. Work done chiefly on CHILI, CIVIL + CALEDONIAN for Map attached "B"
July 9th	Battn ceases to come under orders of 51st Div + Bde + is attached to 7th DIV as Pioneer Battn.	
6 p.m.	Battn moves into the BLUE LINE distributed as follows:— Battn H.Q. 4th railway cutting at H.14.a.18. A + B Coys — " " — H. 7. b. 46 C + D — " — in valley 400 E of railway cutting at H.14.R	vide memo attached "C" E. Ch.

(9 29 6) W 2794 100,000 5/14 HWV Forms/C. 2118/11

Army Form C. 2118.

WAR DIARY
or
INTELLIGENCE SUMMARY
(Erase heading not required.)

Instructions regarding War Diaries and Intelligence Summaries are contained in F.S. Regs., Part II. and the Staff Manual respectively. Title pages will be prepared in manuscript.

Hour, Date, Place	Summary of Events and Information	Remarks and references to Appendices
July 10th	Following L.G. posts for use against hostile aircraft taken over from 52 Inf Bde.	Casualties. Murphy 62 under otherwise sick.
	1 gun at H.14.a.15. 1 gun at H.9.c.65	
	2 guns - H.15.a.19. 1 gun - H.9.a.2.	
July 12th	14 officers & men detached for work under No 1 New Zealand Tunnelling Coy rejoin bath. for duty less Captain H.G. ROBERTS - Batteryman Franklin wounded & accidentally wounded 1 Battalion from their Drill employed as Pioneer Bn Helwan to 7/5 Division (GOC Major General P.R.ROBERTSON) The work being with in proving communication trenches & parapets work past true Hiawata and Jerusalem Chandlier - Drie M.Mann 91 wounded 2 on working parties.	Work Reports "D" Map attached to ties. "E"
July 14th July 15th	" "	
July 16th	Co (Major P.E. Jones) entrained H.9.06. 17th Div. to war. Draft 71 & LCpl	
July 17th	Divine - 1 OR. Rifle & Equip.	

(9 29 6) W 2794 100,000 8/14 HWV Forms/C. 2118/11

WAR DIARY
or
INTELLIGENCE SUMMARY.
(Erase heading not required.)

Army Form C. 2118.

Hour, Date, Place	Summary of Events and Information	Remarks and references to Appendices
July 18th	KENNEDY Capt T D Kennedy OC D Coy sent to Hospital. 2t C E WAITE takes over Coy. Devonshire 1.6.12.	
July 19th	70 men with Drums from Divers went to 8 Ave Battn Canvas at Transport Lines St NICHOLAS in Bermer Rifles. family Irwin Gun & R.B.T.	
July 24th	2 Lieut [name] Indis 2/Lt F T FAIRHURST took over from 7th Division on Kemmel H.A. at LARESSET Dumps — K5 a 91 & K5 b 97 (Sheet 51C).	Battn Strength 24/7/17 34 officers 912 O.R. (inch Coy attached)
July 25	Decrease – 3 evacuated Sick O.R.	
July 26	" – 2 " "	
July 31	Strength – 34 Officers, 708 Other ranks	W.M.

"A" "A"   Copy No. 5

SECRET.

51st. INFANTRY BRIGADE OPERATION ORDER No.172.

Ref.Map 51.b.N.W. 1/20,000.
PLOUVAIN. 1/10,000.

8/7/4

1. The 10th Sherwood Foresters will relieve the 7th Border Regiment plus one company of 3/4th Royal West Kent Regt in the left Bn. front line Sector to-night July 8th. with H.Qrs. in HELFORD.,
    The 7th Border Regiment on relief will move back with two companies to the Black Line with Bn.H.Qrs. in the Black Line, the remaining two companies will move back into the GAVRELLE SWITCH (HURRUM and HELFORD) with Hd Qrs. in HURRUM the name of the O.Cs 2 Companies of 7th Border Regiment in the GAVRELLE SWITCH to be sent to Brigade H.Qrs.
    The 7th Border Regiment will send forward this afternoon an advance party to take over the BLACK LINE from 10th Sherwood Foresters:route GAVRELLE SWITCH--ATHIES Road;also an advance party to take over from 3/4th Royal West Kent Regiment in HURRUM and HELFORD.

2. The 3/4th Royal West Kent Regt will withdraw their Company now under the orders of O.C, 7th Lincolnshire Regt. and the whole Bn on relief will move back to St.NICHOLAS CAMP G. 17.a. with H.Qrs. at St. NICHOLAS CAMP.
    The 3/4th Royal West Kent Regt will send forward advance parties this afternoon,--route GAVRELLE SWITCH--ATHIES ROAD to take over the Camp.

3. Details of relief will be arranged between O.Cs.concerned.

4. No movement is to take place East of the GAVRELLE SWITCH before 10.p.m.

5. Relief will be reported as follows.
    7th Border Regt.   "More Camouflage required."
    10th Sherwood Foresters."Can tracing paper be supplied".
    3/4th Royal 2est Kents. "Angle Irons can be drawn."

6. ACKNOWLEDGE.

                                              C. Fisher Rowe Captain.
Issued at 10.45 a.m.   Brigade Major 51st Infantry Brigade.

Copies to   No.1. 7th Lincolnshire Regt.
            2   7th Border Regiment.
            3. 8th South Staffordshire Regt.
            4. 10th Sherwood Foresters.
            5. 3/4th Royal West Kent Regt.
            6. 51st Machine Gun Company.
            7. 51st Trench Mortar Battery.
            8. War Diary.
            9. Office.
            10. 17th Division.
            11. 183th.Infy Bde.
            12. 50th .Infy Bde.
            13. 78th Bde.R.F.A.
            14. Staff Captain.
            15. B.T.O.
            16. Bde Signals.

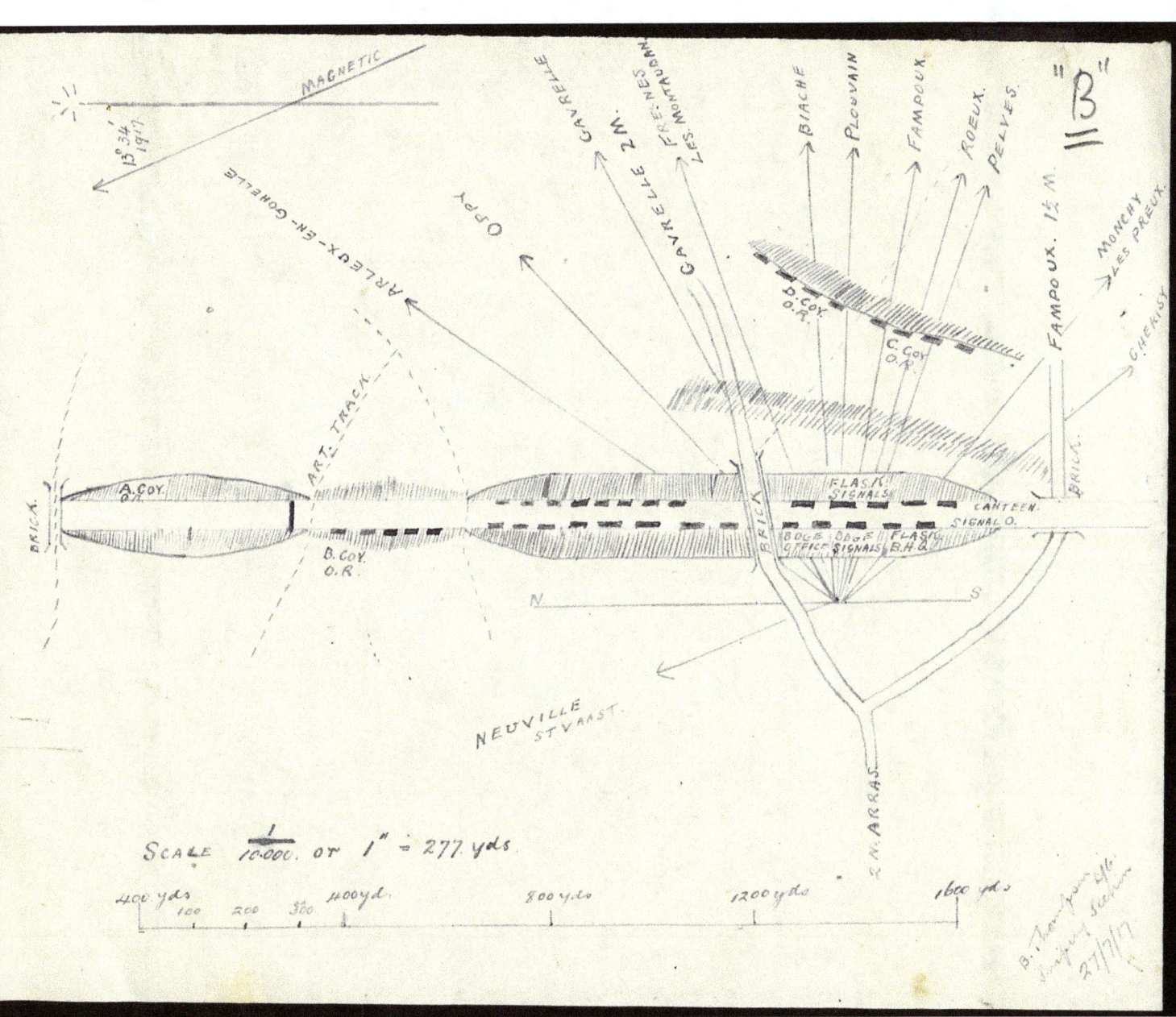

Sheet I "D"

W 9

WORK REPORT

Night 11/12 - 7 - 17. The foll. parties worked under direction of 77th Field Coy. R.E.

"A" Coy - 2 officers } CIVIL C.T. 200' widened &
110 O.R.   } duck-boards laid
1 officer   } CIVIL C.T. sump pits dug
25 O.R.

"B" Coy - 1 officer } CALEDONIAN C.T. 300'
130 O.R.   } widened + deepened - duck-
                  boards carried + dumped.

"C" Coy - 2 officers } CABLE C.T.
all available crew }

"D" Coy.   } CAMOUFLAGE C.T. improved.
                    sump pits made
                  CAMEL TRENCH. 200'
                  cleaned + levelled over 100'
                  duck-boards placed

Morning 12.7.17
During the morning Coy. billeting areas further improved.

12.7.17.   J.A. Fleming Lt.
In the field.   B.I.O.

Sheet I

W 8

WORK REPORT

Night 10/11-7-17.   The follg. parties worked
under direction of 77th Field Coy. R.E.

"A" Coy   1 Officer } CIVIL TRENCH — 150' widened
           50 O.R.   } & levelled + duck-boards placed

"B" Coy   1 officer } 250 sandbags filled & placed
           50 O.R.   } 50' of duck-board laid
                        50' of trench widened & deepened

"C" Coy   2 Officers } CABLE C.T. cleaned &
           50 O.R.   } deepened

"D" Coy   2 Officers } CAMOUFLAGE C.T. levelled,
           50 O.R.   } drained. bottom sandbagged.
                        Duckboards unloaded & placed
                        alongside trench ready for
                        permanent fixing.

Morning 11.7.17. Under Coy. arrangements
                  billeting areas cleaned &
                  improved.

11.7.17.
In the field

J.H. Leuring
B.T.O. 21

Sheet I

W 10

WORK REPORT

Night 12/13 - 7 - 17

"A" Coy   CIVIL C.T. 300' deepened
                 widened for duck-boards.
                 Rly. cutting improved.

"B" Coy.   CALEDONIAN C.T. 300'
                 widened & prepared for
                 duck-boards.
   (Morning 13th) → widened further - 31 duck-
                 boards laid.

"C" Coy. 2 officers ⎫ CABLE C.T.
         98 O.R.   ⎬
(Morning 2 N.C.Os   ⎬ Under 93rd F.C. R.E.
  13th) 20 others ⎭
         1 N.C.O.   ⎫ Reported to Area Commander.
         12 men   ⎭

"D" Coy.   CAMEL 160' deepened &
                 widened.
                 FAMPOUX - GAVRELLE RD.
                 Shell holes filled, road improved.

Morning 13th Coy. billeting area improved.

13.7.17
In the field.
                                J. Fleming ?/
                                  Bto Flnk

Sheet I

W11

WORK REPORT

Night 13/14 – 7 – 17

"A" Coy.   CIVIL C.T. 150ʸ improved
prepared for d-bs
50 dbs carried 500ʸ up
C. C.T. from dump

"B" Coy.   } CALEDONIAN C.T. 200ʸ
100 men } improved – duck-boards
20   "   } carried from dump to C.T.
(Day wk.) } 60 db. laid – 12 db.
           } relaid.

"C" Coy.   } CABLE C.T.
98 O.R. }
2 NCOs } to 93 FC R.E.
20 men } for work

"D" Coy.   CAMEL C.T. 200ʸ
            improved

14.7.17.
In the Field

J.R. Cumming Lt
B.O. FLASK

Sheet I

W 12

WORK REPORT

Night 14/15 - 7 - 17

"A" Coy.   CIVIL C.T.   100Y further
                        improved

"B" Coy. 2 officers } CALEDONIAN C.T. 160Y levelled
          105 OR   } widened. duck-boards carried
                        & laid. (R.Es 20 mins. late)

"C" Coy.   } CABLE C.T.
          80 OR   }
  morning 1 M.O.   } To Area Commander   2 M.Os } To 93rd/c.
          15th 12 men }   20 men } R.E.

"D" Coy.   CABLE C.T. deepened &
                        levelled. duck-boards laid
                        (carried from CAMOUFLAGE DUMP)

15.7.17   J.Fleming Lt.
In the field   BIG FLASK

Sheet I

W 13

WORK REPORT

Night 15/16 - 7 - 17

A Coy.   CIVIL C.T. 300' widened
                          + deepened.

B Coy. 1 Officer ⎫ CALEDONIAN C.T. 50 d.b.
        100 O.R.   ⎬ carried - 150' widened + deepened.
        Day pty.   ⎭ 50 d.b. laid.

C Coy. 1 Officer ⎫ CABLE C.T.   improved
        80 O.R.   ⎬
        1 Officer ⎫
        30   ⎬ Day CABLE C.T. —"—
        2 N.C.O.   ⎪
        20 men   ⎭

D Coy   CAMEL C.T. 160' drained,
                          levelled, + duck-boarded
                          Road mending under R.E.

16.7.17
In the field

                                    J.S.Fleming Lt.
                                    B10 FLASK

Sheet I

W 14

WORK REPORT

Period 4 p.m. 16th – 4 p.m. 17.) 17
Weather fine – ground inclined to be heavy

"A" Coy.
Night 2 Officers } Reported R.E. 10.15 p.m. Left work 2 am
95 O.R. } CIVIL C.T. 300' deepened etc.
60 d.b. carried from dump.
Sandbagging in SUNKEN ROAD.

Day 1 Officer } Reported R.E. 9.30 am.
25 O.R. } Left 1.45 pm.
CIVIL C.T. Six sump pits
dug, trench graded.

"B" Coy.
Night 2 Officers } Reported R.E. 10 p.m.
100 O.R. } Left 1 am.
CALEDONIAN C.T. 150' improved,
50 d.b. carried from dump.

Day 1 Officer } Reported R.E. 9 am.
25 O.R. } Left 3 pm.
80 d.b. laid

"C" Coy. see over.

(Contd)

Sheet II

W 14

"C" Coy.

Night   1 officer } Reported 10.15 pm.
       40 O.R. } Left   2.15 am.
                     CABLE C.T. 150' cleared etc.
                     60 d.t. carried

Day   1 officer } Reported 8.15 am
        50 O.R. } Left   4. pm.
                     CABLE C.T. improved

        1 N.C.O. } Area Commandant
        12 men } (Salvage fatigue)

"D" Coy.

Night   2 officers } Reported 10.15 pm
       72 O.R. } Left   1.40 am.
                     CUBA & CASH C.T. timber
                     carried up for do.s

Day   2 N.C.O.s } Reported 8 am
        6 O.R. } Left   4.45 pm.
                     CAMEL C.T. cleared for d-b

In the field

J. Fleming Lt.
B.I.O. FLASK

Sheet I

W 15

WORK REPORT

Period 4 p.m. 17th - 4 p.m. 18.7.17.
Weather fine - ground heavy.

"A" Coy.
Night 2 Officers } Reported R.E. 10.15 p.m.
       100 O.R.   } Left   1.15 a.m.
                    CIVIL C.T. 300ʸᵈ deepened
                    50 d-b collected & laid
Day   1 Officer } Reported R.E. 9.15 a.m.
       25 O.R.   } Left   1.30 p.m.
                    CIVIL C.T. six dugouts made.

"B" Coy.
Night 2 Officers } Reported   10 p.m.
       100 O.R.   } Left   1.45 a.m.
                    CALEDONIAN C.T. 125ʸᵈ deepened
                    50 d-b carried
Day   1 Officer } Reported   9 a.m.
       25 O.R.   } Left   2.45 p.m.
                    CALEDONIAN C.T. 50 d-b laid

(contd)

Sheet II.   W 15

"D" Coy
night 2 officers } Reported 11 pm.
       85 OR.   } Left   2 am.
                     CAMEL 144' deepened &
                     parapets made up,
                     drainage trench dug
                     78 R.B. laid, further brought
                     up
Day   2 N.C.O.   } Reported 8 am.
       6 men   } CAMEL C^T d-b laid
       1 N.C.O.   }
       12 men   } To Area Commandant

18.7.17;   J A Cuming Lt
In the field.   B^O. FLASK

Sheet I

WORK REPORT   W 16

Period: 4 pm. 18th – 4 pm. 19/7/17
Weather fine – ground heavy

A Coy.
Night   2 Officers } Reported 10.15 pm.
        82 O.R.   } Left   1 am.
                    CIVIL C.T. 300ʸ widened
                    + deepened

B Coy.
Night   2 Officers } Reported 10 pm.
        83 O.R.   } Left   1.45 am.
                    CALEDONIAN C.T. 100ʸ
                    deepened + widened
                    50 d-b carried

Day   1 Officer   } Reported 9 am.
        25 O.R.   } Left   3 pm.
                    CALEDONIAN C.T.
                    42 d-b collected. Arid

C Coy.
Night   1 Officer   } R. 10.15 pm.
        38 O.R.   } L. 1.30 am.
                    CABLE C.T. 50ʸ widened
                    200ʸ cleared.

Day   1 N.C.O.   } To Area Commandant
        12 men   }   (Salvage fatigue)

(contd.)

Sheet II

W 16

D Coy.

Night   2 officers } R. 10.15 pm.
        54 OR.   } L. 2 am.

CUBA & ASH carrying parties

Day   2 N.C.O.   } R. 8 am
       6 men   } L. 4.15 pm

CAMEL C.T. digging & carrying

19.7.'17.
In the Field

J.S. Fleming Lt.
B10 FLASK

Sheet I

WORK REPORT W 17

Period 4 pm. 19th – 4 pm. 20.7.17
Weather fine – ground heavy

A & B Coys.   Baths

C Coy.
Night   2 officers } Reported R.E. 10.15 pm.
        64 O.R.   } Left   2.15 am.
                      CAM C.T. deepened & widened
Day   1 N.C.O.   } R. 12.30 pm.
        12 men   } L.
                      CABLE C.T.

D Coy.
Night   2 N.C.Os   } attached to C Coy.
        6 men   }
Day   1 officer } R. 1.00 pm
        53 OR   } L. 7.10 pm.
                      CABLE C.T. just widened &
                      deepened. Batten given to
                      both sides.

20.7.17
In the field

                            J. Fleming Lt.
                            B10 FLASK

Sheet I

WORK REPORT   W 19

Period 4 pm. 21ˢᵗ – 4 pm. 22.7.17.
weather fine – ground good.

A Coy
Night   3 officers } Reported R.E. 10 pm.
      108 O.R. } Left work 2 am.
               New trench dug from CHILI-
               CUBA – 120'0" to depth of
               3'9" – 4' × 4'

Day   Work in Coy. billeting area

B Coy
Night   2 officers } Reported 10 pm
      67 O.R. } Left 2 am
               New trench (as A Coy)

      1 officer } Reported 9.30
      28 O.R. } Left 12.30
               Carried & laid 39 iron pipes
               for water

C Coy
Night   1 officer } Reported 10.15 pm.
      48 O.R. } Left 2.15 am.
               CAMOUFLAGE C.T. deepened 2'
               fm 35.Y

Day   1 officer } R. 8.15 am.
      25 O.R. } afr work on CAMOUFLAGE

(contd.)

Sheet II

W 19

D Coy.
night   1 officer } Reported 10.15 p.m.
-        36 O.R.   } Left   1.45 a.m.
         CAMEL C.T. } 5' deepened,
         levelled, d-bs laid.
1 N.C.O. } ~~CAMEL~~ R. 10.30 p.m.
10 men   } L. 2.30 a.m.
CASH sandbags carried &
emptied - repaired.

22.7.17
In the field

J. Fleming Lt.
B.S.O.

Sheet I.   W.20

WORK REPORT
Period 4 pm. 22nd — 4 pm. 23/7/17.
Weather fine — ground Good.

"A" Coy.
Night   2 officers } Reported R.E. 10 pm.
         105 O.R. } Left   2 am.
                  New trench (see w.19) contd.
                  to average depth 5'.

"B" Coy.   1 officer } R. 10 pm.
Night   50 O.R. } L. 2 am.
                  New trench (see w.19) contd.

         1 officer } R. 10 pm.
         30 O.R. } L. 1.30 am.
                  Carried & laid 900' water-pipe
                  Dug 120' 3"×1"

         1 officer } R. 9.45 pm.
         30 O.R. } L. 2.45 am.
                  Laid 20 sets of rails
                  Took up scarred 36 sets.
                  Loaded 2 G.S. wagons

"C" Coy.
Night   1 officer } R. 10.15 pm.
         47 O.R. } L. 1.30 am.
                CAMOUFLAGE C.T.
                CABLE   C.T.

Day   1 N.C.O. } Reported area Command. 9 am
       12 O.R. }   Salvage fatigue
      1 officer } Reported R.E. 8.15 am.
      30 O.R. }   (contd)

Sheet II   W 2.D

D Coy.
Night   2 Officers } Reported R.E.   10.15 p.m.
         44 O.R.   } Left
                       CAMEL C.T. 80' cleared, deepened,
                       widened - db brought up.
         1 N.C.O.   } CASE carrying party
         10 men.   }

Day   2 N.C.O. } R.   8 am
         8 men.   } P.   - 4 pm.

23.7.17
In the field   J.B. Fleming Lt.
                                            B Coy. T.J.

Sheet I   (As number W21)
                                                  W 22

WORK REPORT

Period 4 pm 23rd — 4 pm. 24.7.17.
Weather fine; ground dry.

A Coy.
night   2 Officers } Reported R.E. 10 pm
        100 OR   } Left   2 am.
                      CHILI C.T. new sector
                      to SUBA deepened & widened

Day   work on Coy billets

B Coy.
night   1 Officer   } R. 9.45 pm
        29 OR   } L. 1.15 am
                      8½" water pipe carried stores
                      Dug report 1' x 2½'

        1 Officer   } R. 10 pm
        50 OR   } L. 2.15 am
                      CHILI CT. completed new sect

        1 Officer   } R. 9.45 pm
        30 OR   } L. 3 am
                      Laid 100' track took o
                      carried 100' do

C Coy.
night   1 Officer   } R. 10.15 pm
        55 OR   } L. 2.15 am
                      Sandbags from CAMOUFLAGE
                      emptied
                      D.C. pickets carried to CAM
                      to IS

Sheet II   W22

C Coy (cont.)
Day   1 Offr. } R. 8.15 am.
      30 OR. } work on CAMOUFLAGE
      1 N.C.O.} To Area Commandant
      12 men

D Coy.
Night 1 Offr. } R. 10.15 pm
      50 OR.   } L. 2 am.
CAMEL C.T. deepened
ordered, dbs, stakes,
sandbags carried.
CASH sandbagging.

24.7.17
In the field   [signature]
                              B/o

Sheet I   W.23

WORK REPORT
Period 4 pm. 24th – 4 pm. 25.7.17.
Weather fine, ground dry.

A Coy.
night 1 Officer } Reported 9.50 pm.
       9 O.R.   } Left   1.30 am.
                CIVIL C.T. 200' widened &
                HOOD bridges deepened.
                shell holes filled.
day work on Coy. billets

B Coy.
night 1 Officer } R. 10 pm.
       49 O.R.   } L. 1.40 am.
                CALEDONIAN C.T. 60' improved
                40 d.b. carried laid.
                trench bridge carried to
                HURRUM

       1 Officer } R. 10 pm.
       32 O.R.   } L. 2.15 am.
                Carried 20 1½" water pipes
                        30 2"   "
                Dug 50' 3' x 1'

       1 Officer } R. 10 pm.
       30 O.R.   } L. 2 am.
                Loaded unloaded 5 G.S. wagons
                Carried 30 sets rails
                Laid 25 prs.   "
                Prepared track 80'   (contd)

Sheet II   W 23

"C" Coy
Night 1 Officer } R. 10.15 pm.
       38 O.R. } L. 2.30 am.
                   CAMEL C.T. 150' deepened
                   + widened; 500 sandbags
                   emptied.

Day   1 Officer } R. 8.15 a.m. work
      30 O.R.   } on CAMOUFLAGE
       1 N.C.O. } Area Commandant
      12 O.R.   }

"D" Coy
Night 2 Officers} R. 10.15 pm.
      75 O.R.   }
                   work on CAMEL, CINEMA,
                   CASH; carrying to R.E.
                   H.Q.

25/5/17 "In the Field"
                                    J. Fleming Lt.
                                         B/O.

Sheet I   W.24

WORK REPORT

Period 4 pm 25th — 4 pm 26.7.17.
Weather fine, ground sticky.

A Coy.
night   1 officer } Reported   10 pm.
       103 O.R. } Left   2 am.
              CIVIL C.T. 150 Y widened
                 & deepened.

B Coy.
night   1 officer } R. 10.15 pm.
        47 O.R. } L. 2.30 am.
             CALEDONIAN C.T. 50 sb.
             emptied. 40 db. canned laid.

       1 officer } R. 10 pm.
       31 O.R. } L. 2 am.
            2000' piping laid
            60' 3'x1' dug

       1 officer } R. 10 pm.
       30 O.R. } L. 1 am.
            100' picked up & prepared
            80' parallels
            20 prs rails taken up & strained

(contd)

Sheet II   W 24

"C" Coy.   1 Offr } R. 10.15 pm
night   50 OR } L. 2.15 am
                     CAMEL C.T. 150' improved
                     sandbags from CAMOUFLAGE
                     emptied

Day   1 Offr } R. 8.15 am.
            25 OR } work on CAMOUFLAGE
            1 W.O. } To Area Commandant
            12 men }

"D" Coy.   1 Offr } R. 10.15 pm.
night   49 OR } L. 2 am.
                     CAMEL + CASH improved
                     work on R.E. H.Q.

            1 Offr } Reported R.E. H.Q. "CAM"
            20 OR } 4.30 am. - 10.30 am.
            2 W.O. } R. 8 am
            8 men } L. 4 pm.
                     CAMEL 50' laying &
                     dto. pegging

26.7.'17   S.Fleming Lt
In the field   B.O.

Sheet I

WORK REPORT KF 1

Period 4 pm. 26ᵗʰ – 4 pm. 27ᵗʰ July '17
Weather fine – ground dry.

A Coy.
Night 1 Officer } Reported R.E. 10 pm.
       920 OR } Left   1.30 am
                 Mule track made N. Scivu
                 1000' shell holes filled, wire
                 cut removed.

B Coy. 1 Officer } R. 10.5 pm.
Night 49 OR   } L. 1.30 am.
                  CALEDONIAN bit improved
                  40 dts carried laid
                  120 sb emptied

        1 Officer } R. 10 pm
        32 OR   } L. 2.15 am
                  1800' piping carried laid
                  354 1"x3" dug.

C Coy. 1 Officer } R. 9.45 pm.
        31 OR   } L. 1.30 am
                  Loaded 5 G.S. wagons
                  Unloaded laid 25 pr rails
                  Covered 70' track, prepared
                  100' track

(contd)

Sheet II

C Coy
Night   1 Officer }   R. 10.15 p.m.
        66 O.R.   }   L. 2.15 a.m.   Abt. 150Y CAMEL improved

Day   1 Officer }   R. 8.15 a.m.
        25 O.R.   }   fr work on CAMEL
        work on bg. dos

D Coy
Night   2 Sgts.   }   R. 10.30 p.   CASH –
        20 men   }   L. 2.30 a.   Sandbagging
        1 Officer }   R. 10.15 p.   CAMEL –
        60 O.R.   }   L. 2. a.   Improved
        1 NCO   }   R. 10.15 p.   B.H.Q.
        8 men   }   L. 2. a.   Dug out
Day   2 NCOs   }   R. 10 a.   (50' db. laid
        8 men   }   L. 4 p.   CAMEL

24 hr. shift
        2 NCOs }
        8 men }   CASH TRENCH
        2 NCOs }   dug out
        14 men }   filling sbs

2) R. 17 field   J Henry Lt.
                                  B.T.O.

Sheet I

WORK REPORT   KF2

Period 4 pm. 27th - 4 pm 28.7.17.
Weather fine - ground dry.

"A" Coy
Night { 1 Officer } Reported R.E. 10 pm.
       { 84 OR.   } Left   1.45 am.
                      600' LIMBER TRACK made
                      N. of CIVIL

"B" Coy { 1 Officer } R. 10 pm.
Night   { 44 OR.   } L. 2 am.
                       CALEDONIAN 80' deepened
                       tendered 20 dk. carried
                       laid 170 s'b. emptied

         { 1 Officer } R. 9.45 pm.
         { 32 OR.   } L. 1.00 am.
                       Carried 500' pipe - laid
                       1000' 1½" pipe.
                       Dug 50' 3' x 1'.

         { 1 Officer } R. 9.45 p.
         { 31 OR.   } L. 2.30 a.
                       Loaded 5- O.S. wagons
                       Unloaded carried 26 pr. rails
                       laid 26 pr.
                       Prepared 400' kalk -
                       moved 100' track.

(Contd.)

Sheet II   K.F. 2

"C" Coy.   1 Offr. } R. 10.15 p.
Night 59 OR. } L.   2.15 a.
                     CAM improved 200 Y
Day   2 Offrs. } R. 8.15 a.
       40 OR. }   work on CAMEL

"D" Coy.
24 h. shift 1 Offr. }
             2 hrs }   D.O.I in CASH
             14 hrs }
             2 hrs }
             14 hrs }
Night 1 Offr. } R. 10.15 p.
       19 OR. } L. 2 a.
                  CAM 40Y improved
       2 Sects. } R. 10.30
       20 hrs   } L. 2.30
                  CASH improved
Day   2 NCOs }
      8 hrs }
                  CAMEL 50Y d.b. laid

In the field   J.A.Cumming Lt.
28.7.17.   B.W.

Sheet 1   WM 110

WORK REPORT

Period 4 pm 28/7/17 – 4 pm 29/7/17
Weather fine ground hard

"A" Coy nil (bathes)

"B" Coy 1 officer } reported R.E. 10 pm
       & 30 OR } left   12 midnight
            carried 25 2" pipes; unloaded
            25 1½" pipes

"C" Coy 1 officer } reported R.E. 10.15 pm
       & 64 OR } left   2 am
            150x CAM widened & deepened.

"D" Coy (10 pm – 10 pm)
       24 hour shifts (6 hours per shift)
            4 NCOs & 28 men
            reported 4.30 pm, 10.30 pm, 4.30 am,
                10.30 am.
            Work on CASH dug outs
            2 NCOs & 8 men reported 8 am
                       left 4 pm
            duckboarded 50x CAMEL

Sheet 2

2 NCOs 20 men & 2 SB
reported 10.15 pm left 2.30 a.m.
carried material to CASH & prepared
trench for sandbagging

1 officer 9 men 2 SB. reported 10.15 pm left
2.30 a.m.
deepened & widened CAM.

4 men reported 10.30 pm left 2.30 a.m.
loaded & unloaded duckboards on CAMEL.

W.J. Macklin
Lt/Attr
for B.10.

In the Field
31/7/17

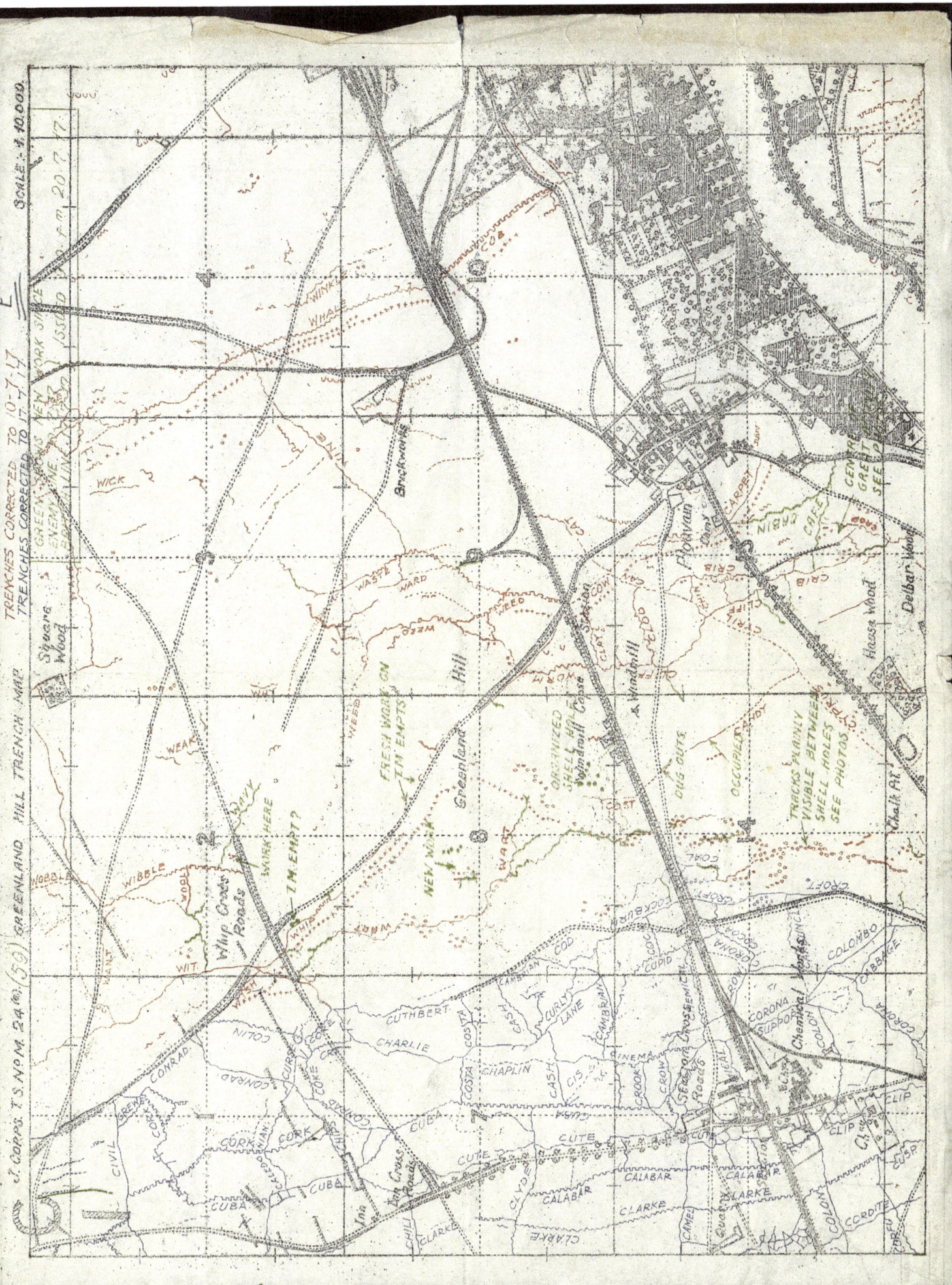

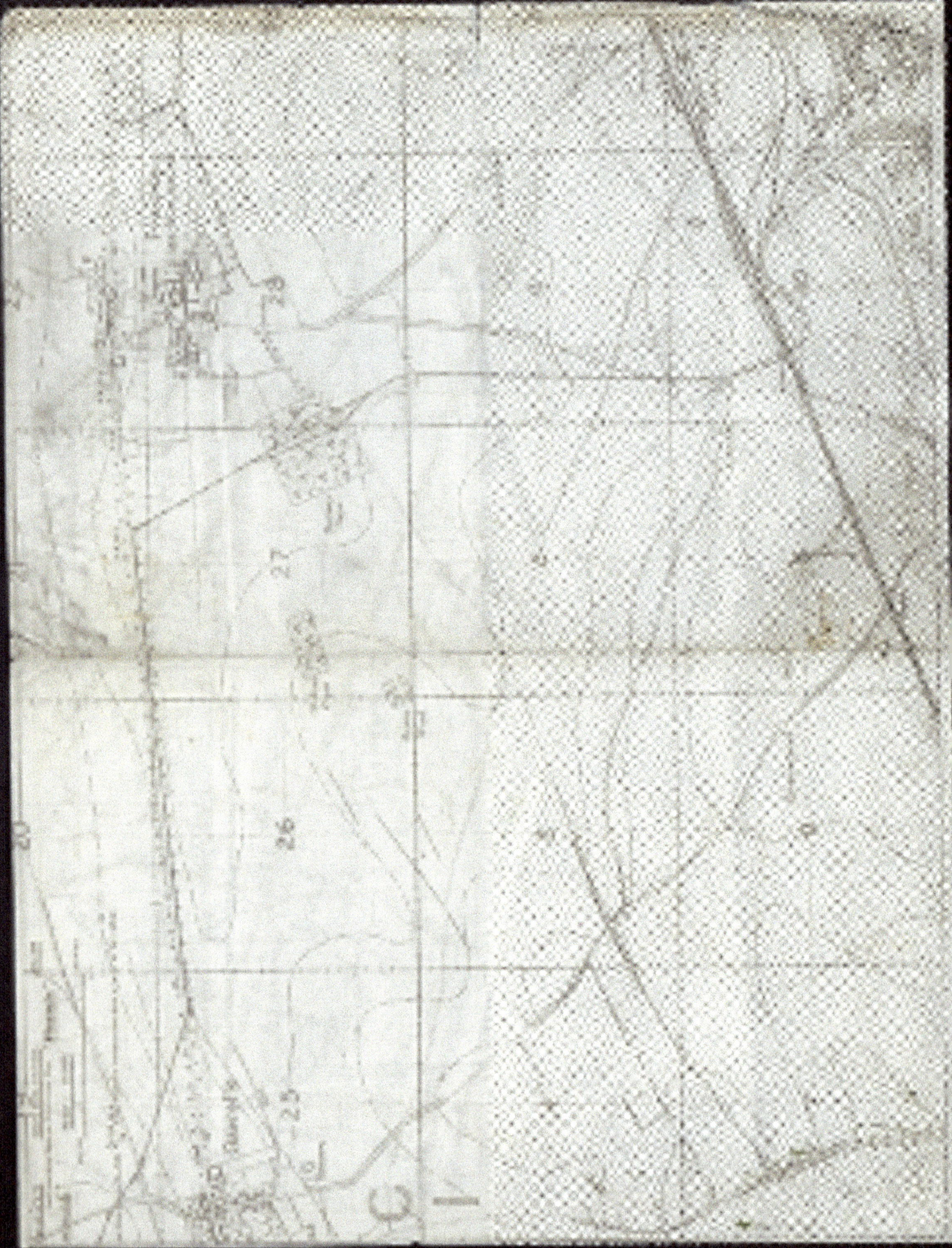

SECRET

Copy No...6.

17TH. DIVISIONAL ORDER NO. 179.

Headquarters, 17th. Division.
28th. July 1917.

The 50th. Infantry Brigade will relieve the 52nd. Infantry Brigade in the GREENLAND HILL Sub-sector of the Divisional front on the night July 31st./1st. August, under arrangements to be made by G.Os.C. 50th. and 52nd. Infantry Brigades direct.

Reliefs will be completed by 4 a.m. August 1st. and completion will be reported to D.H.Q.

Command of the GREENLAND HILL Sub-sector will pass from G.O.C., 52nd. Infantry Brigade to G.O.C., 50th. Infantry Brigade at 7 a.m. on the 1st. August.

On relief, 52nd. Infantry Brigade will move to ST. NICHOLAS Camp and become the Divisional Reserve.

3. A proportion of the personnel of 50th. M.G. Coy. will be sent up into the line on July 30th. under arrangements to be made between G.Os.C. 50th. and 52nd. Infantry Brigades, to learn the situation prior to actual relief of M.G. Coys.

4. A C K N O W L E D G E.

Lieut. Col., G.S.,
17th. Division.

Issued at 10.30 a.m.

Copy No. 1 to 50th. Inf. Bde.
,, 2   51st. "   "
,, 3   52nd. Inf. Bde.
,, 4   C. R. A.
,, 5   C. R. E.
,, 6   3/4th. R.W. Kents.
,, 7   A.D.M.S.
,, 8   XVII Corps.
,, 9   do.
,, 10   XVII Corps H.A.
,, 11   4th. Div.
,, 12   12th. Div.
,, 13   63rd. Div.
,, 14   New Zealand Tunnelling Co.
,, 15   A.P.M.
,, 16   A. & Q.
,, 17   do.
,, 18   17th. Div. Tn.
,, 19   Signals.
,, 20   D.O. File.
,, 21   War Diary.

SECRET.
Copy No. 4

17TH. DIVISIONAL ORDER NO. 182.

Headquarters, 17th. Division.
31st. July 1917.

1.   9th. Bn. Northumberland Fusiliers will be transferred from 17th. Division to 34th. Division by bus, under orders which will be issued later, and will be replaced in 52nd. Infantry Brigade by 3/4th. Royal West Kent Regiment.

2.   9th. Northumberland Fusiliers will be prepared to move at any time on or after August 2nd.

    Orders for 3/4th. Royal West Kent Regiment to join 52nd. Infantry Brigade will be issued later.

3.   A C K N O W L E D G E.

E. M. Birch
Lieut. Col., G.S.,
17th. Division.

Issued at 10 p.m.

	Copy No.	to	
	1		50th. Inf. Bde.
,,	2		51st. " "
,,	3		52nd. " "
,,	4		3/4th. R.W. Kents.
,,	5		C. R. A.
,,	6		C. R. E.
,,	7		XVII Corps.
,,	8		do
,,	9		XVII Corps H.A.
,,	10		Signals.
,,	11		A. & Q.
,,	12		do.
,,	13		A.D.M.S.
,,	14		A.P.M.
,,	15		Camp Comdt.
,,	16		D.O. File.
,,	17		War Diary.

Army Form C. 2118.

WAR DIARY
or
INTELLIGENCE SUMMARY.
(Erase heading not required.)

3/4th R.W. Kents 52/17

Instructions regarding War Diaries and Intelligence Summaries are contained in F.S. Regs., Part II. and the Staff Manual respectively. Title pages will be prepared in manuscript.

Hour, Date, Place	Summary of Events and Information	Remarks and references to Appendices
August 1. 1917	Battn Strength as on July 31	
August 2. 1917	Major H.J. KING 10th Battn R.W.K. takes command of the Battn.	
9 a.m. August 3. 1917	Battn leaves Railway Cutting H.14.a.09 (51 B.W.W.) and ceases to be employed as Pioneer Battn to 17th Division being taken into 52nd INF BDE (Brigadier General EDEN) in place of 9th W.F: their remain in 17th Division. Battn in Camp in St NICHOLAS in Divisional Reserve.	Quarter Orders attached marked "A".
August 4. 1917	B.O.R. "B" Coy attached to N.Z. Tunnelling Coy at FAMPOUX for duty.	
August 6. 1917	10 O.R. attached to 52 BDE M.G. Coy; 10 O.R. attached to 52 Trench Mortar Battery for duty. In each case down from all coys except B.	
August 8. 1917	The Battn (less D Coy) relieves 7th Border Regt in the GAVRELLE SWITCH with HQ at H.11.a.6.2 as Support Battn in the CHEMICAL WORKS sector. "D" Coy attached to the 10th LANCS	Operation Orders attached marked "B".

Army Form C. 2118.

WAR DIARY
or
INTELLIGENCE SUMMARY
(Erase heading not required.)

Instructions regarding War Diaries and Intelligence Summaries are contained in F.S. Regs., Part II. and the Staff Manual respectively. Title Pages will be prepared in manuscript.

Place	Date	Hour	Summary of Events and Information	Remarks and references to Appendices
	8/8/17		Fusiliers (D Coy. consisting of 120 O.R. + 3 officers under Lt. C.E. White.) Lancashire Fusiliers relieve 7th LINCOLNS with H.Q. in CADIZ on the left front of the CHEMICAL WORKS: on "D" Coy. disposed as follows. 2 Platoons COCKBURN, 1 Platoon CURLY, 1 Platoon "D.S.P.", 1 Platoon CADIZ Trench. Strength of Battn. 36 officers + 889 O.R.	Map attached marked "C"
H.11.a.6.2	9/8/17		Captain a/Lt. Colonel E. JAMES, LINCOLNSHIRE REGT., Commanding 6th DORSETS takes command of the Battn. vice Lt. Colonel H.J. KING, posted to command 10th SHERWOOD FORESTERS. "D" Coy. 1 O.R. wounded.	
	12/8/17	9.30 P.M.	Battn. relieves 10th LANCS. FUSILIERS in the left front of the CHEMICAL WORKS sub-sector with A resting on the railway cutting on the right, B in the Centre, C on the left & D Coy in Reserve. Bn. H.Q. in CADIZ trench (H 18 b 5.7). Battn. in the front line as a Battn. for the first time.	Map attached marked "D"
	13/8/17		Enemy T.M's active on 'A' Coy Front: Our artillery called on for a few rounds. Casualties. A Coy 2 O.R. wounded.	Op. orders marked "E"
	15/8/17		Casualties. Wounded O.R. - A Coy 1, B Coy 1, D Coy 7. Battalion Strength 36 officers 897 O.R.	
	16/8/17	9.30 PM	Battn. relieved by 10th L.F. return to GAVRELLE SWITCH as support Battalion	Op. orders attached marked "F"

Army Form C. 2118.

WAR DIARY
INTELLIGENCE SUMMARY
(Erase heading not required.)

Place	Date	Hour	Summary of Events and Information	Remarks and references to Appendices
	18/8/17		with H.Q. at H11a62: C.Coy left in CADIZ under 10th L.F. for tactical purposes	
	21/8/17		12 O.R. attached to 181 Tunneling Coy. Baltn Casualties 2 Men & wounded, 6 wounded - on carrying party for TMB : A Coy.	Operation orders attached marked "G"
	22/8/17		Batn again relieves 10th L.F. with H.Q. in CADIZ in left front of CHEMICAL WORKS Sector — B Coy on the right, A in the centre, D on the left, C Coy remaining in reserve in CADIZ. Casualties 2 O.R. wounded, B Coy. Strength of Battalion 34 Officers and 858 O.R.	
	23/8/17		Casualties 2 O.R. killed, 6 O.R. wounded.	
	24/8/17		Battalion is relieved by the 10th West Yorkshire Regt. (50th Infantry Brigade) and returns to Divisional Reserve at LANCASTER CAMP. ST. NICHOLAS after a quiet tour of trenches.	Operation orders attached marked "H"
	26/8/17		Battalion Strength 34 Officers + 829 O.R.	
	31/8/17		Battalion Strength 33 Officers + 825 O.R.	

Ack
HBbb 3/8/17

SECRET.   *For War Diary*   Copy No. 13

52ND INFANTRY BRIGADE ORDER No. 176.
****

Ref. Maps.
LENS and ST
QUENTIN
1/100,000

1st August 1917.

1. In continuation of 52.G.2969 of date (issued to Northumberland Fusiliers only).

    The Transport of 9th Northumberland Fusiliers will move by road as follows:-

    AUGUST 2nd.

    Destination ..... BAPAUME - To report to Town Major for billets.

    Route ..... ARRAS - BAPAUME Road.

    AUGUST 3rd.

    Destination ..... BOUVENCOURT (6 miles S.E. of PERONNE) to report to H.Q. 103rd Brigade.

    Route ..... BAPAUME - PERONNE.

    Rations to and for 4th August will be carried.

2. The remainder of 9th Northumberland Fusiliers who will be assembled under Brigade arrangements, will move by bus on August 3rd under instructions to be notified later, for duty with 103rd Infantry Brigade, 34th Division.

    on Aug 2/3rd

3. 3/4th R.W. Kent Regt is posted to 52nd Infantry Brigade vice 9th Northumberland Fusiliers with effect from midnight August 2/3rd and will be withdrawn from the line on the night Aug 2nd/3rd and join 52nd Infantry Brigade on August 3rd after departure of Northumberland Fusiliers, under Orders to be issued later.

    ACKNOWLEDGE.

    Issued at 11.30.pm.

    Copy No 1 to Bde H.Q.
    2 to War Diary.
    3 to Staff Captain.
    4 to B.T.O.
    5 to North'd Fus.
    6 to Lancs Fus.
    7 to W Rid R.
    8 to Manch Regt.
    9 to M.G.Coy.
    10 to T.M.Bty.
    11 to No. 4.Coy Train.
    12 to Supply Officer.
    13 to 3/4 RW Kent

J.G. Turner
Captain,
Brigade Major,
52nd Infantry Brigade.

SECRET.
Copy No. 4

17TH. DIVISIONAL ORDER NO. 183.

Headquarters, 17th. Division.
1st. August 1917.

Ref: Map LENS &
ST. QUENTIN,
1/100,000.

In continuation of 17th. Divisional Order No. 182;

1. Transport of 9th. Northumberland Fusiliers will move by road as follows :-

August 2nd. -

  Destination ... BAPAUME - To report to Town Major for billets.

  Route .... ARRAS - BAPAUME Road.

August 3rd. -

  Destination .... BOUVENCOURT (6 miles S.E. of PERONNE) to report to H.Q., 103rd. Inf. Bde.

  Route .... BAPAUME - PERONNE.

Rations to and for August 3rd. will be carried and rations for August 4th. will be drawn from R.S.O. BAPAUME.

2. The remainder of 9th. Northumberland Fusiliers who will be assembled on August 2nd. under Brigade arrangements, will move by bus on August 3rd. under instructions to be issued by 'Q' Branch 17th. Division, for duty with 103rd. Infantry Brigade, 34th. Division.

3. 3/4th. R.W. Kent Regiment is posted to 52nd. Infantry Brigade vice 9th. Northumberland Fusiliers, with effect from midnight August 2nd./3rd. and will be withdrawn from the line on the night August 2nd./3rd. and join 52nd. Infantry Brigade on August 3rd., after the departure of the 9th. Northumberland Fusiliers, under instructions to be issued by G.O.C., 52nd. Infantry Brigade.

4.   A C K N O W L E D G E.

Lieut. Col., G.S.,
17th. Division.

Issued at 5 p.m.

  Copy No. 1 to 50th. Inf. Bde.
  " 2 51st. " "
  " 3 52nd. " "
  " 4 3/4th. R.W.Kents.
  " 5 C. R. A.
  " 6 C. R. E.
  " 7 XVII Corps.
  " 8 do.
  " 9 XVII Corps H.A.
  " 10 Signals.
  " 11 A. & Q.
  " 12 do.
  " 13 A.D.M.S.
  " 14 A.P.M.
  " 15 Camp Comdt.
  Copy No. 16 D.O. File.

"Secret" Copy No 14

Ref. O.S.
Sheet - LENS 11
$\frac{1}{100,000}$

3/4 R. West Kent Regt
Orders No. 1.   2/8/17

1. The Battalion will take over the camp now occupied by the 9th N.F's tomorrow morning the 3rd inst. "B" "C" & "D" Coys & HQ Staff will occupy the main camp vacated by the 9th N.F; A Coy will occupy the Transport Lines already vacated.

2. The Battalion will move in accordance with the following time table, intervals of 200x being maintained between Platoons :—

Sheet 2

Coy	Starting Point	Time of passing
A	Road junction	9.0 am
B	250x W of the	9.10 am
C	cutting –	9.20 am
D	3 J 8366	9.30 am
HQ		9.40 am

Dress – Full Marching Order.

The Q.M. will detail guides to meet each Coy & HQ at the CANDLE FACTORY.

3. Officers' kits, mess stores, M.O. stores, Signals stores, Lewis Guns, & water tins will be at a Dump to be formed at road junction 250x W of the cutting – 3J8366 – by 8.15 a.m. on the 3rd inst. 2/Lt D. B. BROOK will take charge of the Dump & will

Sheet 3

superintend the loading of the stores into the Battalion Transport. Each O.C. Coy will detail 1 N.C.O. & 4 men to report to 2/LT BROOK at the Dump at 8.0 am to load, proceed with the Transport, & unload in camp. The Transport will be clear of the Dump by 8.50 a.m.

4. All cooks not in the Blue Line will report to 2/LT BROOK at the Dump at 8.30 am & will march with the Transport.

5. Breakfast rations will be delivered in the Blue Line tonight as usual. The remainder

Sheet 4

of tomorrow's rations will be issued by C.Q.M.S.s in camp.

6. O.C. A Coy. will detail 1 Sergt & 2 men to report at Battery Hill in the cutting at 8.0 am on the 3rd inst to hand over the area in the Blue Line to the 50th Brigade. Full day's rations then will be sent to O.C. A Coy for these O.R. tonight.

7. The Anti-Aircraft stations will be relieved by the 50th Brigade. O.s C Coys concerned will warn NCOs in charge of these stations to report with their parties, when

Sheet 5

relieved, to the RSM at the Transport Lines. The RSM will direct them to their Coys.

8. The usual certificates will be rendered by O's C Coys to Battalion HQ by 3 pm on the 3rd inst that they left their lines clean & tidy.

9. Arrangements will be made direct between OC A & B Coys for a salvage Dump for these coys: similar arrangements will be made by O.C C & D Coys. O's C Coys will render a return by 3 pm on the 3rd inst to Battalion HQ of the approximate amount of salvage deposited by them in their Dump with location.

Sheet 6

10. Tools drawn from R.E. will be returned under Coy arrangements before 8.0 am tomorrow 3rd inst.

[signature]
Lt & Adjt

By order
3/4 R West Kent Regt

Copies to — 1 CO
2 Major Jones
Copy 15 to 2/Lt BROOK   3 OC A Coy
4 " B "
5 " C "
6 " D "
7 O i/c Sigs
8 MO
9 TO
10 QM
11 Intelligence Officer
12 RSM
13 FILE
14 War Diary

Secret (FILE) War Diary Copy No. 1.
12/8/17

3/4 R. West Kent Orders No 3

1. Relief. The Battalion will relieve the Lancs Fusiliers in the left Sub-sector of the CHEMICAL WORKS SECTOR tonight 12/13 August.

2. Details of Relief. "C" Coy will take over from "D" Coy of this Battn on the left of the Battalion front.
"B" Coy will take over from "A" Coy of the Lancs Fusiliers in the centre.
"A" Coy will take over from "B" Coy of the Lancs Fusiliers on the right.
"D" Coy now attached to Lancs Fusiliers will move back to CADIZ and will be in reserve.

Order of March — "C" Coy
— "B" Coy
— "A" Coy
— H.Q.

Time. Head of column moves off at 9.40 p.m.

ROUTE :- LEMON – CAMEL thence to Battn H.Q at junction of CAMEL - CADIZ where Coys will be met by guides of the Lancs Fusiliers.

Sheet 2.

3. Lewis Guns. O.C. Coys will arrange to send in Lewis Guns by Daylight, 3 men to go in with each gun.
These parties will report to 2/Lt. W.C. CLIFFORD at junction of CAMEL – LEMON at 6.0 p.m. and will be taken by him to H.Q. Lancs Fusiliers where guides will be provided.

4. Observers. The Battn Intelligence Officer will arrange for 6 observers + 1 N.C.O. to move off at 6.0 p.m. to take over the Battn. O.P. from the Lancs Fusiliers.

5. Signals. The Officer i/c Signals will arrange for 1 N.C.O. & 1 Signaller for each station to proceed at 6.0 p.m. to take over signal stations.

6. Patrols. The Battalion will be responsible for patrolling after relief. O.C.'s A & C Coys will find officer's patrols tonight.

Sheet 3

7. Rations — Details as to the transport of rations for tomorrow will be issued later.

8. Trench Stores — Duplicate receipts for Trench Stores will reach Battn. H.Q. by 6.0 a.m. tomorrow the 13th inst.

9. R.A.P. — The R.A.P. will be at the QUARRY I.13.a.

2.55/p.m.

W M Mueller
Lieut + Adjt.
3/4 R. W. Kent Regt.

Copies to. 1 Adjt
2 O.C. A Coy
3 – B –
4 – C –
5 – D –
6 – Lancs Fusiliers
7 File

SECRET.   Copy No. 18

3/4th. Battn. Royal West Kent Regiment.

                                                                      8-8-17.

OPERATION ORDER NO. 2.

Reference :- Ordnance Survey Sheet 51b, N.W., 1/20,000.

1. The 3/4th. Royal West Kent Regiment - less one Company - will relieve the 7th. Border Regt. on the night of 8/9th. August 1917 in the GAVRELLE SWITCH with Headquarters at H 11.A.62.

2. "A" Coy. will relieve "A" Coy. of the 7th. Border Regt., "B" Coy. will relieve "B" Coy. and "C" Coy. will relieve "C" and "D" Coys. 7th. Border Regt. Relief complete will be reported to Battalion Headquarters by the following code words :- "A" Coy. "AXM", "B" Coy. "BAT", "C" Coy. "CAT".

3. "D" Coy. consisting of 120 Other Ranks under the command of Lieut. C.E. Waite with the following Officers :- 2/Lieut. V.A. Meeks, 2/Lieut. E.F. Annetts and 2/Lieut. E.W. Tuft, will be attached to the 10th. Lancashire Fusiliers until further orders. The company will report on parade ground of 10th. Lancashire Fusiliers at 8.0 p.m. 8th. inst. prepared to move into the trenches. This company will be rationed by 3/4th. R.W. Kent Regt. and one limbered wagon will be loaded with their supplies and join Transport of the Lancashire Fusiliers nightly, taking orders direct from that Battalion.

4. The R.S.M. and all the C.S.M's will reach Battalion Headquarters in the GAVRELLE SWITCH by 1.0 p.m. today the 8th. inst, to take over the Trench Stores and to make the necessary preparations for the relief.

5. O I/c. Signals will take his section into the GAVRELLE SWITCH during the afternoon of the 8th. inst. and will ensure that all runners are acquainted with the Battalion, Companies and Brigade Headquarters. O.C. Coys. will arrange to send one runner each to O I/c. Signals for the same purpose.

6. The Battalion, less "D" Coy., will parade on the Battalion Parade Ground at 9.15 p.m. today the 8th. inst., and will move off at 9.30 p.m. by half companies at 200 yards distance in the order "A", "B", "C" Coys. H.Q. ROUTE :- St. Nicholas, ATHIES, FAMPOUX Road; Guides will meet companies 300 yards East of GAM VALLEY and direct them to their positions in the line.

7. The Lewis Gun Officer will arrange for the Lewis Guns of "D" Coy. to be loaded in the Transport wagon proceeding with the 10th. Lancashire Fusiliers. Guns of the other coys. will proceed to the Battalion Dump, under the direction of the Transport Officer.

8. Rations and water for the 9th. inst. will be brought up in limbers on the night of the 8/9th. inst. under arrangements made by the Transport Officer. Orders for transporting "D" Coys. rations and water will be given by the O.C. 10th. Lancashire Fusiliers.

9. R. Aid Post will be at TANK DUMP H 11a.

                                                    O.J. Needham
                                                    Lieut. & Adjutant
                                          3/4th. Battn. Royal West Kent Regiment.

Issued at _____

Copies to :-

1. C.O.	9. Adjutant.	17. File.
2. 2nd. in Command	10. Intelligence Officer	18. War Diary.
3. O.C. "A" Coy.	11. Lewis Gun Officer	
4. O.C. "B" Coy.	12. Bombing Officer	
5. O.C. "C" Coy.	13. Transport Officer	
6. O.C. "D" Coy.	14. M.O.	
7. Asst. Adjt.	15. Q.M.	
8. O.C. Signals	16. R.S.M.	

SECRET.   Copy No. 8

Ref maps.   52nd INFANTRY BRIGADE ORDER No.176.
51.B.N.W.
1/20,000
Div.Map.
FAMPOUX
T.13.
1/20,000
                                                           8th August 1917.

1.   Reference Warning Order issued to units
concerned under 52.G.3040 dated 8th inst, the 52nd
Infantry Brigade will relieve the 51st Infantry Brigade
in the CHEMICAL WORKS Sector on the night 8/9th Aug.
in accordance with attached march table.

2.   Details of relief will be arranged mutually
between O's.C. Concerned.

3.   The 51st Brigade will be responsible for
patrolling the front till 12.30.am 9th inst, after
which time relieving Battalion will carry out patrol
work.

4.   Intelligence summaries up to time of relief
will be taken over from opposite Battalions and
Intelligence and patrol reports submitted to Bde.H.Q.
at the usual times.

5.   Work programmes will be carefully taken over
and continuity of all work in progress must be
ensured.

6.   Units will take over the 51st Brigade "Warning
Order in case of a German withdrawal to the DROCOURT
- QUEANT Line" and the defence scheme from opposite
Commanders.

7.   Brigade Headquarters will close at ST NICOLAS
at 7.am 9th inst. and reopen same time in the
Gavrelle switch (H.16.D.1.7.)

8.   Completion of reliefs will be reported to
Bde H.Q. in D.A.B.Code.

            ACKNOWLEDGE.

        Issued at 10.30.am.

Copy No.1 to Bde H.Q.
        2 to War Diary
        3 to Staff Captain.
        4 to O.C.Signals.
        5 to B.T.O.
        6 to Lancs Fus.
        7 to W Riding R.   Captain,
        8 to R.W.Kents.   Brigade Major,
        9 to Manch Regt.   52nd Infantry Brigade.
       10 to M.G.Coy.
       11 to T.M.Bty.
       12 to Fld Coy R.E.
       13 to 50th Brigade.
       14 to 51st Brigade.   17 to 17th Division.
       15 to 10th Brigade.   18 to No.4.Coy Train.
       16 to 79th F.A.Bde.   19 to Supply Officer.

MARCH TABLE Issued with O.O.176.

Ser. No.	Unit.	Date	From	To	Unit Relieving.	Route	Starting Point.	Time	Remarks.
1	Lancs Fus. Plus one Coy. R.W.Kents	Aug. 8th	ST NICHOLAS CAMP.	Left Subsector	Lincolns.	Overland to Gav. Switch - Camel Tr.	Camp.	9.0.pm.	
2.	W.RId.R.	8th.		Reserve Bn. H.Q. & 2 Coys Rly. Cutting, 2 Coys Gav. Switch S of R.W.Kents.	So Staffs.	Overland to Gav. Switch.	Camp	10.0.pm	
3.	R.W.Kents. less 1 Coy.	8th.		Support Bn. in Gav. Switch.	Borders.	Overland to Gav. Switch.	Camp	9.0.pm	
4.	Manch R.	8th.		Right Subsector.	Sherwoods	Canal Bank - Chemical Tr.	Camp	9.0.pm	
5.	M.G.Coy.	8th		Forward Area.	51st M.G. Coy.	Athies - Fampoux Rd.	Camp		As many guns as possible should be relieved during daylight by sending small parties at a time.
6.	T.M.Bty.	8th.		Forward Area.	51st T.M. Batty.	Athies - Fampoux Rd.	Camp.		As for M.G.Coy.

SECRET*

Lancashire Fusiliers.
West Riding Regt.
Royal West Kent Regt.
Manchester Regt.
Machine Gun Company.
Trench Mortar Batty.

H.Q.,
52ND INFANTRY BDE.

WARNING ORDER.

The 52nd Infantry Brigade will relieve the 51st Infantry Brigade on the Front Line on the night 8/9th Aug. Battalions will take up the following dispositions:-

Right Front Manchester Regt relieve 10th Sherwood Foresters. H.Q. in CRETE Trench.

Left Front. Lancashire Fusiliers with one Coy Royal W Kent Regt.(to be detailed by O.C. R.W.Kents) relieve 7th Lincolns. H.Q. CADIZ.

Dispositions to be taken up in the Left Subsector from Right to Left will be as follows:-

Lancashire Fusiliers.
  1 Platoon COAL Tr. (N and S of embankment)
  ½ Platoon COCKBURN.
  ½ Platoon CUPID.
  1 Coy.

  1 Platoon COCKBURN
  ½ Platoon CUPID
  ½ Platoon "C" S.P. in CINEMA.
  1 Coy.

  1 Platoon CINEMA
  1 Platoon QUARRY (Q.13.A.).
  1 Coy.

  1 Coy CADIZ Trench.

R.W.Kents (attached Lancs Fus).
  2 Platoons COCKBURN (Left Boundary)
  ½ Platoon CURLY
  ½ Platoon "D" S.P.
  1 Platoon CADIZ Trench.

Support Bn.
  R.W.Kents (3 Coys.) relieve 7th Border Regt. in GAVRELLE SWITCH H.Q. H.11.A.8.2.

Reserve Bn.
  Duke of Wellingtons. R. Relieve 8th So Staffs. - 2 Coys GAVRELLE SWITCH, 2 Coys Railway Cutting. H.Q. H.7.D.8.5.

The G.O.C. wishes Battn Commanders, M.G.Coy and T.M.Bty. Comdrs. to arrange details of relief tomorrow. Company Commanders of battalions proceeding into Front Line should also visit their opposite numbers in the Front Line. Machine Gun Company and Trench Mortar Batty.

(2).

Commanders should arrange to relieve during daylight

    Battalions will leave their Camps on 8/9th inst. as follows:-

Lancashire Fusiliers.	....	9.0.pm.
Manchester Regt.	....	9.0.pm.
Royal West Kent R.	....	9.30.pm.
Duke of Wellingtons R.	....	10.0.pm.

                                  Captain,
                                Brigade Major,
6/8/17.   82nd Infantry Brigade.

GREENLAND HILL & CHEMICAL WORKS SECTORS

"C"
"D"

GREENLAND HILL

SCALE, 1:10,000.

MAP B III

Ack H.B.E
11/8/17

FILE   W Diary

SECRET.   Copy No 8

52ND INFANTRY BRIGADE ORDER NO.179.

Ref. Maps
51.B.N.W.
1/20,000
PLOUVAIN
1/10,000

11th August 1917.

1. Three Companies of the Royal West Kent Regt. will relieve the Lancashire Fusiliers and one Company Royal West Kent Regt. in the Left Subsector of the CHEMICAL WORKS SECTOR tomorrow night 12/13th August.

2. Details of relief to be arranged between O's.C concerned.

3. The Lancashire Fusiliers and one company Royal West Kent Regt on relief will take up the present disposition of the three companies Royal West Kent Regt. in the GAVRELLE SWITCH.

4. The Lancashire Fusiliers will be responsible for the patrolling of their front up to the time of relief when the Royal West Kent Regt will take over the responsibility.

5. All Intelligence up to the time of relief, maps (including Sun-print issued to front Battns., on 9th inst.), Air photographs, Company Patrol Books, sniper suits etc. also work in progress will be taken over from opposite Battalion. The relieving unit will forward Intelligence summaries to Brigade Headquarters at the usual times.

6. Completion of relief will be reported in B.A.B. Code to this Office.

7. ACKNOWLEDGE.

Issued at 9.pm.

Copy No. 1 to Bde H.Q.
2 to War Diary
3 to Staff Captain.
4 to Signals.
5 to B.T.O.
6 to Lancashire Fusiliers.
7 to West Riding Regt.
8 to Royal West Kent Regt.
9 to Manchester Regt.
10 to Machine Gun Company.
11 to Trench Mortar Batty.
12 to 93rd Fld Co R.E.
13 to 50th Brigade.
14 to 10th Brigade.
15 to 79th Bde R.F.A.
16 to 17th Division.

J. T. Turner
Captain,
Brigade Major,
52nd Infantry Brigade.

SECRET.   Copy No. 16

52nd INFANTRY BRIGADE ORDER NO.181.

Ref. Maps.
51.S.N.W.
1/20,000,
PLOUVAIN
1/10,000.

18th August 1917.

1. The Lancashire Fusiliers will relieve three companies of the Royal West Kent Regt. in the Left Subsector of the CHEMICAL WORKS SECTOR tonight, 16/17th August.

2. Details of relief to be arranged between O's.C. concerned.

3. The one Company Royal West Kent Regt. not relieved will be disposed in the CADIZ RESERVE and COLT RESERVE Lines. The Company will be under the Command of O.C. Lancashire Fusiliers for tactical purposes only.
Detail of work for the Company will be issued from Brigade Headquarters.

4. The three Companies Royal West Kent Regt. on relief will take up the present disposition of the Lancashire Fusiliers. in the GAVRELLE SWITCH.

5. All intelligence up to the time of relief, maps (including Sun-print issued to Front Battalions on 9th inst.), Air Photographs, Company Patrol books, Sniper suits, etc., also work in progress will be taken over from opposite Battalion. The relieving unit will forward Intelligence summary etc, to Brigade Headquarters at the usual times.

6. Unit to be relieved will be responsible for patrolling its front until relief, when the relieving unit will take over the duty.

7. Relief complete will be reported to this Office in S.A.B. Code.

8. ACKNOWLEDGE.

Issued at 11.15.am

Copy No. 1 to Bde H.Q.
        2 to War Diary.
        3 to Staff Captain,
        4 to Signals
        5 to E.T.C.
        6 to Lancs Fus.
        7 to W Riding R.
        8 to .anch Regt.
        9 to M.G.Coy.
       10 to T...Batty.
       11 to 93rd Fld Coy R.E.
       12 to 50th Brigade.
       13 to 10th Brigade.
       14 to 79th F.A.Bde.
       15 to 17th Division.
       16 to Royal W. Kent R.

S.G. Turner
for Captain
Brigade Major,
52nd Infantry Brigade.

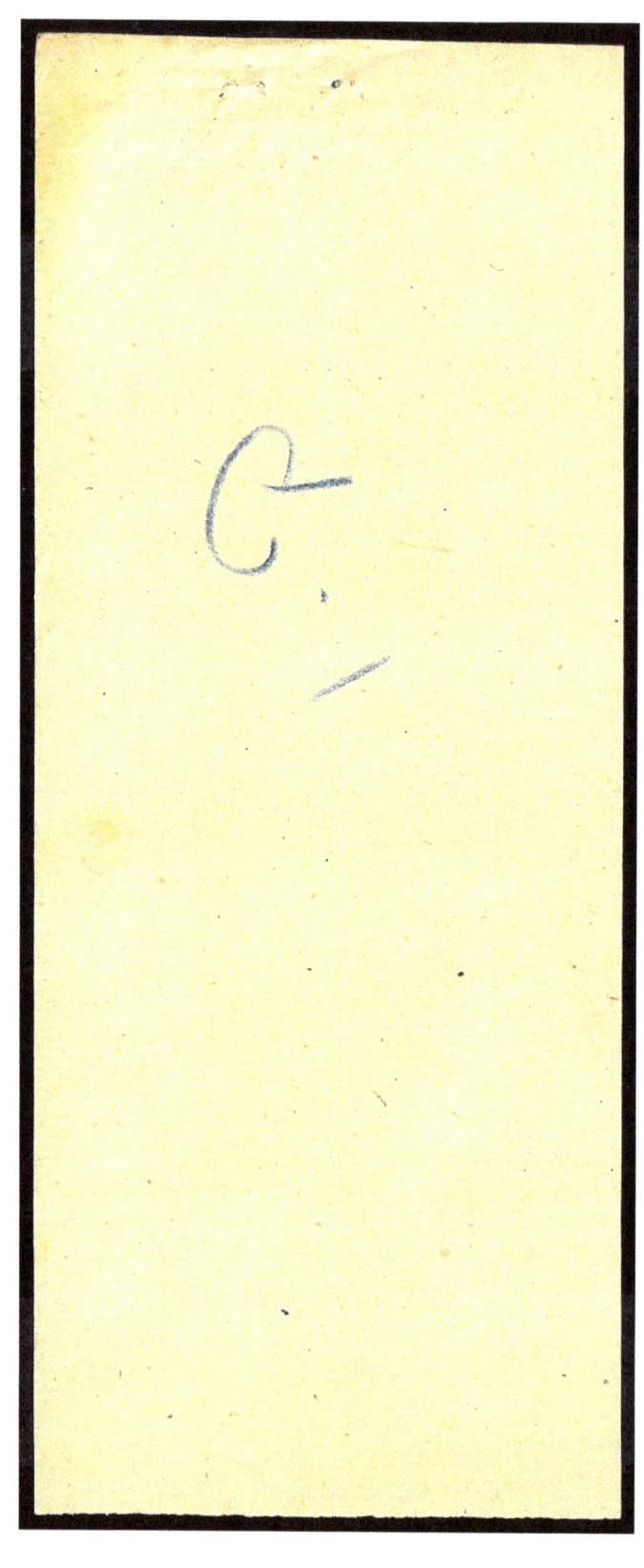

SECRET.   Copy No. 8

Ref. Maps   52ND INFANTRY BRIGADE ORDER No. 182.
51.B.N.W.
1/20,000
PLOUVAIN
1/10,000.
                                                        19th August 1917.

1.   The Duke of Wellington Regt will relieve the
    Manchester Regt in the Right subsector of the
    CHEMICAL WORKS Sector on the night 20/21st inst.
            The Royal West Kent Regt. will relieve the
    Lancashire Fusiliers in the Left Subsector on the
    night 21/22nd August.

2.   The Manchester Regt will detail one
    Company to remain in the line to relieve "C" Coy.
    Duke of Wellingtons, for work with the R.E. in
    CORFU.
            The Lancashire Fusiliers will leave one
    Company in the line to relieve the Company of
    Royal West Kent Regt in COLT RESERVE.

3.   Details of relief to be arranged between
    O's. C. concerned.

4.   The Manchester Regt on relief will take up
    the present disposition of the Duke of Wellingtons,
    Viz. one Company in the Railway Cutting, two Coys.
    GAVRELLE SWITCH.
            The Lancashire Fusiliers on relief will take
    up the present disposition of the Royal West Kents.

5.   Units to be relieved will be responsible for
    patrolling their front until relief, when the
    relieving unit will take over the duty.

6.   All intelligence up to time of relief, Air
    photographs, Company Patrol books, Sniper Suits,
    etc. also work in progress will be taken over from
    opposite Battalion. The relieving unit will forward
    Intelligence summary etc. to Brigade Headquarters at
    the usual time.

7.   Completion of reliefs will be reported to
    this Office in B.A.B. Code.

8.   ACKNOWLEDGE.

    Issued at 4.pm

    Copy. No.1 to Bde H.Q.
           2 to War Diary.
           3 to Staff Captain.
           4 to Signals
           5 to B.T.C.
           6 to Lancs Fus.
           7 to W Rid. R.
           8 to R.W.Kent R.
           9 to Manch Regt.
          10 to M.G.Coy.
          11 to T.M.Bty.
          12 to 93rd Fld Coy R.E.
          13 to 79th F.A.Bde.
          14 to 50th Brigade
          15 to 10th Brigade
          16 to 17th Division.

                                            Captain,
                                        Brigade Major,
                                       52nd Infantry Brigade.

SECRET.

Lancashire Fusiliers.
Royal West Kent Regt.

Reference para 2 of Brigade Order No.182.

The Royal West Kent Regt. will leave one Company in Cadiz Reserve, and the Lancashire Fusiliers one Company in Colt Reserve.

Captain,
Brigade Major,
52nd Infantry Brigade.

20/8/17.

SECRET.   Copy No. ___

52ND INFANTRY BRIGADE ORDER No. 184.

Ref. Maps
51.B.N.W.
1/20,000
PLOUVAIN
1/10,000

22nd August 1917.

1. The 52nd Infantry Brigade will be relieved by the 50th Infantry Brigade in the CHEMICAL WORKS Sector of the Divisional Front on the night 24/25th August, in accordance with the attached table. Reliefs will be completed by 4.am and reported to Brigade Headquarters in B.A.B. Code.

2. On completion of relief the 52nd Infantry Brigade will move to ST NICHOLAS and become the Divisional Reserve.

3. Advanced parties of 50th M.G.Coy and T.M.Bty. will be sent up on the night 23/24th August.

4. Units in the line will be responsible for patrolling the front till 1.am Aug. 25th after which the responsibility will devolve upon incoming units.

5. Defence Scheme - Warning Order in case of a German withdrawal - patrol books - and air photographs will be handed over, also camouflage suits, Dummy figures and rattles, and receipts obtained.

6. All details of relief - guides etc, will be arranged between O's. C. concerned.

7. Command of the line will pass to Brigadier General Commanding 50th Infantry Brigade at 7.am 25th August.

8. The policy of work will be thoroughly explained to opposite numbers by C.O's. and Coy. Commanders to ensure continuity of work.

9. ACKNOWLEDGE.

Issued at 1.pm.

Copy No 1 to Bde H.Q.
       2 to War Diary.
       3 to Staff Captain.
       4 to Signals
       5 to S.T.O.
       6 to Lancs. Fus.
       7 to W Riding R.
       8 to R.W.Kent R.
       9 to Manch Regt.
      10 to M.G.Coy.
      11 to T.M.Bty.
      12 to 93rd Fld Coy.
      13 to 50th Brigade
      14 to 51st Brigade.
      15 to 10th Brigade.
      16 to 79th F.A.Bde.
      17 to 17th Division.
      18 to No. 4.Coy Train.
      19 to Supply Officer
      20 to D.T.M.O.

M.C. Hagan
Captain,
Brigade Major,
52nd Infantry Brigade

W D

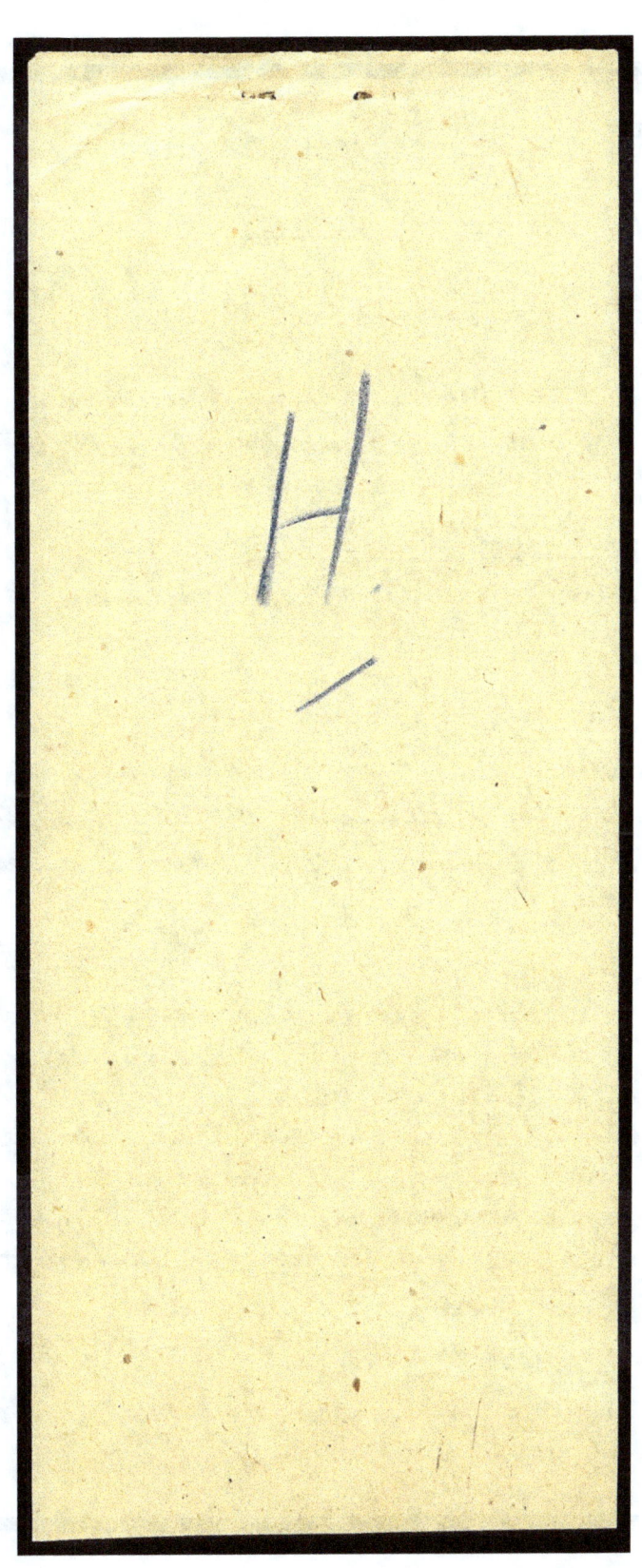

Secret.   3/4th R. West Kent   Copy No 7
                Orders No 6   20/8/17

Ref: PLOUVAIN
Sheet 51B NW
& S.W. 1/10000

1. The Battalion will be relieved in the Front line to-night and will return to St Nicholas Camp and be in Divisional Reserve

2. Details of Relief :-
   Right :-   "B" Coy will be relieved by "D" Coy West Yorkshire Regt
   Centre :- "A"   "   "   "   "   "A"   "   "   "
   Left :-   "D"   "   "   "   "   "C"   "   "   "
   Reserve :- "C"   "   "   "   "   "B"   "   "   "

   One Officer per Coy of West Yorkshire Regt will report to O.C. Coys by daylight to take over trench stores. The relieving Coys will probably arrive at the Front Line at about 11.30 p.m.

3. Guides
   5 Guides will be required :- (one from each Coy and one from H.Qrs. These guides will report to Lieut. J. S. Fleming at Bn. H.Qrs at 9.15 p.m. Lieut. J. S. Fleming will then proceed with the guides to point H.18.a.1.1. on the Fampoux Road. where he will meet the West Yorkshire Regt at 9.45 p.m., and hand over the guides as required to the incoming companies.

4. Transport & Horses
   Lewis Gun Limbers will meet Coys on Fampoux Road at JUNCTION with YORK St. Only two limbers

Sheet 2

4. Contd. will be available. Each limber will carry the guns and ammunition of two Coys. Each Coy will supply 3 men to accompany their Lewis Guns.

<u>Maltese Cart</u> will leave Quarry Dump at 1 a.m.

<u>Salvage & Water tins</u> 2 limbers will leave Quarry Dump at 10.30 p.m. with Salvage & empty water tins, and Yukon packs. Coy Mess Boxes may be sent on these limbers.

<u>Officers Chargers</u> (with the exception of that of O.C. "B" Coy) will be on Pamsoux Road at junction with YORK St. by 1.0.a.m.

5. <u>Completion of Relief</u> :- will be reported by fullerphone as follows:-

   "A" Coy - WE
   "B" Coy - WANT
   "C" Coy - <u>BLINKY</u>
   "D" Coy - <u>BILL</u>

In addition each Coy Commander will send an Officer to report personally to Bn HQrs in CADIZ when his company has passed to the West of CADIZ trench. These Officers will bring with them when they report :- Patrol reports & copies of receipts for trench stor'. Coys will march back to St Nicholas Camp independently.

Sheet

6. **Petrol Tins** All petrol tins now on charge of Coys and H.Qrs must be taken to the Quarry Dump by 8.0 p.m. this evening. Even tins which are slightly damaged will be sent as it will be possible to replace these with good tins.

7. **Trench Stores** Patrol Books, Air Photographs, Camouflage suits, Dummy figures and rattles will be handed over on relief.

8. **Sanitation** Coy Commanders will ensure that all latrine tubs are emptied before leaving and that dug outs & trenches are all left clean & in good order.

9. **Patrol** The Battalion will be responsible for the patrolling of the Bn. Front until 1.0 a.m. on the 25th inst. Patrols will be sent out as follows:-
   D Coy. 1 Officer & 8. O.Rs. Patrol to cover front from left of "D" Coys sector to centre of "A" Coys sector.
   B Coy. 1 Officer & 6. O.Rs. Patrol to cover front from centre of "B" Coys front to centre of "A" Coys Front.

10. **Salvage** In addition to the Salvage referred to in para VI O's.C. Coys will see that each man brings out of trenches a light piece of salvage.

11. **ACKNOWLEDGE**

Copies to O.C. A Coy - No 1   File 7-
         B   - 2
         C   - 3
  A.D.T.R.Works - 4
     T.O.B. - 5

W.T.M[...]
Lieut & Adjutant
3/4th R. West. Kent. Regt.

WAR DIARY
or
INTELLIGENCE SUMMARY

(Erase heading not required.)

Army Form C. 2118.

Place	Date	Hour	Summary of Events and Information	Remarks and references to Appendices
St Nicholas	1/9/17	By night	Battalion Strength 33 Officers 825 O.R. Battalion relieves 8 South Staffordshire Regt (51st Infantry Brigade) in support on the right Battalion subsector of the GREENLAND HILL subsector with Battalion H.Q. in HUDSON (H.11.b.6.8.) Trench Strength, 18 Officers 484 O.R.	Operation orders attached marked "A"
H.11.b.6.8.	5/9/17	3 P.M. to 8 P.M.	Battalion relieves 10th Lancashire Fusiliers in the right Battalion front of the GREENLAND HILL subsector with Battalion H.Q. in CHILI (H.12.b.1.9.) In the front line from right to left: B.D. + C. Coys: A Coy in reserve	Operation orders attached marked "B"
H.12.b.1.9.	9/9/17	10 P.M.	Manchester Regt on our left, raid the German front line WIT. They were to have pushed up WOOL but failed to do so. A slight and ragged barrage was put down at 10.3. which included our lines (front + support) + a more powerful one at 11.0 P.M. — Artillery + T.M.B. being engaged we suffered Casualties. — 3 killed (all D. Coy.) + 5 wounded.	
	10/9/17	9.0 P.M.	Fighting patrol — 2/Lt. E.M. WILLIAMS, SERGT. BETTS + 10. O.R. enter enemy bombing post at I.1.d.9.2. but finds it unoccupied.	

Army Form C. 2118.

WAR DIARY
or
INTELLIGENCE SUMMARY
(Erase heading not required.)

Instructions regarding War Diaries and Intelligence Summaries are contained in F.S. Regs., Part II. and the Staff Manual respectively. Title Pages will be prepared in manuscript.

3/4th R.W. Kent

Vol 4

Place	Date	Hour	Summary of Events and Information	Remarks and references to Appendices
H.12.6.19.	11/9/17	3 P.M. to 8 P.M.	Battalion is relieved in the front line by the 10th Lanc. Fus. & return to the GAVRELLE SWITCH with H.Q. in HUDSON (H.11.6.6.8.)	Operation Orders attached marked 'C'
	14/9/17	3 P.M. to 8 P.M.	Battalion relieves the 10th Lancs Fus. in the front line with H.Q. in CHILI. H.12.6.19. Front line held by D.C.A. from right to left. B in reserve.	Operation Orders attached marked 'D'
H.12.6.19.	16/9/17 midnight	Manchester Regt. raid their main successfully on our left, 9 dugouts bombed & prisoners taken.	Operation Orders attached marked 'E'
H.12.6.19.	17/9/17 night	Battalion relieved in front line by 7th Yorkshire Regt. (Lt. Col. MAIRIS, D.S.O) 50th Brigade returns to Divisional Reserve at LANCASTER Camp ST NICHOLAS Casualties during 16 days tour. Killed O.R. 5 - Wounded O.R. 26. Queen Town.	
	19/9/17		Draft of 73 O.R. from 2/5 R WEST KENT Regt received	
	22/9/17	10 A.M. to 4 P.M.	Battalion moves by Brigade march route to WANQUETIN to rest in billets - Ref. 51.C., K.32. Central	March Orders attached marked 'F'
			Draft of 100 O.R. from 3/10th Middlesex Regt. received.	
	25/9/17		Draft of 33 O.R. from 2/5 R WEST KENT REGT received.	
WANQUETIN	26/9/17	7.30 A.M. to 12.30 P.M.	Battalion moves by march route to LUCHEUX - ref. 51.C. T.16.C.	March Orders attached marked 'G'
	28/9/17		Draft of 6 O.R. from 2/5 R WEST KENT REGT received	
LUCHEUX	30/9/17		Battalion strength 33 Officers 997 O.R.	

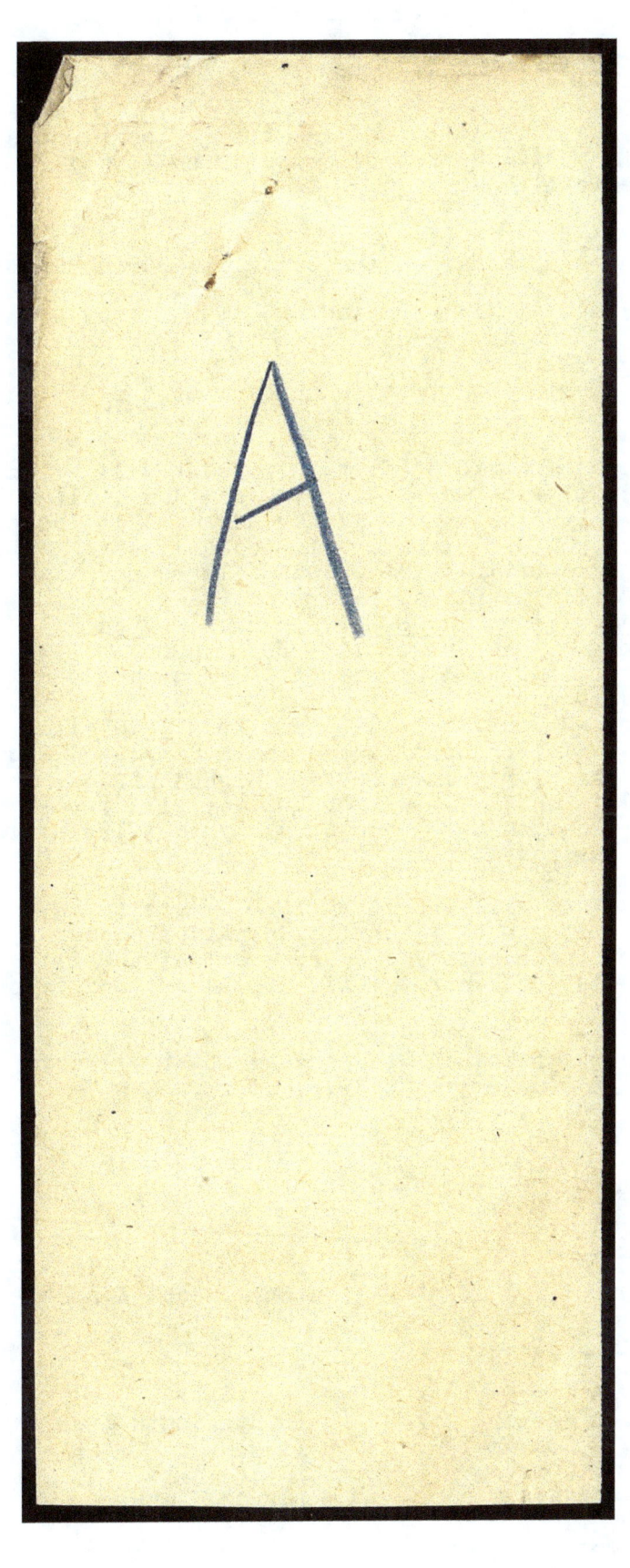

SECRET.

Copy No. 13.

3/4th. Battn. Royal West Kent Regt.

1-9-17.

OPERATION ORDER NO. 6.

Reference :- Map 51 BNW. 1/20000.
             PLOUVAIN   1/10000.

1. The Battalion will go into the line tonight as right support Battalion in the GREENLAND HILL Subsector and will relieve the 8th. South Staffordshire Regt.

2. Details of relief :-
The Battalion will parade on the Battalion Parade Ground at 7.35 p.m.
Route :-
February Circus - ATHIES - FAMPOUX Road - Railway Arch - CAM Valley - CAMEL Trench - HUDSON Trench.
Order of March :-
H.Q., D, C, B, A, relieving opposite numbers of the 8th. South Staffordshire Regt.
Lewis Guns :-
2 limbers from the South Staffordshire Regt. will be on the Battalion Parade Ground at 7.15 p.m. to carry Lewis Guns, half a limber for each company - A and B in one limber, C and D in the other.
3 men for each gun will parade with these limbers. 2/Lieut. W.C. Clifford will be in charge of the party. Guns will be unloaded at TANK DUMP.
Water bottles will be filled before starting.
Battalion Headquarters and R.A.P. in Hudson Trench.
Battalion Dump :- TANK DUMP H 11 a 56.
Completion of relief will be reported by runner to Battalion H.Q.
Trench Stores :-
Sergt Brooker and Corpl. Bolwell and 2 policemen will proceed at 4.0 p.m. to take over Battalion Dump. The Signals Sergt. and 2 Signallers will proceed with this party to take over Signal Office.
2/Lieut. E.W. Tuft and 1 N.C.O. per Company will proceed at 4.0 p.m. to take over for Headquarters. and Coys. 2/Lieut. Tuft will be in charge of the above parties starting at 4.0 p.m.
Company Schemes :-
Company Commanders will submit by 10.0 a.m. tomorrow the 2nd. inst. a brief scheme of the work which they consider necessary for the improvement of their sector : special attention will be paid to cookhouses, ablution benches, Officers Messes and accommodation for the men.
Trench Stores :-
A duplicate copy of Trench Stores taken over will be rendered tomorrow morning by each O.C. Company by 9.0 a.m.

3. ACKNOWLEDGE.

Captain & Adjutant
3/4th. Battn. Royal West Kent Regiment.

Issued at _____ p.m.
Copies to :-
1. O.C. "A" Company.
2. O.C. "B" Company.
3. O.C. "C" Company.
4. O.C. "D" Company.
5. O.C. Signals
6. L.G. Officer.
7. 2/Lieut. E.W. Tuft
8. M.O.
9. T.O.
10. 8th. South Staffs Regt.
11. Q.M.
12. R.S.M.
13. War Diary
14. File.

SECRET   Copy No. 8.

52nd INFANTRY BRIGADE ORDER No. 185.

Ref Maps
51.B.N.W.
1/20,000
PLOUVAIN
1/10,000.

August 31st. 1917.

1. The 52nd Infantry Brigade will relieve the 51st Infantry Brigade in the GREENLAND HILL SECTOR of the Divisional Front on night 1st/2nd September

2. Details of relief to be arranged between O's.C. concerned.

3. Relief to be complete by 4.am on the 2nd September, and completion to be reported in B.A.B. Code.

4. Advanced parties of one officer and 8 N.C.O's, with proportion of observers of Battalions proceeding into the Front Line, will be sent up during daylight of the 1st prox. to take over stores, dumps and work in progress.

5. The 52nd M.G.Coy and T.M.Batty. will send up a proportion of their personnel on the night 31/1st, the remainder proceeding to forward area during daylight of the 1st Sept., small parties going forward at a time.

6. The 51st Brigade Front Line Battalions will be responsible for patrolling the front until 12 midnight when the relieving battalion will carry on the duty.

7. Intelligence Summaries up to the time of relief, patrol reports, scheme of work, Defence Scheme, Orders in case of enemy withdrawal and patrol books will be taken over from units to be relieved. Intelligence and patrol reports will be forwarded to Brigade Headquarters at usual time.

8. Brigade Headquarters will close at ST NICHOLAS at 7.am on the 2nd September and reopen at same hour at GAVRELLE SWITCH.

9. ACKNOWLEDGE.

Issued at 10.pm.

Copy No. 1 to B de H.Q.
        2 to War Diary.
        3 to Staff Captain.
        4 to Signals.
        5 to B.T.O.
        6 to Lancs Fus.
        7 to W.Riding. R.
        8 to R.W.Kent R.
        9 to Manch Regt.
      10 to M.G.Coy.
      11 to T.M.B ty.
      12 to 77th F.Coy R.E.
      13 to 78th F.A.Bde.
      14 to 50th Brigade.
      15 to 51st Brigade.
      16 to 17th Division.
      17 to No.4.Coy Train.
      18 to Supply Officer.

                                                        Captain,
                                                   Brigade Major,
                                              52nd Infantry Brigade.

MARCH TABLE Issued with O.C. 185.

Serial No.	Unit.	Date	From	To	Unit Relieving.	Route	Starting Point.	Time	Remarks
1.	Lancs. Fus.	1st. Sept.	ST NICHOLAS CAMP.	Right Subsector	Lincolns	Overland Route to Gavrelle Switch – CALEDONIAN and CLYDE.	Railway Cutting.	8.p.m	
2.	W.Rid R.	1st. Sept.		Left Support.	Borders.		do	8.30.pm	
3.	Manch Regt	1st Sept		Left Subsector	Sherwoods		do	8.15.pm	
4.	E.W.Kents	1st Sept.		Right Support.	So. Staffs		do	8.45.pm	
5.	M.G.Coy.	1st Sept.		Forward Area	51st M.G. Company.		G.E.		As many guns as possible to be relieved during daylight by sending small parties forward at a time.
6.	T.M.Bty.	1st Sept.		Forward Area	51st T.M.B.		Camp.		as for M.G.Coy

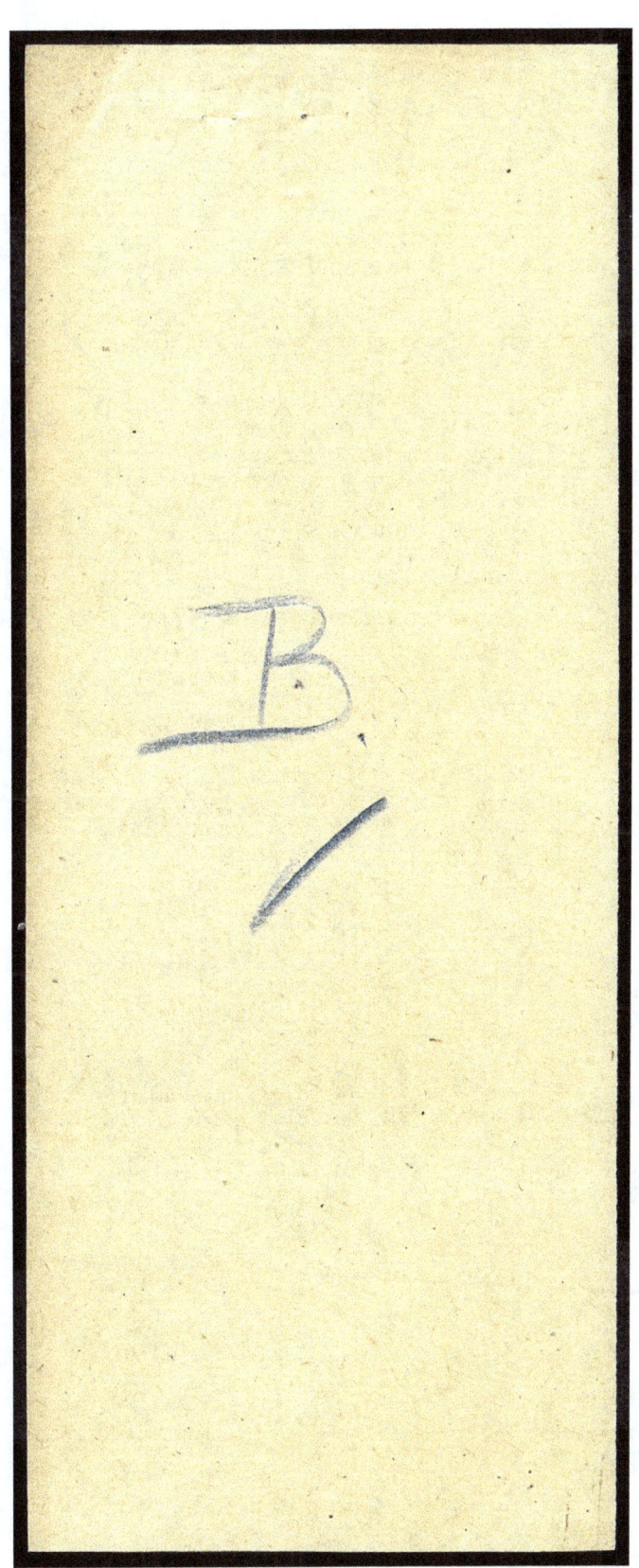

SECRET.   Copy No: 8

Ref.Maps
Corps
1/10,000
GREENLAND HILL
and FALFOUX.

52nd INFANTRY BRIGADE ORDER No: 187.

4th September 1917.

1. The Royal West Kent Regiment will relieve the Lancashire Fusiliers in the right Sub-sector of the Brigade Front during the hours of 3 p.m. and 8 p.m. on the 5th instant.

2. On relief the Lancashire Fusiliers will occupy positions vacated by the Royal West Kent Regiment in the GAVRELLE SWITCH.

3. Details of relief to be arranged between O's Commanding concerned.

4. Intelligence Summary, up to time of relief, Air Photos, Company Patrol Report Books, Sniper Suits, Dummy Figures and Work in progress will be taken over from opposite Battalion and Intelligence and Patrol Reports forwarded to Brigade Headquarters at the usual time.

5. Completion of reliefs will be reported to Brigade Headquarters in BAB Code.

3. ACKNOWLEDGE.

Issued at 9-0 p.m.

Copy No 1 to Bde. H.Q.
       2 to War Diary.
       3 to Staff Captain.
       4 to Signals.
       5 to B.T.O.
       6 to Lanc. Fus.
       7 to W.Rid.R.
       8 to R.W.Kents.
       9 to Manch: R.
      10 to M.G.Coy.
      11 to T.M.Bty.
      12 to 77th F.Coy.,R.E.
      13 to 78th F.A.Bde.
      14 to 50th Bde.
      15 to 189th Bde.
      16 to 17th Division.

Captain,
Brigade Major,
52nd Infantry Brigade.

4-9-1917.

SECRET　　　　　　　/2 Q West Kent Regt.　　　　Copy No 9
　　　　　　　　　　　Orders No 9　　　　11-9-17.
FILE W.D.

Reference:
GREENLAND HILL
Trench Map
1/10000.

Relief　　　1. The 10th Bn. Lancs. Fus. will relieve the
　　　　　　　　Bn. in the Right Sub-sector of the
　　　　　　　　GREENLAND HILL sector during daylight on
　　　　　　　　the 11th inst between the hours of 3.0pm
　　　　　　　　and 8.0pm.

Dispositions　2. B coy on the right will be relieved by D coy L.F.
　　　　　　　　D coy in the centre　————————— B coy L.F.
　　　　　　　　C coy on the left　————————— A coy L.F.
　　　　　　　　A coy in support　————————— C coy L.F.

Guides　　　3. As B coy will send 2 guides each to
　　　　　　　　report to the Adjutant at 2.45p.m. to
　　　　　　　　direct the relieving coys to their new
　　　　　　　　dispositions. The Lancs. Fus will move
　　　　　　　　in the following order - D, B, A, C -
　　　　　　　　by the following route
　　　　　　　　　(a) D coy Lancs. Fus. will enter trenches
　　　　　　　　　　　by CASH ALLEY
　　　　　　　　　(b) B & A coys by COSTA ALLEY

Cont. (Guides).	3.	O's C Coys will take particular care to insure that their guides know which coy Lancs Fus they are sent to direct, and are thoroughly clear about the route to be followed.
Time	4.	The Lancashire Fus. will begin to pass B'n H.Q. in CHILI at 3·0pm & the rear of their column will pass the same spot at about 3·30pm O's C Coys will see that when relief is complete no move is made from the trenches until an order to that effect is received from Battn H.Q. This order to move will be given by the code word "EAST GRINSTEAD".
Route	5.	On relief the B'n will return to the GAVRELLE SWITCH with H.Q in HUSSAR. Coys will receive the order to move in the following order A, D, C, B, reoccupying the positions evacuated on 3rd inst. H.Q will move when relieved. Route for all – CHARLIE SUPPORT – COSTA – CAULDRON – CHILI.
Trench Stores & Accommodation	6.	1 Officer & 1 N.C.O per Coy. & 1 Officer from H.Q. will proceed in the morning to t...

cont. 6. over accommodation & stores. The R.S.M.
will make the necessary arrangements in
respect of Bn Dumps.
Copies of receipts must be sent to O.R.
with returns on morning of 12th

Relief complete   7. Relief complete will be wired as follows.

     A Coy   ANTONY
     B ...   FRIENDS.
     C ...   ROMANS
     D ...   COUNTRYMEN.

   8 ACKNOWLEDGE.

             W Mucklg

             Capt. Adjt.
              RODENT.

Issued at
  a.m

By Runner   Copies to   1 OC 10th Bn Lancs Fus
           2 A Coy
           3 B ---
           4 C ---   9 FILE.
           5 D ---
           6 B.I.O
           7 MO
           8 R.S.M

SECRET.   Copy No. 9

52ND INFANTRY BRIGADE ORDER No. 189.

Ref. Maps
Corps 8/10,000
FAMPOUX &
GREENLAND-HILL.
                                                    10th September 1917.

1. The Lancashire Fusiliers will relieve the Royal West Kent Regt. in the Right Subsector of the GREENLAND HILL Sector during daylight on 11th inst., between the hours of 3.0.pm and 8.0.pm.

2. On relief the Royal West Kent Regt. will occupy the positions in the GAVRELLE SWITCH, vacated by the Lancashire Fusiliers.

3. Details of relief to be arranged between O's.C. concerned.

4. Intelligence summary, up to time of relief, Air photographs, Company Patrol Report Books. Sniper suits, dummy figures etc. and work in progress will be taken over from opposite Battalion, and Intelligence and patrol reports forwarded to Brigade Headquarters at the usual time.

5. Completion of relief will be reported to Brigade Headquarters in B.A.B.Code.

6. ACKNOWLEDGE.

Issued at 4.pm.

Copy No. 1 to B de H.Q.
        2 to War Diary.
        3 to Staff Captain.
        4 to Signals.
        5 to B.T.O.
        6 to Lancs Fus.
        7 to W Rid. R.
        8 to R.W. Kent R.
        9 to Manch Regt.
       10 to M.G. Coy.
       11 to T.M. Bty.
       12 to 77th F. Coy R.E.
       13 to 78th F.A. Bde.
       14 to 51st Brigade.
       15 to 188th Brigade.
       16 to 17th Division.
       17 to 93rd F. Coy. R.E.

                                        F.R. Lindley Captain.
                                          a/Brigade Major,
                                          52nd Infantry Brigade.

FILE 6D

SECRET   Copy No. 8

52ND INFANTRY BRIGADE ORDER No. 190.

Ref. Maps
Corps 1/10,000
FAMPOUX and
GREENLAND HILL.   11th September 1917.

1. The Manchester Regt will relieve the West Riding Regt in the Left Sub/Sector of the GREENLAND HILL SECTOR during daylight 12th September between the hours of 3.pm and 8.pm.

2. On relief the West Riding Regt will occupy positions in the GAVRELLE SWITCH vacated by the Manchester Regt.

3. Details of relief will be arranged direct between O's.C. concerned.

4. Intelligence summary, up to time of relief, Air photographs, Company Patrol Report Books, Sniper suits, dummy figures etc. also work in progress will be taken over from opposite Battalion and Intelligence Summary, patrol reports etc. forwarded to Brigade Headquarters at the usual times.

5. Completion of relief to be reported to Brigade Headquarters in B.A.B.Code.

6. ACKNOWLEDGE.

Issued at 1.0.pm.

Copy No.1 to Bde H.Q.
     2 to War Diary.
     3 to Staff Captain.
     4 to Signals.
     5 to B.T.O.
     6 to Lancs Fus.
     7 to W.Riding R.
     8 to R.W.Kent R.
     9 to Manch Regt.
    10 to M.G.COY.
    11 to T.M.Batty.
    12 to 77th F.Coy R.E.
    13 to 93rd F.Coy R.E.
    14 to 78th F.A.Bde.
    15 to 51st Brigade.
    16 to 188th Brigade.
    17 to 17th Division.

                                               J.R.Lindley Captain,
                                                   a/Brigade Major,
                                             52nd Infantry Brigade.

SECRET.   Copy No. 8

Ref Maps.   52ND INFANTRY BRIGADE ORDER No. 191.
Corps 1/10,000
GREENLAND HILL   13th September 1917.
& FAMPOUX.

1.   The West Riding Regt will relieve the
Manchester Regt. in the Left Subsector of the GREENLAND
HILL Sector during daylight Sept. 14th between the hours
of 8.am and 12.noon.
        The Royal West Kent Regt will relieve the
Lancashire Fusiliers in the Right Subsector of the
GREENLAND HILL Sector during daylight Sept 14th
between the hours of 3.pm and 8.pm.

2.   On relief that portion of the Manchester Regt
which will not actually be engaged in the forthcoming
operations will occupy positions in the GAVRELLE
SWITCH vacated by the WestRiding Regt; the remainder
will move back to the Railway Cutting in small groups
during the afternoon of the 14th Sept.
        The Lancashire Fusiliers on relief will occupy
the positions in the GAVRELLE SWITCH vacated by the
Royal West Kent Regt.

3.   Details of relief will be arranged direct
between O's.C.concerned.

4.   Intelligence summaries up to time of relief,
Air photographs, Company Patrol Report Books, Sniper
suits, dummy figures also work in progress will be
taken over from opposite Battalions and Intelligence
and patrol reports forwarded to Brigade Headquarters
at the usual times

5.   Completion of relief between R.W.Kents and
Lancs Fus. will be reported to Bde H.Q. in B.A.B.Code.
        Completion of relief between Manchester Regt
and West Riding Regt, and the establishment of H.Q.
of the Manchester Regt in the Railway Cutting will be
reported to this Office in B.A.B.Code.

6.   ACKNOWLEDGE.

Issued at 1.0.pm.

Copy No. 1 to Bde H.Q.
        2 to War Diary.
        3 to Staff Captain.
        4 to Signals.
        5 to B.T.O.
        6 to Lancs Fus.
        7 to W.Riding Regt.
        8 to W.R.Kent R.
        9 to Manch Regt.
       10 to M.G.Coy.
       11 to T.M.Bty.
       12 to 77th F.Coy R.E.
       13 to 93rd F.Coy R.E.
       14 to 78th F.A.Bde.
       15 to 51st Brigade.
       16 to 188th Brigade.
       17 to 17th Division.

                                        F.R. Lindley Captain,
                                            a/Brigade Major,
                                         52nd Infantry Brigade.

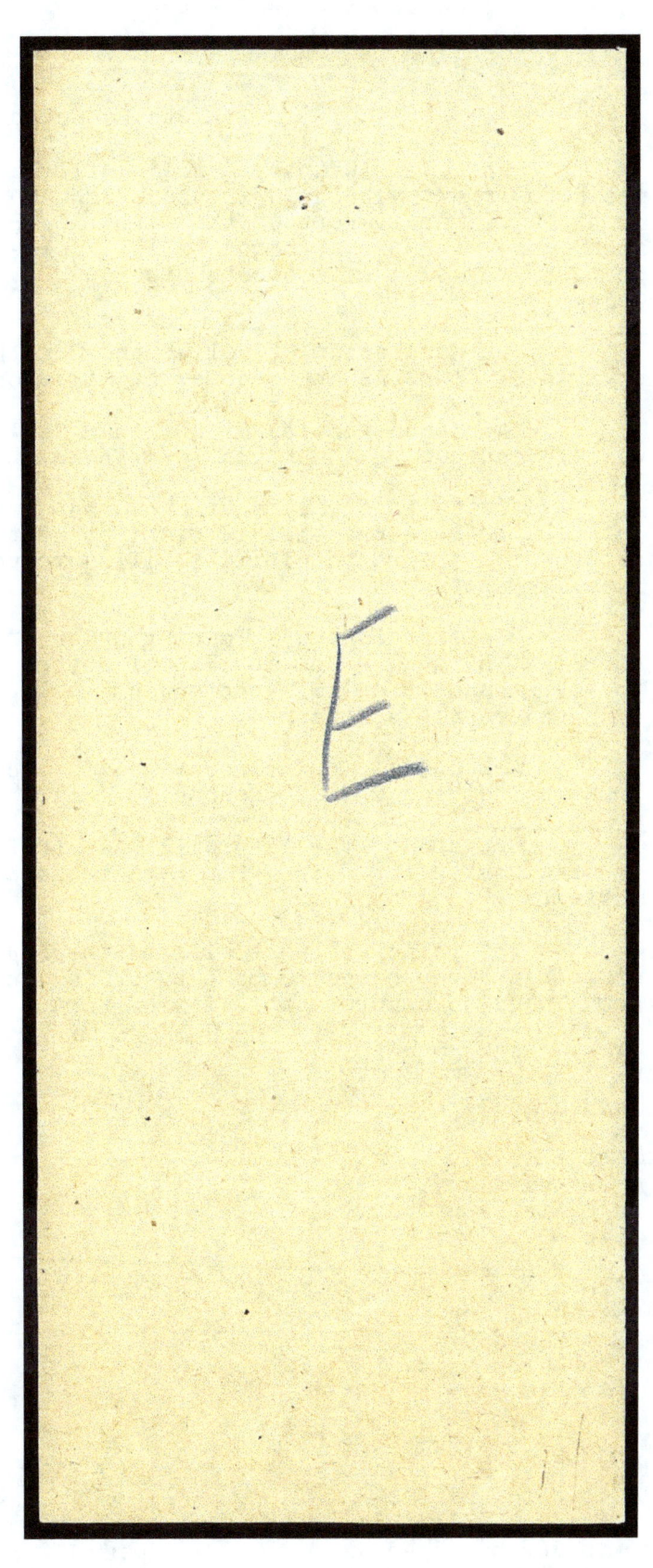

SECRET.  Copy No. 8

Ref.Maps
Corps FAMPOUX
&GREENLAND
HILL 1/10,000,
51.B.N.W.
1/20,000

52ND INFANTRY BRIGADE ORDER No.193.

16th September 1917.

1. The 52nd Infantry Brigade will be relieved by the 50th Infantry Brigade in the GREENLAND HILL Sector of the Divisional Front on the night 17/18th Sept. in accordance with the attached table. Reliefs will be completed by 4.am and reported to Bde H.Q. in B.A.B. Code.

2. On completion of relief the 52nd Brigade will move to ST NICHOLAS and become the Divisional Reserve.

3. Advanced parties of 50th M.G.Coy. and T.M.Bty. will be sent up on the night 16/17th inst.

4. Units in the line will be responsible for patrolling the Front till 12 midnight Sept. 17th. after which the responsibility will devolve upon incoming units.

5. Defence Scheme - Warning Order in case of a German withdrawal - Company Patrol Report Books - Sector maps only and air photographs will be handed over and receipts obtained.

6. All details of relief - guides etc. will be arranged between O's.C.concerned.

7. Command of the Line will pass to Brigadier General Commanding 50th Infantry Brigade at 7.am 18th September.

8. The policy of work will be thoroughly explained to opposite numbers by C.O's. and Company Commanders to ensure continuity of work.

9. ACKNOWLEDGE.

Issued at 1.pm.

Copy No.1 to Bde H.Q.
2 to War Diary.
3 to Staff Captain.
4 to B.T.O.
5 to Signals.
6 to Lancs F us.
7 to W.Riding R.
8 to R.W.Kent R.
9 to Manch Regt.
10 to M.G.Coy.
11 to T.M.Bty.
12 to 77th F.Coy R.E.
13 to 93rd F.Coy R.E.
14 to 50th Brigade
15 to 51st Brigade.
16 to 182nd Brigade.
17 to 78th F.A.Bde.
18 to No.4.Coy Train
19 to Supply Officer.
20 to 17th Division

F.R. Findley Captain,
a/Brigade Major,
52nd Infantry Brigade.

TABLE OF MOVES issued with O.O. 193.

Ser. No.	UNIT	FROM	TO	RELIEVED BY	Route of incoming unit forward of GAVRELLE SWITCH.	Time to arrive GAV. SWITCH.	REMARKS.
1.	Lancs Fus.	GAVRELLE SWITCH.	ST NICHOLAS CAMP.	E.Yorks R	------	9.0.pm.	
2.	Duke of Wellingtons	Left Sub-sector.		Dorset R.	CALEDONIAN and CIVIL C.T's.	8.45.pm	
3.	R.W.Kent R.	Right Subsector.		Yorkshire R	CHILI C.T.	8.30.pm	
4.	Manch.Regt.	GAVRELLE SWITCH.		W.Yorks R.	------	9.15.pm.	
5.	L.G.Coy.	Forward Area.		50th M.G.C.	To be arranged between O's.C.	During daylight.	
6.	T.M.Bty.	Forward Area.		50th T.M.B.	To be arranged between O's.C.		Interchange of guns in the line to take place.

Secret   7/L R.W. Kent Regt. (W)   Copy W.

Orders No. 11   17-9-17

Ref GREENLAND HILL
1/10000 51B.N.W

Relief	1	The 7th Bn the Yorkshire Regt. will relieve this Bn in the right sub sector of the GREENLAND HILL sector on the night 17/18 September.
Move	2	On completion of relief the Bn will move to LANCASTER CAMP St Nicholas in Divisional Reserve
Details of relief	3	A Coy 7th Bn Yorkshire Regt will relieve A Coy. B --- --- --- --- C --- H --- --- --- --- D --- C --- --- --- --- B ---
Time of relief	4	The 7th Bn Yorkshire Regt will leave the GAVRELLE SWITCH at 8.35pm in the order A, B, H, C.
Guides	5	2 guides each per coy, for HQ (detailed by O/C Signals) will

report to Lt. J.S FLEMING at HQ at 7.45pm punctually. Each guide will have a chit signed by his coy. officer, showing the coy of the Yorkshire Regt which he is detailed to guide. Lt FLEMING will see that these guides are ready at TANK DUMP at 8.15c.

Relief complete 6. Relief complete will be reported to Bn HQ as follows:—

    A coy   ALL
    B ...   POLICEMEN
    C ...   BIG
    D ...   FEET

Order of move 7. Coys will move out in the order B,D,C,A. immediately on relief. The usual distances will be maintained between platoons. Subject to the order of starting, coys will move independently

Reports 8. The Officer o. NCO in rear of each coy will report to the Adjutant when his coy. has passed Bn HQ

Route 9. (a) To TANK DUMP
COSTA - CALDRON - CHILI
Avenue. The mule track can be used.

(b) From TANK DUMP
CABLE - CASTLE LANE - CAM
VALLEY - St NICHOLAS.
Overland track may be used as
an alternative.

10. ACKNOWLEDGE

W Mackley
Capt & Adjt.
4 R West Kent Regt.

Issued at
on

Copies 1 A Coy
2 B "
3 C "
4 D "
5 OC 7th Bn Jemadar Regt.
6 File.

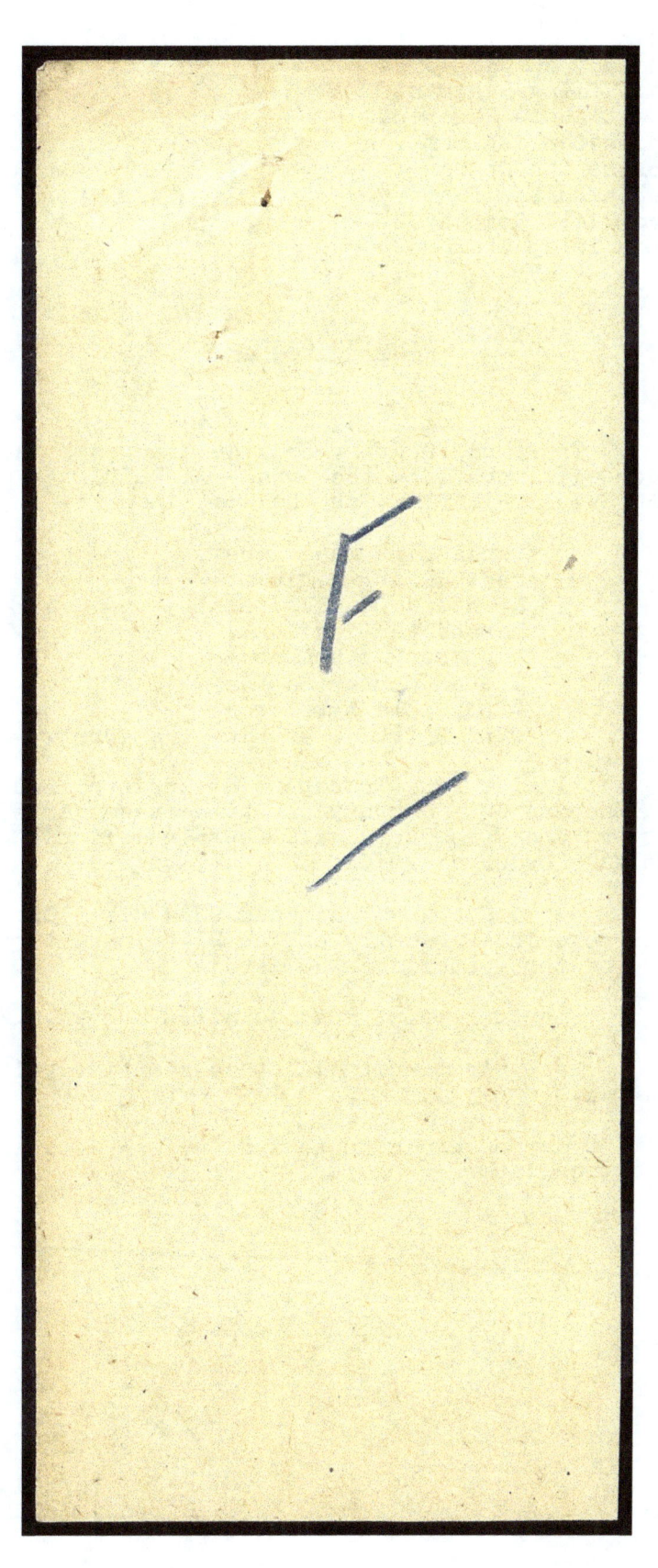

SECRET.   FILE W.D

H.Q.
52ND INFANTRY BDE.
52.G.
3751.

Lancashire Fusiliers.
West Riding Regiment.
R. West Kents Regiment.
Manchester Regiment.
Machine Gun Company.
Trench Mortar Battery.
93rd Field Company R.E.
52nd Field Ambulance.

Ref. Maps.
51.B.& 51.C.
1/40,000.

WARNING ORDER.

1. The 52nd Infantry Brigade Group composed as under will move into the area - WANQUETIN - FOUSEUX - HAUTEVILLE - LATTRE, on the ~~21st~~ 22nd instant:-

   Lancashire Fusiliers.
   West Riding Regiment.
   R. West Kents Regiment.
   Manchester Regiment.
   Machine Gun Company.
   Trench Mortar Battery.
   52nd Field Ambulance.
   52nd Brigade, 1st line Transport.

2. All 1st line Transport of Infantry Battalions and Machine Gun Company except Maltese Carts, Cookers and Mess Carts will be brigaded and march in the same order as Units.

3. No. 4 Company Train and 93rd Field Company R.E. will move independantly on the ~~21st~~ 22nd instant, or in case of the latter when relieved.

4. Starting point road junction C.15.D.2.2.

5. First unit will pass starting point at 11.0.am.

6. Order of March, route and further details will be issued later.

20:9:17.

J.R. Lindley
Captain.
a/Brigade Major.
52nd Infantry Brigade.

SECRET.　　　　　　　　　　　　　　　　　　　　Copy No. 8

52ND INFANTRY BRIGADE ORDER No. 196.
****

Ref Maps
51.B.N.W.
1/20,000
51.C.
1/40,000

September 21st 1917.

1. The 52nd Infantry Brigade Group will march to the area WANQUETIN - FOSSEUX - HAUTEVILLE - LATTRE, on the 22nd inst.
   Starting Point - Road junction G.15.D.2.2.

2. Movements will be carried out by march route in accordance with attached table

3. All 1st Line Transport of Infantry Battalions and Machine Gun Company except Maltese Carts will be Brigaded and march in the same order as units.
   Baggage wagons will march with the 1st Line Transport of units.

4. A distance of 200 yards will be maintained between units and Brigade Group of transport until after the 1st halt when the Brigade transport will proceed independently.
   A distance of 30 yards will be maintained between the Machine Gun Company and the Trench Mortar Battery.

5. The 93rd Field Company R.E. will march at 2.pm under orders issued by O.C. Company.

6. No. 4 Company Train will move off independently before 11.am

7. In addition to the usual halts there will be a special halt of half an hour from 1.30.pm to 2.pm.

8. Reports to Brigade Headquarters ST NICHOLAS up to 11.am after that hour to head of the column.
   Brigade Headquarters will reopen at FOSSEUX at 5.pm.

9. For march on 23rd inst head of column will pass FOSSEUX Chateau at 10.am.

ACKNOWLEDGE

Issued at 8.pm. (9.30)

Copy No. 1 to Bde H.Q.
         2 to War Diary.
         3 to Staff Captain.
         4 to Signals.
         5 to B.T.O.
         6 to Lancashire Fusiliers.
         7 to West Riding Regt.
       ✓ 8 to Royal West Kent Regt.
         9 to Manchester Regt.
        10 to Machine Gun Company.
        11 to Trench Mortar Battery.
        12 to 93rd F.Coy R.E.
        13 to 52nd F.Ambce.
        14 to No. 4.Coy Train.
        15 to O.C.Supplies.
        16 to 17th Division.

F. R. Findley
Captain,
a/Brigade Major,
52nd Infantry Brigade.

MARCH TABLE to accompany Brigade Order No. 196.

Ser. No.	Unit.	From.	To	Route to Starting Point G.15.D.2.2.	Time to reach S.P.	Route.
	52nd Bde 1st Line transport & Baggage Sect.	St Georges Camp	---	Rd. junct. G.16.A.70.45 – Rd. junct. G.9.C.75.00 – St CATHERINE.	11.a.m.	Dead Man Corner – Rd Junct L.1.D.6.8. from thence for each unit as below.
2.	Bde H.Q.	Reserve Bde H.Q.	FOSSEUX	Across Valley to ROCLIN-COURT Rd. B.9.C. – ST CATHERINE	11.15.am	Dead Man Corner – Rd Junct L.1.D.6.8. – HABARCQ – WANQUETIN – FOSSEUX.
3.	W Rid R.	Bull Camp.	–do–	BAILLEUL Rd. – Cross Rds G.16.C.65.90 Rd. Junct G.16.A.00.50 – Rd.junct G.9.C.75.00 – ST CATHERINE	11.16.am	– do –
4.	Manch Regt	Grimsby Camp	HAUTEVILLE	As for Ser No. 2.	11.21.am	Dead Man Corner – Rd Junct L.1.D.6.8. – HABARCQ – LATTRE – HAUTEVILLE.
5.	Lancs Fus.	Lichfield Camp	LATTRE	As for Ser.No.2.	11.26.am	Dead Man Corner – Rd Junct L.1.D.6.8. – HABARCQ – LATTRE.
6.	W.Kent R.	Lancaster Camp	VANQUETIN	As for Ser No. 2.	11.31.am	Dead Man Corner – Rd Junct L.1.D.6.8. – HABARCQ – WANQUETIN.
7.	M.G.Coy.) T.M.Bty.)	Grimsby Camp	LATTRE.	As for Ser. No.2.	11.37.am	As for Ser No.5.
8.	F.Ambce.	ARRAS.	WANQUETIN	Join column at Dead Man Corner, follow T.M.Bty.	Approx. 11.48.am	As for Ser.No.6.
9.	93rd F.Coy	St Nicholas	HAUTEVILLE	As for Ser No.2.	Approx. 2.pm.	As for Ser No.4.
10.	No.4.Coy Train	---	WANQUETIN	March independently starting before 11.am		Rd.junct. L.1.D.6.8.–any Route

SECRET

Ref. Maps. FILE W.D. Copy No. 6.
51.B. 51 C.
1/40000

WARNING ORDER.

1. The 53rd Inf. Bgde. will move to Billets tomorrow in the FOSSEUX area, and will probably move the following day to another area.

2. Probable time of parade 10.20 a.m.

3. 1st Line Transport.
(a) Mattress cart, cookers & mess cart will move with the Battalion, remaining transport moving under Brigade arrangements.

(b) Officers Kits.
Valises containing only blankets & sufficient necessaries for one night will be stacked outside H.Q's Mess hut by 6.45 a.m tomorrow morning. 30 lbs. per Officer will be the maximum allowed with these kits.

All kit surplus to the above will be stacked outside H.Q's Mess by 6 p.m this evening.

Mess boxes will be carried tomorrow with the Battalion & will be available tomorrow night, but Mess Presidents

3. (b) will have them made as light
(continued) as possible. Surplus stuff will
be stacked by 6 p.m tonight with
surplus kits.

4. Camp cleaning.
(a) 2 N.C.O.'s & 25 men from each Coy
will parade at 2 p.m today on
Bell Parade ground under orders of the
Quartermaster.
(b) Mess Presidents will ensure that
Officers servants & mess staffs have
all refuse, bottles etc burnt today and
that the Mess huts are thoroughly cleaned
(c) Major A. E. Jones will inspect the
Camp at 5 p.m. One Officer from
each Coy will report to him at that hour,
also 2/Lt. Flemming to represent H.Q. Coy
mess.

5. Coys. will be at the disposal of
Coy commanders from after dinner
today for the purpose of seeing that
all equipment is properly fitted,
special attention being paid to
the men's packs, which must be
carried well up on the shoulders.
Water bottles straps will be filled
today.

6. Acknowledge.

Issued by Orderly
at 11.45 a.m.

Copies to:—

No 1 — A Coy
No 2 — B —
No 3 — C —
No 4 — D —
No 5 — Transport Off. A.M.
No 6 — File.

[signature]
Capt. & Adjt.
3/4" Royal West Kent Rgt.

File

S E C R E T.

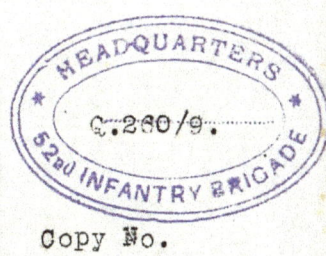

Copy No.

REFERENCE ADMINISTRATIVE INSTRUCTIONS NO.17.

September 21st. 1917.

The following is location of Units tomorrow night:-

Lancashire Fusiliers.	LATTRE ST. QUENTIN.
West Riding Regt.	FOSSEUX.
Royal West Kent Regt.	WANQUENTIN.
Manchester Regt.	HAUTEVILLE.
52nd. Machine Gun Coy.	LATTRE ST. QUENTIN.
52nd. Trench Mortar Battery.	LATTRE ST. QUENTIN.
52nd. Field Ambulance.	WANQUENTIN.
93rd. Field Coy. R.E.	HAUTEVILLE.
No. 4. Coy. Train.	WANQUENTIN.

All billetting parties are to report to their respective Town Majors at 9.0 a.m. 22nd. inst.

Units with interpreters must send them forward with their billetting parties.

Units make their own arrangements for guides to lead them to billets on arrival.

Copies to :-

1. Lan.Fus.
2. W.Rid.R.
3. R.W.Kent.R.
4. Manch.R.
5. M.G.Coy.
6. T.M.Bty.
7. 52nd. Fld. ambce.
8. 93rd. Fld. Coy.R.E.
9. No. 4 Coy. Train.
10. G.O.C.
11. Brigade Major.
13. Bde. Supply Officer.

Captain,
a/Staff Captain,
52nd. Infantry Brigade.

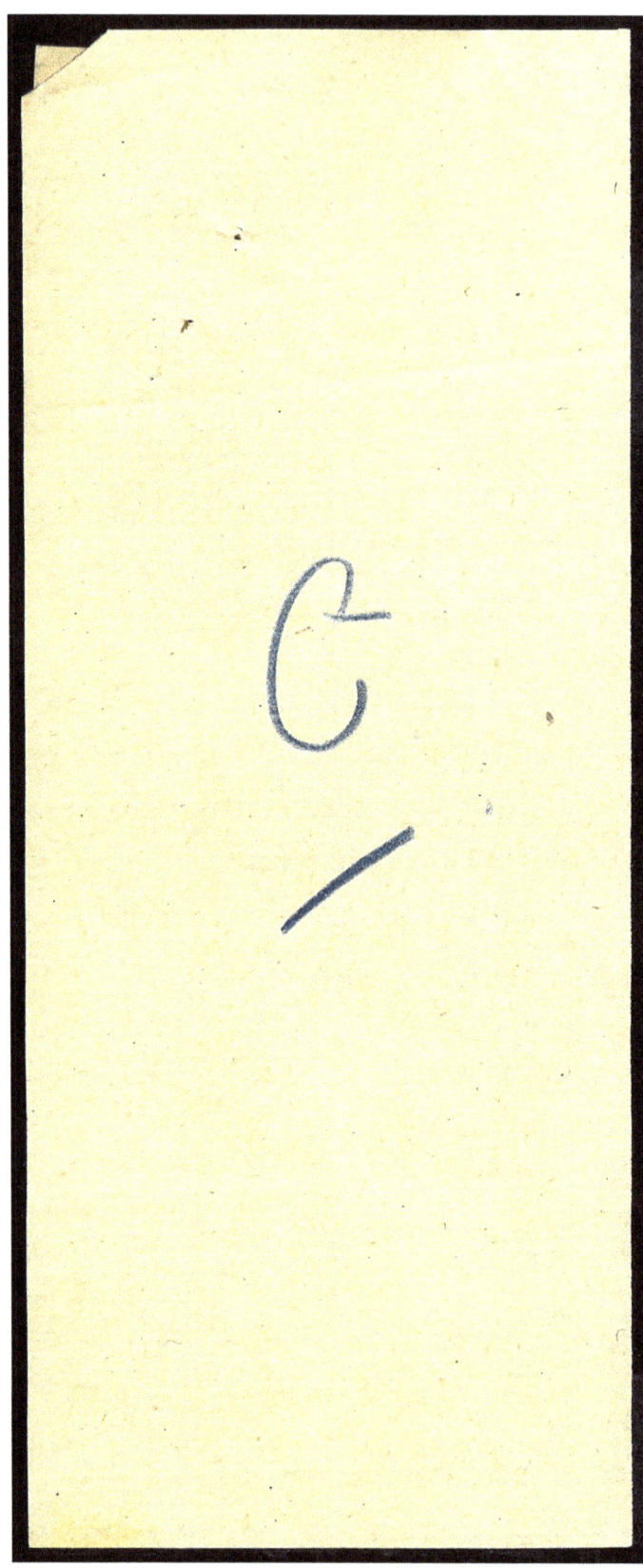

FILE W.D.

SECRET.   Copy No. 8

52ND INFANTRY BRIGADE ORDER No. 197.

Ref. Map
51.C.
1/40,000

September 25th 1917.

1. The 52nd Infantry Brigade will move to the area LUCHEUX - BREVILLERS - LE SOUICH on the 26th inst.

2. Units will move by march routes in accordance with the attached table.

3. All 1st Line Transport and Baggage wagons will accompany their respective units.

4. No.4 Company Train will move independently.

5. The usual reports will be rendered to Brigade Headquarters on arrival in Billets.

6. The usual 10 minute halts will be strictly observed.

7. Brigade Headquarters will close at FOSSEUX at 10.am on the 26th inst and reopen at LUCHEUX at the same hour.

ACKNOWLEDGE.

Issued at 8.am.

Copy No. 1 to Bde H.Q.
2 to War Diary.
3 to Staff Captain.
4 to Signals.
5 to B.T.O.
6 to Lancs. Fus.
7 to W.Riding R.
8 to R.W.Kent R.
9 to Manch Regt.
10 to M.G.Coy.
11 to T.M.Bty.
12 to 52nd F.Ambce.
13 to No.4.Coy Train.
14 to O.C.Supplies.
15 to 17th Division.

T.R.Lindley Captain,
a/Brigade Major,
52nd Infantry Brigade.

P.T.O.

MARCH TABLE to accompany Brigade Order No.197.

Ser. No.	Unit.	From	To	Starting Point	Time to reach Starting Point	Route.
1.	Manch. Regt.	HAUTEVILLE	BREVILLERS	Road Junction AVESNES le Comte J.31.B.1.1.	8.0.am.	AVESNES le Comte to GRAND RULLECOURT - Cross Rds.0.20.A. - SUS St Leger - IVERGNY - Le SOUICH
2.	Lancs Fus.	LATTRE	LE SOUICH	As for Ser.No.1	8.15.am.	As for Serial No. 1.
3.	M.G.Coy.	LATTRE	LUCHEUX	As for Ser.No.1	8.30.am.	AVESNES le Comte - GRAND RULLECOURT - Cross Rd.0.20.A. -
4.	T.M.Bty.	LATTRE	LUCHEUX	As for Ser.No.1	8.40.am	As for Serial No. 3.
5.	W Riding R.	FOSSEUX	LE SOUICH	Road Junction P.16.A.25.25.	7.0.am.	BARLY - SOMBRIN - SUS St Leger. - IVERGNY.
6.	Bde H.Q.	FOSSEUX	LUCHEUX	As for Ser No.5.	7.15.am	BARLY - SOMBRIN - Cross Roads 0.20.A.
7.	R.W.Kent R.	WANQUETIN	LUCHEUX	As for Ser No. 5.	8.35.am.	As for Serial No. 6.
8.	52nd F.Ambce	WANQUETIN	LE SOUICH	As for Ser.No.5.	8.45.am.	FOSSEUX - BARLY - SOMBRIN - Sus St Leger.
9.	No.4.Coy Train	-	BOUQUEMAISON		independently any route.	

Secret   7/4 Royal West Kent Regt.   Copy No. 9.

March Orders No. 1.   25-9-17.

Reference.
Sheet 51.c. 1/40,000.

Move 1. The Battalion will move by march route to Billets in LUCHEUX tomorrow the 26th inst.

Route 2. BARLY – SOMBRIN – cross roads O.20.c.

Starting Point 3. Junction of HAUTEVILLE – WANQUETIN and FOSSEUX – WANQUETIN roads. K.31.D.3.3

Time 4. The head of the column will pass the starting point at 7.30 a.m.

Order of March 5. H.Q. – B – C – Band – D – A.

Meals 6. Breakfasts 5.30 am
Small haversack ration will be carried on the march.
Dinners on arrival.

Baggage 7. All Baggage will be stacked outside billets at 6.0 am and sufficient loading parties ready, detailed by O.C. Coys concerned.

Transport 8. 1st Line Transport will march in rear of the Battalion.

Reports 9. Reports to head of column.

10. ACKNOWLEDGE

L. M. [signature]
Capt. & Adjutant
7/4 Royal West Kent Regt.

Issued through Signals
p.m.

Copies to   1. HQ   6. QM
            2. A   7. T.O.
            3. B   8. File
            4. C   9. W.D.
            5. D

SECRET.

H.Q.
52ND INFANTRY BDE.
52 G
3767.

Copy No. 8

The 52nd Infantry Brigade will remain in the present area until the 26th inst. when it will move to the LUCHEUX Area.

Para 10 of Brigade Order No. 193 is therefore cancelled.

Tomorrow, 23rd inst, will be employed in cleaning up, reorganising and inspections.

Copies to all recipients
of Brigade Order No. 196.

22/9/17.

J. R. Lindley Captain,
a/Brigade Major,
52nd Infantry Brigade.

Vol. 4.
52/17

War Diary
of
3/4th Bn: Royal West Kent:
October 1917.

Cosmographic

Vol Step 5
Chung Action
Lib Attender October December 1919
January s February 1920

Army Form C. 2118.

3/4 RW Kent 52/17
Vol 4

WAR DIARY
or
INTELLIGENCE SUMMARY

(Erase heading not required.)

Instructions regarding War Diaries and Intelligence Summaries are contained in F.S. Regs., Part II. and the Staff Manual respectively. Title Pages will be prepared in manuscript.

Place	Date	Hour	Summary of Events and Information	Remarks and references to Appendices
LUCHEUX	1/10/17		3/4th R.W.Kents/ Battalion Strength 33 Officers + 998 O.R.	
	2/10/17		Draft of 64 O.R. from 2/5th + 3rd R.W. Kent Regt.	
LUCHEUX	4/10/17	9.42 p.m.	Battalion (less "B" Coy) entrains at MONDICOURT.	Orders attached marked "A"
	5/10/17	9.20 A.M.	Battalion (less "B" Coy) detrains at PERSIA Camp F.16.d.85. (ref Belgium France 27 1/40,000)	
		1.42 p.m.	"B" Coy entrains at MONDICOURT	
		11.0 p.m.	"B" Coy detrains at PROVEN + joins Battalion in Persia Camp.	Orders attached marked "B"
PROVEN	10/10/17	11.0 A.M.	Battalion (less Transport) entraining at PROVEN detraining at EVERDINGHE at 12.45 p.m. Thence moved by Light march into DUBLIN Camp A.11.c.3.5. Transport moves by road from PROVEN to same destination. Battalion (with rest of 52 Infantry Bde.) in Divisional Reserve, 17th Division relieves 29th Division in the line N.E. of LANGEMARCK	Orders attached marked "C"
DUBLIN Camp.	14/10/17	2.15 P.M.	Battalion (less Transport) moves by march route to PARROY Camp B.10. c. 4.7 Transport was moved by road to B.17.d. H.1. (ref Belgium 28 N.W. 1/20,000)	Orders attached marked "D"

Elcomb[?] Lt
A/Adjt Royal West Kents

[signature] Lt Col
Comdg 3/4 Royal West Kents
9/11/17

Army Form C. 2118.

WAR DIARY
or
INTELLIGENCE SUMMARY
(Erase heading not required.)

Instructions regarding War Diaries and Intelligence Summaries are contained in F. S. Regs., Part II. and the Staff Manual respectively. Title Pages will be prepared in manuscript.

Place	Date	Hour	Summary of Events and Information	Remarks and references to Appendices
PARROY Camp.	16/10/17		Battalion commenced work under 183 Tunnelling Coy on PILCKEM Ridge to LANGEMARCK Church, working in two shifts, one from 5.0 AM — 11 O. AM. and the other from 11 O AM. till 5.0. PM. One Coy resting per day.	Orders from Gilbert Bigs Attached Marked "E"
	21/10/17		Battalion continued work but under direction of 173 Tunnelling Coy. in place of 183rd.	Orders attached marked "F"
	26/10/17	6.30 pm	Battalion moved by train (less Transport) to DRAGON Camp A.16.C.4.9. (26. B.N.W.) detraining at International Corner. Transport moved by route march to BUYSSCHEURE. Casualties during road work - P/Lt. E.G. Roe wounded. 14 O.R. Killed 14 O.R. wounded. 2 O.R. Wounded at duty.	Orders attached marked "G"
DRAGON Camp.	27/10/17	3.15 AM	Battalion moves to LA PANNE in the NORDAUSQUES area (ref. HAZEBROUCK 5" A) by route march to PROVEN thence by train. Transport reaches LA PANNE by route march.	
	29/10/17		Draft of 12 Officers + 20 O.R. received	
LA PANNE	31/10/17		Strength 42 Officers + 1024 O.R.	

2449 Wt. W14957/M90 750,000 1/16 J.B.C. & A. Forms/C.2118/12.

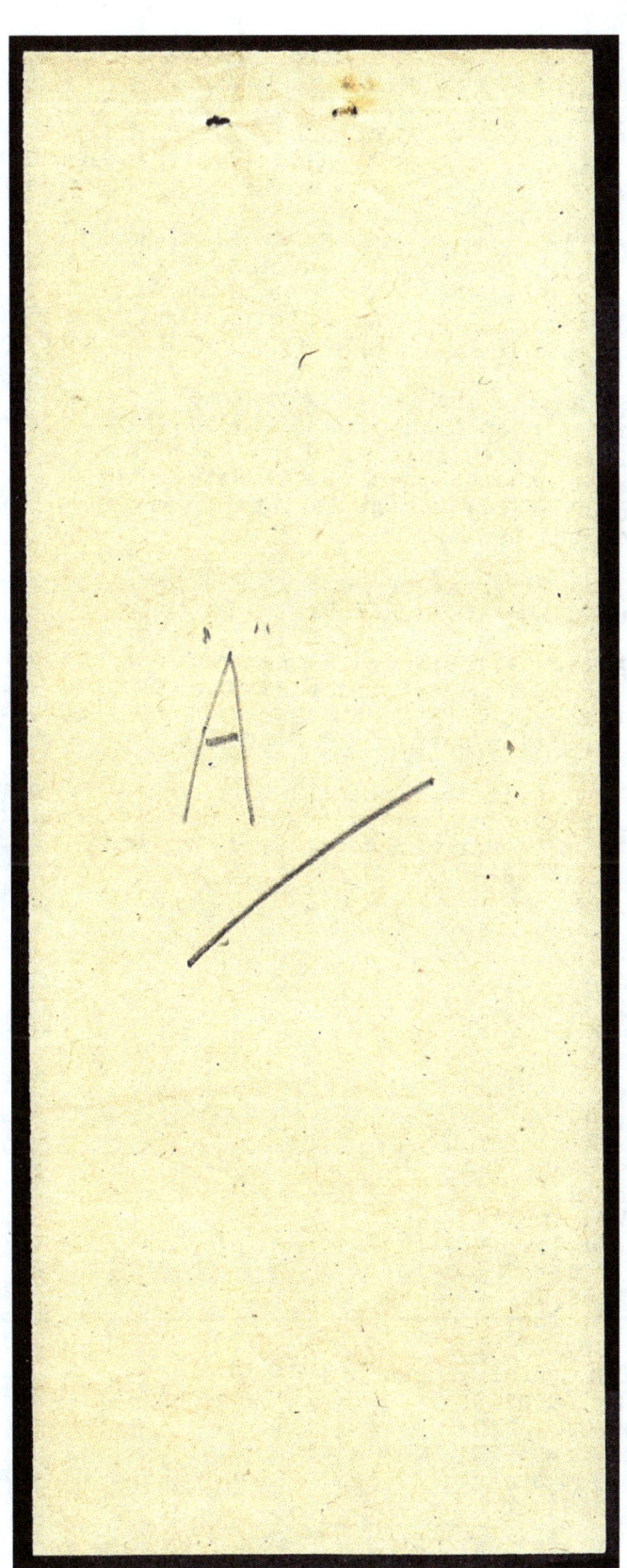

ENTRAINING (Contd).

(e). Major W.E. ROYDS, Manchester Regt. is detailed as Entraining Officer, Major S.DARBY West Riding Regt. is detailed as D etraining Officer.

(f). Officers Commanding Trains from LONDICOURT will be as follows :-

1st. Train.	-	G.O.C. 52nd.Inf.Bde.
2nd. Train.	-	O.C. 51st. Field Ambce.
3rd. Train.	-	O.C. 52nd. Field Ambce.
4th. Train.	-	O.C. 53rd. Field Ambce.
5th. & 6th. Trains)	-	To be detailed by Camp Commandant.
7th. Train.	-	O.C. Royal West Kent R.
8th. Train.	-	O.C. Manchester Regt.
9th. Train.	-	O.C. Lancashire Fusiliers.
10th. Train	-	O.C. West Riding Regt.
11th. Train	-	Major W.E. ROYDS, Manchester Regt.

Entraining Strengths are to be handed to each O.C. Train by the senior officer of each unit which has troops proceeding on the train, immediately on arrival at Entraining Station. O.C. Train will hand a consolidated return to R.T.O. showing total number of animals, vehicles, other ranks and officers proceeding on the train.

3. SURPLUS KIT :- Address of Dump at FREVENT is c/o Madame DERAY, 23 Rue d'Hesdin, FREVENT.

4. VILLAGE STORES :- All village stores and range stores are to be handed over to Town Majors and receipts obtained. O.C. Lan. Fus. will arrange direct with Town Major, BOUQUEMAISON, to hand over stores in Recreation Room at LE SOUICH.

5. CLAIMS :- As it will be impossible for units to leave behind the usual Rear Parties, every effort must be made to settle all claims before units leave the present area. All billets are to be left clean.

Copies to :-
1   G.O.C.
2   Brigade Major.
3   Staff Captain.
4   A/St ff Captain.
5. B.T.O.
6&7. Lan. Fus.
8&9. W.Rid. R.
10&11. R.West Kent Regt.
12&13. Manch. R.
14. 52nd.Fd.Ambce.
15. 93rd.Fd.Coy. R.E.
16. 52nd.Bde. Signals.
17. 52nd.M.G.Coy.
18. 52nd.T.M.Bty.
19. No.4 Coy. Train.
20. Supply Officer, No.4 Coy.Train.
21. R.T.O. LONDICOURT.
22. Major W.E.ROYDS, Manch. R.
23. Major. S.DARBY, West Riding Regt.
24. Camp Commandant, 17th.Division)   For information.
25. 1st .Division C.   )
26. Town Major, BOUQUEMAISON.

S. H. Smith
Captain,
Staff Captain,
52nd.Infantry Brigade.

SECRET.

ADMINISTRATIVE INSTRUCTIONS No.19.   C.320/10.

1st October 1917.

The following instructions are issued in connection with 17th.Division Administrative Instructions No.35 dated 30.9.17.

1. **BILLETING PARTIES :-** Units of Brigade Group will send following billetting parties from FREVENT early to-morrow, 2nd. inst. at a time to be notified later.

Bde. H.Q.	1 Officer.	3 Other ranks.	2 bicycles.
Each Battn.	1 "	6 " "	3 "
M.G.Coy.	1 "	2 " "	3 "
T.M.Bty.	1 "	2 " "	3 "
52nd.Fd.Ambce.	1 "	5 " "	3 "
93rd.Fd.Coy.R.E.	1 "	6 " "	3 "
No.4 Coy.Train.	1 "	3 " "	3 "
T O T A L	10	46 "	29 "

Officers servants are included in the above figures and must act as members of the billeting party. Manchester Regt. will detail a Captain as their billeting Officer and this officer will be in charge of the Brigade Group Billeting Party. All units billeting parties will report to this officer at FREVENT to-morrow for entraining.

Billeting parties report on arrival to Area Commandant, PROVEN (and not St.SIXTE as stated in Divisional Instructions). O.C. Billeting Parties will ascertain from R.T.O. PROVEN time of arrival of trains and will arrange that billeting parties meet their units on arrival at PROVEN and conduct them to camps.

2. **ENTRAINING :-** (a). It is not anticipated that there will be any halts on the journey for watering and feeding. Units with horse transport will therefore place petrol tins full for each horse in the horse trucks. Horses will be watered by their drivers and grooms with buckets from these petrol tins. Petrol Tins required for this purpose may be drawn from mobile reserve, but **must** be replaced on transport vehicles at the end of the journey. Horses must be watered just before entraining. There are good troughs at LE GROS TISON farm and in MONDICOURT next to the Chocolate Factory.

(b). Transport Officers must ensure that the floors of all trucks used for animals are sprinkled with shingle or cinders, of which there is a supply at MONDICOURT Station. Breast ropes must be obtained from Divisional Headquarters if units have not sufficient on hand.

(c). O.C. Manchester Regt. will detail 1 Coy. which must parade as strong as possible, to act as entraining party for all trains leaving MONDICOURT Station. Company to be rationed up to night of 5th. inst., and to report to R.T.O. MONDICOURT 3 hours before departure of first train from MONDICOURT. As entraining will probably commence in the afternoon of 3rd inst. the Company must be prepared to move to MONDICOURT any time after 9 a.m. 3rd. inst. The Coy. will be billetted by R.T.O. MONDICOURT and will entrain on the last train leaving MONDICOURT.

(d). Similarly O.C. Lan. Fus. will detail 1 Coy. for detraining at PROVEN, similarly rationed. This Coy. will proceed in first train leaving MONDICOURT, and will report to R.T.O. PROVEN, and to Detraining Officer on arrival at PROVEN.

P.T.O.

- 2 -

                (1) <u>Returns.</u>   Entraining strength will be handed in by the Senior Officer of each Unit which has troops moving by the train, to O.C. Train who will hand a consolidated return to R.T.O. shewing total number of animals, vehicles, O.R. & Officers proceeding by the train.

Surplus Kits.   The address of the dump at FREVENT is :-
                         C/o Madame DERAY,
                           23, Rue d'HESDIN,
                             FREVENT.

Claims.   2nd-Lieut. E. C. Vise will report to the Adjutant to-morrow at 2.15 p.m. with a view to dealing with claims forthwith.   <u>No Rear Party will be left.</u>

Stoves.   All village & range stoves will be handed over to Town Major, LUCHEUX, by 9.0 a.m., 3rd. instant, and receipts forwarded to Battn. H.Q. by noon the same day.

Billets.   Billets & streets in the vicinity will be left thoroughly clean.

                                                         ACLovett 2/Lt
                                                           Asst Adjt
                                            for Captain & Adjutant,
                             3/4th. Battn. Royal West Kent Regiment.

Issued at 9-45 p.m.

Copies to :-

1. C.O.   9. T.O.
2. O.C., "A" Coy.   10. M.O.
3. O.C., "B" Coy.   11. 2/Lt. E.M. Williams.
4. O.C., "C" Coy.   12. Asst. Adjutant.
5. O.C., "D" Coy.   13. 2/Lt. E.C. Vise.
6. Capt. T.L. Tanner.   14. R.S.M.
7. H.Q. Officers' Mess. 15. W.D.
8. Q.M.   16. File.

SECRET.

3/4th. Battn. Royal West Kent Regiment.

ADMINISTRATIVE INSTRUCTIONS.
No. 3.

Copy No. 15

W D

1-10-17.

The following administrative instructions are issued with reference to the impending move of the Battalion :-

1. Billeting Party. 2nd-Lieut. E.M.Williams & batman, 1 N.C.O. for H.Q. and 1 N.C.O. per Coy. will report to O.i/c.Bde. Group Billeting Party (an officer of the MANCHESTER REGT.) FREVENT early to-morrow, the 2nd. instant. On arrival 2nd-Lieut. WILLIAMS will report to the Area Commandant, PROVEN, and ascertain from R.T.O. PROVEN, the time of arrival of the trains conveying this Unit and arrange for the billeting party to meet them.

Entraining.
(a) Entraining Station. MONDICOURT.
(b) Destination. PERSIA CAMP.
 P 5 Area PROVEN.
(c) Trains. No.7 will convey the Battn. less "B" Coy., with its cooker & team.
O.C. Train - O.C., 3/4th.R.W.Kent Regt.
No. 11 will convey "B" Coy. with its cooker & team. O.C. Train Major W. E. BOYDS, Manchester Regt. G.T. WILKES
(d) Train-load. Each train consists of one passenger coach to hold 30 Officers,
30 covered vans " " 40 men or 8 L.D.horses, or 6 H.D.horses.
17 flats to hold 4 to 5 axles.
(e) Time-table. All transport & animals (except Officers' chargers) will reach entraining station 3 hours before the train is due to start; all personnel will arrive 1½ hours before the train is due to start. In all cases an Officer will reach station ¾ of an hour before troops.
(f) Watering & Feeding. No halts are probable on the way for watering & feeding. Petrol tins full must be placed in the horse trucks for each horse; horses will be watered by buckets from these tins by their drivers or grooms. Such petrol tins may be drawn from mobile reserve, but must be replaced after the journey. Horses must be watered just before entraining. Food troughs exist at LE GROS TISON Farm and in MONDICOURT next to the Chocolate Factory.
(g) Horse Trucks. The floors of all horse trucks will be sprinkled with cinders or shingle under arrangements made by the T.O. A supply is available at MONDICOURT Station. Breast ropes must be obtained from Divisional H.Q. if there are not enough in possession.
(h) Baggage & Supply Wagons. These will be entrained full with units.
(i) Rations. The unexpended portion of the day's ration will be carried on the man and on the horse or in the First Line Transport.
(j) Ammunition. Mobile reserves must be complete.
(k) Water. Water-carts & water-bottles will be full at the time of entrainment.

(See Sheet 2)

SECRET.

C.320/17.

MOVE TO PROVEN AREA.

COPY NO. 7.

October 2nd. 1917.

1.   52nd. Infantry Brigade Group, including 236th. M.G.Coy., will move by rail to PROVEN Area (Fifth Army, XIV Corps) on 3rd., 4th. and 5th. inst., entraining at MONDICOURT and detraining at PROVEN.

2.   Detailed instructions for the move have been issued to all concerned in 17th. Divisional Admin. Instrons. Nos. 35 and 36, and in 52nd. Infantry Brigade Admin. Instrons. No.19, which must be closely adhered to.

3.   Entraining Tables have been issued to all Units. Attached Table shows in addition, composition of each train and Officer Commanding Train.

4.   There are no restrictions as to times or routes to entraining station, but units must arrive at the Station at the precise time stated. If units arrive too early there is bound to be congestion at the station.

5.   Billeting Parties have been sent on in advance and will meet units at detraining station.

6.   The Brigade Group on arrival will be accomodated in PROVEN No. P.5 Area, which is administered by P.5 Area Commandant, who lives at PROVEN.

7.   Supply Arrangements will be as laid down in 17th. Div. Admin. Instrons. No.36. Railhead for 4th. inst. is PREVENT. Railhead for 5th. inst. is PROVEN.

8.   Brigade H.Q. will close at LUCH EUX at 5 p.m. on 3rd. inst., and open at POONA Camp, P.5. Area, PROVEN, at noon October 4th.

9.   ACKNOWLEDGE.

Issued at 4.0 p.m.

Copy. No. 1 - War Diary.
      2 - Bde. Major.
      3 - Staff Captain.
      4 - B. T. O.
      5 - Lan. Fus.
      6 - W. Rid. R.
      7 - R.W.Kent R.
      8 - Manch. R.
      9 - 52nd. M.G. Coy.
    10 - 52nd. T.M. Bty.
    11 - 52nd. Fd. Ambce.
    12 - 93rd. F d. Coy. R.E.
    13 - 236th. M.G.Coy.
    14 - B de. Signal Officer.
    15 - No. 4 Coy. Train.
    16 - Supply Officer, No.4 Coy. Train.
    17 - Major S. DANBY, W. Rid. R.
    18 - Major W.T. WILKES, Manch. R.
    19 - 17th. Division Q.
    20 - 17th. Division G.
    21 - Town Major, LUCHEUX.
    22 - Town Major, BOU QUEMAISON.

S. H. Smith

Captain,
Staff Captain,
52nd. Infantry Brigade.

S E C R E T.

ENTRAINING TABLE. 52nd. INFANTRY BRIGADE.

C.320/17
HEADQUARTERS 52nd INFANTRY BRIGADE

Entraining Station.	Train No.	Date.	Time of departure.	UNIT.	Officer Cmdg. Train.
MON DICOURT	1.	3.10.17.	9.42 p.m.	Brigade H.C. and Signal Section, M.G.Coy.,and T.M.Bty., 1 Coy., 1 Cooker, and 1 Team of Lan.Fus.	Brig-Genl. A.J.F.EDEN D.S.O.
Do.	3.	4.10.17.	2.42 a.m.	77th.Fd.Coy.R.E., 51st. Field Ambce.	O.C.51st.Fd.Ambce.
Do.	5.	4.10.17.	5.42 a.m.	93rd.Fd.Coy.R.E., 52nd.Fd.Ambce.	O.C.52nd.Fd.Ambce.
Do.	7.	4.10.17.	9.42 a.m.	78th.Field Coy.R.E., 53rd.Field Ambce.	O.C.53rd.Fd.Ambce.
Do.	9.	4.10.17.	1.42 p.m.	236 M.G.Coy., 218 E.E.Coy., H.C.Divl.Train, and 29th.M.V.S.	Detailed by Div.H.Q.
Do.	11.	4.10.17.	5.42 p.m.	Div. H.C., H.C.Div.Engineers, H.C. and No.1 Section Signal Coy.	Do.
Do.	13.	4.10.17.	9.42 p.m.	R.W.Kent R.,(less 1 Coy., 1 Cooker and 1 Team).	O.C. R.West Kent R.
Do.	15.	5.10.17.	1.42 a.m.	Manch. R., (less 1 Coy., 1 Cooker and 1 Team).	O.C. Manch. R.
Do.	17.	5.10.17.	5.42 a.m.	Lan. Fus. (less 1 Coy., 1 Cooker and 1 Team).	O.C. Lan. Fus.
Do.	19.	5.10.17.	9.42 a.m.	W.Rid. R. (less 1 Coy., 1 Cooker and 1 Team).	O.C. W. Rid. R.
Do.	21.	5.10.17.	1.42 p.m.	1 Coy., 1 Cooker and 1 Team of W.Rid. R. 1 Coy., 1 Cooker and 1 Team of R.W.Kent R. 1 Coy., 1 Cooker and 1 Team of Manch. R. No.4 Coy. Train.	Maj.C.T.WILKES, Manch. R.

✸ Copies of S.S.554 have been issued to each Battn. and to Maj. WILKES. Further copies will be issued if received.

2.10.17

S. H. Smith
Captain,
Staff Captain,
52nd. Infantry Brigade.

DISTRIBUTION.

INSTRUCTIONS.

50th. Brigade. - 12 for Units, Fd.Coys., Fd.Amb. & Train Coy.
51st.   "   12 "   "   "   "   "   "
52nd.   "   13 "   "   "   "   "   "   and
                                                            236th.M.G.Coy.

"G" (3) C.R.E.(1) Signals.(1) A.D.M.S.(1) Train.(1) S.S.O.(1)
A.P.M.(1) Dumps Off.(1) D.A.D.V.S.(1) Camp Cdt.(1) Salvage.(1)
Emply.Coy.(1) Baths Off.(1) S.C.F.(C.of E.)(1) S.C.F.(Non C of E)(1)
Supply Col.(1) D.A.D.R.T.AVNES. R.T.Os. SAULTY and MONDICOURT.

TIME TABLE.

50th. Brigade. - 10 :- Bde.H.Q.(1)Bns.(1)Fd.Coy.(1)Fd.Amb.(1)
                       Train Coy.(1)Entraining Off.(1) Detraining
                       Off.(1)

51st.Brigade.   do.   do.   do.   do.   do.   do.

52nd.Brigade.   11.   do.   do.   do.   do.   do.   and
                                                    236th.M.G.Coy.

H.Q.,Divl.Train.(1) C.R.E.(1)A.D.M.S.(1)C.Cdt.(1) D.A.D.V.S.(1)
D.A.D.O.S.(1) 47th.Supply Col.(1) "G"(1)

S.S.524. 6 per Bde. Extra Copy to be forwarded later.

SECRET.
A/1001.

ADMINISTRATIVE INSTRUCTIONS.

No. 36.
(In continuation of No. 35.)

1. MOVE BY RAIL.

(a) Time Table of railway moves from SAULTY and MONDICOURT is attached.
The following small alterations from original table will be noted :-

1st. Train now leaves from MONDICOURT. It was originally arranged that trains would leave SAULTY first. In other respects the table is identical.

The following additions will be made to Appendix "A" of Administrative Instructions No. 35.

6th. Train from SAULTY.	H.Q., No. 3 Coy. Train.
11th. Train from MONDICOURT.	H.Q., No. 4 Coy. Train.
12th. Train from SAULTY	H.Q., No. 2 Coy. Train.

(b) With reference to Administrative Instructions No. 35 of 30th. September, para. 3, entraining sub-paras (h) (1) (j) the companies responsible for entraining will now report 3½ hours before the departure of the trains from SAULTY and MONDICOURT.

DETRAINMENT.
(c) Brigade Staffs will be responsible for the entraining and detraining of their Brigade groups. Detraining must be expeditiously carried out and in accordance with the wishes of the R.T.O. Particular care must be taken to prevent the blocking of Station exits and roads to camps from detraining stations.
Guides from the billeting parties must be at the detraining stations to meet all parties of their units and guide them to their camp.

WATER FOR HORSES.
(d) SAULTY - Water is available in a field adjoining the Station.

MONDICOURT - Water is available in the village, near to the Chocolate Factory, and at GROS TISON FARM on the LUCHEUX Road.

COOKERS.
(e) All fires will be drawn before Cookers are entrained.

DISCIPLINE.
(f) Attention is directed to A.R.O. No. 1119 - Copies of S.S. 534, for distribution to O.C. Trains, are attached.

(MOTOR VEHICLES.

- 2 -

2. MOTOR VEHICLES.

See Foot-Note.
The 47th.Supply Column and Motor Ambulance Cars will proceed on 4th.October by road to PROVEN. Route - ST.POL - PERNES - LILLERS - HAZEBROUCK - STEENVOORDE.

Motor Ambulance Cars will proceed in one party, starting point BUNEVILLE, 4 miles S. of ST.POL at 11:30 a.m.. They will rejoin Field Ambulances on arrival in new area.

47th.Supply Column will not leave LIENCOURT before 11:30 a.m. and will proceed in one party. Advance party of 47th.Supply Column will report to S.M.T.O.,XIV Corps at ST.SIXTE on 2nd.October.

3. SALVAGE.

On no account is any salvage to be left in the present area. All salvage must be sent to D.A.D.O.S. Store.

4. DIRTY CLOTHING.

All dirty clothing from baths and any surplus clean clothes must be returned by 6 p.m. 2nd.inst. The clean clothing store will close as far as issues are concerned at 10 a.m. 2nd.instant.

5. YUKON PACKS - PACK CRATES.

All Yukon Packs and Pack Crates now in possession of units will be taken to the new area.

6. PACK SADDLES.

All Pack Saddles loaned for practice purposes will be collected at Bde.H.Q. by 2 p.m., 2nd.instant. D.A.D.O.S. will arrange to collect and deliver to O.O., 17th.Corps Troops.

7. BILLETING PARTIES.

All Billeting Parties will proceed rationed to such time as their units will arrive.

8. SUPPLY ARRANGEMENTS.

(i) On October 3rd.Supply Wagons will deliver supplies as usual. The Supply Wagons of all Units entraining on and before 18.48 hours on the 4th.inst. will refill with supplies for consumption 5th.inst. and join their units by 2 p.m. 3rd.inst.

(ii) On October 4th. supply wagons of all units entraining after 18.48 hours on the 4th.inst. will deliver supplies as usual, return to refilling points and load up rations for consumption 6th.inst. & join their units by 2 p.m.,4th.inst.

(iii) Supplies for units in para.1 for consumption 6th.inst. will be taken to the new area by 47th.Supply Column and dumped under orders to be issued by O.C.,17th.Divisional Train.

NOTE:- One M.A. car per Field Ambulance to be placed at the disposal of respective Infantry Brigades until entrainment is completed. Cars will then report to D.H.Q. in PROVEN.

L. R. Nicholson

1st.October,1917.

Lieut-Colonel.
A.A. & Q.M.G.,17th.Division.

STRATEGICAL MOVE OF 17th DIVISION (LESS ARTILLERY).

From THIRD ARMY   To. FIFTH ARMY.

A. HEUDICOURT   A. PROVEN

B. SAULTY   B. PESCHENDEL

All trains will be consigned to HAZEBROUCK for regulation.

Train No. From Stations		SERIAL NUMBER	Date 1917	Marche	Time of Dept.	Time due to arrive	Remarks
A.	B.						
1	2	3	4	5	6	7	8
1	-	1730-1731a-1735-1736-1737	3/10	T.64(DA.248)	21.42		
-	2	1720-1721a-1725-1726-1727	"	T.66(DA.268)	22.42		
3	-	1731-1736	4/10	T.68(DA.8)	1.42		
-	4	1721	"	T.70(DA.28)	2.42		
5	-	1733-1737	"	T.72(DA.56)	5.42		
-	6	1722	"	T.74(DA.76)	6.42		
7	-	1732-1738	"	T.52(DA.104)	9.42		
-	8	1723	"	T.54(DA.124)	10.42		
9	-	1708-1709-1775-1790	"	T.56(DA.152)	13.42		
-	10	1724	"	T.58(DA.172)	14.42		
11	-	1701-1703-1705	"	T.60(DA.200)	17.42		
-	12	1722a-1723a-1724a-1777	"	T.62(DA.220)	18.42		
13	-	1735	"	T.64(DA.248)	21.42		
-	14	1710-1711a-1715-1716-1717	"	T.66(DA.268)	22.42		
15	-	1734	5/10	T.68(DA.8)	1.42		
-	16	1713	"	T.70(DA.28)	2.42		
17	-	1731	"	T.72(DA.56)	5.42		
-	18	1711	"	T.74(DA.76)	6.42		
19	-	1752	"	T.52(DA.104)	9.42		
-	20	1712	"	T.54(DA.124)	10.42		
21	-	1732a-1733a-1734a-1778	"	T.56(DA.152)	13.42		
-	22	1714	"	T.58(DA.172)	14.42		
-	23	1712a-1713a-1714a-1776	"	T.62(DA.220)	18.42		

All trains will be Type Omnibus i.e. 1 Coach 30 Covers 17 Flats.

F.T.Baron
Captain,
Traffic Officer,
THIRD ARMY.

AVESNES
1st October 1917.

SECRET.

17th DIVISION (Less Artillery).

TABLE "D"

UNIT	SERIAL NUMBER	DESCRIPTION
DIVISIONAL UNITS	1701	Divisional H.Q.
	1703	H.Q. Divisional Engineers.
	1705	H.Q. and No. 1 Section Divisional Signals.
	1708	236th Machine Gun Company.
	1709	218th Divisional Employment Company.
50th INFANTRY BRIGADE	1710	Brigade Headquarters.
	1711	10th W.Yorks R. less 1711a.
	1711a	1 Co., 1 Cooker & Team of 10th W.Yorks R.
	1712	7th E.Yorks R. less 1712a
	1712a	1 Co., 1 Cooker & Team of 7th E.Yorks R.
	1713	7th Yorks R. less 1713a
	1713a	1 Co., 1 Cooker & Team of 7th Yorks R.
	1714	6th Dorset R. less 1714a
	1714a	1 Co., 1 Cooker & Team of 6th Dorset R.
	1715	Brigade Signal Section.
	1716	Brigade Machine Gun Company.
	1717	Brigade Trench Mortar Battery (Light).
51st INFANTRY BRIGADE	1720	Brigade Headquarters.
	1721	7th Linc. R. less 1721a
	1721a	1 Co, 1 Cooker & Team of 7th Linc. R.
	1722	7th(West.& Cumb.Yeo)Bord.R. less 1722a.
	1722a	1 Co., 1 Cooker & Team of 7th Bord. R.
	1723	8th S.Staff. R. less 1723a
	1723a	1 Co., 1 Cooker & Team of 8th S. Staff. R.
	1724	10th Notts. & Derby R. less 1724a
	1724a	1 Co., 1 Cooker & team of 10th Notts & D.R.
	1725	Brigade Signal Section.
	1726	Brigade Machine Gun Company.
	1727	Brigade Trench Mortar Battery (Light).
52nd INFANTRY BRIGADE	1730	Brigade Headquarters.
	1731	10th Lancs. Fus. less 1731a
	1731a	1 Co., 1 Cooker & Team of 10th Lanc. Fus.
	1732	9th W.Rid. R. less 1732a.
	1732a	1 Co., 1 Cooker & Team of 9th W.Rid. R.
	1733	3/4th R.W.Kent R. less 1733a
	1733a	1 Co., 1 Cooker & Team of 3/4th R.W.Kent R.
	1734	12th(D of Lancaster's Yeo)Manc.R.less 1734a.
	1734a	1 Co., 1 Cooker & Team of 12th Manch. R.
	1735	Brigade Signal Section.
	1736	Brigade Machine Gun Company.
	1737	Brigade Trench Mortar Battery (Light).

SECRET.

UNIT	SERIAL NUMBER	DESCRIPTION
DIVISIONAL TRAIN.	1775	H.Q., Divisional Train.
	1776	No. 2 Company.
	1777	No. 3 Company.
	1778	No. 4 Company.
DIVISIONAL ENGINEERS.	1781	77th Field Company R.E.
	1782	78th Field Company R.E.
	1783	93rd Field Company R.E.
MEDICAL UNITS.	1786	51st Field Ambulance.
	1787	52nd Field Ambulance.
	1788	53rd Field Ambulance.
VETERINARY UNIT.	1790	29th Mobile Veterinary Section.

U R G E N T.

Bde. H.Q.
W.Rid. R.
R.West Kent R.
Manch. R.
52nd. M.G.Coy.

52nd.T.M.Bty.
52nd.Fd.Ambce.
93rd.Fd.Coy. R.E.
No.4 Coy. Train.
A/Staff Captain.

N 320/16

Reference para. 1 of this office Admin. Instrcns. No.19 of yesterday:- Billeting Parties :-

1. One Officer and one other rank of each unit in Brigade Group will be conveyed by motor-bus to-day direct to PROVEN. No Officers kits, beyond haversack and pack can be taken on this bus.

2. Bus will call at Headquarters as follows :-

   12.30 p.m.   Bde H.Q. - For 93rd.Fd.Coy. R.E. M.G.Coy.,
                           T.M.Bty., R.West Kents, and Bde.H.Q.

   12.45 p.m. - H.Q. Manch. R. - for Manch. Regt.

   1.0 p.m.   - H.Q. W.Rid. R.- for Lan. Fus., W.Rid. R., and
                                 52nd.Fd.Ambce.

   1.15 p.m. - Town Major, BOUQUEMAISON - for No.4 Coy.Train.

   Party proceeding on bus will be in charge of Capt. F.W. EVANS, Asst. Staff Captain, and must take rations to night of 5th. inst.

3. Remainder of billeting parties of units must report to R.T.O. F REVENT, at 10.0 p.m. to-night ready to proceed. No transport is available to send them to PREVENT. O.C. Manch. Regt. will detail 1 additional officer to take charge of this party and all units parties will report to him at PREVENT Station at 10.0 p.m. to-day. He should take with him blank Movement Order in triplicate. Parties to be rationed to night of 5th. inst.

L 68, 69-70.

S. H. Smith

2/10/17

Captain,
Staff Captain,
52nd.Infantry Brigade.

Q 320/14

QM/134

SECRET.

MOVE OF 17TH DIV. DEPOT BATTALION TO FIFTH ARMY.

1. The 17th Divisional Depot Battalion, consisting of approximately 10 officers, 300 O.R. and 5 tons of baggage, will move on the 2nd inst by rail from SAVY to BOLLEZEELE

2. Entraining Station - SAVY-BERLETTE.
   Detraining Station - ARNEKE.

3. The train (T.C.8289) is timed to leave SAVY-BERLETTE at 23.46 hours.

4. All personnel with baggage will arive at the Station 1 hour before the time of departure. An officer will be detailed to report to the R.T.O. 1½ hours before the time of departure of the train.

5. Rations up to and for consumption 4th inst will be taken

6. The XIV Corps have been asked to send guides and transport for baggage to ARNEKE to meet the train.

7. Attention is directed to S.S.554.

Mark Phillips
Captain,

1/10/1917.
D.A.Q.M.G., 17th Division.

Copies to :-

17th Div Depot Bn.
50th Brigade.
51st Brigade.
52nd Brigade.
"G".
Traffic AVESNES-LE-COMTE.
R.T.O. SAVY-BERLETTE.
R.T.O. ARNEKE.
XIV Corps.
XVII Corps.
VII Corps.

SECRET.

Lan. us.
West Riding Regt.
R.West Kent Regt.
Manchester Regt.
52nd M.Gun Coy.
52nd T.M.Battery.
236th M.Gun Coy.
17th Division. Q.,)
A.D.M.S.,17th Div.) for information.
Area Commandant, MONDICOURT.

Reference impending move of Brigade Group:-

1. The Staff Captain will remain in the present area till the last train leaves MONDICOURT on th instant.   Messages intended for him should be sent to Office of Area Commandant, MONDICOURT, between -0 p.m. on 3rd instant and Noon on th instant.

2. Our Motor Ambulance Car is at the disposal of the Brigade to convey men unable to march to entraining Station. This Car will call at Units' Headquarters in accordance with following table and will return to Office of Area Commandant, MONDICOURT after completion of last journey on 4th instant.

Oct. 4th.   H.Q.,   R.WEST KENT REGT.   1-0 p.m.

     4th.   "   MANCHESTER REGT.   3-0 p.m.

     4th.   "   LANCASHIRE FUS.   5-0 p.m.

     4th.   "   WEST RIDING REGT.   8-0 p.m. (for West Riding Regt and No. 4 Coy. Train)

On no account is the Car to be overloaded or used except for really necessitous cases.

                                    Captain,
                                Staff Captain,
2 -10-1917.   52nd Infantry Brigade.

SECRET.   Copy No. 13

3/4th. Battn. Royal West Kent Regiment.

March Orders No. 2   3-10-17.

Ref.:- Belgium
       HAZEBROUCK 5a - 1/100,000

1. **Move.** The move of the Battn. foreshadowed in Administrative Instructions No. 3 of the 1st. instant, will take place to-morrow, the 4th inst., and Friday, 5th. inst.

2. **Train Arrangements.**
   (a) Train No. 13 from MONDICOURT Station, Serial No.1733, will convey the Battn. (less "B" Coy. with cooker & team) and is timed to start at 9.42 p.m. on the 4th instant.
   (b) Train No. 21 from MONDICOURT Station, Serial No.1733a, will convey "B" Coy. with cooker & team and is timed to start at 1.42 p.m. the 5th instant.

3. **Order of March.** The Battn. (less "B" Coy. & Transport) will march in the following order, H.Q., "D", "C", Band, "A".

4. **Starting Point.** Starting Point will be Battn. H.Q.

5. **Time of Parade.** The head of the column will pass the Starting Point at 6.20 p.m.

6. **Transport.** First & Second Line Transport (less officers' chargers which will proceed with the Battn. and "B" Coy.'s cooker & team) will reach MONDICOURT Station at 6.42 p.m., the 4th instant ready to entrain. The T.O. will make his own arrangements for the march.

7. **"B" Coy..** O.C. "B" Coy. will arrange for his Coy. cooker & team to reach MONDICOURT Station by 10.42 a/m., the 5th instant, and for his Coy. (less cooker & team) to reach the same Station by 12.12 p.m., the 5th instant.

8. **Entraining.** Special attention is drawn to Administrative Instructions No. 3, dated 1-10-17, para.2, which will be strictly adhered to, and to the following additions thereto :-
   (a) **Rations.** Rations for the 5th. instant will be carried on the man. Rations for the 6th. instant will be on the supply wagons which will report by 2.0 p.m. on the 4th. instant.
   (b) **Railhead.** Railhead for the 4th. instant will be PREVENT and for the 5th instant PROVEN.
   (c) **Cookers.** All fires will be drawn before cookers are entrained.
   (d) **Salvage.** No salvage will be left in the LUCHEUX Area.
   (e) **Loading Transport.** 1st. Line Transport will be loaded by 12.0 noon, the 4th instant and inspected by the Adjutant at that hour.
   No.1 Baggage Wagon will reach Q.M.Stores at 10.0 a.m. & No.2 Baggage Wagon at 10.15 a.m. on the 4th instant. Os.C. "A" & "B" Coys. will detail one N.C.O. & 6 men each to report to Q.M. at 10.0 a.m. as loading party.
   No. 1 Baggage Wagon will report at Battn.H.Q., "B" & "C" Coys. H.Q. for Officers' kits at 10.30, 10.45 & 11.0 a.m. respectively. Loading parties will be ready detailed by Os.C. Coys. concerned.
   No. 2 Baggage Wagon will report at "D" & "A" Coys. H.Q. at 10.45 a.m. & 11.15 a.m. respectively. Loading parties will be ready detailed by Os/C.Coys. concerned.
   Both wagons will return to Transport Lines when loaded.

                                              W.Macklin
                                              Captain & Adjutant,
                                              3/4th.Battn.Royal West Kent Regiment.

Issued at 4.50 p.m.
Copies to :-
1. C.O.	5. O.C. "D" Coy.	10. M.O.
2. O.C. "A" Coy.	6. Capt.T.L.Tanner.	11. Asst. Adjutant.
3. O.C. "B" Coy.	7. H.Q. Officers' Mess.	12. R.S.M.
4. O.C. "C" Coy.	8. Q.M.	13. W.D.
	9. T.O.	14. File.

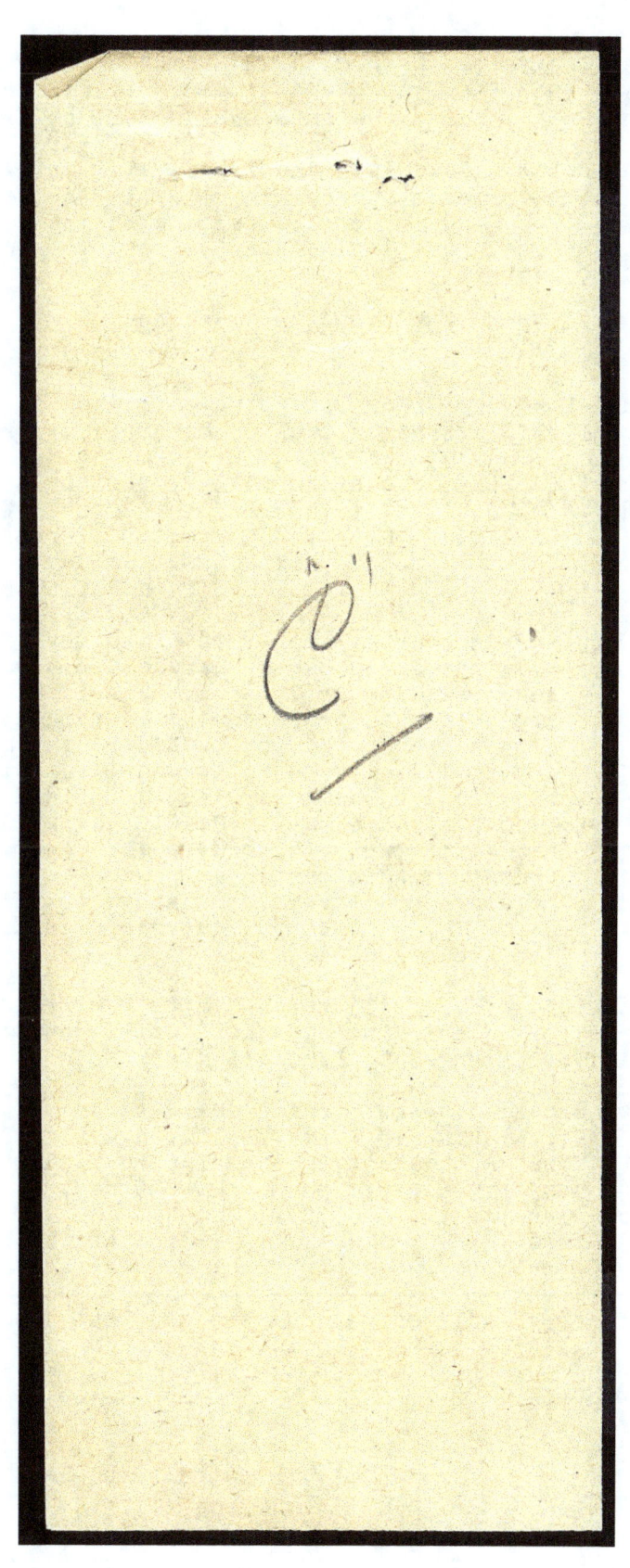

SECRET.

Copy No. 14

3/4th. Battn. Royal West Kent Regiment.

March Orders No. 3.   9-10-17.

Ref.:- Belgium & France 27   1/40,000.
   Belgium 28 N.W.   1/20,000.
   do. 28 S.W.   1/20,000.

1.	Move.	52nd. Infantry Brigade Group (less certain units) will move into staging camps to-morrow, 10th instant. The Battn. will move into DUBLIN Camp by train. A.11.c.35.
2.	Time, Parade & Starting Point.	The Battn. (less 1st Line Transport & details in para.5) will be formed up in column of route on the WATOU - HAANDEKOT Road (W. of the Camp) with the head of the column at the road junction F.16.b.8.2. at 9.0 a.m. to-morrow, the 10th instant.
3.	Order of March.	H.Q. - "C" - "D" - Band - "A" - "B".
4.	Dress.	Full Marching Order with blanket rolled in waterproof sheet and secured on pack by supporting straps.

5.	Detachment.	The following detachment will proceed by train leaving PROVEN at 8.0 a.m. to-morrow, the 10th instant :-
		(a) Billeting Party. 2nd-Lieut.D.B.Brook & batman.
		  1 N.C.O. per Coy.
		  1 N.C.O. detailed by R.S.M. for H.Q.
		(b) Working Party. For 93rd.Field Coy. R.E. This party will parade on Battn. Parade Ground at 6.0 a.m. and reach station by 7.0 a.m. 2nd-Lieut.D.B.Brook will proceed ahead to reach the Station at 6.30 a.m. Sergt. Sachs, "B" Coy., will be in charge of the party till he reports to 2nd-Lieut.D.B.Brook at the Station. Names for (a) will reach the Adjutant by 6.30 p.m. to-night. Os.C.Coys. will verify the names for party (b) before that hour.
		Dress :- as in para. 4.
		Separate orders will be issued to Billeting Officer. Party (b) will carry and retain cooking utensils (to include 2 Dixies).

6.	Transport.	Separate Orders will be issued to the Transport Officer. Transport (including bicycles) will proceed by road. Cooks will accompany 1st. Line Transport.
7.	Meals.	(a) Breakfasts for parties detailed in para.5. :- 5.0 a.m. Breakfasts for Battn.:- 7.0 a.m. (b) Bread & cheese haversack ration will be carried on the man for consumption on the journey. (c) Dinners. :- 4.30 p.m. (d) Teas. :- 7.0 p.m. Some of the bread should be retained by the men for this meal.
8.	Baggage.	Officers' valises will be stacked outside H.Q.Mess by 8.30 a.m., 10th. instant, ready for loading.
9.		ACKNOWLEDGE.

Captain & Adjutant,
3/4th.Battn.Royal West Kent Regt.

Issued at   p.m.
Copies to :-
1. C.O.
2. O.C. "A" Coy.
3. O.C. "B" Coy.
4. O.C. "C" Coy.
5. O. C."D" Coy.
6. Capt.T.L.Tanner.
7. H.Q. Officers' Mess.
8. Q. M.
9. T. O.
10. M. O.
11. Asst.Adjutant.
12. R.S.M.
13. 2/Lt.D.B.Brook.
14. War Diary.
15. File.

```
Lan. Fus.
W.Rid. R.
R.W.Kent R.
Manch. R.
M.G.Coy.
L.T.M.B.
236th M.G.Coy.
No. 4 Coy. Train.
```

H.Q.,
52ND INFANTRY BDE.
52.G.3935.

Reference Table 'B' issued with O.O.198.:-

For Map Reference F.1.c.4.0.(Sheet 20) read F.1.c.4.0.(Sheet 27).

Captain,
Brigade Major,
52nd Infantry Brigade.

9-10-17.

SECRET.

ADMINISTRATIVE INSTRUCTIONS NO.22.

Sept. 9th. 1917.

1. **R.E. PARTY.** Reference 17th.Division Admin. Instrons. No.39, para 1 (a), and this office Admin. Instrons. No.21, para 8 :- Map reference B.14.b.3.2 should read B.14.b.9.2, B.16.b.8.2 should read B.14.b.8.2., and B.24.a.9.5 should read B.14.a.9.5.
   Parties for work with O.R.E. will therefore report to O.C. 93rd.Fd.Coy.R.E. at B.14.b.8.2 and not at B.13.b.8.2. as previously stated.

2. **EXTRA STRETCHER BEARERS.** Reference 17th.Division Admin. Instrons. No.39., para. 1 (b). Lancashire Fusiliers, Royal West Kent R., and Manchester Regt. will each detail 2 N.C.Os. and 20 men for employment with 52nd.Field Ambulance in case of need as extra stretcher bearers. These men will remain with their units until Brigade Depot is formed, when they will move to Brigade Depot and remain there until ordered to join 52nd.Field Ambulance. They will join Brigade Depot with rations for day following date of joining, and similarly will later join 52nd.Field Ambulance with rations for day following date of joining. In each case they will join with a proportion of cooking utensils.

3. **EVACUATION OF SICK.**
   (a). Any sick requiring evacuation to-morrow from the present area will be evacuated by 53rd.Field Ambulance, and, in the case of units proceeding by first train, must be left in charge of a N.C.O. at unit's present camp. Ambulance will collect sick from all camps about 9.0 a.m. Any N.C.Os. left in charge of sick must proceed by 2.0 p.m. train from PROVEN and rejoin their units in new area
   (b). In the next area sick will be evacuated daily by 53rd. Field Ambulance from camps, as soon after 9.0 a.m. as possible.
   (c). Commanding Officers will inform their Medical Officers of above arrangements.

Copies to :-

Lan. Fus.
W.Rid. R.
R.West Kent R.
Manch. R.
52nd.L.G.Coy.
52nd.T.M.Bty.
93rd.Fd.Coy.R.E.
52nd.Fd.Ambce.
O.C.52nd.Bde. Depot.
Brigade Major.
No.4 Coy.Train.
236th.M.G.Coy.
53rd.Fd.Ambce.
17th.Division C (for information).

S. H. Smith
Captain,
Staff Captain,
52nd. Infantry Brigade.

SECRET.

LAN. FUS.
W.RID. Regt.
R.W.KENT Regt.
MANCH. Regt.
M.G.COY.
L.T.M.B.
STAFF CAPTAIN.
O.C., SIGNALS.
BDE. INTEL: OFFICER.

H.Q.
52ND INFANTRY BDE.
52.G.3939.

FILE WD

WARNING ORDER.

1. Provided the operation today meets with the success anticipated, the following forecast of moves appears probable.

    (a) The Divisional front may be taken over on the night 13/14th by the 50th Brigade, in which case the 52nd would probably become Brigade in Support, with two Battalions in neighbourhood of PILCHEM and two near the CANAL.

    (b) The Divisional front may be taken over by 50th Brigade and 52nd Brigade, in which case the probable dividing line between Brigades will be:- V.7.b.87. - V.2.d.40.75. - 52nd Brigade on the Right.

2. As regards para. 1 (a), the two leading Battalions will be R.W.Kent R. and the Lan. Fus.

    As regards para. 1 (b), the R.W.Kent R. will take over the Brigade front on a two Company frontage and the Lan. Fus in close support, each Battalion distributed in depth.

    The Manch. R. and the W.Rid. R. will be in Brigade Support.

3. It can also be anticipated that a further attack will be made on the enemy in a few days time, in which case the two leading Battalions will be prepared to carry out the attack.

    Acknowledge.

12-10-1917.

Captain,
Brigade Major,
52nd Infantry Brigade.

SECRET.

FILE W.D.

Copy No. 8

Ref. Maps
Sheets
19,20,27
& 28.
1/40,000.

52ND INFANTRY BRIGADE ORDER No. 198.
****

9th October 1917.

1. The 17th Division will relieve the 29th Division in the line on 'Z' night, relief to be completed by 6-0 a.m. 'Z' plus 2 days. 52nd. Infantry Brigade will be in Divisional Reserve.

2. The 52nd Infantry Brigade Group, less 52nd Field Ambulance and 93rd Field Company, R.E., and plus 236th Machine Gun Company (dismounted personnel) will move into staging Camps on the 10th instant in accordance with attached entraining Table 'A'. Horses and vehicles will move by road vide march Table 'B'.
   Administrative instructions will be issued separately.

3. On reaching 29th Divisional Area, formations and Units will come under the tactical Command of G.O.C., 29th Division until command of the Divisional front passes to G.O.C., 17th Division.

4. Units will detail the following number of Officers and men for attachment to the 93rd Field Company, R.E., on the 10th instant.
   These parties will go by the <u>first train</u> on the <u>10th instant, (8-0 a.m.)</u>, detrain at ELVERDINGHE, march to B.16.b.8.2., and report to the 93rd Field Company. :-

Lan. Fus.	1 Off.	40	O.R.
W.Rid. R.	1 "	30	"
R.W.Kent R.	-	40	"
Manch. R.	1 "	40	"

   Officers may be detailed from those already detailed for Brigade Depot.

5. Brigade Depot will be established at DRAGON I Camp. Orders for joining will be issued separately.

6. Brigade Headquarters will close at 6-0 a.m., 10th instant at present location and re-open at CARIBOU CAMP on arrival there.

7. <u>ACKNOWLEDGE.</u>

Issued at 8-0 a.m.

Copy No 1 to Bde. H.Q.
   2 to War Diary.
   3 to Staff Captain.
   4 to Signals.
   5 to B.T.O.
   6 to Lan. Fus.
   7 to W.Rid. R.
   8 to R.W.Kent R.
   9 to Manch. R.
   10 to 52nd M.G.Coy.
   11 to 52nd T.M.B.
   12 to 93rd F.Coy.,R.E.
   13 to 236th M.G.Coy.
   14 to No. 4 Coy. Train.
   15 to Supply Officer.
   16 to 17th Division.
   17 to 52nd Field Ambulance.

H.C. Morgan
Captain,
Brigade Major,
52nd Inf. Brigade.

MARCH TABLE 'A' issued with O.O. No. 198.

Ser. No.	Date.	Unit.	From.	To	Time of starting.	Remarks.
1.	Oct. 10.	Ede. H.C.	PROVEN STN.	CARIBOU CAMP.	8-0 a.m.	
2.	10.	Lan. Fus.	PROVEN STN.	ROUSSEL CAMP.	½ Bn. 11 a.m. ½ Bn. 2 p.m.	Detrain at INTERNATIONAL CORNER.
3.	10.	W.Rid.R.	PROVEN STN.	CARIBOU CAMP.	8-0 a.m.	
4.	10.	R.W.Kent R.	PROVEN STN.	DUBLIN CAMP.	11-0 a.m.	
5.	10.	March. R.	PROVEN STN.	DRAGON II.	2-0 p.m.	Detrain at INTERNATIONAL CORNER.
6.	10.	M.G.Coy.	PROVEN STN.	CARIBOU CAMP.	8-0 a.m.	
7.	10.	T.M.Bty.	PROVEN STN.	CARIBOU CAMP.	8-0 a.m.	
8.	10.	236th M.G.C.	PROVEN STN.	COPPERNOLLE.	8-0 a.m.	

NOTES :—
1. Detraining will be at ELVERDINGHE except where otherwise stated.
2. Lan. Fus. will arrange for the Middlesex Regt. (29th Division) to rest for a short period

P.T.O.

NOTES (2) continued :-

in ROUSSEL Camp on their way out of the line, if desired.
3. Time of starting is the time of actual departure of the trains by which Units must be completely entrained.
4. The following intervals on the march will be adhered to :-
West of the POPERINGHE-PROVEN Road - 500 yards between Units.
East of this Road - 200 yards between Companies.

SECRET.

17th. Division.
A/1001.

ADMINISTRATIVE INSTRUCTIONS.

NO.30.

ADDITIONAL PERSONNEL. R.E. PARTIES.

(a) The additional personnel required for R.E. parties will report as follows :-

NUMBER.	FROM.	TO.	DATE.	PLACE.
4 Officers 150 O.R.	50th.Inf.Bde.	O.C.78th.Fd.Co.R.E.	Noon 10th. Oct.	B.14.b.3.2.
Ditto.	51st.Inf.Bde.	O.C.77th.Fd.Co.R.E.	Noon 11th. Oct.	B.24.a.9.5.
Ditto.	52nd.Inf.Bde.	O.C.93rd.Fd.Co.R.E.	Noon 10th. Oct.	B.16.b.8.2.

The above will take rations for day following date of journey. They will subsequently be rationed by Field Company to which they are attached. A proportion of cooking utensils will be taken.

(b) EXTRA STRETCHER BEARERS.

The additional personnel required for Extra Stretcher Bearers will be detailed as follows :-
Each Infantry Brigade will detail 66 fit N.C.Os and men for employment with 52nd.Field Ambulance in case of need as extra stretcher bearers. These men will temporarily remain with Brigade Depots.
The date to join 52nd.Field Ambulance will be notified later. They will join with rations for day following date of joining and will take cooking utensils with them.

(c) TRAFFIC.

The Traffic Officer to be found by 51st Infantry Brigade, will report to the A.P.M. at Div. H.Q. ELVERDINGHE at 9 a.m. 11th inst.

24. AMMUNITION DUMPS.

The Ammunition Dump for completion of extra S.A.A., Grenades etc for the 51st and 50th Infantry Brigades has been established at B.14.b.3.6. near ELVERDINGHE.
Units of 51st Infantry Brigade will be completed on detrainment.
15,000 sandbags are at B.14.b.8.2. near ELVERDINGHE, opposite the Church, and may be drawn by the 51st and 50th Infantry Brigades from the West Riding Field Co. R.E.

3. EXTRA RATIONS.

Solidified Paraffin and Whale Oil have been issued to the 50th and 51st Inf. Brigades.

P.T.O.

4. ENTRAINING.

Dismounted personnel of Field Ambulances may travel by any train except 8 a.m. train on Z + 1 day. Senior Officer of party to report to entraining officer.

78th and 93rd Field Coys will travel on the 8 a.m. train on Z + 1 day. Train for 77th Field Coy. will be notified later.

Billeting Parties of 51st and 50th Inf. Brigades will travel by the first trains at INTERNATIONAL CORNER and PROVEN respectively on the 9th inst.

5. BRIGADE DEPOTS.

Personnel of Brigade Depot. of 51st Inf. Brigade will concentrate at DRAGON I CAMP, A.9.d.9.3. at 3 p.m. 9th October. This Camp will not be cleared by 29th Division before 2.30p.m.

Personnel of Brigade Depots of 50th and 52nd Inf. Brigades will concentrate at same Camp at a date to be notified later.

Para. 5 (b) of Administrative Instructions No. 38 is cancelled.

H. A. Nicholson

Lieut-Colonel,
A.A. & Q.M.G., 17th Division.

8/10/1917.

DISTRIBUTION.

"G".
50th Brigade.)
51st Brigade.) Copies for all Units in Brigade Groups.
52nd Brigade.)
C.R.E.
A.D.M.S.
Signals.
A.P.M.

S E C R E T.

C.342/10

ADMINISTRATIVE INSTRUCTIONS NO.21.

Reference impending move of Brigade Group :-

1. **BLANKETS**.

    When the Brigade Group moves no transport will be available to carry blankets. Each man must therefore carry his own blankets with him to entraining point and from detraining point to new camp.

2. **T.M.BTY.**

    O.C. 52nd.M.G.Coy. will as usual lend 6 mules to 52nd.T.M.Bty. to draw handcarts of the latter. Details to be arranged between units concerned. Mules to rejoin 52nd.M.G.Coy. on completion of the march. O.C.52nd.T.M.Bty. will detail 2 men to each handcart on the march.

3. **TRANSPORT.**

    All Units are to move with Echelons full. No stores are to be left behind in present area. Mobile reserve of petrol tins is to be carried on vehicles.

4. **BRIGADE DEPOT.**

    Orders as to assembly of Brigade Depot will be issued later. O.C. Lan. Fus. will detail 2 men as cooks. O.C. W.Rid. Regt. will detail 2 men as sanitary men. O.C. R.West Kent Regt. will detail 2 men as orderlies and clerks. O.C. Manch.Regt. will detail 1 N.C.O. as Depot Q.M.S., and 1 man as storeman.

    The above will report to O.C. Bde.Depot immediately on its assembly at DRAGON Camp.

    Each Battalion will send with its contingent proportion of cooking utensils, including Dixies at the rate of 1 for every 16 men. All N.C.Os. and men proceeding to Bde.Depot will carry their blankets with them.

5. **ENTRAINING.**

    (a). Major G.W.THACKER, Lan. Fus. is detailed as entraining officer at PROVEN, and will report to R.T.O. PROVEN, at 6.30 a.m. on day of entrainment of Bde. Group. All units entraining will send an officer ahead who will report to Entraining officer at PROVEN Station, with the units entraining strength, 90 minutes before departure of train on which unit is moving. Entraining Officer will proceed by last train from PROVEN.

    (b). Capt. T.B.FORWOOD, Manch. Regt. is detailed as Detraining Officer at ELVERDINGHE Station, and will proceed on first train on day of entrainment. He will report to R.T.O. ELVERDINGHE immediately on arrival. He will rejoin his unit after detrainment of last train at ELVERDINGHE.

    (c). All units entraining are to arrive at Entraining Station 1 hour before time of departure of train.

    (d). Train Time-Table and composition of each train as given in attached Table A.

    (e). Units will detrain as expeditiously as possible and march off at once to their camps.

6. **BILLETING PARTIES.**

    (a). Billeting Parties of all units moving by train on 1 day will proceed by the first train and will conduct their units to camps on arrival. Billeting parties of Manch.Regt. and half Lan.Fus. detraining at International Corner must meet their units on arrival at International Corner. Billeting Parties of other units will meet their units at ELVERDINGHE Station. Each unit will send 1 Officer and 6 men as it billeting party.

P.T.O.

(b). Guides for First Line Transport are to meet the units transport on arrival at a point to be determined by each Commanding Officer for his own unit. These guides are to be included in the 1 Officer and 6 other ranks from each unit mentioned in preceding paragraph.

7. TRANSPORT LINES.

It is anticipated that units will occupy transport lines adjacent to their camps. It is possible, however, that all of these will not be vacated on the day on which the Bde.Group moves. In that case Transport Lines (except 236th.M.G.Coy.) will probably all be at A.16.a.5.3. (north side of road), and Quartermasters Stores will be at units camps, as the accomodation for personnel at A.16.a.5.3 is bad. Units will be informed as soon as possible whether their Transport Lines will be at A.16.a.5.3. Unless orders to the contrary are received Transport Lines will be those alongside camps, and units have reconnoitred on that assumption. In any event, Transport Lines of 236th.M.G.Coy. will be at COPPERNOLLE Camp.

8. PARTIES ATTACHED TO O.R.E.

These parties will proceed on the first train from PROVEN on 10th.inst., and will detrain at ELVERDINGHE, marching thence to quarters of 93rd.Fd.Coy.R.E. at B.16.b.8.2. They will report to O.C.93rd.Fd.Coy.R.E. there at noon on 10th.inst. A proportion of cooking utensils is to be sent with each party. Parties will proceed rationed to night of 10th.inst. only (and not as stated in 17th.Div. Admin.Instrns.No.39) Rations for the parties for consumption 11th. inst. will be delivered to O.C.93rd.Fd. Coy.R.E. under Divisional arrangements. Parties will carry their own blankets with them.

9. BICYCLES.

Bicycles will accompany First Line Transport.

10. BAGGAGE WAGONS.

O.C. No.4 Coy.Train will return all Baggage Wagons to units by 3 p.m. to-day, 9th.inst. He will also send extra forage wagons to Bde.H.Q. by 6 p.m. to-day. All Baggage Wagons are to rejoin No.4 Coy.Train by noon on Z ∓ 2 day.

11. PRESENT CAMPS.

Present Camps are to be handed over to the Camp Wardens of the Area Commandant and receipts obtained for tentage handed over. Receipts to be forwarded to this office.

12. ACKNOWLEDGE.

Copies to :-

No. 1 G.O.C.
    2 Bde.Major.
    3 Staff Captain
    4 B.T.O.
5, 6 Lan. Fus.
7, 8 W.Rid.R.
9,10 R.West Kent R.
11,12 Manch. R.
13,14 52nd.M.G.Coy.
   15 52nd.T.M.Bty.
   16 52nd.Fd.Amboe.
   17 93rd.Fd.Coy.R.E.
   18 236th.M.G.Coy.

No.19 No.4 Coy.Train.
   20 Supply Officer, No.4 Coy.Train.
   21 Major THACKER.Lan.Fus.
   22 Capt.FORWOOD.Manch.R.
   23 R.T.O. PROVEN.
   24 R.T.O.ELVERDINGHE.
   25 O.C.52nd.Bde.Depot.
   26 78th.Fd.Coy.R.E.
   27 Bde.Signal Officer.
   28 17th.Div.C.(for information).

L. H. Smith

Captain,
Staff Captain,
52nd.Infantry Brigade.

SECRET.

FILE (W)

Q.342/9.

ADMINISTRATIVE INSTRUCTIONS No.20.

8th.October 1917.

1. Units of Brigade Group will occupy the following Camps in the next Area :-

Serial. No.	Unit.	Camp.	Map reference.
1.	Brigade Headquarters	CARIBOO	A.11.d.7.7
2.	West Riding Regt.	"	"
3.	52nd.M.G.Coy.	"	"
4.	52nd.T.M.Bty.	"	"
5.	Lancashire Fusiliers.	ROUSSEL	B.13.a.2.4
6.	Royal West Kent R.	DUBLIN	A.11.c.3.5
7.	Manchester Regt.	DRAGON II	A.10.c.
8.	236th.M.G.Coy.	COPPERNOLLE	A.16.b.4.8

2. The above Units must send billeting parties to reconnoitre these Camps to-morrow, 9th. inst. Billeting parties of all units to be billeted in CARIBOO Camp will meet Staff Captain at DIE WUPPE Cross Roads (A.11.b.3.2) at 11.30 a.m. to-morrow. Billeting parties of other units will proceed direct to their respective camps, and reconnoitre them. All billeting parties will rejoin their units in present area to-morrow after reconnaissance.

3. Transport Lines of 236th.Machine Gun Coy. will be at COPPERNOLLE Camp.

4. Transport Lines are alongside each Camp.

Copies to :-

Lancashire Fusiliers.
West Riding Regt.
Royal West Kent R.
Manchester Regt.
52nd.M.G.Coy.
52nd.Lt.T.M.Bty.
93rd.Fd.Coy. R.E.
52nd.Fd.Ambce.
No.4 Coy. Train.
Supply Officer,No.4 Coy. Train.
236th.M.G.Coy.
B.T.O.
Brigade Major.
Brigade Signal Officer.
17th.Division C. (for information).
50th.Inf.Bde. (for information).
246th.

S. M. Smith
Captain,
Staff Captain,
52nd.Infantry Brigade.

T A B L E A.
****

Serial No.	UNIT.	DATE.	PLACE OF ENTRAINING.	TIME OF DEPARTURE OF TRAIN.	PLACE OF DETRAINING.	ESTIMATED ENTRAINING STRENGTH.	
						Officers.	Other Ranks.
1.	52nd.Brigade H.Q.	Z ‒ 1 day.	PROVEN STATION.	8.0 a.m.	ELVERDINGHE	8	96
2.	52nd.M.G.Coy.	"		8.0 a.m.	"	8	160
3.	52nd.T.M.Bty.	"		8.0 a.m.	"	1	40
4.	W.Rid.R.	"		8.0 a.m.	"	25	600
5.	Billeting parties.	"		8.0 a.m.	"	9	54
6.	R.E. Party	"		8.0 a.m.	"	4	150
7.	256th.M.G.Coy.	"		8.0 a.m.	"	9	150
8.	93rd.Fd.Coy.R.E.	"		8.0 a.m.	"	6	100
9.	78th.Fd.Coy.R.E.	"		8.0 a.m.	"	6	150
10.	R.West Kent R.	"		11.0 a.m.	"	25	800
11.	2 Coys.Lan.Fus.	"		11.0 a.m.	"	12	345
12.	H.Q. & 2 Coys. Lan.Fus.	"		2.0 p.m.	INTERNATIONAL CORNER	13	400
13.	Manch.R.	"		2.0 p.m.	"	27	720

S.H.Smith.
Captain,
Staff Captain,
52nd.Infantry Brigade.

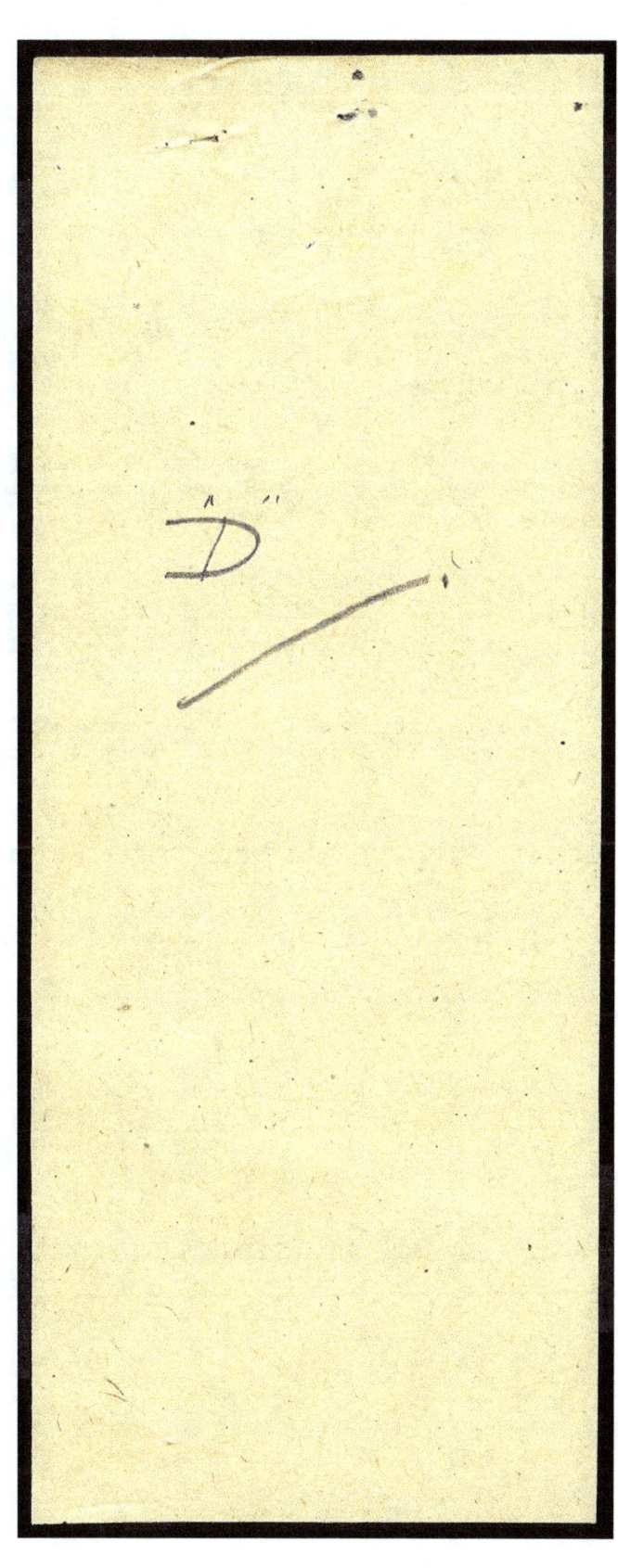

SECRET.   No. 15

3/4th. Battn. Royal West Kent Regiment.

WARNING ORDERS No. 3.

Reference 28 N.W.,
1/40,000

(1) The Battalion, less 1st. Line Transport, will move to-morrow by Route March to PARROY CAMP, B.10.c.4.7., leaving the present billets at 2.15 p.m.

(2) One N.C.O. per Coy. and One (to be detailed by the R.S.M.) for Headquarters, will report to 2nd-Lieut. E. C. Vise at Battalion Headquarters at 9.0 a.m. to-morrow, the 14th instant, and proceed as billeting party to PARROY CAMP.

(3) The Transport Officer will arrange to draw from the Area Officer's Stores, ELVERDINGHE, 2 Tents and 10 Shelters and convey them to Transport Lines, B.17.d.6.5., and have them erected by 4.0 p.m.

(4) All Transport will have left present Lines, finally, before 2.0 p.m.

(5) The Q.M. Stores will move to new Transport Lines to-morrow, but a proportion of Stores may be left in present area under a guard.

(6) Supplies will be delivered after 4.0 p.m. to-morrow to Q.M.Stores in the New Area.
Blankets will be stored in the present area. Great-coats, Packs & Officers' Valises will be taken to the new area.

(7) ACKNOWLEDGE.

[signature]

Captain & Adjutant,
3/4th.Battn.Royal West Kent Regt.

Issued at   p.m.
Copies to
1. C.O.   ~~6. Capt. T. L. Tanner.~~   11. Asst. Adjutant.
2. O.C. "A" Coy.   7. B. I. O.   12. 2/Lt. F.C.Vise.
3. O.C. "B" Coy.   8. Q. M.   13. R. S. A.
4. O.C. "C" Coy.   9. T. O.   14. W. D.
5. O.C. "D" Coy.   10. M. O.   15. File.

SECRET   3/4th. Battn. Royal West Kent Regt.   Copy No. 14

14-10-17.

March Orders No.4.

Reference :- 28 N.W.
              1/40000.

1. The move indicated in Warning Orders issued last night will take place today in accordance with attached March Table.

2. "B" Echelon constituted as usual and including the Band will be accommodated at new Transport Lines B.17.d.4.1. (Not B 17d.6.5.)

3. Blankets will be taken to Q.M. Stores under Coy. arrangements, rolled in bundles of 10 and labled before 12.45 p.m. today.

4. Baggage wagons and the Mess Cart will report at Company and Battn. Messes, to be loaded at 1.15 p.m. O.C.Coys will see that loading parties are ready. Baggage wagons will be returned to O.C.No4 Coy. Train tonight.

5. O I/c. Signals will issue correct time to all concerned at 1.30 P.M.

6. The Band will march over to new Transport Lines this morning with Transport, and will stack their instruments today at present Q.M. Stores under the guard.

7. ACKNOWLEDGE.

                                       W.T. Monckton

                                         Capt. & Adjutant
                 3/4th. Battn. Royal West Kent Regiment.

Issued at   a.m.

Copies to ;-

1. C.O.	9. M.O.
2. O.C. "A" Coy.	10. Asst. Adjutant
3. O.C. "B" Coy.	11. 2/Lieut. E.C. Vise.
4. O.C. "C" Coy.	12. R.S.M.
5. O.C. "D" Coy.	13. Sergt. Underdown
6. B.I.O.	14. War Diary.
7. Q.M.	15. File.
8. T.O.	

MARCH TABLE.

Coy.	Starting Point.	Time of Starting.	Route.	Remarks.
H.Q.	"D"Coy.H.Q. on the POPERINGHE - WOLSTAN Road	2.15 p.m.	ONDANK EAST - B.1.c.9.1 - ELVERDINGHE - FARROY CAMP B.10.c.4.7.	Distance of 200 yards between platoons will be maintained.
"D"		2.17 p.m.		
"C"		2.25 p.m.		
"A"		2.33 p.m.		
"B"		2.40 p.m.		

NOTE.
1. O.C.Coys. will be careful to reach Starting Point at times stated and NOT before.
2. All Platoon Commanders will make careful study of the route on the map this morning.
3. Dress :- Full Marching Order.

MARCH TABLE.

Coy.	Starting Point.	Time of Starting.	Route.	Remarks.
H.Q.	"D"Coy.H.Q. on the POPERINGHE - WOLSTAN Road /	2.15 p.m.	ONDANK EAST - B.1.c.9.1 - ELVERDINGHE - PARROY CAMP B.10.c.4.7.	Distance of 200 yards between platoons will be maintained.
"D"		2.17 p.m.		
"C"		2.25 p.m.		
"A"		2.33 p.m.		
"B"		2.40 p.m.		

NOTE.
1. O.C.Coys. will be careful to reach Starting point at times stated and NOT before.
2. All Platoon Commanders will make careful study of the route on the map this morning.
3. Dress :- Full Marching Order.

MARCH TABLE.

Coy.	Starting Point.	Time of Starting.	Route.	Remarks.
H.Q.	"D"Coy.H.Q. on the POPERINGHE - WOLSTAN Road/	2.15 p.m.	ONDANK EAST - B.1.c.9.1 - ELVERDINGHE - FARROY CAMP B.10.c.4.7.	Distance of 200 yards between platoons will be maintained.
"D"		2.17 p.m.		
"C"		2.25 p.m.		
"A"		2.33 p.m.		
"B"		2.40 p.m.		

NOTE.
1. O.C.Coys. will be careful to reach Starting Point at times stated and NOT before.
2. All Platoon Commanders will make careful study of the route on the map this morning.
3. Dress :- Full Marching Order.

MARCH TABLE.

Coy.	Starting Point.	Time of Starting.	Route.	Remarks.
H.Q.	"D"Coy.H.Q. on the POPERINGHE - WOLSTAN Road /	2.15 p.m.	ONDANK EAST - B.1.c.9.1 - ELVERDINGHE - DARROY CAMP B.10.c.4.7.	Distance of 200 yards between platoons will be maintained.
"D"		2.17 p.m.		
"C"		2.25 p.m.		
"A"		2.33 p.m.		
"B"		2.41 p.m.		

NOTE.
1. O.C.Coys. will be careful to reach Starting Point at times stated and NOT before.
2. All Platoon Commanders will make careful study of the route on the map this morning.
3. Dress :- Full Marching Order.

SECRET   Copy No. 8

52ND INFANTRY BRIGADE ORDER No.200.

Ref. Maps
Sheet 20
1/40,000   13th October 1917.

1. On the relief of the 51st Infantry Brigade in the line by the 50th Infantry Brigade, the 52nd Infantry Brigade will be in Support to the 50th Infantry Brigade.

2. UNITS OF The 52nd Infantry Brigade will move on the 13th and 14th in accordance with the attached table.

3. On completion of move, the following will be the distribution of the 52nd Infantry Brigade on October 14th:-

    52nd Infy. Bde H.Q. —————— WHITE MILL Camp.
    Lancs. Fus.   PILKEM II.
    W.Riding R.   CANAL B.18.A.7.7.
    R.W.Kents R.   PARROY B.10.C.4.7.
    Manch Regt.   WHITE MILL
    52nd M.G.Coy.   WHITE MILL
    52nd T.M.Bty.   WHITE MILL .

The following distance will be maintained on the march :-

    East of the Canal - between platoons 100 yards interval.
    West of the Canal - between platoons 200 yards interval.

4. Arrivals of Battalions at respective Camps will be reported to Brigade Headquarters.

5. ACKNOWLEDGE.

Issued at 4.pm.

Copy No. 1 to Bde. H.Q.
    2 to War Diary.
    3 to Staff Captain.
    4 to O.C.Signals.
    5 to B.T.O.
    6 to Lancs Fus.
    7 to W.Riding R.
    8 to R.W.Kent R.
    9 to Manch Regt.
    10 to M.G.Coy.
    11 to T.M.Bty.
    12 to No. 4.Coy Train.
    13 to O.C.Supplies.
    14 to 53rd F.Ambce.
    15 to 17th Division.

J. Turner
for Captain,
Brigade Major,
52nd Infantry Brigade.

MARCH TABLE TO ACCOMPANY 52ND INFANTRY BRIGADE ORDER NO. 200.

Date.	Unit.	From.	To.	Time of starting.	Route.	Remarks.
Octr. 13th.	Lan. Fus.	ROUSSEL.	PILKEM II. C.2.Central.	2-45 p.m.	ELVERDINGHE-BOESINGHE,	To arrive PILKEM Camp at 7-0 p.m.
14th.	H.Q. 52nd Bde.	CARIBOU.	WHITEHILL.	2-45 p.m.	B.1.c.9.1.,ELVERDINGHE.	
13th.	R.W.Kent R.	DUBLIN.	PARROY.	2-15 p.m.	ONDANK CAMT.,L.1.c.9.1. ELVERDINGHE.,B.10.c.4.0.	
14th.	W.Rid. R.	CARIBOU.	CANAL.	2-0 p.m.	B.1.c.9.1.,ELVERDINGHE —BOESINGHE.	

SECRET.   Copy No. 7

Ref. Maps   52ND INFANTRY BRIGADE ORDER No.199.
SCHAAP BALIE   ********************************
  and
Special Map   11th October 1917.

~~17th Division Order No 234 issued on the 10th
Oct. with reference to future operations.~~
:-:-:-:-:-:-:-:-:-:-:-:-:-:-:-:-:

1.   XIV Corps will resume the attack on the 12th October at an hour to be notified later.

2.   The attack will be carried out by the Guards, 17th and 4th Divisions. on the Left Centre and Right of the Corps Front.

3.   The attack will be made in two bounds, the First to the Green Line and the second to the Red Line vide attached map (issued to units of 52nd Brigade only) strong points on the 17th Divisional Front will be established at GRAVEL FARM, TURENNE CROSSING, BERTHIER FARM, COLIBRI FARM, ADEN HOUSE, TAUBE FARM, SENEGAL FARM, V.1.C.5.0., V.7.A.85.80.

4.   (a)   The attack by the 17th Division will be carried out by the 51st Infantry Brigade, the 50th Brigade in Support and the 52nd Brigade - Divisional Reserve.

        (b)   3 Battalions of the 51st Brigade will carry out the attack, the remaining Battalion will move forward in rear of the attacking line and make a line 800 yards in rear of the Red Line.
                This Battalion will be used in the event of a counter attack.

        (c)   One Battalion 50th Brigade will be placed at the tactical disposal of the G.O.C. 51st Brigade.

5.   Special parties will be detailed to keep touch with flanking divisions.

6.   The attack will be made under cover of artillery and machine gun barrages arranged by G.O.C. R.A. and D.M.G.O.
        The barrage will begin to creep at zero plus 8 minutes at the rate of 100 yards in 8 minutes throughout.

7.   (a)   Adequate mopping up parties will be arranged to deal with enemy dugouts and strong points.

        (b)   In the event of a unit on either flank or within the Brigade being held up, adjoining units will not check their advance, but will follow the barrage, taking care to protect their flank.

8.   Tanks may co-operate.

9.   (a)   Contact aeroplanes will fly over the Corps front at stated times, red flares in bunches of three will be lit when called for either by Klaxon horns or white light.

(2).

9 (contd)(b)   A protective aeroplane will be up continuously during daylight whose mission will be to detect the approach of enemy counter attacks.
A smoke bomb bursting into a white parachute flare, which descends slowly leaving a long trail of brown smoke about a foot broad behind it, will be dropped whenever this patrol observer hostile parties of more than 100 moving to counter attack and it will be dropped over that portion of the front to which the enemy is moving.

(c)   Each Brigade and Battalion headquarters will be marked by authorised ground sheet and code letter.

10.   S.O.S. signal will be a succession of rifle rockets each bursting into four Red Stars.

11.   The 52nd Machine Gun Company will be employed under the D...G.O.

ACKNOWLEDGE.

Issued at

Copy No. 1 to Bde H.Q.
    2 to War Diary.
    3 to Staff Captain
    4 to O.C. Signals.
    5 to Lancs Fus.
    6 to W.Rid R.
    7 to R.W.Kents
    8 to ...nch Regt.
    9 to ..G.Coy.
    10 to T.M.Bty.
    11 to

M.E. Morgan
Captain,
Brigade Major,
52nd Infantry Brigade.

SECRET.   Copy No. 8

52ND INFANTRY BRIGADE ORDER NO. 201.

Ref Maps
Sheet 27
& 28.
1/40,000.

14th October 1917.

1.   The 17th Division will be relieved in the Line, by the 34th and 35th Divisions on the night 16th/17th October.

2.   Battalions of the 52nd Brigade will remain in the forward area between ELVERDINGHE and the CANAL, in their present Camps except the Manchester Regiment who will move to PARROY CAMP on the 16th instant.

    Advance parties of the Manchester Regiment will take over this Camp tomorrow at 10-0 a.m.

    All Battalions will start work under C.E. XIV Corps on the dates given in attached Table.

3.   Relief of the Guns of the 52nd Machine Gun Company will be arranged by the D.M.G.O.

    On completion of relief, the 52nd Machine Gun Company will move back to the PROVEN Area.

4.   52nd Trench Mortar Battery will also move to the PROVEN Area on the 17th instant.

5.   Brigade Depot will move into the Camp to be vacated by the Manchester Regiment on the 16th instant.

6.   Brigade Headquarters will remain at WHITE MILL.

7.   ACKNOWLEDGE.

Issued at 8-30 p.m.

Copy No. 1 to Bde. H.Q.
        2 to War Diary.
        3 to Staff Captain.
        4 to O.C., Signals.
        5 to B.T.O.
        6 to Lan. Fus.
        7 to W.Rid. Regt.
        8 to R.W.Kent Regt.
        9 to Manch. Regt.
      10 to M.G.Coy.
      11 to T.M.Bty.
      12 to No.4 Coy.Train.
      13 to O.C.,Supplies.
      14 to 51st F.Amboe.
      15 to 17th Division.

H.C. Morgan
Captain,
Brigade Major,
52nd Infantry Brigade.

TABLE OF RELIEFS.

UNIT.	CAMP.	Starting Date of work.	In relief of.	Remarks.
Lancashire Fus.	CANAL.	15th inclusive.	29th Divisional Pioneers.	
West Riding Regt.	CANAL.	ditto.	63rd Divisional Pioneers.	
R.West Kent Regt.	PARROY.	16th inclusive.	4th Divisional Pioneers.	
Manchester Regt.	PARROY.	17th inclusive.	1st Bn. Guards Pioneers.	

Instructions for work will be issued from C.E. XIV Corps through Brigade.

S E C R E T.

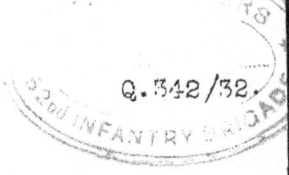

Q.342/32.

ADMINISTRATIVE INSTRUCTIONS No.25.
******* **********************

Oct. 13th, 1917.

1.   Reference 17th.Div.Admin. Instrons. No.41 para.1 (b), and Bde. Admin. Instrons. No.24 para 1 :- Map Reference of New Transport Lines should read B.17.d.4.1 and not B.17.d.6.5. These lines are better than those at B.17.d.6.5 and have a certain amount of accomodation already made. Lan. Fus will take over lines now occupied by Lincolns, and Manch. R. will take over lines now occupied by Sherwood Foresters. Lines of other units have been shown to Transport Officers.

2.   52nd.M.G.Coy. (with Transport and Q.M. Stores) will move to-morrow afternoon to COPPERNOLLE CAMP now occupied by 50th. M.G.Coy. and not to WHITE MILL, 52nd.M.G.Coy. to be clear of CARIBOO CAMP by 2.0 p.m.

3.   52nd.T.M.Bty. will move to WHITE MILL CAMP to-morrow, leaving CARIBOO CAMP at 2.55 p.m. 52nd.M.G.Coy. will lend 52nd.T.M.Bty. 6 mules to assist in the move. Details to be arranged between Commanding Officers concerned. Billeting party of 52nd.T.M.Bty. to meet Staff Captain at WHITE MILL CAMP at 11.0 a.m. to-morrow. Q.M.Stores of 52nd. T.M.Battery will be at WHITE MILL Camp.

4.   Rations for 52nd.M.G.Coy. will be delivered by No.4 Coy. Train at COPPERNOLLE CAMP from to-morrow inclusive. Rations for Bde. H.Q. and T.M.Bty. will be delivered to WHITE MILL by No.4 Coy. Train. Rations for all other units will be delivered to Transport Lines at B.17.d.4.1.

6.   Units moving to CANAL, PARROY and PILKEM II Camps will make their own arrangements about sending an advance party to take over the Camps.

Copies to :-

Lan. Fus.
W.Rid. R.
R.West Kent R.
Manch. R.
52nd.M.G.Coy.
52nd.T.M.Bty.
B.T.O.
No.4 Coy. Train.
Supply Officer, No.4 Coy. Train.
53rd.Fd.Ambce.
17th.Division Q. (for information).
51st. Inf. Bde. (for information).

S. H. Smith.
Captain,
Staff Captain,
52nd.Infantry Brigade.

ADMINISTRATIVE INSTRUCTIONS.
NO. 42

A/1001
SECRET.

1. LOCATION OF UNITS.

Div H.Q.	PROVEN Central.
C.R.A.	"
D.A.D.O.S.	"
236th M.G. Co.	P.1 Area

50th Inf. Brigade.H.Q.	POONA CAMP.	
10th West Yorks.	PATALIA CAMP. "	
7th East Yorks.	PATINA "	P.5. Area.
7th Yorks.	PERSIA "	
6th Dorsets.	PERA "	
50th M.G. Co.	PARANA "	
50th T.M. Bty.	PRETORIA "	

51st Inf Brigade H.Q.	POUNDON CAMP.	
7th Lincolns.	PITCHCOTT "	
7th Borders.	POODLE "	P.1. Area.
8th South Staffs.	PIDDINGTON "	
10th Sherwoods.	PRATTLE. "	
51st M.G. Coy.	PILCH "	
51st T.M. Bty.	PRESTWOOD "	

52nd Inf Brigade.	ELVERDINGHE AREA.
77th Field Co. R.E.	ELVERDINGHE AREA.
78th Field Co. R.E.	PATAGONIA CAMP. P.5. Area.
93rd Field Co. R.EM	ELVERDINGHE AREA.
51st Field Ambulance.	SOLFERINO FARM.
52nd Field Ambulance.	P.1. Area.
53rd Field Ambulance.	PANAMA CAMP. P.5.Area.
Div Train H.Q.	PROVEN.
No. 2 Co.	PARDO CAMP P.5 Area
No. 3 Co.	P.1.Area
No. 4 Co.	ELVERDINGHE
S.A.A.Section.D.A.C.	P.1.Area.
29th M.V. Section.	PROVEN.
Railhead.- Supplies.	PROVEN. (From 17th inst.)
Div. Baths.	COOTHOF.
Cinema.	PROVEN. (Church Army Tent).
"Duds".	POPERINGHE.

2. ENTRAINING.

The Division will entrain for the PROVEN Area as follows :-

Formation or Unit.	Date.	Entraining Station.	Time.	Detraining Station.
51st Bde. H.Q.	16th	ELVERDINGHE.	Time	PROVEN.
M.G. Coy.	"	"	to be	"
T.M.Bty.	"	"	noti-	"
8th S.Staffs.	"	"	fied	"
7th Borders.	"	"	later.	"
7th Lincolns.				

10th Sherwoods/

- 2 -

10th Sherwoods.	16th.	INTERNATIONAL CORNER.		PROVEN.
226th M.G. Coy.	"	"	Time	"
50th Inf Bde Group less Fld.Amb.	17th	BOESINGHE.	to be noti-	"
52nd Field Amb.	"	"	fied	"
53rd " "	"	"	later.	INTERNATIONAL CORNER.
Div H.Q.	"	ILVERDINGHE.		PROVEN.

Officer Commanding 53rd Field Ambulance will advise R.T.O. BOESINGHE before entraining that he wishes to detrain at INTERNATIONAL CORNER.

Units of 51st Inf Brigade Group must arrive at their entraining Station at least three quarters of an hour before the time of departure of train.

Entraining Officers must report to R.T.O. with entraining states three-quarters of an hour before time of departure of train.

One Officer must be sent on ahead to supervise detraining.

2. (b) <u>Billeting Parties.</u>

Billeting Parties will proceed 24 hours ahead of units. They will report as follows :-

50th and 51st Inf Brigade Groups to Area Commandants of P.3 and P.1. Areas respectively at PROVEN by 7 p.m. on October 15th.

The 51st Inf. Bde will arrange accommodation in their area for the 52nd Field Ambulance and the S.A.A. Section of the D.A.C. and 226th M.G.Coy.

3 52nd Inf. Bde & 77th and 93rd Field Coys, R.E.

(a) The above troops will be located as follows:-

```
        Bde H.Q.                    WHITE MILL CAMP
        Bde Depot                        -do-
        52nd M.G.Coy                     -do-
        No. 4 Coy. Divl Train       ILVERDINGHE
        First Line Transport        B.17.D.5.1
        77th Fd Coy. R.E.)
        93rd     -do-     )         CANAL BANK
```

(b) The 52nd Infantry Brigade will be administered by the 34th Divn

This includes all arrangements for Supplies and R.E. Material

Ordnance Stores will be issued by D.A.D.O.S., 17th Division, stores being sent by lorry to First Line Transport

All routine correspondence will be sent in to H.Q., 17th Divn. and all casualty reports will be <u>repeated</u> to 17th Division.

(c) Applications for the use of the ILVERDINGHE Baths will be made to 35th Divl H.Q. at ILVERDINGHE CHATEAU

(d) The Brigade will take over the Soup Kitchen at CACTUS CAUSEWAY by midday 16th instant

4 CAMPS/

CAMPS.

Particular care will be paid to the handing over of all camps in the back area in a thoroughly sanitary condition

It is important that the tents handed over should be carefully checked and receipts obtained, a copy of the receipts will be forwarded to Divisional Headquarters.

In those cases in which camps are not taken over by any relieving unit, the tents now in them are to be struck and handed in to the Area Commandant, at ELVERDINGHE CHATEAU.

5 PERSONNEL.

(a) Brigade Depots will proceed as follows:-

50th Infantry Brigade will move to P.5 Area by march route on morning of October 16th under arrangements to be made by 50th Infantry Brigade

51st Infantry Brigade will rejoin their units on the afternoon of October 15th

52nd Infantry Brigade will proceed to WHITE MILL CAMP on the morning of October 17th under arrangements to be made by the 52nd Infantry Brigade

(b) R.E. Working Parties.

Infantry personnel attached to Field Companies, R.E. will rejoin their units when Division is relieved.

C.R.E. will arrange direct with Infantry Brigades concerned as to time and place of rejoining.

(c) Extra Stretcher-Bearers.

The A.D.M.S. will arrange direct with Infantry Brigades for the return of the additional personnel to their Brigades

The 50th and 51st Infantry Brigades stretcher bearers will rejoin from detraining stations in PROVEN AREA

The 52nd Infantry Brigade will rejoin in ELVERDINGHE Area.

(d) Corps Employment.

The following Corps employed men will remain in forward area and will be administered by the 52nd Infantry Brigade:-

Nature of Employment	Place	Number	Found by
Water Point Guards	WHITE HOPE CORNER	1 N.C.O. 4 Men	50th Inf.B.
	BOESINGHE	-do-	-do-
	S.23.c.6.4	1 N.C.O. 3 Men	-do-
	A.3.B.6.0	-do-	-do-
Church Army Hut	DAWSONS CORNER	1 Man	51st -do-
SWISS COTTAGE R.E.DUMP	A.7.c.4.7	2 N.C.Os.12 Men	52nd -do-
Carpenters	25th San.Son ST.SIXTE	6 Men	52nd -do-

(e) Employed Men

All other employed men will proceed with the Division to the PROVEN Area

Barrack Wardens will remain until last unit of 17th Division vacate their camps, they will rejoin their own units at the first available opportunity.

14/10/17.

Lieut-Colonel.
A.A. & Q.M.G., 17th Division.

SECRET.
17th Division.
A/1001
————

ADMINISTRATIVE INSTRUCTIONS.
NO:41.

1. CAMPS AND TRANSPORT LINES.

(a) CAMPS. The following tent shelter camps have been, or are being pitched :-
PILKEM.   2 Camps, each to take a Battalion.

West of Canal. 1 Battalion Camp. B.18.A.7.8
             1 Battalion Camp. B.18.8 6.4

As soon as possible these will be provided with drying rooms.

Proper sanitary arrangements will be made by the Units in occupation, until more permanent fixtures can be made.

(b) TRANSPORT LINES.
(i) First Line Transport of Infantry Brigades complete will move to camps stated below, moves to be completed by 4 p.m. 14th.instant.

50th.Infantry Brigade.   B.17.d.3.3.
51st.   do.   do.   B.23.A.5.8.
52nd.   do.   do.   B.17.d.6.5.

(ii) Brigades will draw from the Area officers store, ELVERDINGHE, 10 tents and 50 trench shelters.

(iii) The Divisional Train will move by the same date as follows :-
(iv)   H.Q. Div.Train.   ELVERDINGHE.
       No.2 Coy.Train.   A.18.b.8.6.
       No.3. "   "   A.12.3.4.3.
       No.4. "   "   A.16.a.5.4.

(v) In order to lessen the danger of casualties by bombs to animals as well as to men, traverses of earth or sandbags will be constructed at frequent intervals in all horse lines.

(vi) Supply Railhead is expected to move forward to ELVERDINGHE on the 15th.October.

(vii) The 47th.Divl.Supply is at X.27.a.3.6.(Sheet 19) and not as stated in Administrative Instructions No.40.

2. CAMP WARDENS.
Lieut.F.T.FAIRHURST has been appointed Area Commandant EAST Area. He will be responsible for all camps East of ELVERDINGHE (Inclusive)

Capt.SMYLY has been appointed Area Commandant, WEST Area. He will be responsible for all camps West of ELVERDINGHE (Exclusive)

Each Camp will have 2 Camp Wardens who will be responsible for all tents or tent shelters allotted to the Camp

(3. Burials

3. BURIALS.

(a) Burial Party will be located at Canal Bank - C.13.c.2.9. - The front and supporting Brigade will find such personnel as the Burial Officer may require.

(b) CEMETERIES to be used are situated at U.28.c.1.2 and U.26.a.2.2. Mortuaries are being started at C.1.c.8.8. (ARTILLERY Wood) and C.13.b.9.9. (CEASERS Nose) in conjunction with the Cemeteries at these two places.

Whenever possible full use should be made of Divisional Tramways for bringing down bodies, and attention must be paid to salving the equipment (especially boots) of men who have been killed.

4. SALVAGE.
The Divisional Salvage Dump has been established at B.14.b.9.1.
Every effort must be made to send back salvage.
Brigade dumps should be formed and if necessary additional transport will be provided to assist clear these dumps.
Particular attention must be apid to the salving of all Machine and Lewis Guns and their spare parts. These are urgently required.

5. SOLIDIFIED ALCOHOL.
The present allotment for the Division is 1200 tins = 9600 rations per week. This will be divided equally between the three Brigades. For the 14 days 7th. - 21st.October 2400 tins have been drawn, and will be distributed as follows :-

    50th.Brigade.   (600 tins already issued.
                         (200 tins to be issued on 14th.

    51st.Brigade.   (600 tins already issued.
                         (200 tins to be issued on 14th.

    52nd.Brigade.   (600 tins to be issued on 13th.
                         (200 tins to be issued on 14th.

There is a small Divisional Reserve which will be issued on demand to this office, but only under very special circumstances.
Units can augment this supply by making a substitute for solidified alcohol from dripping, paraffin and sawdust.

6. BATHS.
The Baths at ELVERDINGHE CHATEAU are now working - capacity 100 men per hour.
Applications to be made to Baths Officer, Divl.H.Q.

7. CASUALTIES TO EQUIPMENT.
All casualties to animals, Vickers and Lewis Guns must be reported immediately to this office.
If machine guns are reported as damaged by shell fire, it must be stated whether they are out of action or not.

8. FUEL.
Charcoal is available, demands should be made to Brigade Supply Officers.

L. W. Nicholn

Lieut-Colonel,
A.A. & Q.M.G., 17th.Division.

12-10-17.

Distribution
    Area Commandants. Divl.Area Commandants.
    As for Administrative Instructions No.40.

SECRET.

ADMINISTRATIVE INSTRUCTIONS No.26.

October 15th 1917

1. **LOCATIONS :-**
   The following will be the locations of units from 17th. inst :-

BDE. H.Q.	WHITEMILL	B.14.d.6.5
BDE. DEPOT.	"	B.14.d.8.4
52nd.M.G.COY.	"	B.14.d.8.4
52nd.T.M.BTY.	"	B.14.d.8.4
LAN. FUS.	CANAL CAMP	B.12.c.9.1
W.RID.R.	" "	B.17.b.9.5
MANCH. R.	PARROY II CAMP	B.16.c.8.5
R.W. KENT R.	PARROY I "	B.16.d.3.5
51st.FD. AMBCE.	SOLFERINO FARM.	
93rd.FD.COY.R.E)	CANAL BANK.	
77th.FD.Coy. R.E)		
First Line Transport)	B.17.d.5.1.	
of Brigade.		

2. **BLANKETS :-**
   Units will move their blankets and all other stores from the stores in CARIBOO CAMP area to their present camps to-day and will use them in the present area.

3. **M.G. COY.**
   52nd.M.G.Coy. will move from COPPERNOLLE CAMP to WHITEMILL Camp to-morrow 16th. inst., clearing COPPERNOLLE Camp by noon. Billeting Party to report to Staff Captain at Bde. H.Q. at 11.0 a.m. 16th. inst. Transport Lines of M.G.Coy. will be at site to be selected by B.T.O. and notified by him to M.G.Coy. and Train to-day.

4. **BRIGADE DEPOT :-**
   The Brigade Depot will move to WHITEMILL Camp by march on the morning of the 17th. inst., clearing DRAGON Camp by 11.0 a.m. Depot to march in parties less than 50 strong at intervals of 200 yards. O.C. Royal West Kent R. will detail two limbers to report to O.C.Bde. Depot at 9.0 a.m. 17th. inst. to assist Depot to move. O.C. Bde. Depot will send billeting party to report to Staff Captain at Bde. H.Q. at 11.0 a.m. 17th.inst. Supply arrangements of Bde.Depot will continue as hitherto.

5. **DETACHED MEN :-**
   Parties now employed with 52nd.Fd.Ambce. as extra stretcher bearers will rejoin their units to-morrow. Parties attached to C.R.E. will also probably rejoin to-morrow. Units must adjust ration indents accordingly.

6. **CORPS EMPLOYMENT :-**
   The following Corps employ parties will be found by units of the Bde. in relief of men of 50th. Inf. Bde.

	Employ.	Place.	Number.	Found by.
(1).	Water Point Guards.	WHITEHOPE CORNER	1 N.C.O. & 4 men.	Lan. Fus.
(2).	"	BOESINGHE	1 N.C.O. & 2 men.	Manch. R.
(3)	"	S.28.c.6.4	1 N.C.O. & 3 men.	R. West Kents
(4)	"	A.3.b.6.0	1 N.C.O. & 3 men.	W.Rid. R.
(5)	Church Army Hut.	DAWSONS CORNER	1 man.	Manch. R.

   All the above will report at their respective places of employment by noon 18th. inst., rationed to night of 17th. inst. From 18th. inst. inclusive parties 1, 2 and 5 will be rationed by Bde. H.Q., and 1 man from each party must be sent to Bde. H.Q. at 5.0 p.m. daily to draw rations. Parties 3 and 4 will be rationed under Divisional arrangements.

7. SOUP KITCHEN :-
O.C. Lan. Fus. will detail 1 N.C.O. and 3 men to take over Soup Kitchen at CACTUS CAUSEWAY at 9.0 a.m. on 16th. inst. L.T.O. will detail transport every alternate day from 18th. inst. to take soup and fuel to the kitchen from Refilling Point. Supply Officer will arrange that the proper amounts of soup and fuel are available at Refilling Point on alternate days from 18th. inst. inclusive.

8. EVACUATION OF SICK :- O.C. 51st. Fd. Ambce. at SOLFERINO FARM (Corps Main Dressing Station) will be responsible for collection and disposal of sick of the Brigade Group and 77th. Fd. Coy. R.E. Detailed arrangements will be notified later.

9. GRENADES AND TOOLS :-
The extra grenades drawn by units from Brigade Temporary Dump will be returned to Main Div. Grenade Dump by noon to-morrow. Units will retain sandbags drawn and use them on their present camps. S.O.S. bombs will also be retained by units.

COPIES TO :-

Lan. Fus. - 2 copies.
W.Rid. R. - 2 copies.
R.West Kent R. 2 "
Manch. R. 2 "
52nd.M.G.Coy. 2 "
52nd.T.M.Bty. 2 "
G.O.C.
Bde. Major.
L.T.O.
A/Staff Captain.
93rd.Fd.Coy. R.E.
No.4 Coy. Train.
Supply Officer, No.4 Coy. Train.
51st. Fd.Ambce.
17th.Division Q. (for information)
34th.Division Q. (for information)
50th. Inf. Bde. (for information)
Div. Dump Officer.
77th.Fd.Coy. R.E.
O.C. Bde. Depot.
O.C. Signals.

S H Smith
Captain,
Staff Captain,
52nd. Infantry Brigade.

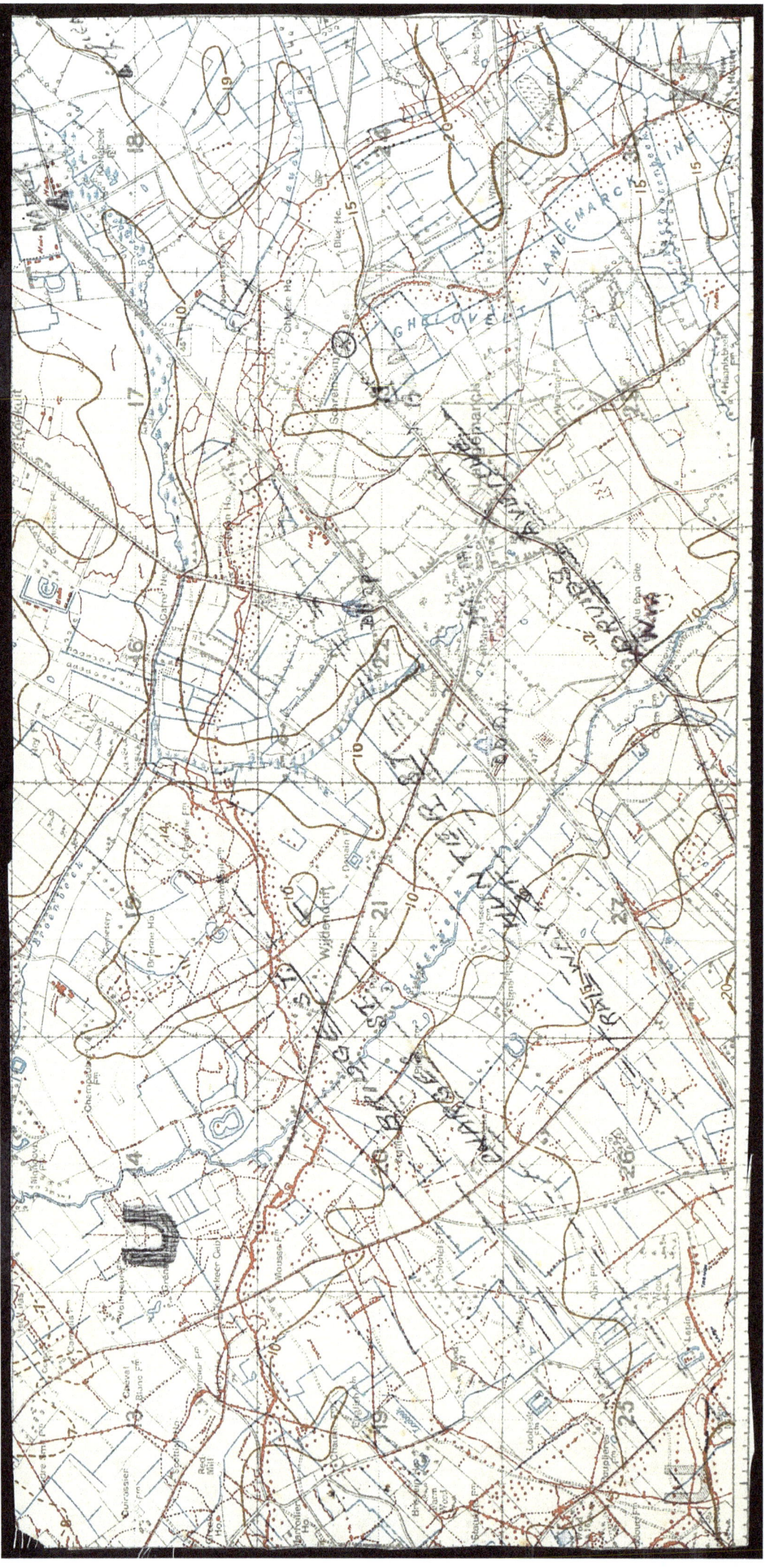

Bergtun 20 SW.
Skala 1/20000

"C" Form (Quadruplicate).   Army Form C. 2123 A.

MESSAGES AND SIGNALS.

No. of Message..........

FILED

Charges to Pay

Office Stamp

ARMY TELEGRAPHS ZEB -14.X.17.

Service Instructions.

Handed in at the .... Office, at 7.15 p.m. Received here at ....

TO   3/4 West Kents

Sender's Number	Day of Month	In reply to Number	AAA
G 118	14	G 11	

You will work from 16 inst inclusive under the technical direction of 183rd Tunnelling Coy aaa for ahon 17 P 9.1 who have been told to send you instructions direct aaa Acknowledge

FROM / PLACE / TIME

CE 11th Corps

GALE & POLDEN, LTD. PRINTERS, ALDERSHOT.
(69,017). Wt. 7931—448. 40,000 Pads. 4/13. W

SECRET.　　　　　　　　　　　　　　　　　　　　　　　　　　　　　　　　Copy No. 14

3/4th. Battn. Royal West Kent Regiment.

March Orders No. 5.

26-10-17.

Ref. Sheet 28. N.W.
1/20000.

1. **Move.** The Battalion will move to-day to DRAGON Camp, A.16.b.4.9. The Battalion (less Transport) will leave by train leaving BOESINGHE Station at 6.30 p.m. Transport will proceed by route march.

2. **Parade.** The Battalion will be ready to move off at 5.0 p.m. March table showing exact times will be issued later. Dress :- Full Marching Order with blanket rolled in water-proof sheet.

3. **Billeting Party.** Lieut. J. S. Fleming with the 4 C.Q.M.Ss. will report to Area Commandant, CARDOEN Camp, A.18.a.9.9. at 2.0 p.m. as billeting party. Lieut. Fleming will send guides to meet the Battalion at detraining point, INTERNATIONAL Corner, and the Transport at DE WIPPE CABARET, A.11.b.3.3.

4. **Rations.** Rations for the 27th instant will be carried on the man.

5. **Transport.** The following Transport will leave Battn.H.Q. at 5.0 p.m. and proceed to DRAGON Camp by route march :-
   - 4 travelling kitchens.
   - 1 water cart.
   - 2 baggage wagons.
   - Mess Cart.
   - Officers' chargers.
   - Bicycles.

   meeting a guide as detailed in para. 3.
   Mess Cart & baggage wagons will report at Officers' Lines at 4.0 p.m. and will be loaded at once.
   The remainder of Transport proceeded this morning under the T.O., and will rejoin the Battalion at the final destination to-morrow, 27th instant.

6. **Warning Order.** The Battalion will entrain tomorrow, the 27th instant, at PROVEN for LA PANNE in the NORDAUSQUES Area.

7. **ACKNOWLEDGE.**

　　　　　　　　　　　　　　　　　　　　　　　[signature]
　　　　　　　　　　　　　　　　　　　　　Captain & Adjutant,
　　　　　　　　　　　　　　　　　3/4th. Battn. Royal West Kent Regiment.

Issued at　　a.m.

Copies to :-

1. C.O.
2. O.C. "A" Coy.
3. O.C. "B" Coy.
4. O.C. "C" Coy.
5. O.C. "D" Coy.
6. B. I. O.
7. Q. M.
8. T. O.
9. M. O.
10. Asst. Adjutant.
11. 2/Lieut. V.A.Weeks.
12. R. S. M.
13. Sergt. Underdown.
14. War Diary.
15. File.

War Diary

BATTALION ORDERS by Lieut. Colonel ....
.... Commanding 3/4th Battn. Royal East Kent Regiment.

1. Church. The Battalion will now to-day for Church Para. A 10.A.M.
The Battalion (less Drummers) will form up in a mass in front
ROSAMOND Cottage at 9.50 a.m. "Drums" on will pass at the
rear march.

2. Parade. The Battalion will be ready to move off at 2.0 p.m.
March table showing march timed will be issued later.
Dress:- Full marching order with Great.... rolled in
waterproof sheet.

3. Billeting. Lieut. J. E. Fleming with the 4 Cpl./..... will report
to Area Commandant, CANDOR Inn, AYLESFORD at 4.0 p.m.
as billeting party. Lieut. Fleming will draw guides to
meet the Battalion at detraining point, BUCKLAND JUNCTION
Dover, and the Transport at SNARGATE WHARF, A.11.b.5.2.

4. Rations. Rations for the 27th instant will be carried on the men.

5. Transport. The following Transport will leave Maidstone W.H.T. at 8.0 a.m.
and proceed to DRAGON Camp by route march:-
   Travelling kitchens.
   1 water cart.
   2 baggage wagons.
   Mess Cart.
   Officers' chargers.
   Bicycles.

Having a guide as detailed in para 3.
Mess Cart & baggage wagons will report at Officers' Mess
at 7.0 p.m. and will be loaded at once.
The remainder of Transport preceded this evening under
the T.O. and will rejoin the battalion at the final
destination to-morrow, 27th instant.

6. Warning The Battalion will entrain tomorrow, the 27th instant, en
Order. route for 14 DAYS in the NORTH-EASTERN Area.

7. Signallers.

Captain & Adjutant,
3/4th Battn. Royal East Kent Regiment.

Issued at .... a.m.

Copies to :-
1. C.O.   9. M.O.
2. O.C. "A" Coy.   10. Asst. Adjutant.
3. O.C. "B" Coy.   11. 2/Lieut. V.A. Herts.
4. O.C. "C" Coy.   12. T.O.K.
5. O.C. "D" Coy.   13. Sergt. Butcher.
6. R.S.M.   14. War Diary.
7. E.S.M.   15. Mil.
8. T.O.

O.C. 173rd Tunnelling Coy, R.E.
O.C. 183rd Tunnelling Coy, R.E.
O.C. Cavalry Pioneer Battn.
O.C. 12th Manchester Regt.
O.C. 3/4th West Kent Regt.

    From tomorrow 20th instant inclusive road parties will be re-arranged as follows :-

 1. 12th Manchester Regt. and 3/4th West Kent Regt. will work under the technical direction of the O.C. 173rd Tunnelling Company, R.E. Their task will be as given in para. 2 of my E.S/250 dated 11-10-17.

 2. The Cavalry Pioneer Battalion will work under the technical direction of the O.C. 183rd Tunnelling Company, R.E. Their task will be as given in para. 1 of my E.S/250 dated 11-10-17.

 3. The allotment of transport from 33rd Reserve Park, the Detachment 5th Aux. M.T. Company and 7th (Horsed) Pontoon Park remains the same as given in para. 4 of my E.S/250 dated 11-10-17.

19th October 1917.

Captain, R.E.
S.O. R.E.
for Chief Engineer, XIVth Corps.

C.E. XlVth Corps No. E.S/250.

O.C. 173rd Tunnelling Coy.
O.C. 183rd Tunnelling Coy.
O.C. 20th Army Troops Coy.
O.C. 16th Bn. Royal Scots.
O.C. 1/2nd Monmouth Regt.
O.C. 14th Worcestershire Regt.
O.C. 21st West Yorks.
O.C. 33rd Reserve Park.
O.C. 7th (Horsed) Pontoon Park.
O.C. Det. No. 5 Aux. H. T. Coy.
****

With reference to my E.S/238 of 5-10-17 and E.S/243 of 7-10-17, work on forward roads will be re-arranged as follows from the 12th instant inclusive.

1. The 21st West Yorks and 1/2nd Monmouth Regt. will work under the technical direction of the 183rd Tunnelling Company, R.E. Their task will be as follows :-
   (a). To continue the maintenance, clearing and improvement of the road from IRON CROSS to SCHREIBOOM.
   (b). To work small parties only along the SCHREIBOOM-POELCAPPELLE road.
   (c). To continue the planking and improvement of the road from LANGEMARCK to WHITE HOUSE.
   (d). To continue the repair of the road from LANGEMARC to ALOUETTE FARM as far as U.29.b.00.15.

2. The 14th Worcestershire Regt. and the 16th Bn. Royal Scots will work under the technical direction of the O.C. 173rd Tunnelling Company, R.E. Their task will be as follows :-
   (a). To carry out the maintenance, repair and improvement of the road from FOURCHE FARM-WIJDEN DRIFT-LANGEMARCK STATION-U.22.b.00.35.-NEY CROSS ROADS, and to work small parties forward along the

road to KOEKUIT.

(b).   To maintain and improve the road from U.27.c.1.8. to MARTINS MILL via TUFFS FARM.

3.   The 133rd, 109th and half the 174th Labour Companies will work under the O.C. 20th Army Troops Company, R.E. on the task already allotted to him by my E.S/238 of 5-10-17.

4.   Transport from the 33rd Reserve Park; the Detachment 5th Aux. H.T.Company and 7th (Horsed) Pontoon Park is allotted as from the 12th instant as follows :-

To O.C. 183rd Tunnelling Company, R.E.

    45 G.S.wagons from the 33rd Reserve Park.

To O.C. 20th Army Troops Company, R.E.

    33 G.S.wagons from the 33rd Reserve Park, including 10 tip carts.

To O.C. 173rd Tunnelling Company, R.E.

    30 G.S.wagons from the Detachment 5th Aux. H.T. Company, and

    15 Pontoon wagons from the 7th (Horsed) Pontoon Park.

5.   Transport will be ordered direct from 33rd Reserve Park, the Detachment 5th Aux. H. T. Company and 7th (Horsed) Pontoon Park by the O's C. 173rd and 183rd Tunnelling Companies and 20th Army Troops Company, R.E.

The above allotment is the maximum available; if it is found that all these cannot be worked with convenience, the O's C. concerned must use only such wagons as they consider advisable.

6. The map locations of the 33rd Reserve Park, the Detachment 5th Aux. H. T. Company and the forward sections of the 7th (Horsed) Pontoon Park are as follows :-

    33rd Reserve Park ... ... A.18.d.4.9.
    Det. 5th Aux.H.T.Company ... ... B.22.b.8.2.
    7th (Horsed) Pontoon Park ... ... B.24.c.9.9.

7. ACKNOWLEDGE.

(Sgd). P.K.BOULNOIS.
Captain, R.E.
S.O. R.E.
for Chief Engineer, XIVth Corps.

19th October 1917.

War Diary

3/4th Royal West Kents

November 1917

War Diary
of
3/4 Royal West Kent Regt.

from November 1st 1917. to November 30th 1917.

WAR DIARY or INTELLIGENCE SUMMARY

Army Form C. 2118.

Place	Date	Hour	Summary of Events and Information	Remarks and references to Appendices
LA PANNE	1/4/17		Batt. Strength 42 officers & 1024 O.R.s	
	6/11/17		17th Division relieves the 57th Division on the right sector of the XIX Corps front between POELCAPELLE & the YPRES-STADEN Railway, the 52 Inf Bde taking over the front line from the 172 Bde on the night 6/7/11.	About strength marched "A"
		4.30a.m.	Battalion moves by march route to AUDRUICQ thence by march route to SOULT Camp (C28.a.2.0 or 28.N.W.17000)	
SOULT Camp	7/11/17		Other Battalions using march route to MARSOUIN Camp in reserve	One attached at the 13
MARSOUIN Camp & BESACE Farm	8/11/17		Battalion relieves the Lewis Tug in the front line in the right sector of the Divisional front, A&B Coys in the front line with HQ at FERGUSON & C&D in support, C&D with HQ at LOUIS FARM. C.O. inspected H.Q., MARSOUIN Camp & BESACE Farm inspected S.A. & Lewis Gun & at MILLERS Houses inspected	

Army Form C. 2118.

WAR DIARY
or
INTELLIGENCE SUMMARY

(Erase heading not required.)

Instructions regarding War Diaries and Intelligence Summaries are contained in F. S. Regs., Part II. and the Staff Manual respectively. Title Pages will be prepared in manuscript.

Place	Date	Hour	Summary of Events and Information	Remarks and references to Appendices
LOUIS FARM U.24.c.50.95	11/11/17		Battalion relieved in the front line by the Lancs Fusiliers move to Camp in reserve (C.7.d.1.3)	Arrow attached misc. 1.
HUDDLESTONE Camp	13/11/17		52 Bde relieved in the line by the 50th Bde moves into Divisional Reserve. The Battalion proceeds by march route to DUBLIN Camp (A.M. unless cancelled), in the train killed O.R. 4: wounded O.R. 28. JANUARY Battn casualties. 2/Lt ST JAMES M.C. proceeds on leave. Lt (a/Major) 1ST. MONCKTON assumes Company command. 2/Lt Burton.	Arrow attached misc. 2
DUBLIN Camp	19/11/17		Battn moves into BRIDGE Camp in support to 51 Bde in the front line. 52 Bde moving into support.	Arrow attached misc. 3
BRIDGE Camp	23/11/17		Battn moves into the front line (52 Bde relieving 51st Bde) in relief of 7th Bn Border Regt to the right subsector of the Divisional	Arrow attached misc. 4

Army Form C. 2118.

WAR DIARY
or
INTELLIGENCE SUMMARY
(Erase heading not required.)

Place	Date	Hour	Summary of Events and Information	Remarks and references to Appendices
BENNETTS	25/26		[illegible handwritten entries]	
	26/27			
BEAUREGARD	27	6.30 am		

WAR DIARY
or
INTELLIGENCE SUMMARY

(Erase heading not required.)

Army Form C. 2118.

Place	Date	Hour	Summary of Events and Information	Remarks and references to Appendices
LEVIS Pt 2	28/11/17		Battn relieved in the front line 1/c Lan of Fr by 1/5 Leys. A & B Coys Oppo attached (reported "K")	
			2 A.C in BKRU Trench & DOUBLE COTES, C & D Cops in own OLD Trench.	
Double Cotes	30/11/17		Battn Hq/k Afrais 41 D2, 8824	

Signed,
LIEUT. COL.
Comdg. 1/4th Bn. R. W. Kent Regt.

Lan. Fus.
W.Rid. Regt.
R.W.Kent Regt.
Manch. Regt.
M.G.Coy.
T.M.Bty.
E.Yorks. Regt.

H.Q.,
52ND INFANTRY BDE.

52.G. 4138

Reference Brigade Order No. X.2.

It is probable that there will be a Conference of all COMPANY COMMANDERS on the ground after the Exercise.

Commanding Officers of W.RIDING REGT. and R.WEST KENT REGT. will remain with Brigade Headquarters after forming up has taken place.

3/11/1917.

Captain,
Brigade Major,
52nd Infantry Brigade.

SECRET.

Lan. Fus.
W. Rid. Regt.
R. W. Kent Regt.
Manch. Regt.
M.G. Coy.
T.M. Bty.

H.Q.,
52nd INFANTRY BDE.

52.G.....

WARNING ORDER.

It is likely that the 52nd Brigade will be moving into the FORWARD AREA on the 6th instant and take over the Divisional front with one Battalion in the front line, (LANCASHIRE FUSILIERS) one Battalion in Support, (WEST RIDING REGIMENT) and two Battalions in Reserve on the night of 7/8th instant.

The BRIGADE BOUNDARY will be as follows :-

RECQUETTE FARM on the right and BROEMBEEK on the left.

The Support Battalion is believed to be *disposed* somewhere in the vicinity of a line running through OLGA HOUSES.

The two Reserve Battalions are believed to be encamped between PILCKEM and the CANAL.

No further details are at present available.

M.C. Hogan

Captain,
Brigade Major,
52nd Infantry Brigade.

3/11/1917.

S E C R E T. Copy No. 7.

Ref Maps
HAZEBROUCK 5A.1/100000 52ND INFANTRY BRIGADE O.O.No.202.
Sheet 28.N.W.1/40,000
and
SCHAAP BALIE 1/10,000.

FILE WD

****

1. The 17th Division (less Artillery) will relieve the 57th Division (less Artillery) in the right Sector of XIX Corps front on 6th., 7th., and 8th. November.

2. The 52nd Infantry Brigade will move in accordance with attached Tables "A" and "B".
Administrative Instructions have already been issued for the move of the TRANSPORT and entrainment.
TRANSPORT will detrain at BOESINGHE.

3. ENGINEER, SIGNAL and MEDICAL reliefs will be carried out under arrangements to be made by C.R.E., O.C.,SIGNALS and A.D.M.S. respectively, with C.R.E., O.C.Signals, and A.D.M.S. 57th Division.

4. D.M.G.O. will arrange for relief of barrage Guns in the forward area, and A.A. Guns in the Artillery area during November 7th; relief to be completed by 6.0 p.m.

5. Battalions will each detail 1 Officer, 5 N.C.O's and 45 men to report to 93rd Field Coy., R.E. at a time and date to be notified later, as permanent WORKING and CARRYING PARTIES.

6. A BRIGADE SCHOOL will be established at HOUNSLOW Camp on the 7th instant after Breakfast. Captain BENNETT, West Riding Regiment will command the School. Further instructions on this matter will be issued later.
MACHINE GUN COMPANY and TRENCH MORTAR BTY. will send 10% of their trench Strength to the School.

7. BRIGADE HEADQUARTERS will close at NAUDAUSQUES at 6.30 a.m., 6th instant and re-open at B.23.c.6.6. on arrival.

Acknowledge.

Issued at 2-20 pm.

Copy No 1 to Bde.H.Q.
2 to War Diary.
3 to Staff Captain.
4 to O.C.Signals.
5 to Eas. Fus.
6 to W.Rid. Regt.
7 to R.W.Kent Regt.
8 to Manch. Regt.
9 to M.G.Coy.
10 to T.M.Bty.
11 to D.M.G.O.
12 to 93rd F.Coy., R.E.
13 to 51st F.Ambce.
14 to 172nd Bde.
15 to No.4 Coy.Train.
16 to O.C., Supplies.
17 to 17th Division.

S. G. Turner
Captain,
Brigade Major,
52nd Infantry Brigade.

5th NOVEMBER 1917.

"TABLE "A".
****

Serial No.	UNIT.	Date. 1917. NOVR. 8th.	From.	To.	In relief of.	Remarks.
1.	Brigade Headquarters.	8th.	NORDAUSQUES.	B.23.c.8.6.	Bde.H.Q., 171st Bde)	57th Division. Entraining Station, AUDRUICQ.
2.	Lancashire Fusiliers.	do.	do.	MARSOUIN.	A Bn., 172nd Bde.	Detraining Station, ELVERDINGHE.
3.	West Riding Regt.	do.	ZOUAFQUES.	HUDDLESTONE.	B Bn., 172nd Bde.	
4.	Royal West Kent Regt.	do.	LA PANNE.	SOULT.	3 Bn., 171st Bde.	On arrival, 52nd Brigade group comes under the tactical control of 57th Division.
5.	Manchester Regiment.	do.	LUCHES.	WOLFE.	A Bn., 171st Bde.	
6.	Machine Gun Company. Trench mortar battery. C. & D. Batteries.	do.	(AUTINGUES. do. GRASSE PAYELLE.	MARSOUIN.		

TABLE "5".
****

Serial No.	UNIT.	Date. 1917. NOVR.	From	To.	In relief of.	Remarks.
1.	Brigade Headquarters.	7/8th.	L.23.c.6.6.	Adv.H.Q.,STRAY FARM. Rear H.Q.,Fusilier House)	172nd.Brigade.	
2.	Lancashire Fusiliers.	7/8th.	MARSOUIN.	Front line.	C Bn.,172nd Bde.	
3.	West Riding Regiment.	do.	HUDDLESTONE.	Support line.	D Bn.,172nd Bde.	
4.	Royal West Kent Regt.	do.	SOULT.	MARSOUIN.	Lancashire Fus.	
5.	Manchester Regiment.	do.	WOLFE.	HUDDLESTONE.	West Riding Regt.	
6.	Machine Gun Company.) Trench Mortar Battery.)	do.	MARSOUIN.	Front line.	Opposite Nos. of 172nd Bde.	
7.	C & D Batteries.	do.	do.	do.	57th Division barrage and A.A.Guns.	

The following intervals will be maintained on the march.:-

EAST of the CANAL - Between Platoons 100 yards interval.

WEST of the CANAL - Between Companies 200 yards interval.

SECRET. Copy No..1..

3/4th. Battn. Royal West Kent Regiment.

MARCH ORDERS NO. 6.

5-11-17.

Reference HAZEBROUCK 5A 1/100000.
28 B N.W.1/40000.

MOVE. The Battalion will move into SOULT Camp tomorrow and into MARSOUIN Camp on the 7th. inst.

PARADE. The Battalion (less Transport) will pass road junction S.E. corner of stubble field adjoining "B" Coy. at 4.15 a.m.
Order of march :- Band, H.Q., "B", "C", "A", "D".
Water Bottles must be full.

BREAKFASTS. Breakfasts, 3.15 a.m.

BICYCLES. Bicycles will proceed to the station with Battalion, but will remain there, under one man only, and proceed with the transport train.

BLANKETS. Blankets must be stacked at H.Q. before breakfast.

PAILLASSES. Paillasses must be stacked at "B" Coy. barn before breakfasts and not at "C" Coys. C.Q.M.S's Stores as ~~advised~~ ORDERED in Administrative Instructions No.4.

LOADING PARTY. The T.O. will detail 1 N.C.O. and 10 men to report to Sgt. Ward at Battalion H.Q. at 7.15 a.m. to load lorries. The loading parties ordered in Administrative Instructions No.4 para.3 are not now required.

EMPLOY. Reference Administrative Instructions No.4 para.8 and 9, 2/Lieut. S.H. Webb and 2/Lieut. H.A. Southgate are transposed.
In addition to the employs ordered in Administrative Instructions No.4, O.C. "A" Coy. will detail 1 Officer, 2 N.C.O's and 12 men to work under Sub Area Commandant Right Division. 1 N.C.O. must be a good map reader, and the other, a Sergeant. Names will reach the Adjutant tonight.
This party will proceed by the first omnibus train, and will reach AUDRUICQ Station at 9.30 a.m. This party will report at dug out 62 East Bank Canal, B 24. c.9.8. with two days rations and will be rationed by "A" Coy. till the night of the 11th. inst.
O.C. "C" Coy's party for Area Commandant MALAKOFF Area referred to in Administrative Instructions No.4 para7, will proceed by the same train.
All employed parties are to be in possession of full written instructions, and each man in such parties is to know exactly what his party is.

PUNCTUALITY. It is essential that all orders for the move are punctually carried out.

DRYING ROOM PARTY. O.C. "B" Coy. will detail 1 N.C.O. and 3 men to be in charge of the drying room at SOULT Camp. This party will proceed with the Battalion, but will remain at SOULT Camp when the Battn. moves on.

TIME TABLE. Train time table with serial Nos. is issued herewith.

ACKNOWLEDGE.

Capt. & Adjutant
3/4th. Battn. Royal West Kent Regiment.

Issued at 7.30 p.m.
Copies to all recipients of Administrative Instructions No.4.

TRAIN TIME TABLE.

Train.	Serial No.	Party.	To reach Station	Time Train leaves.
No.1 Personnel Train	5.	Traffic Control Officer.	6.0 a.m.	7.0 a.m.
No.2 Personnel Train	9.	The Battalion.	6.30 a.m.	8.0 a.m.
No.1 Omnibus Train	18.	"C" Coys. MALAKOFF Area Commandant party.	9.30 a.m.	11.0 a.m.
No.1 Omnibus Train	19.	"A" Coys. Party for Sub. Area Commandant Right Division.	9.30 a.m. *8.0 a.m.*	11.0 a.m.
No.2 Omnibus Train	21.	Transport.	11.0 a.m.	2.0 p.m.

SECRET.   3/4th.Battn.Royal West Kent Regiment.   Copy.No.- 15

ADMINISTRATIVE INSTRUCTIONS NO.4.

                                                              In the Field
                                                              5-11-17.
Ref. HAZEBROUCK 5 A 1/100000.

1. **MOVE.**
    The Battalion (less 4 limbered wagons which proceeded by route march today), will move tomorrow 6th.inst. to ELVERDINGHE by No.2 train, time of which will be notified when received.

2. **1st.LINE TRANSPORT.**
    1st.Line Transport will be loaded this afternoon. All tools will be returned to Q.M.Stores at 4.0 p.m.today. Tool limbers will report at Battn.H.Q. for SIGNAL STORES at 5.0 p.m. Lewis Gun Limbers will be loaded at Battn.H.Q. at 5.15 p.m.

3. **LORRIES.**
    Two lorries will report at Battn.H.Q. at 7.30 a.m. tomorrow the 6th.inst to convey :- No.1 Lorry, Band Instruments, Officers Valises, and Orderly Room Stores. No.2 Lorry, Blankets.
    All these stores will be ready stacked outside Battn.H.Q.at 7.15 a.m. and loading parties furnished as follows :-
    (a). For Band Instruments, 1 N.C.O. and 2 men supplied by O I/c.Band.
    (b). For Officers Valises, Officers' own batmen.
    (c). For Orderly Room Stores, O.R.Staff.
    (d). For blankets, (which must be securely labelled and tied in bundles of 10), 1 N.C.O. and 4 men per Coy. Three men from the Q.M.Staff and three from the O.R.Staff will travel by lorry. No additional personnel will travel by lorry.

4. **RATIONS.**
    Rations for the 6th. will be carried on the man, for the 7th. on the cookers.

5. **PAILLASSES.**
    No paillasses will be taken out of the present area, They will be taken to the barn at Billet Warden's quarters (at "C"Coy. C.Q.M.S Stores), at a time to be notified later.
    Empty paillasses will be rolled in bundles of 10.

6. **SANITATION.**
    The M.O.has inspected billets today with C.Q.M.S's who will report defects to O.C.Coys. The area is to be left absolutely clean, and O.C.Coys. and Lieut.Fleming for H.Q.will arrange to have billets inspected by an Officer tomorrow, before the Battalion moves.

7. **EMPLOYED MEN.**
    O.C."C"Coy. will detail 1 N.C.O.and 10 Other Ranks for duty with Area Commandant MALAKOFF. Area (B.23.c.8.3). Two days rations will be carried. The party will proceed by No.1 train tomorrow, time of which will be notified when received. The N.C.O. will report to Major G.T.THACKER, Lancashire Fusiliers (Brigade Entraining Officer), ½ hour before train moves. Nominal roll will reach the Adjutant by 6.30 p.m tonight.

8. **R.E.WORKING PARTY.**
    2/Lieut.S.H.Webb with 50 Other Ranks, detailed as follows will be held in readiness to work under C.R.E. at short notice:-
    "A"Coy., 1 Sergt.,1Cpl.or L/c. and 15 men.
    "C"Coy., 1 Cpl.or L/c.and 15 men. "D"Coy., 1 Sgt., 1 Cpl.or L/c.& 15 men.
    Nominal Rolls will reach the Adjutant by 6.30 p.m.tonight.

9. **TRAFFIC.**
    2/Lieut.H.A.Southgate will report to Capt.Grove at AUDRUICQ Station 1 hour before departure of No.1 train on 6th.inst. for Traffic Control duties, with his servant and kit. Two days rations will be taken.

10. **PROTECTION OF CAMPS.**
    Immediately on arrival in the new area steps will be taken by O.C.Coys. to construct revetment of sandbags, earth or other material round all tents and huts occupied.

11. **HUTTING SECTION.**
    The Hutting Section whose names have been checked by O.C. Coys. will be kept ready to proceed to D.O.R.E. at short notice.

                                        [signature]
                                        Capt.& Adjutant.
                                        3/4th.Battn.Royal West Kent Regt.

Issued at........
Copies to :- 1.C.O.   6.Major A.E.Jones.   11.2/Lt.S.H.Webb.
              2.O.C."A"Coy. 7.H.Q.Off's Mess.   12. " H.A.Southgate.
              3.O.C."B"Coy. 8.Q.   13.Officer I/o.Band.
              4.O.C."C"Coy. 9.T.O.   14.R.S.M.   15. M.D.
              5.O.C."D"Coy. 10.M.O.   16.File.

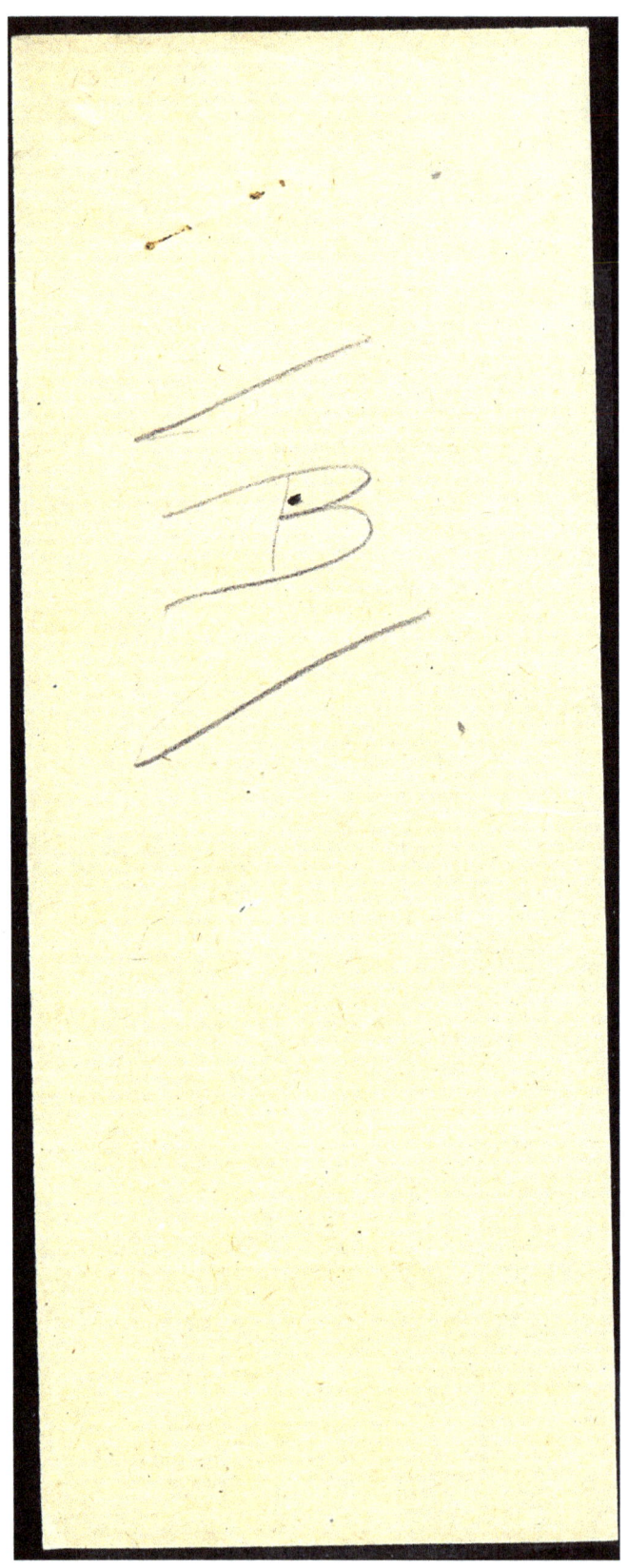

"A" Form.
MESSAGES AND SIGNALS.

Army Form C. 2121 (in pads of 100).

Secret

Copy No 7.

TO Relief of 172nd Inf Brigade by 59nd Inf Brigade

Sender's Number: BM 1
Day of Month: Nov 6th

AAA

(1) The 59nd Inf Brigade will relieve the 172 Inf Brigade in the front line on the night 7/8th inst in accordance with attached table aaa Relief to be completed by 6 am 8th inst aaa

(2) Guides for the Lancs Fus and West Riding Regt will report at their present camps at 12 noon tomorrow (1 per platoon 1 per Coy Hdqs and 1 for Battn Hdqs.)

(3) The R West Kent Regt and Manchester Regt will arrange for their own guides and will reconnoitre the routes before marching

(4) The command of the sector will pass from G.O.C 172nd Inf Brigade to G.O.C 59nd Inf Brigade on completion of relief.

"A" Form.
MESSAGES AND SIGNALS.

Army Form C. 2121 (in pads of 100).

Prefix ...... Code ...... m	Words	Charge	This message is on a/c of:	Recd. at ...... m
Office of Origin and Service Instructions.				Date ......
	Sent		...... Service.	From ......
	At ...... m.			
	To			
	By		(Signature of "Franking Officer.")	By ......

TO { (2) }

| Sender's Number. | Day of Month. | In reply to Number. | A A A |

(5) Brigade Hdqs will close at B.23.c.6.6 at 4 pm and reopen at STRAY FARM at same time.

(6) The following arrangements will be made to deal with low-flying enemy aeroplanes
(a) Front & Support lines by Lewis Guns
(b) 2 Vickers Guns between Support and Reserve Lines.
(c) Battns in Support and Reserve will detail 4 Guns for A.A duty.

(7) Lancs Fus and W. Riding Regt will send forward 1 Officer per Coy and 1 N.C.O per platoon during daylight tomorrow to take over Coy and platoon stores and to ~~ascertain~~ learn as much as possible about the dispositions in their respective areas.

From
Place
Time

The above may be forwarded as now corrected. (Z)

Censor. Signature of Addressor or person authorised to telegraph in his name

"A" Form.
MESSAGES AND SIGNALS.

Army Form C. 2121 (in pads of 100).

TO ③

they will await the arrival of their Companies

(8) Details of relief other than those laid down will be arranged between OsC. concerned.

(9) Relief complete will be reported to Bde H.Qs in B.A.B. code

ACKNOWLEDGE. ✓ fOL.
Issued at 7.0 pm
Copies to 1. War Diary   11. 172 Inf Brigade
         2. Bde H.Q.   12. 57 Division
         3. Staff Captain 13. 17 Division
         4. D. of Signals
         5. Lanc Fus
         6. N. Lod Regt
       ✓ 7. R. West Kent Regt
         8. Manchester Regt
         9. M.G. Coy.   H.C. Morgan
        10. T.M. Bty.   Captain
                             Brigade Major
                             5nd Inf Bde.

MARCH TABLE.

Ser. No.	UNIT.	Date. 1917. Novr.	From.	To.	In relief of.	REMARKS.
1.	Brigade Headquarters.	7.	E.23.c.6.6.	STRAY FARM.	172nd Inf.Bde.	To be established at 4 pm.
2.	Lancashire Fus.	do.	7/8th. MARSOUIN.	Front line. H.C.LOUIS Fm.	2/4th S.L.R.	Leading platoons to pass STRAY FARM at 2.30 pm. Tracks "A" and "B".
3.	West Riding Regiment.	do.	HUDDLESTONE.	Support. H.C.,2/5th S.L.R. U.23.d.3.2. DOUBLE COT.		Leading platoons to pass STRAY Farm at 4 p.m. Tracks "A" and "B".
4.	E.West Kent Regt.	do.	7th. SOULT.	MARSOUIN.	Lan. Fus.	Leading platoon to start from Camp at 1 pm. Track "B".
5.	Manchester Regt.	do.	WOLFE.	HUDDLESTONE.	W.Riding Regt.	Leading platoons to start from Camp at 2.30 pm. Track "A".
6.	Machine Gun Coy.	do.	MARSOUIN.	Front line.	Guns of 172nd Inf. Brigade.	Only 6 Guns are in position & these only to be relieved at present. O.C.,M.G.Coy. will meet O.C.,172nd M.G.Coy. at 10.30 am. at STRAY FARM tomorrow and arrange details of relief. The 6 Guns should arrive at STRAY FARM at 2 pm. ready to be guided up.
7.	T.Mortar Battery.	do.	do.	CANAL BANK CAMP.	do.	No Guns are at present in the line. For location of CANAL CAMP, O.C., T.M.B. will report to Staff dept. 172nd Inf.Bde. at FUSILIER-HORSE, C.13.c.0.0. Relief to be completed by 3 pm. A RECONNAISSANCE of the line will be made by the O.C.,T.M.B. tomorrow with a view to establishing 2 Guns each at GRAVEL FARM and BESACE FARM.

Following INTERVALS will be maintained EAST of the CANAL. 100 Yards.

"A" Form.
MESSAGES AND SIGNALS.

Army Form C. 2121 (in pads of 100).

Prefix...Code...m	Words	Charge	This message is on a/c of:	Recd. at...m
Office of Origin and Service Instructions.				Date...
Secret	Sent		W	From...
By hand	At...m		Service.	
	To		(Signature of "Franking Officer.")	By...
	By			

TO RELIEF ORDERS BY 52ND INF BDE

| Sender's Number. | Day of Month. | In reply to Number. | AAA |
| *B.M.1 | 8/11 | | |

① The following reliefs will take place on the night 9/10th Nov

② The R West Kent Regt will relieve the Right centre and Supports Coys of the Lancs Fus also the Right forward Coy of the West Riding Regt

③ The 12 Manch Regt will relieve 2 Coys of the 6th N.F. (149th Inf Bde) in front and support lines between V.7.3. 5.5 and Railway at TURENNE CROSSING (R.Y inclusive) also Left Coy Lancs Fus in front line and Left forward Coy West Riding Regt

④ The Lancs Fus on Completion of relief will occupy HUDDLESTONE camp
The Two forward Coys West Riding Regt will occupy MARSOUIN camp on relief

From
Place
Time

The above may be forwarded as now corrected. (Z)

Censor. Signature of Addressor or person authorised to telegraph in his name
* This line should be erased if not required.

"A" Form.
MESSAGES AND SIGNALS.

Army Form C. 2121
(in pads of 100).
No of Message ....

Prefix .... Code .... m	Words	Charge	This message is on a/c of:	Recd. at .... m
Office of Origin and Service Instructions.				
....	Sent		.... Service.	Date ....
....	At .... m.			From ....
....	To			By ....
....	By		(Signature of "Franking Officer.")	

| TO { | | ② | | |

| Sender's Number. | Day of Month. | In reply to Number. | |
| | | | AAA |

(5) 52nd M.G. Coy will relieve two guns 149th M.G. Coy at BERTHIER FME and V.7.A.1.3

(6) Guides from 6th NF to lead the two Manch Coys will be where Rly track crosses WIJDEN DRIFT — LANGEMARCK Road at 4.30 p.m. Guides for M.G. Coy will at same place at 4 pm. Guides from Lanc Fus and West Riding Regt for R West Kent Regt and Manch Regt in proportion of 1 per platoon 1 per Coy HQ 1 per Bn HQ will report at Bn HQ at 2.30 pm where they will meet relieving Coys on the duckboards

From
Place
Time

The above may be forwarded as now corrected. (Z)

Censor. Signature of Addressor or person authorised to telegraph in his name

"A" Form.
MESSAGES AND SIGNALS.

Army Form C. 2121.
(In pads of 100.)

Prefix......Code......in	Words.	Charge.	This message is on a/c of:	Recd. at ...... m.
Office of Origin and Service Instructions.				
	Sent			Date......
......	At......m.		......Service.	
	To......			From......
......	By......		(Signature of "Franking Officer.")	By......

TO {

Sender's Number. | Day of Month. | In reply to Number. | **A A A**

(7) Details of relief other than laid down will be arranged between O.C. concerned.

(8) Route for the 2 Coys Manch Regt relieving the 6" NF will be along RAILWAY STREET Duckwalk Route for R West Kent and remaining two Coys Manch Regt will be along "A" and "B" tracks and a time table will issue later to those concerned. Leading platoon of Manch Regt will pass STRAY FARM (Bn HQ) at 2.30 p.m. Intervals of 100 between platoons will be maintained.

(9) Completion of reliefs will be reported to Bn HQrs in BAB code

From
Place
Time

The above may be forwarded as now corrected. (Z)

Censor. Signature of Addressor or person authorised to telegraph in his name.

※ This line should be erased if not required.

"A" Form.
MESSAGES AND SIGNALS.

Army Form C. 2121.
(In pads of 100.)

Sender's Number.	Day of Month.	In reply to Number.	A A A

(10) Command of the sector taken over from 149th Inf Bde will pass from f.o.c 149 Bde to f.o.c 53rd Inf Bde on completion of relief

(11) One Officer per Coy and one N.C.O per platoon from each of the relieving Coys should be sent up to take over Coy stores and to learn the situation during daylight

(12) H.Q" of the West Riding Reg" will remain at present location (DOUBLE (07 75) Acknowledge
Copies to — Lancs Fus   M.G Coy
West Rid R   T.M Batts
8 West Rid R

From. Manch Reg"
Place 149 Inf Bde
Time Staff Capt 53rd Bde

(Z) M C Moyan Capt

Bd Adjt 53rd Inf Bde

"A" Form.
MESSAGES AND SIGNALS.

Army Form C. 2121.
(In pads of 100.)

TO	Lancs Fus	R.W. Kent Regt
	West Rid Regt	Manct Regt

Sender's Number.	Day of Month.	In reply to Number.	AAA
BM 2	9		

Continuation of BM 1 8th inst aaa Leading platoon of Manct Regt will pass STRAY FM at 2.30 pm, last platoon to pass by 2.55 pm. R West Kent Regt may use same tracks from 3 pm. Owing to air raid activity on duckboards platoons should march at 200 yds intervals with 100 yds.

M. Morgan Capt

From 52nd Bde
Time 8.0 am

Secret H.P.   Copy No 11

              3/4 R West Kent Regt
              Order No. XI.   9/1/17

        Ref. 28 B NW 1/20000
             SCHAAP-BALIE

Relief   1. The Battalion will relieve the
             Right Centre & Support Coys of
             1st Lancashire Fusiliers and the
             right forward Coy of the West
             Riding Regt Today the 9th inst
             and will take over the right sector
             of the Brigade front.

Dispositions 2. A Coy will relieve Right Coy 1st Fus
              B "   "   "   Centre "   "
              C "   "   "   Support "   "
              D "   "   "   Right forward Coy
                                  West Riding Regt.

March   3. The Battalion will leave camp
             at 2.30 pm in the following
             order A,B,C,D, HQ 200 yards
             distance will be maintained
             between Platoons.

Guides 4. Guides from the coys to be relieved will meet the Battalion on the duckboard track near Bde HQ STRAY FARM in the proportion of 1 per platoon 1 per coy HQ & 1 per Bn HQ

Route. 5. B tracks to Bn HQ where Guides meet Battn.

Advance 6. Major JONES with 1 NCO. from
party HQ 1 Officer per coy & 1 NCO. per Platoon will proceed to the new area at 12.45 pm to take over stores & reconnoitre the positions.

Runners 7 1 HQ runner will accompany each coy to coy HQ and will return to Bn HQ with 2 coy runners each who will be returned to their coy.

SOS Bombs 8. Coys will draw from ROM first morning & will take up

8. to lire SOS Bombs Very
lights or Ground Flares. In
addition 2 sandbags per
man will be taken up.

SAA. 9. 30 boxes SAA will be
taken up to Bn HQ. Coys
can draw in the proportion
of 1 extra bandolier per
man.

Lewis guns 10. Lewis gun teams will carry
up their guns & ammunition

Rations 11. Rations up to the night of the
4th will be taken up on
the man.

Water 12. Water will be taken up
to Bn HQ from which
coys will draw it. Water
bottles must be taken up
full.

Packs & 13. Packs & Officers Blankets will
kit

be stacked at present Bn HQ
before 12.30 pm & will be
taken to B Echelon in baggage
wagons.

R.A.P. 14. R.A.P will be at Louis Farm

Bn HQ 15 Bn HQ will be at LOUIS FARM
until further orders.

Patrols 16 A & B Coys will each find
an Officer's patrol & one
NCO's patrol tonight
9th – 10th, one before &
one after midnight.

ACKNOWLEDGE

Issued at 11.45 am   W M Lauchlan
                              Capt & Adjt
Copies to 1. Lan Fus.   3/4 R. West Riding
         2. Dukes Riding Regt
         3-6 Coys   9. QM & TO
         7 HQ   -10 RQM
         8 MO   11 WD
                         12 52 Bde (thro' inf.)

Lancs Fus.
W. Rid. R.
R.W. Kent R.
Manch Regt
M.G. Coy
T.M. Bty
17th Division
Staff Captain
O.C. Sigs
174th Brigade
54th Brigade
O.C. 2 Coys W Rid R Marsouin Camp.

Secret

H.Q.,
52ND INFANTRY BDE.
5254204.

A "Coy"
B "Coy / O.C. House

1. The following reliefs will take place tonight 10th inst and the new distribution in accordance with attached table taken up.

2. The Lancs Fus. will take over the Headquarters of the Royal West Kent Regt. at OLGA HOUSE and take over the whole of the Brigade Front and Support lines from 2 Coys R.W. Kent R. and 2 Coys Manch Regt.

The Manch Regt (Less 2 Coys) will remain in the line as Support Bn with H.Q. at U.18.c.13.6. having attached to them 2 Coys of the W. Rid. R, now at MARSOUIN Camp.

One Coy Manch Regt will garrison the line of defended posts at the points indicated in the table

Two Coys W. Rid. R. will occupy the line. 19 Metre Hill — U.12.D.20. respectively.

One Coy Manch Regt will occupy EAGLE TRENCH

3. The W. Rid. R, less 2 Coys, will occupy MARSOUIN Camp having attached to them 2 Coys Manch Regt.

The R.W. Kent Regt will occupy HUDDLESTONE Camp on completion of relief

2

4. The M.G. Coy will detail one gun for each of the defended posts and also place 5 guns at approx the following points for the defence of the front line V.13.B.3.5., V.7.D.3.2. and V.1[?].45.90. (two of these guns will do A.A. work during the day)
Three guns will be in Brigade Reserve.

5. ROUTES & GUIDES

The Lancs Fus. will move along "A" and "B" tracks leading platoons to pass STRAY FARM at 3.30 pm. 200 yards interval being maintained between platoons.

Guides from the Royal W Kents (2 front line Coys) will meet incoming coys on the tracks A & B where they will pass over the railway running through MILLERS HOUSES, CONDE HOUSE, TRANQUILLE HOUSE at 4 pm.

Guides from the Manchester 2 front Coys will meet incoming Coys at OLGA HOUSE at 4.15 pm.

Lancs Fus. Bn. H.Q. will not require guides.

The two Coys W. Rid. R will move along "D" track leading platoon passing STRAY FM at 3.0 pm.

The Manch Regt will supply guides for the Coy occupying the position V.12.D.2.0. to meet at OLGA HOUSE at 4.45 pm.

The R. W. Kent Regt will supply guides to meet the Coy occupying 19 metre Hill at Drop House at 3.30 pm.

One Coy. of the R. W. Kent R. now occupying positions near MILLERS HOUSES will move back at 8.0 pm as this Coy will not be actually relieved by anyone.

When the Manchester Coy takes over EAGLE TR, both the W. Rid. R Coys will move back to MARSOUIN CAMP.

Relief complete will be reported to Bde H.Q. in R.A.B. code.

Acknowledge.

R.C. Hergest
Captain
Brigade Major

11.11.17.

Start

Copy No 16

3/4 R. West Kent   11/11/17

Orders No X 2

Ref 28 B.N.W. 1/20000
SCHAAP-BALIE 1/10000

Relief. 1. The Battalion will be relieved in the front line tonight as follows

Details 2. A & B Coys will each be relieved by a coy of the Lewes Fus: C
By D Coy — West Riding — Coy by a Coy of the ~~West Riding~~ Regt. Position now occupied will be given up after tonight. D Coy will remain in position until 8 p.m. when they will move off.

Guides 3. Guides who have already been sent to Bn HQ will meet incoming Platoons of relieving unit. Further arrangements to be made by Bn HQ.

Relief Complete 4. Coys connected by telephone will report relief complete to BAB and in addition all coys will send an officer to report personally at Bn HQ at LOVES FARM on their way out from the line. These officers except D Coy will each bring a chit signed by the officer commanding the incoming coy that the relief has been carried out.

March 5. Coys will then march back independently by platoons to HUDDLESTONE Camp. 1 guide per platoon & 1 for Battn HQ will meet the Battn at the HQ occupied by the Battn when at MARSOUIN Camp.

Lewis Guns 6. There will be limbers on the road near present Battn HQ to take back Lewis Guns. 2 Lewis Gunners per Coy with

accompany the guns. RSM Martin
with detail Cpl. LIEUT HEWISTER to
take charge of the guns & accompany
them to camp.

batteries 7. All batteries & food containers will
be put in the lorries.

Tea. 8. Tea will be provided for the
men on arrival in camp.

9. ACKNOWLEDGE

                                    W. Macklin
                                    Capt. Major
 Copies at   from
                              3/4 R. West York Regt
 Copies to 1. CO.   11 RSM
           2-5 Coys   12 52 Inf Bde
           6 M. Men   13 Lan Fus
           7 MO   14
           8 QM   15 West Riding Regt
           9 TO   15 FILE
          10 Chaplain   16 W.O.

Secret.   3/4 Royal West Kent Rgt.   Copy No

Ref map
Sheet 28 NW   "Irish" XZ   12/4/17
1/20000

1. Move — The Battalion will move to DUBLIN CAMP tomorrow.

2. March Orders — Order of march :- H.Q, "A", B, C, D

Starting Point & Route. West along road running through present camp, thence by CACTUS BRIDGE - & DAWSONS CORNER, - EWERTINGHE - DROMORE CORNER - DE WIPPE CABARET to DUBLIN CAMP. Head of column will pass starting point at 8.0 am. Intervals of 50 yards between platoons.

3. Reveille   Reveille 5.30 am
   Breakfasts Breakfasts 6.30 am.

4. Packs & Blankets.
  (a) Packs will be carried by transport & will be stacked on the side of the road under arrangements to be made by the Regtl. Sgt. Major, by 7.15 am.
  (b) Blankets to be rolled in bundles of 10 & stacked under arrangements as in (a).

4 cont'd. (c) Officers valises to be stacked alongside dumps (a) & (b) by 7.30am.
Dress:- Fighting Order

5 Stragglers. Lieut Waite will march in rear of the Battn, & will take charge of any stragglers.

6 Taking Over. 2/Lt V Weeks will proceed in advance of the Battn, & will arrive at DUBLIN CAMP by 8.30am to take over from the Dorsetshire Regt. 1 NCO per Coy & 1 per H.Q. will be detailed to report to 2/Lt Weeks at 6.30am, & will proceed with him.

7 Transport The Transport Officer will arrange to carry packs, blankets & valises. Details as to loading will be issued separately.

Medical 8. The Medical Officer will remain behind
Officer to arrange for the evacuation of sick, & will join the Battalion later in the day

9 ACKNOWLEDGE.

Issued at   pm
Copies to 1-4 D. & C Coys
           5 2/Lt Weeks
           6 Q.M.
           7 T.O.
           8 M.O.

Capt & Adjt
HUGE

12-11-17

SECRET.   Copy No. 7.

52ND INFANTRY BRIGADE O.O. NO. 202.
****

Ref Maps
17th Div. Map
T.1.,
1/10,000.
Sheet 28.N.W.
1/20,000.

12th November 1917.

1.   The 52nd Infantry Brigade will be relieved in the front line by the 50th Infantry Brigade on the Night, 13/14th November.

2.   Movements will be carried out in accordance with attached TABLE "A".

3.   The 52nd Infantry Brigade, (LESS the ROYAL WEST KENT Regiment, WEST RIDING REGIMENT (LESS 2 Companies) and TRENCH MORTAR BATTERY) will entrain at BOESINGHE at 5.0 a.m., 14th instant, under arrangements to be made by the STAFF CAPTAIN.
    The three Units above mentioned will proceed to their new Camps by march route on relief – INTERVALS of 100 yards between Companies will be maintained on the Roads WEST OF CANAL.

4.   Special Instructions as regards Routes and Guides for INCOMING UNITS are attached marked "B" & "C".

5.   PATROLLING of the line will not be interfered with during relief.
    The LANCASHIRE FUSILIERS will be responsible for patrolling the Company fronts until Companies have handed over the Posts correct.

6.   PATROL BOOKS and all AEROPLANE PHOTOGRAPHS will be handed over on relief.

7.   WORK IN PROGRESS, and the general policy of work will be carefully handed over, as also the provisional DEFENCE SCHEME.

8.   COMMAND of the Brigade Sector will pass from G.O.C., 52nd Infantry Brigade to G.O.C., 50TH INFANTRY BRIGADE at............ 10 A.M. 14th inst. Relief complete will be reported to Bde HQ in BAB code.

9.   ACKNOWLEDGE.

Issued at.. 11.A.M.

Copy No 1 to Bde.H.Q.
        2 to War Diary.
        3 to Staff Captain.
        4 to O.C., Signals.
        5 to Lan. Fus.
        6 to W.Rid. Regt.
        7 to R.W.Kent Regt.
        8 to Manch. Regt.

Copy No 9 to M.G.Coy.
        10 to T.M.Bty.
        11 to 54th Inf.Bde.
        12 to 174th Inf.Bde.
        13 to 17th Div.
        14 to 50th Inf.Bde.
        15 to O.C., Supplies.
        16 to No.4 Coy.Train.

                Captain,
                Brigade Major,
                52nd Infantry Brigade.

Secret

Reference 52nd Infy Bde. Order No. 202 the following amendment is made:-

Table "A" Delete Serial No. 3 and Substitute

Ser. No.	Date	Unit	From	To	Relieved by	Starting point	Time	Route	Remarks
3	1917 (a) 13th	W. Rid. R.	(a) H.Q. & 2 Coys MARSOUIN	CARIBOU	(a) E. Yorks Regt	(a) SOULT	(a) 1.0 pm	(a) "B" Track	Intervals of 200 yards [illegible]
	(b) 14th	W. Rid. R.	(b) 2 Coys Front Area	CARIBOU	(b) W. Yorks. Regt	(b) Where tracks "A" and "B" cross PILCKEM ROAD in C. E. A.	(b) 3.45 pm	(b) "A" Track	[illegible]

Serial no. 5. read East Yorks R instead of West Yorks R

Copies to all recipients of B.O. 202

12. 11. 17

G. Tyrrell
for Captain
Brigade Major
52nd Infantry Brigade

TABLE "C" issued with O.O.No.202.
✳ ✳ ✳ ✳ ✳ ✳ ✳ ✳ ✳ ✳ ✳

SPECIAL GUIDE INSTRUCTIONS.
=✳=✳=✳=✳=✳=✳=✳=✳=✳=✳=✳=✳

The Lancashire Fusiliers, Manchester Regt. and two Companies West Riding Regiment will provide GUIDES as follows :-

    2 per Battalion Headquarters.
    1 " Company Headquarters.
    1 " Platoon.

These Guides will come out of the line tonight, 12TH INSTANT, and will be accommodated at MARSOUIN CAMP under arrangements to be made by the O.C., West Riding Regiment.

All Guides will RENDEZVOUS at 2.0 p.m., 13th instant at the Junction of "B" track with the PILCKEM ROAD in C.8. a.

An Officer from the above Battalions will also be detailed to meet Officers of relieving Battalions at same place, and time, calling at Brigade Headquarters on their way down.

Guides will be given a WRITTEN CHIT before coming out of the line with Companies distinguished as follows :-

<u>Lancashire Fusiliers.</u>   <u>(Companies from RIGHT to LEFT.)</u>

RECQUETTE COY.	RECQUETTE COY. H.Q.
BESACE COY.	BESACE COY. H.Q.
BERTHIER COY.	BERTHIER COY. H.Q.
TURENNE X. COY.	TURENNE X. COY. H.Q.

<u>Manchester Regiment.</u>

DEFENDED POST COY.	DEFENDED POST COY. H.Q.
MILLERS HOUSES COY.	MILLERS HOUSES COY. H.Q.
"A" EAGLE TRENCH COY.	"A" EAGLE TRENCH COY. H.Q.
"B" " " "	"B" " " " H.Q.

<u>West Riding Regiment.</u>

19 METRE HILL COY.	19 METRE HILL COY H.Q.
S.W. TRANQUILLE HO. COY.	S.W. TRANQUILLE HO. COY. H.Q.

LANCASHIRE FUSILIERS., Battalion Headquarters.
MANCHESTER REGIMENT.,   "   "

W.Rid. R will provide 2 guides to take E/ko HQ. to Double Cotts

TABLE "A". Issued with O.O.No.202.

Ser.No.	Date. 1917	Unit.	From.	To.	Relieved by.	Starting point.	Time.	Route.	Remarks.
1.	NOV. 13/14.	Bde.H.Q.	STRAY FM.	CARIBOU.	50th Brigade.	-	-	-	-
2.	13/14.	Lan.Fus.	Front line.	ROUSSEL.	(a) A Yorks.Rt. (b) B W.Yorks.Rt.	Where "A" & "B" tracks cross PILCKEM ROAD in C.8.a.	(a) A 3.15 pm. (b) B 2.30 pm.	a A.& B. tracks. b 'A' track.	Intervals of 200 yds. to be maintained between Pns. along tracks.
3.	(a) 13. (b) 13/14.	W.Rid.Rt.	A H.Q. & 2 Coys. MARSOUIN. B 2 Coys. front area	CARIBOU.	E.Yorks.Rt.	(a) SOULT. (b) As for Ser No.2.	(a) A 1.0 pm. (b) B 3.45 pm.	a B track. b A track.	-do.-
4.	13.	R.W.Kent R.	HUDDLESTON.	DUBLIN.	Dorset Rt.	ELVERDINGHE.	9.30 am.	-	-do.-
5.	13/14.	Manch.Rt.	Front area.	DRAGON.	(a) A Yorks.Rt. (b) B W.Yorks.Rt.	As for Ser. No.2.	(a) A 3.15 pm. (b) B 2.30 pm.	a A.& B. tracks. b A.track.	-do.-
6.	13.	M.G.Coy.	Front area.	CARIBOU.	50th M.G.Coy.	-	-	A & B tracks.	Details of relief during daylight to be arranged between Os.C. concerned.
7.	13.	T.M.Bty.	CANAL BK.	ROUSSEL.	50th T.M.B.	-	-	-	50th T.M.B. may not be taking over the same accommodation

9:30 Elondyke

June $7.45
Beulfast 6:30
Reville 6.0 am

Brackets
Pins &
Valises

SECRET.   52ND INFANTRY BRIGADE O.O. No.204.   Copy No. 7.

Ref Maps
28.N.W.,
1/20,000.   18th November 1917.

1.   The 52nd Infantry Brigade will relieve the 51st Infantry Brigade in the LANGEMARCK II area on the 19th. November, and be in Support to the 51st Brigade in the line.

2.   Movements will be carried out in accordance with attached Table.

3.   Each Unit will send a small advance party today to take over its new Camp from opposite number of 51st. Infantry Brigade.

4.   C.M. Stores will be at Transport lines and not in Camps.

5.   No Stores of any kind are to be left in present area.

6.   Rations for Units of 50th Infantry Brigade moving into this Brigade present area on 19th and 20th instants, will be delivered at Camps in this area by Supply Officer, 50th Brigade today. Units now in the Camps will arrange to accommodate.
        Representatives of Units of 50th Brigade will report at present Camps to take over the Rations on arrival.

7.   Brigade Headquarters will move into WHITEMILL Camp at 10.0 a.m., 20th instant.

        ACKNOWLEDGE.
Issued at 12.30 p.m.

Copy No 1 to Bde.H.Q.
        2 to War Diary.
        3 to Staff Captain.
        4 to O.C.,Sigs.
        5 to Lan. Fus.
        6 to W.Rid. Regt.
        7 to R.W.Kent Regt.
        8 to Manch. Regt.
        9 to M.G.Coy.
       10 to T.M.Bty.
       11 to 50th Inf.Bde.
       12 to 51st Inf.Bde.
       13 to S.O.,52nd Inf.Bde.
       14 to No.4 Coy.Train.
       15 to 17th Division.

                                                    Captain,
                                                Brigade Major,
                                            52nd Infantry Brigade.

MARCH TABLE ISSUED WITH O.O.204.

Ser.No.	Date.	Unit.	From.	To.	In relief of.	Route.	Remarks.
1.	NOVR. 20th.	Bde.H.Q.	CARIBOU Camp.	WHITEMILL.	51st Inf.Bde.	DE WIPPE.	
2.	19th.	Lan.Fus.	ROUSSEL	WHITEMILL Cmp.	Border Regt.	CABT. CORNER.	Leading Company will arrive WHITEMILL at 10.45 a.m.
3.	19th.	W.Rid.Regt.	CARIBOU "	BRIDGE Camp.	Sherwood Foresters.	DROMORE CORNER.	Leading Company will start from present Camp at 11.0 a.m.
4.	19th.	R.W.Kent R.	DUBLIN "	BRIDGE Camp.	Staffords'	ELVERDINGHE.	Leading Company will start at 11.30 a.m.
5.	19th.	Manch.Regt.	DRAGON Camp.	SOULT Camp.	Lincolns'	DAWSONS CORNER.	Leading Company will start at 2.0 p.m.
6.	19th.	M.G.Coy.	CARDOEN Camp.	MORTAR CAMP B.15.c.35.65.	51st M.G.Coy.		Start moving at 2 pm.
7.	19th.	T.M.Bty.	CARDOEN Camp.	REDAN Camp. (B.22.d.5.8.)	51st T.M.Bty.		Start moving at 2.30 p.m.

SECRET.   3/4th. Battn. Royal West Kent Regiment.   Copy No. 14

18-11-17.

MARCH ORDERS, NO. 7.

Ref. 28 B. N.W. 1/20000

1. **Move.** The Battalion will move into BRIDGE Camp to-morrow, 18th instant.

2. **Parade.** Coys. will pass the Q.M. Stores, DUBLIN Camp, in the following order :- H.Q., "D", "C", "A", "B", Head of the Column to pass the Stores at 11.30 a.m. Intervals of 200 yards will be maintained between Coys.
Dress :- Full Marching Order. 1 blanket per man will be carried on top of the pack. Route, DE WIFFE CABARET - "B" ECHELON.

3. **Blankets.** The second blanket per man will be rolled in bundles of 10, securely labelled and stacked at Q.M. Stores, DUBLIN Camp, before 9.0 a.m.

4. **Loading.** The Assistant Adjutant will be in charge of loading. 1 N.C.O. and 4 men per Coy., will be detailed to report to him at 7.45 a.m. at Orderly Room.
All Stores for loading, except Mess Stores and Medical Stores, will be at Q.M. Stores, DUBLIN Camp, by 9.0 a.m. No Stores are to be left in the present area.

5. **Sanitation.** The Camp will be left thoroughly clean. The C.O. will inspect Huts, etc., at 10.0 a.m.

6. **Salvage.** Os. C. Coys. will see that no Salvage is left behind.

7. **Unloading Party.** An unloading party of 1 N.C.O. and 3 men per Coy., will leave Camp under the Battalion Orderly Sergeant at 9.0 a.m.

8. ACKNOWLEDGE.

                                  (Signed) F. C. LOVETT,
                                        2nd-Lieut. & Acting Adjutant,
                        3/4th. Battn. Royal West Kent Regiment.

Issued at _____ p.m.

Copies issued to :-

1. C.O.	9. M.O.
2. O.C. "A" Coy.	10. Asst. Adjutant.
3. O.C. "B" Coy.	11. R.S.M.
4. O.C. "C" Coy.	12. Sergt. Underdown, H.J.
5. O.C. "D" Coy.	13. Sergt. Speake, T.
6. Acting Adjutant.	14. War Diary.
7. Q.M.	15. File.
8. T.O.	

SECRET.   Copy No. 14

3/4th. Battn. Royal West Kent Regiment.

                                                                     24-11-17.
ADMINISTRATIVE INSTRUCTIONS, NO. 6.

Ref. 28 B. N. W. 1/20,000.

1. **Routine to-morrow.**
   - 6.30 a.m. Reveille.
   - 7. 0 a.m. Roll Call, and Cleaning of Rifles, &c.
   - 7.45 a.m. Breakfasts.
   - 10. 0 a.m. Voluntary Holy Communion Service in Hut to be cleaned and prepared by O.C. "B" Coy..
   - 12.0 noon. Dinners.
   - 4.30 p.m. Teas in HUDDLESTONE Camp from "C" & "D" Coys.' Cookers.
   - 7.30 p.m. Tea in HUDDLESTONE Camp from "B" Coy. Cooker.

2. **Issue.**
   Os. C. Coys., through their C.Q.M.Ss., will draw and issue to their men to be carried into the line -
   - 2 days' rations,
   - 1 extra water-bottle, per man,
   - 1 tommy's cooker per man.
   - S. O. S. Bombs, "B", "C" & "D" 6 each, "A" & H.Q. 3 each.
   - Ground Flares, 30 per Coy. in front line, and 15 "B" Coy.

3. **Hot Food & Water.**
   Transport, with hot food and petrol tins of water, will reach Battalion Headquarters not later than 8.0 a.m. daily, and Coys can draw their share at any time after that hour. The carrying party will bring back to H.Q. empty containers, water-bottles, and tins, wet socks (for which they will obtain receipt), and salvage. The supply of petrol tins is very low indeed and every effort must be made to get all tins back.

4. **Rations for 28th.**
   Rations for consumption on the 28th instant, will reach EAGLE Dump by 6.0 a.m. on the 27th instant. "A" & "B" Coys. will draw theirs before relieving "C" and "D". "C" & "D" will draw before or after relief as Os. C. Coys. desire. Q.M. will leave 1 N.C.O. and 2 men in charge of the rations until all are drawn.

5. **Kitchens.**
   3 kitchens and one water-cart will reach HUDDLESTONE Camp to-morrow by 4.30 p.m., and will return after the Battalion has left the Camp.

6. **Taking Over.**
   O. C. "C" Coy. will detail an Officer to reach HUDDLESTONE Camp by 1.0 p.m. to-morrow, to take it over from the Sth. Staffs. Regt. The same Officer will hand it over to the Manchester Regt. in the evening.

7. **Socks.**
   There is a Sock Drying Store at HUDDLESTONE Camp. Coys. will send down wet socks daily to Battalion H.Q. These will be dried at the Store and returned under arrangements made by the Q.M.

8. **Sanitation.**
   (1) Os. C. Coys. will see that each separate detachment uses one marked shell-hole as a latrine in the forward area when properly dug latrines do not exist
   (2) The present camp will be left absolutely clean. The C.O. will inspect camp at 11.30 a.m.

(See Sheet 2).

- 2 -

9. Candle Trench. Os. C. "C" & "D" Coys. on their return to CANDLE Trench will find blankets in the drying room at MARSOUIN Camp. They must be returned to Drying Room daily by 10.0 a.m. for redrying and re-issue.

10. Handing over BRIDGE Camp. Q.M. will hand over present Camp to relieving Unit, and forward receipts to Staff Captain by 4.0 p.m. on 26th instant.

11. Blankets, etc. Blankets, packs and all stores for transport to "B" Echelon will be stacked near the road at a spot chosen by the R.S.M. before 12.0 noon to-morrow, 25th instant. The Band will load, and unload at "B" Echelon.
No stores will be left in this camp.

Lelow

2nd-Lieut. & Acting Adjutant,
5/4th.Battn. Royal West Kent Regiment.

Issued at 8.0 p.m.

Copies to :-

1. C. O.
2. Act.Adjutant.
3. O. C. "A" Coy.
4. O. C. "B" Coy.
5. O. C. "C" Coy.
6. O. C. "D" Coy.
7. Asst.Adjutant.
8. M. O.

9. Q. M.
10. T. O.
11. O. i/c. Signals.
12. Band.
13. R. S. M.
14. War Diary.
15. File.

SECRET.   Copy No. 15

3/4th. Battn. Royal West Kent Regiment.

OPERATION ORDER, NO. 9.   24-11-17.

Ref. Map:
SCHAAP BALIE,
1/10,000.
BROEMBEEK.
1/10,000
Sheet 28.
1/40,000

(1) RELIEF.   The Battalion will relieve the 7th. Battn. the Border
                Regt. in the front line in the right sub-sector of the
                Divisional front, on the night 25/26th. November.

(2) Stage I.   The Battalion will parade on the road from WHITE MILL
                facing SIEGE Junction in column of Route (in file).
                Order of march, "D", "C", "B", "A", H.Q.
                Route :- Bridge Camp, Siege Junction, Magenta Circus,
                thence by duck-board track to BARDS CAUSEWAY -
                HUDDLESTONE CAMP.
                Intervals of 100 yards will be maintained between Coys.
                on the march.
                Os. C. Coys. and I.O. will each have route reconnoitred
                before 12.0 noon, 25th instant.

(3) Guides.   Guides in the proportion of 2 per Battalion H.Q., 1 per
                Coy. H.Qs., and 2 per Platoon, will be at BARD'S CAUSEWAY
                at 1.0 p.m., on the 25th instant for Stage II.
                The I.O. will report at 'Fusilier House' to the Staff
                Captain, 51st. Brigade at BARD'S CAUSEWAY, at 12.45 p.m.
                to apportion out guides.

(4) Stage 2.   The Battalion will leave HUDDLESTONE CAMP for the front
                line in accordance with time-table below :-
                Route, "B" Track and "A" Track E. of SCHREIBOOM.
                Intervals of 300 yards will be rigidly maintained between
                platoons.
                Time-table :-
                  8. 0 p.m.   Leading platoon, "D" Coy.
                  8.20 p.m.   do.   do., "C" Coy.
                  8.40 p.m.   do.   do.   "B" Coy.
                  9. 0 p.m.   do.   do.   "A" Coy.
                  9.20 p.m.   H.Q.

(5) Dispositions. "D" Coy. will relieve "A" Coy., the Border Regt., in
                the front line on the left.
                   "C" Coy. will relieve "B" Coy., the Border Regt., in
                the front line on the right.
                   "B" Coy. will relieve "C" Coy., the Border Regt., in
                the line of defended posts.
                   "A" Coy. will relieve "D" Coy., the Border Regt., in
                Battalion Reserve at MILLERS HOUSES.

(6) Lewis Guns. Lewis Guns will be taken to HUDDLESTONE CAMP by limber,
                under arrangements made by L.G.O., and T.O., distributed
                there under arrangements made by L.G.O. & Coys.

(7) Grenades & Coys. will draw and carry under their own arrangements
    S.O.S.   Grenades as required. S.O.S. Bombs will be drawn
    Bombs.   at the rate of 6 per Coy., and Ground Flares at the
                rate of 30 per Coy. from the Q.M.

(8) Relief   Relief complete will be notified where possible by Wire,
    Complete.   in B.A.B. Code, and elsewhere by Runner.

                        (See Sheet 2).

- 2 -

(9) Rations. Two days' rations will be carried on each man, one extra water-bottle filled will be carried by each man, This second water-bottle should be used first and the bottles returned to Battalion H.Q.

(10) R.A.P. R.A.P. will be at LOUIS FARM.

(11) Reports. Reports will be rendered to Battalion Headquarters at LOUIS FARM.

ACKNOWLEDGE.

J.B. Lowth

2nd-Lieut. & Acting Adjutant,
3/4th.Battn.Royal West Kent Regiment.

Issued at <u>5-0</u> p.m.

Copies to :-

(1) C.O.
(2) Actg.Adjutant.
(3) Asst.Adjutant.
(4) O.C. "A" Coy.
(5) O.C. "B" Coy.
(6) O.C. "C" Coy.
(7) O.C. "D" Coy.
(8) L.G.Officer.
(9) M.O.
(10) 7th.Battn.Border Regt.
(11) T.O.
(12) Q.M.
(13) O. i/c.Signals.
(14) R.S.M.
(15) War Diary.
(16) File.

SECRET.
==========

Copy No. 6

52ND INFANTRY BRIGADE O.O. NO.205.
****

Ref Maps
Schaap Balie,
   1/10,000.
Broembeek,
   1/10,000.
Sheet 28,
   1/40,000.

23rd November 1917.
----

1.   The 52nd Infantry Brigade will relieve the 51st Infantry Brigade in the front line on the night 25/26th November in accordance with attached Table.

2.   DETAILS OF RELIEF other than those laid down will be arranged by C. Os. concerned.

3.   PRIORITY OF WORK will be the wiring of the Post line running through STRING HOUSE – COMPROMIS FARM – SENEGAL FARM – TAUBE FARM – V.7.a.5.6., with special attention paid to all possible lines of approach.
     Work in progress, and details as regards wire available in Dumps in the forward area, will be carefully taken over.
     Further instructions will be issued on the subject of wiring.

4.   GUIDES in the proportion of 2 per Battalion Headquarters, 1 per Company Headquarters, and 2 per Platoon will be at BARD'S CAUSEWAY at 1.0 pm. 25th. instant for Battalions proceeding E. of the STEENBEEK.
     These Battalions will send an Officer Representative to report at FUSILIER HOUSE to the Staff Captain, 51st Brigade at BARD'S CAUSEWAY at 12.45 pm. to apportion out respective Guides.

5.   INTERVALS of 200 yards between Platoons along the duck-boards E. of the Canal will be rigidly adhered to, and allowance will also be made for Platoons spreading out on the way up.

6.   NOS. 1 OF M.Gs. will proceed into the line tomorrow 24th instant to learn the Situation.

7.   SPECIAL ATTENTION will be paid to vigorous offensive measures against low flying Aeroplanes, in the forward area.

8.   AEROPLANE PHOTOS and PATROL BOOKS will be taken over.

9.   BRIGADE HEADQUARTERS will close at WHITEMILL Camp at 9.30 am. 26th instant and re-open same time at STRAY FARM.
     Command of the Brigade Front will pass from G.O.C., 51st Brigade to G.O.C., 52nd Brigade at 10.0 am. 26th inst.
     Completion of relief to be reported to Bde HQ in BAB code.

10.   ACKNOWLEDGE.

Issued at 10.0 pm.

Copy No 1 to Bde. H.Q.
     2 to War Diary.
     3 to Staff Captain.
(continued overleaf)

M.C. Mosah
Captain,
Brigade Major,
52nd Infantry Brigade.

Copy No. 4 to Lan. Fus.
5 to W.Rid. Regt.
6 to R.W.Kent Regt.
7 to Manch. Regt.
8 to M.G.Coy.
9 to T.M.Bty.
10 to 50th Bde.
11 to 51st Bde.
12 to Supply Offr; 52nd Bde.
13 to O.C., No.4 Coy.Train.
14 to O.C.,Signals.
15 to B.T.O.
16 to 17th Division.

TABLE "A" (FIRST STAGE).

Ser. No.	Date	Unit	From	To	Route	In relief of	Remarks.
1.	1917. NOV. 25th.	West Rid. R.	BRIDGE.	CANDLE & CLAY trenches.	via BARDS CAUSEWAY.	Sherwoods. (2 Coys)	BRIDGE CAMP to be cleared by 1.30 pm.
2.	do.	R. West Kent R.	do.	HUDDLE-STONE.	do.	South Staffords.	Camp cleared by 2.30 pm.
3.	do.	Lan. Fus.	WHITE MILL.	Site of old MARSOUIN Camp.	do.		Camp cleared by 3.30 pm. MARSOUIN Camp will be a resting stage.

TABLE "B" (SECOND STAGE).

Ser. No.	Date	Unit	From	To	Route.	In relief of	Remarks.
1.	NOVR. 25th.	Lan. Fus.	MOERS-QUIN.	(a) H.Q. & 2 Coys. DOUBLE COTTS & EAGLE trench line. (b) 2 Coys to CANDLE & CLAW.	via LANGEMARCK Road to DROP HOUSE, thence "A" track if desired. 2 Coys for CANDLE trench will proceed along "B" track.	(a) H.Q. & 2 Coys Sherwoods. (b) 2 Coys West Riding Regt.	"A" track between STRAY FARM and DROP HOUSE is in bad condition and is to be avoided. Leading Platoon of (b) to arrive 7.45 pm. at CANDLE trench. (a) starts 8.30 pm.
2.	do.	W.Rid. R.	CANDLE R. & CLAW trench.	Left subsector.	do.	Lincolns.	Leading Platoon will start from CANDLE trench at 7.45 pm.
3.	do.	R.W. Kent R.	HUDDLE-STON.	Right subsector.	"B" track and "A" track E. of SCHREIBOOM.	Border R.	Leading Platoon will start at 8.0 pm.
4.	do.	Lanch. R.	SOULT.	HUDDLESTON.	via EARDS CAUSE-WAY.	R.W.Kent R.	Leading Platoon to arrive HUDDLESTON at 8.0 pm.
5.	do.	M.G. Coy.	MORTAR Camp.	Front line.	do.	51st M.G.Coy.	Relief to be carried out as far as possible during daylight in small parties. Camp to be cleared by 1.0 pm.
6.	do.	T.M. Bty.	REDAN Camp.	EAGLE trench.	do.	do.	The Battery will be attached to the Coys. of Lan.Fus. at EAGLE trench for discipline & work & will conform to movements of Lan.Fus for Relief. Camp to be cleared by 3 pm.

K.

Secret   Relief   L401

         OC A Coy
         OC D Coy   27/4/17

Relief   1. A Coy will relieve D Coy in the
                front line on the left of the
                Divisional subsector by/for the
                27/28th.

Details   2. The first platoon will not
                arrive at D Coy till 8.0 p.m.
                There will be ½ hour intervals
                between platoons. OC D Coy will
                send to OC A Coy at MILLERS
                HOUSES by 7.0 pm 1 guide per
                platoon & 1 for Coy HQ.
                Route – A track.

Relief   3. Relief complete will be notified to
Complete   Bn HQ by wire by the code
                word ARABY.

Rations   4. A Coy will obtain rations for
                consumption 28th before relief.
                D Coy before & after relief as
                desired. Similarly with hot food
                water &c.

Handover. 5. Special care will be taken in handing over dispositions to see that they are fully understood. Jerwoth Stores & books in hand will be handed over as usual.

Warning Order 6. The ... will be relieved on the first line tramway night the 28/29th. A & B Coys will thereupon proceed to EAGLE Trench, C & D to CANDLE Trench, Bn HQ to DOUBLE COTTS. Details follow.

ACKNOWLEDGE (by wire)

W Mackln Major
adj. H7/G

Secret   7th Bn R West Kent Regt Orders   Copy No 8
                              No 10   28.11.17

Ref 28 BNW   1/20000
  & SCHAAP BALIE 1/10000

Relief   1 The Battn will be relieved in the front line by
             the Lancs Fus. tonight. On relief 'A' & 'B' Coys
             will move to EAGLE Trench 'C' & 'D' to CANDLE
             Trench. DOUBLE COTTS will be Battn H.Q.

Details   2 'A' Coy Lancs Fus will relieve   'D' Coy
 &   'C' -"-   -"-   -"-   'B' -"-
Relief   'B' -"-   -"-   -"-   'A' -"-
             'D' -"-   -"-   -"-   'C' -"-

Guides   3 Guides have already been ordered & will
             receive written instructions at Battn H.Q.

Time   4 (a) The Coys relieving 'B' & 'D' Coys of this Bn
 of   will reach B & D Coys about 5.0 pm. On
Relief   relief 'D' Coy will occupy 'A' Coys position 1
              EAGLE Trench until the first platoon of
              'A' Coy reaches EAGLE Trench, when 'D' Coy
              will move on to CANDLE Trench. Hot
              food will be available at EAGLE Trench.
            (b) The Coys relieving 'A' & 'C' Coys will arrive
              at those Coys at about 8.30 pm.

Trench   5 Trench stores, patrol reports & intelligence up to
Stores   time of relief will be handed over as usual
             & receipts forwarded by 12 noon tomorrow
             Battn H.Q.

Relief Complete	6.	Relief complete will be notified to Battn H.Q by the code name of the coy concerned.
Lewis Guns	7.	The 2 Lewis Guns on duty at CORK House, now found by the Lancs Fusiliers, will be relieved by O.C "C" Coy by 7.0 am 29th inst
Command	8.	Captain Markey will command the 2 coys in CANDLE Trench as a separate detachment
Salvage	9.	All salvage will be brought down to EAGLE Trench.

ACKNOWLEDGE

LC Rovett 2/Lieut
Actg Adjt

Issued at 1-15 pm   ~~copy~~ 3/4Bn R West Kent Regt

Copies to:-
1. O C A Coy   5. H Q
2. " B "   6. 10th Bn Lancashire Fus
3. " C "   7. 9th Duke of Wellington
4. " D "   (W Riding Regt)
                     8. W D

SECRET   Copy No. 7

52nd INFANTRY BRIGADE ORDER No. 206

                    W.P.

                                        27th November 1917

1.   The Royal West Kent Regt and Wiltshire Regt will be
relieved on the night 28/29th inst in accordance with attached
table.

2.   The Trench Mortar Battery will move back into
Hoddlestone Camp where accommodation will be arranged by the
West Riding Regt.

3.   Details of relief other than those laid down will
be arranged between O's C. concerned.

4.   Patrolling will not be interfered with.

5.   Work in progress will be carefully handed over
to relieving unit.

6.   The usual intervals between platoons will be maintained.

7.   The two Lewis guns on A.A. duty at Cave House will
be taken over from Lancs Fus by West Riding by 9 am 29th.

8.   Completion of relief to be reported to Bde HQ on
B.A.B. Code.

                Acknowledge

                                        H.E. Molyneux
                                        Captain
                                        Brigade Major
                                        52nd Infy Brigade

RELIEF TABLE ATTACHED TO BRIGADE ORDER No 206.

Serial No.	Unit	Date	From	In relief of:-	Remarks
1.	Lancs Hus.	28th	EAGLE & CANDLE TRENCHES	Royal West Kent Regt Right Subsector	Relief of Sqns. in EAGLE Tr. to be carried out between 5 and 8 p.m. Sqns. in CANDLE Tr. will start at 7.30 p.m. "A" track is allotted for this relief as far as DOURE COTTS. after R.arkinds will take up positions indicated by Lancs Hus.
2.	Manch Regt.	28th	HUDDLESTONE CAMP	West Riding Regt Left Subsector	Leading platoon will pass SCHREIBOOM where LANGEMARCK "A" track crosses the SCHREIBOOM - POELCAPPELLE Road at 6 p.m. LANGEMARCK & LANGEMARCK "A" track will be used. On relief W.Rid.R. will occupy positions vacated by Manch. Regt.
3.	T.M. Battery	28th	EAGLE TRENCH	—	Battery will leave EAGLE Trench at 6 p.m. via "B" track.

"A" Form.
MESSAGES AND SIGNALS.
Army Form C. 2121.

Prefix	Code	m.	Words	Charge	This message is on a/c of:	Recd. at	m.
Office of Origin and Service Instructions.			Sent		Service.	Date	
DRLS			At	m.		From	
			To				
			By		(Signature of "Franking Officer.")	By	

TO — HUGE

| Sender's Number. | Day of Month. | In reply to Number. | | AAA |
| R11-3 | 28 | | | |

The	G.O.C	wishes	to	commend
the	action	taken	by	the
two	Sergts	this	morning	leading
to	the	capture	of	two
Officers	and	one	Pte	AAA
	He	wishes	you	to
put	their	names	forward	for
immediate	recognition	as	soon
as	possible	AAA	The	story
can	be	typed	at	Fusilier
House	if	you	will	send
it	in	manuscript	with
full	particulars	as	regards	christian
names	&c.			

M C Hogan Capt

From Husk.
Place
Time 8 pm

attached to November (W.D.)

3/4th. Battn. Royal West Kent Regiment.

TRENCH FEET.

The following steps will be taken to minimise the risk of Trench Feet :-

(1) Os. C. Coys. & H.Q. Sections will inspect boots, socks, and feet every Saturday morning, and on the day before the Battalion goes into the line in accordance with time-table below. The M.O. and the Battalion Chiropodist will attend. The following points are to receive attention :-
    (a) Boots must be dubbined and soft, and fit loosely.
    (b) Laces & spare laces must be in good condition.
    (c) Socks, at the rate of 3 pairs per man, must be clean, dry, and have no holes ; (and fit loosely).

Time-table :-
Headquarters.	9.0 a.m.
"A" Coy.	9.45 a.m.
"B" Coy.	10.30 a.m.
"C" Coy.	11.30 a.m.
"D" Coy.	12.30 p.m.

(2) Foot rubbing will take place daily. Men will work in pairs, rubbing each others feet. On no account will any man in the Battalion miss this foot rubbing on any day.

(3) On the day before going into the line, feet will be washed and socks powdered under the direction of the M.O. The Battalion Chiropodist will be present. Time-table in para.1 will be adhered to.

(4) In the line -
    (a) feet will be rubbed daily with whale oil which will be taken up in water-bottles, carried under Coy. arrangements;
    (b) socks will be changed daily. Clean socks, before being put on, will be powdered. 4 pepperpots of powder will be issued per Coy. for the tour.
    (c) Hot food will be given men daily. Battalion arrangements are being made for cocoa and tea in hot food containers and rum in petrol tins ; Tommy's cookers or substitutes will be issued on the scale of 1 per man.
    (d) Platoon and Section Commanders must take every opportunity for work and movement during hours of darkness, twilight and mist.
    (e) Puttees and boots must <u>not</u> be worn tightly laced or rolled.
    (f) When sitting still every opportunity should be taken to raise feet above level of hip if ever so slightly.

These instructions, which are issued down to section commanders, will be read out and explained to all ranks together with the reasons for them.

                      (Signed) W. T. MONCKTON, Major,
            Temp., Commanding 3/4th. Battn. Royal West Kent Regiment.

In the Field,

22-11-17.

WD 7

Confidential

War Diary

of

3/4 Bn. Royal West Kent Regt.

From 1st December 1917.
To 31st December 1917.

WAR DIARY or **INTELLIGENCE SUMMARY**

Army Form C. 2118.

1st 3/1 R West Rgt (?)

December 1-3/17

Place	Date	Hour	Summary of Events and Information	Remarks and references to Appendices
DOVER COTTS	1/12/17		Battalion Strength Officers 41 O.R. 886. Battalion relieved by the West Yorkshire Regt. and marched to BEOMHE(?) Station and entrained to INTERNATIONAL CORNER thence marched to DUBLIN CAMP at BRIELEN(?). Major E. LUCIE JAMES M.C. assuming command of the Battalion.	Every Officer & man
DUBLIN Camp	2/12/17	8.35 am	Battalion marched to PADDINGTON Camp near PROVEN	
PADDINGTON Camp	3/12/17	5.30 am 7.30 am	Battalion marched to PROVEN Station arriving at 6 am & left there 1.30 am on gt: arrived AUDRUICQ Station 7.30 am & it marched to LA DAMNE.	Every attack ...

WAR DIARY
or
INTELLIGENCE SUMMARY

(Erase heading not required.)

Army Form C. 2118.

Place	Date	Hour	Summary of Events and Information	Remarks and references to Appendices
LA PANNE	12/04/17	9am	Battn marches to MOVILLE: entrain 12½ hrs later to proceed to unknown destination.	order attached marked "D"
MOVILLE	14/04/17		Bttn marches to ARQUES Station. 1 pm & arrives at MIROUMANS nr BAPAUME & 6 am 15th then marches to ACHIET-LE-PETIT to camp	order attached marked "E"
ACHIET-LE PETIT	16/04/17		Battn marches to ROCQUIGNY arriving 5.30 pm. Bttn in Army Reserve. Third Army. engn 2 hours notice to move.	Order attached marks "F"
ROCQUIGNY	21/04/17		52 Bde relieving 519 on the No British Front Line & becomes subalt to the 59th Division	Order attached marked "G"

2449 Wt. W14957/M90 750,000 1/16 J.B.C. & A. Forms/C.2118/12.

WAR DIARY or INTELLIGENCE SUMMARY

Army Form C. 2118.

Place	Date	Hour	Summary of Events and Information	Remarks and references to Appendices
8th British Front Line	27/3/23 8/3/17		Battalion relieves the 5th Lincolns (177th Infantry Bde) in the left S.MN sector. The line at FLESQUIERES.	
FLESQUIERES	27/3/17	10 am	Battalion hands back its Bn in reserve of the Bde in Front MARCOING RAVINE as Battalion Front in the move up to RED MOUNT being relieved by the 5th Yorkshire Regt. B2 in Divisional Reserve. Casualties in support — 2 Lt. MAXEY — wounded. OR killed — wounded.	
BERTINCOURT	30/3/17		Battalion relieves 7th Border Regt in Front line – On W. outskirts of Battn Front N MAURAN COURT & E. MFLESQUIERES. On Bde Res day 1.	
HSDQI	8/3/17		Battalion strength - Officers 47 OR 856	

E.J. Parnell
Lt Col
Comdg 3/4 Royal
30/1/17

"A" Form
MESSAGES AND SIGNALS.

Army Form C. 2121
(in pads of 100).

No. of Message..................

Prefix......Code......m.	Words	Charge	This message is on a/c of	Recd. at.......m.
Office of Origin and Service Instructions.				Date..............
	Sent		.................Service.	From ....
Havre	At......m.			
	To..........			By...............
	By...........		(Signature of "Franking Officer.")	

TO { HUNT HUGE HUMBLE HUMOUR Staff Captain

Sender's Number.	Day of Month.	In reply to Number.	AAA
*BMX 23	1/12		

Ref BO 207 of 30th ult aaa train timed to leave BOESINGHE 3.30 am Dec 2nd will now leave 5.0 am aaa Administrative Orders for entraining issued by Staff Captain hold good //

Ryan Capt

From	HUSK aaa
Place	
Time	12.45

The above may be forwarded as now corrected. **(Z)**

.... Censor. Signature of Addresser or person authorised to telegraph in his name

* This line should be erased if not required.

Wt. W492/M1647 100,000 pads. 4/17. W. & Co., Ltd. (E. 1187.)

Secret   3/4 Bn Royal West Kent Regt (A) Copy No. 8

30-11-17

Orders No 11

Relief 1. The Battn will be relieved in the front line by the 10th Battn. E.W. Yorkshires R. on the night of Dec 1/2nd. Relief to commence at 9.30 p.m. "A" Coy will be relieved by "C" Coy W. Yorks "B"   "   "   "   "   " D "   "   "

On relief the Battn, less "C" & "D" Coys will proceed by train from BOESINGHE to DUBLIN CAMP in Divnl reserve, detraining at INTERNATIONAL CORNER.

"C" & "D" Coys 2. Separate orders have been issued by Bde to O.C the detachment.

Guides 3. Battn H.Q & O.C "A" & "B" Coys will detail guides in the proportion of

2 Guides per Battn H.Q
1 Guide " Coy H.Q
2 Guides " Platoon.

These guides will report to Battn H.Q by 4.45 p 30 inst for written instructions.

Route 4. The "B" track will be used on relief. Great care must be taken that an interval of 300 yds be maintained between platoons.

Trench Stores 5. Ground Flares & S.O.S Bombs.

Ground Flares If not already handed over, these will & S.O.S Bombs. be handed over to relieving Battn.

French Stores (cont'd)	5.	Receipts being taken. Receipts will be rendered to Orderly Room by 12 noon 2nd Dec.
Relief Complete	6.	An officer from each Coy will be detailed to report at Battn H.Q when the whole of the Coy concerned has passed by.
Move	7.	The Battn less 'C & D' Coys will entrain at BOESINGHE (Broad Gauge) by train leaving at 3.30 am on Dec 2nd, detraining at INTERNATIONAL CORNER. Major E.R. THOMPSON Manch Regt will be entraining officer at BOESINGHE and detraining officer at INTERNATIONAL CORNER. No men will entrain without leave from Battn H.Q. If no earlier entrainment is ordered the party will move from the assembly point to the train at 2.50 am.
Assembly	8.	On coming out of the line, before entraining the Battn. less 'C & D' Coys will assemble at B12d3-5 on BOESINGHE – YPRES Road on East side of MANCH. Regt. Capt F.C NEEDHAM and 1 guide per platoon & 1 for Coy H.Q and 2 for Battn H.Q will report at FUSILIER HOUSE by 2.0pm on afternoon of 1st Dec to learn exact site of assembly ground. The guides will report to CAPT F.C. NEEDHAM at Battn H.Q by 11.0 am. Q.M will arrange for a hot meal to be ready on assembly ground.

Transport: 9. The Transport Officer will detail 2 limbers to be at EAGLE Dump at 9.0pm on the night of 1st Dec.
1 limber for Lewis Guns & Signal Stores
1 " — petrol tins, food containers etc.
Coys will make their own arrangements to convey stores to EAGLE Dump, & will detail a party of 1 NCO & 3 men as loaders.

10 ACKNOWLEDGE.

H.R.Lovett
Lieut:
Actg Adjt
7/4 R. West Kent Regt

Issued at 6.30 pm.

Copies to:-
1 CO.
2 Major W.T. MONCKTON
3 OC "A" Coy
4 " B "
5 2/Lt W.C. CLIFFORD
6 QM & TO
7 ~~HQ~~ 10th Battn The West Yorkshire Regt
8 WD

SECRET J Copy No 8

3/4 B? Royal Berkshire Regt
Orders No. 6

27/11/17

Reference France 1/C 20,000

1. The Batta will move into Divisional Reserve
   at BERTINCOURT tonight. It is relieved by
   7th ? ? E. York Regt.

2. ?

3. The relief battalions will have present
   ? independently. An Officer per
   Coy will report at Batta H.Q when the
   whole Company has left the line.

4. Routes via TROISLOUIS + ?. Intervals
   of 100 yards will be maintained between
   Platoons on [route] and ?
   at ROUTE 2.6, where platoons will close up
   & be marched in companies.

5. Guides will meet Batta at ? ?
   Battalion Guides ? conducting to billets

6. All ? bags will ? Transport
   Packs etc will be dumped on road

6(cont) at the Faggot Bundle in K35
before 3.0 pm.

7 Cookers with hot food will be
at the H.Q. - companies in
the new billeting area.

8 ACKNOWLEDGE

issued at 12.45P
copies to:
    [illegible]
  5 HQ
  6 RSM
  7 [illegible] Parachute Regt
  8 WE

[signature]
2/Lieut
Asst Adjt
HQ,E

SECRET.   Copy No. 9

52ND INFANTRY BRIGADE O.O. NO. 207.

Ref Maps   30th November 1917.
17th Div.T.1.
    1/10,000
Schaap Balie,
    1/10,000
Sheet 28.N.W.
    1/20,000.

1. The 52nd Infantry Brigade will be relieved in the line by the 50th Infantry Brigade on the night 1/2nd Dec.
    After relief, 52nd Infantry Brigade will be concentrated in the LANGEMARCK III area and be in Divnl. Reserve.

2. Movements will be carried out in accordance with attached Table.
    Staff Captain will issue instructions as regards entraining.

3. Patrol Books, Patrol Reports, Aeroplane Photos, Intelligence Reports up to time of relief, K.1. Maps, Anti-gas appliances and Defence Scheme will be handed over to relieving Units.

4. All Work in hand will be handed over carefully together with the General Policy to be pursued.

5. O.C., 52nd Machine Gun Company will arrange all details of relief with O.C., 50th Machine Gun Company.
    No. 1 of Gun Teams from 50th Machine Gun Company will arrive on 30th instr. to learn the situation.

6. The Lancashire Fusiliers, Manchester Regiment, Royal West Kent Regiment less 2 Companies will send Guides in the proportion of :-
    2 per Battn. H.Q.
    1 per Coy. H.Q.
    2 per Platoon.
    to be accommodated in HUDDLESTON CAMP under arrangements to be made by the West Riding Regiment on the night prior to relief.
    The above Units will send an Officer to report at FUSILIER HOUSE (Canal Bank) at 4.0 pm. to meet representatives of relieving Units and to proportion out the Guides there.

7. West Riding Regiment will relieve 3 L.Gs. and teams, strength four (O.R.) each of 51st Brigade on A.A. Defence at D.H.Qrs. at 10.0 am., 2nd December. 10 Drums per Gun will be taken. Ammunition will be supplied.

8. Command of the Sector will pass from G.O.C., 52nd Infantry Brigade to G.O.C., 50th Infantry Brigade at 10.0 am. 2nd December at which hour Brigade H.Qrs. will reopen at CARIBOO CAMP.

9. Completion of relief to be reported to Brigade H.Qrs. in B.A.B. Code.

10. ACKNOWLEDGE.
                                                                    Captain,
                                                                Brigade Major,
    Issued at 12.0 Noon.   52nd Infantry Brigade.

                                                                         P.T.O.

-2-

Copy No 1 to War Diary.
    2 to Bde. H.Q.
    3 to Bde. Major.
    4 to Staff Captain.
    5 to O.C., Sigs.
    6 to B.T.O.
    7 to Lan. Fus.
    8 to W.Rid. Regt.
    9 to R.W.Kent Regt.
  10 to Manch. Regt.
  11 to M.G.Coy.
  12 to T.M.Bty.
  13 to 106th Inf. Bde.
  14 to 53rd Inf. Bde.
  15 to 50th Inf. Bde.
  16 to 51st Inf. Bde.
  17 to 17th Div. "G".
  19 to 17th Div. "Q".
  19 to 77th Fld. Coy.,R.E.
  20 to 78th Fld. Coy.,R.E.
  21 to No. 4 Coy. Train.
  22 to Supply Officer.

TABLE issued with 52nd INFANTRY BRIGADE O.O. NO.207.

Ser. No.	Unit	Date	From	To	Relieved by.	Route of incoming Unit.	Remarks.
1.	LAN. FUS.	DEC. 1/2.	Right Sub-Sector	ROUSSEL Camp.	East Yorks.	"B" track to DOUBLE COTTS, thence "A" & "B" tracks. 3 Platoons for Posts at SENEGAL - TAUBE Farms and V.7.a.5.7. will take "A" track to V.13.a.4.0. thence to CONDE HO. thence Railway or SENEGAL.	Leading Platoon of EAST YORKS will pass DOUBLE COTTS at 8.15 pm. 6.45 Train will leave BOESINGHE (broad guage) for ELVERDINGHE at 5.0 am. 3.30
2.	W. RID. R.	1.	HUDDL-ESTON & CADDIE	CARIBOU Camp.	Yorks.		Leading Platoon YORKS. Regt will arrive HUDDLESTON 2 pm. W.RID. R. will proceed by Train leaving BOESINGHE (broad guage) at 3.30 pm. for ELVERDINGHE.
3.	R.W. KENT R.	1/2. 1.	(a)H.Q. & 2 Coys EAGLE line. (b)CAN-DLE Trench.	DUBLIN Camp.	West Yorks.	(a) "B" track. (b) "B" track.	(a) Leading Platoon W.YORKS. will arrive DOUBLE COTTS at 9.30 pm. 3:30 Train leaves BOESINGHE 5.0 am. (broad guage) for INTERNATIONAL CORNER thence to DUBLIN via Cross-roads at A.16.c.1.9. - WOESTON ROAD. (b) Leading Platoon will arrive CANDLE trench at 5.0 pm. Train will leave BOESINGHE Light CONTROL at 7.0 pm. for VOXVRIE near DUBLIN Camp.

TABLE issued with 52nd Infantry Brigade O.O.No.207 (contd).

Ser. No.	Unit	Date	From.	To.	Relieved by	Route of incoming Unit.	Remarks.
4.	Manch.R.	DEC. 1/2.	Left Sub-Sector	DRAGON Camp.	Dorsets.	IRON CROSS - LANGEMARCK - EAGLE DUMP "A" LANGEMARCK track.	Leading Platoon will pass EAGLE DUMP at 9.30 pm 6.30 Train leaves BOESINGHE (broad guage) at 5.0 am. 3.30 for INTERNATIONAL CORNER thence to DRAGON as for Serial No. 3.
5.	52nd M.G. Coy.	1/2.	Front line.	CARIBOU.	50th M.G.Coy.	"A" and "B" tracks.	Details of relief to be arranged between Os. C. concerned. Train as for Serial No.1.
6.	T.M. Bty.	1.	HUDDLE-STON.	ROUSSEL.	Nil.	-	Train as for Serial No. 2.

"A" Form.
Army Form C. 2121.

MESSAGES AND SIGNALS.

Prefix ...... Code ...... m.	Words	Charge	This message is on a/c of:	Recd. at ...... m.
Office of Origin and Service Instructions.				Date ......
Secret	Sent At ...... m.		...... Service.	From ......
D.R.L.S	To By		(Signature of "Franking Officer.")	By ......

TO	HUNT	HUMBLE		
	HUGE	HURRY		

Sender's Number.	Day of Month.	In reply to Number.	AAA
BM 5	29		

WARNING ORDER AAA

The 50th Inf Bde will relieve the 52nd Inf Bde in the front line on the night 1/2nd Dec AAA HUNT HUMBLE and HUGE (HQ & 2 Coys EAGLE TRENCH) will send guides in the proportion of 2 per Bn H.Q 1 per Coy HQ and 2 per Pn AAA Coys less guides to HUDDLESTON camp to be accommodated by HURRY on the night 30/1st p. to guide incoming units AAA Officer representatives of these units will report Inredin House 4 pm

From on 1st prox to point out
Place guides to opposite numbers
Time

The above may be forwarded as now corrected. (Z) McMajor Capt

Censor. Signature of Addressor or person authorised to telegraph in his name.

* This line should be erased if not required.

ADMINISTRATIVE INSTRUCTIONS No. 39.

The following instructions are issued relative to the impending move of the Brigade into Divisional Reserve :-

1. LOCATIONS.

Bde. H.Q. -	CARIBOO Camp.
Lan. Fus. -	ROUSSEL "
W.Rid. R. -	CARIBOO " (1 Coy. at CARDOEN)
Manch. R. -	DRAGON "
52nd.M.G.Coy. -	CARDOEN "
52nd.T.M.Bty. -	CARDOEN. "
All Q.M. Stores & Transport Lines.	- Present sites near BRIDGE JUNCTION.

All units take over the same camps as when Brigade was last in Divisional Reserve. Quartermasters will detail parties to take over Camps, by 10.0 a.m. on December 1st.

2. BLANKETS AND PACKS.

Blankets and packs will be moved under units own arrangements. O.C. No.4 Coy. Train will return remaining baggage wagon to each Battalion on afternoon of 30th. inst. These wagons are to be returned to No.4 Coy. Train on December 2nd.

3. WATER BOTTLES AND HOT FOOD CONTAINERS.

As many as possible are to be handed in to B.T.O. by 9.0 a.m. on 1st. inst. Remainder to be delivered to him early on 2nd. inst. If opposite numbers of 50th. Inf. Bde. wish to take any over in the line this may be done by arrangement between Officers Commanding concerned, but the number so handed over must be wired to this office early on 2nd. inst. It is essential that there should be no deficiency of either water bottles or hot food containers.

4. YUKON PACKS, PACK SADDLES, CRATES and OTHER STORES.

Yukon Packs, pack saddles, crates and other stores taken over from 51st. Inf.Bde. by B.T.O. are to be handed over by him to B.T.O. 50th. Inf.Bde. on 1st. December and receipts forwarded to this office on 2nd.December.

5. S.O.S. SIGNALS and GROUND FLARES.

These will be handed over to relieving units.

6. TRENCH STORES.

Receipts for these will be forwarded to Bde. H.Q. on 2nd. December.

7. OVERHAUL OF MACHINE GUNS AND RIFLES.

The following table shows the dates on which these will be overhauled. Column A. shows date on which the unit concerned will send 4 Lewis Guns to D.A.D.O.S. Column B. gives the date on which the Brigade Armourer Sergeant will visit unit concerned at 9.0 a.m. to overhaul rifles etc. M.G.Coy.

P.T.O.

will send 1 Vickers gun to D.A.D.O.S. daily from 2nd. December.

Unit.	A.	B.
Lan. Fus.	Dec. 4th., 8th. & 12th.	Dec. 5th. & 10th.
W. Rid. R.	Dec. 2nd., 6th. & 10th.	Dec. 2nd. & 7th.
R. West Kent R.	Dec. 3rd., 7th. & 11th.	Dec. 3rd. & 8th.
Manch. R.	Dec. 5th., 9th. & 13th.	Dec. 4th. & 9th.
M.G.Coy.	2 guns daily from Dec.2nd.	Dec. 6th. & 11th.
T.M.Bty.		Dec. 6th. & 11th.
Bde. H.Q.		Dec. 6th. & 11th.

8. BATHS.

Following table gives allotment of Baths. Table C. gives allotment of BRIDGE JUNCTION Baths and Table D. gives allotment of Baths at A.14.b.8.3.

Unit.	C. (BRIDGE JUNCTION) 120 per hour.	D. (A.14.b.8.3) 100 per hour.
Bde.H.Q.	Dec.4th. - 11.0 a.m. to noon	
Lan. Fus.	Dec.3rd.- 9.0 a.m. to 1 p.m. - 4th.- 9.0 a.m. to 11a.m.	
W.Rid.R.		Dec.2nd.- 9.0 a.m. to 1 p.m. & 2 p.m. to 3 p.m.
R.West Kent R.		Dec.2nd-3 p.m. to 4.30 p.m. - 3rd-9 a.m. to 1 p.m.
Manch.R.		Dec.3rd.- 2 p.m. to 4 p.m. - 4th.- 9 a.m. to 1 p.m.
M.G.Coy.	Dec.3rd.- 2 p.m. to 3.30 p.m.	
T.M.Bty.	Dec.3rd.- 3.30 p.m. to 4 p.m.	
Bde.School.		Dec.4th.- 2 p.m. to 4.30 p.m.

9. MOVE OF W.RID.R. and T.M.BTY.

W.Rid.R. and T.M.Bty. will entrain at BOESINGHE (BROAD GAUGE) by train leaving at 3.30 p.m. on Dec. 1st and will detrain at ELVERDINGHE. Troops to be at entraining station at 3 p.m. Major H.GARDINER, D.S.O., W.Rid.R. is detailed as entraining officer and will report to R.T.O. ELVERDINGHE Station at 2.45 p.m. on 1st. December. He will travel on the train and will be in charge of detraining at ELVERDINGHE. The train is for personnel only and no transport vehicles may proceed by it. After detraining units will march direct to camps. Estimated entraining strengths all ranks - W.Rid.R. 490, T.M.Bty. 50.

10. **MOVE OF 2 COYS. R. WEST KENT R. now in CANDLE TRENCH.**

    These two companies will entrain at BOESINGHE (NARROW GAUGE) by train leaving at 7.0 p.m. on Dec.1st., and will detrain at VOX VRIE, near DRAGON Camp, marching to DUBLIN after detraining. Companies to arrive at NARROW GAUGE STATION at 6.40 p.m. Senior Coy. Commander is to act as entraining and detraining officer.

11. **MOVE OF LAN.FUS., MANCH.REGT. M.G.COY. & H.Q. & 2 COYS. R.WEST KENT REGT.**

    (a). These units will entrain at BOESINGHE (BROAD GAUGE) by train leaving at 5.0 a.m. on December 2nd. Lan. Fus. will detrain at ELVERDINGHE ; remainder at INTERNATIONAL CORNER. Major E.R.THOMPSON, Manch.R. is detailed as entraining officer at BOESINGHE, and detraining officer at INTERNATIONAL CORNER. He will report to R.T.O. at BOESINGHE at 3.45 a.m. on Dec.2nd., but will be at FUSILIER HOUSE from midnight yo 3.30 a.m. on Dec.2nd.

    (b) LAN.FUS.& MANCH.R. on coming out of the line will assemble on the same piece of land as last time, i.e., Lan. Fus. at B.12.d.2.4 on west side of BOESINGHE-YPRES road ; Manch. R. at B.12.d.3.5 on east side of same road.

    (c). H.Q. & 2 COYS. R.WEST KENT R. & M.G.COY. will assemble at B.12.d.3.5 just east of Manch. Regt. Each of these units will send an officer to FUSILIER HOUSE on afternoon of Dec.1st. to learn exact site of assembly ground.

    (d). Units will arrange for guides to lead units to Assembly Ground.

    (e). Quartermasters will arrange a hot meal and rum for all ranks to be ready at the assembly ground as men come out of the line. Cookers will proceed by road as soon as units have entrained.

    (f). Units are not to entrain without permission of entraining officer. With his permission if the train is at BOESINGHE Station early, units may entrain as soon as all ranks have arrived at Assembly Ground and had a meal. If units do not entrain earlier, they will march off from Assembly Ground at following times :- Manch. R. 4.0 a.m., Lan.Fus. 4.10 a.m., H.Q. & 2 Coys. R.West Kent R. 4.20 a.m., M.G.Coy. 4.25 a.m.

    (g). Lan. Fus. will detail an officer not below the rank of Captain, to supervise detraining of this train at ELVERDINGHE.

    (h). Estimated entraining strengths all ranks :- Lan. Fus. 430; Manch. R. 380 ; R.West Kent R., 260 ; M.G.Coy. 80.

12. **STRAGGLERS.**

    Stragglers will be directed to Transport Lines.

13. **CASUALTY RETURNS.**

    Units will submit to Bde. H.Q. by 9.0 p.m. 3rd. inst. an accurate casualty return covering the period from noon Nov.24th. to noon Dec.3rd. In a separate column will be shown the number of cases of Trench Feet.

    P.T.O.

14. ACKNOWLEDGE.

Copies to :-

No. 1.	G.O.C.	
2.	Bde. Major.	
3.	Staff Captain.	
4.	Asst. Staff Captain.	
5.	B.T.O.	
6.	Lan. Fus.	
7.	W. Rid. R.	
8.	R. West Kent R.	
9.	Manch. R.	
10.	M.G. Coy.	
11.	T.M. Bty.	
12.	No. 4 Coy. Train.	
13.	Supply Officer, No. 4 Coy. Train.	
14.	T.O. Lan. Fus.	
15.	T.O. W. Rid. R.	
16.	T.O. R. West Kent R.	
17.	T.O. Manch. R.	
18.	T.O. M.G. Coy.	
19.	Q.M. Lan. Fus.	
20.	Q.M. W. Rid. R.	
21.	Q.M. R. West Kent R.	
22.	Q.M. Manch. R.	
23.	Q.M.S. M.G. Coy.	
24.	D.A.D.O.S. 17th. Division.	
25.	Traffic Control Officer, 17th. Division.	
26.	R.T.P. ELVERDINGHE.	
27.	Bde. Armourer Sgt.	
28.	17th. Div. Baths Officer.	
29.	Maj. H. GARDINER, W. Rid. R.	
30.	Maj. E.R. THOMPSON, Manch. R.	
31.	O.C. 52nd. Bde. School.	
32.	Bde. Signal Officer.	
33.	50th. Inf. Bde.)	For information.
34.	17th. Division Q.)	
35.	O.C. Detachment R. West Kent R. (CANDLE TRENCH)	

S. H. Smith
Captain,
Staff Captain,
52nd. Infantry Brigade.

20.11.17.

SECRET.

Supply Officer.   Q.M. Lan. Fus.
Lan. Fus.   Q.M. W.Rid. R.
W.Rid. R.   Q.M. R.West Kent R.
R.West Kent R.   Q.M. Manch. R.
Manch. R.   T.O. 52nd.M.G.Coy.
52nd.M.G.Coy.   Q.M. Sgt. 52nd.T.M.Bty.
52nd.T.M.Bty.   Bde. Major (for information)
B.T.O.

A. Rations and water for consumption December 1st. will be delivered as follows :-

1. <u>For Manch.R., Lan. Fus., H.Q. & 2 Coys. R.West Kent R.</u> - to EAGLE DUMP by 6.0 a.m. 30th. inst.

2. <u>For W.Rid. R. & T.M. Bty.</u> - To HUDDLESTONE CAMP early on 30th. inst.

3. <u>For 2 Coys. R.West Kent R.</u> -To CANDLE TRENCH by noon 30th. inst.

4. <u>For M.G.Coy.</u> - As usual.

A guard is to be left over all rations dumped, till taken over by units. Units in each case are responsible for carrying forward their own rations from dump.

B. Q.M. Manch. Regt. and Q.M. Lan. Fus. can each draw from B.T.O. on 29th. inst. 50 more tins of solidified alcohol. These are to be sent up to EAGLE DUMP with rations on 30th. inst.

C. Extra petrol tins up to 40 per Battalion may be drawn by Quartermasters from B.T.O.

D. Limbers taking rations forward must bring back salvage, empty petrol tins, extra water bottles and hot food containers. No limber should be allowed to come back empty. Units in the line will ensure that empty petrol tins etc. are at EAGLE DUMP by 6.0 a.m. on 30th. inst.

S. H. Smith

28.11.17

Captain,
Staff Captain,
52nd.Infantry Brigade.

S E C R E T & U R G E N T.

Brigade Major.
Lan. Fus.
W. Rid. R.
R. West Kent R.
Manch. R.
52nd. M.G. Coy.
52nd. T.M. Bty.
93rd. Fd. Coy. R.E.
52nd. Fd. Ambce.
No. 4 Coy. Train.
Supply Officer No. 4 Coy. Train.
17th. Division Q.
Area Commandant, PROOSDY area, PROVEN.
Signal Officer.

1. The Brigade Group will move to PROOSDY Area on 5th. inst. Locations will be as follows :-

    Bde. H.Q.   - PENGE Camp   - X.27.a.4.6 (Sheet 19 S.E.)

    Lan. Fus.   -(PORTSMOUTH Camp - W.30.b.1.3 (Sheet 19 S.E.)
               (PITT   " - W.30.d.1.8   " " "
               (PORTOBELLO " - W.30.d.6.9   " " "

    W. Rid. R.   -(PORTSDOWN " - X.25.a.5.3 " " "
               (PRIVET   " - X.25.c.6.4 " " "

    R. West Kent R. - PADDINGTON Camp - F.3.a.1.2 (Sheet 27 N.W.)

    Manch. R.   -(PETWORTH   " - X.25.d.2.7 (Sheet 19 S.E.)
               (PARTRIDGE " - X.26.c.1.4 " " "

    M.G. Coy.   - PUTNEY   " - X.27.a.2.1 " " "

    T.M. Bty.   - PICCADILLY " - X.20.d.7.3 " " "

    93rd. Fd. Coy. R.E. - PORTLAND   " - X.28.a.1.9 " " "

    52nd. Fd. Ambce - PORTSEA   " - F.1.b.3.2 (Sheet 27 N.W.)

    No. 4 Coy. Tn. - POPLAR   " - F.2.a.6.3 (Sheet 27 N.W.)

Transport Lines are alongside Camps in each case.

2. Each unit will detail a billeting party under an office to report to AREA COMMANDANT. PROOSDY AREA, at his office at PROVEN (F.7.a.4.4, Sheet 27 N.W.) at 2 p.m. 4th. inst. to take over camps. These parties will remain night 4/5th. in new camps and meet units on arrival.

3. Supplies for consumption 5th. inst. will be delivered at above camps not before 4 p.m. on 4th. inst. Units will detail 1 N.C.O. and 1 man of their billeting party to take over these supplies on delivery at new Camps, and to remain on guard over them till units arrive on 5th. inst.

                                                    S. H. Smith

3.12.17
                                                    Captain,
                                                    Staff Captain,
                                                  52nd. Infantry Brigade.

SECRET.   Copy No. 6

52ND INFANTRY BRIGADE ORDER NO.208.

Ref Maps
Sheets 28,
27 and 19.
1/40,000.   4th December 1917.

1. The 52nd Infantry Brigade will move from the LANGEMARCK III area to the PROOSDY area, PROVEN on Dec. 5th in accordance with attached Table "A".

2. Transport will be brigaded and will march under the Orders of the B.T.O. in accordance with Table "B". Cookers and Mess Carts will accompany Units.

3. Intervals as laid down in 2nd Army Traffic Orders will be strictly adhered to.

4. Brigade Headquarters will close at CARIBOU Camp at 10.30 a.m. and reopen at PENGE Camp on arrival.

5. ACKNOWLEDGE.

Issued at 12, Noon.

Copy No. 1 to Bde. H.Q.
         2 to War Diary.
         3 to Staff Captain.
         4 to O.C., Sigs.
         5 to B.T.O.
         6 to Lan. Fus.
         7 to W.Rid. Regt.
         8 to R.W.Kent Regt.
         9 to Manch. Regt.
        10 to M.G.Coy.
        11 to T.M.Bty.
        12 to 93rd F.Coy.,R.E.
        13 to 52nd Fld.Ambce.
        14 to No.4 Coy. Train.
        15 to O.C., Supplies.
        16 to 17th Division.

                                            Captain,
                                          Brigade Major,
                                      52nd Infantry Brigade.

TABLE "B" to accompany 52ND INFANTRY BRIGADE ORDER NO.208.
****

TRANSPORT.

Ser. No.	Date.	UNIT.	Starting Point.	Time.	Route.	Remarks.
1.	DEC. 5th.	Bde. H.Q. M.G.Coy. T.M.Bty.	INTERNATIONAL CORNER.	12.15 p.m.	As for Infantry.	B.T.O. will issue more detailed Orders as regards times of leaving respective Transport lines.
2.	5th.	Lan. Fus.		12.25 p.m.		
3.	5th.	W.Rid. R.		12.35 p.m.		
4.	5th.	R.W.Kent R.		12.45 p.m.		
5.	5th.	Manch. R.		12.55 p.m.		

TABLE "A" to accompany 52ND INFANTRY BRIGADE ORDER NO.206.

Ser. No.	Date.	UNIT.	From.	Route.	To.	Starting Point.	Time.
1.	DEC. 5th.	March. Regt.	DRAGON II.	INTERNATIONAL CORNER. Road Junct. F.11.b.6.8. Road Junct. F.21.a.2.6.	(PITWORTH. (PARTRIDGE.	INTERNATIONAL CORNER.	9.30 a.m.
2.	5th.	R.W.Kent R.	DUBLIN.		PADDINGTON.		9.55 a.m.
3.	5th.	W.Rid. Regt.	CARIBOU.		(PORTSDOWN (PRIVET.		10.20 a.m.
4.	5th.	M.G.Coy.	CARIBOU.		PUTNEY.		10.45 a.m.
5.	5th.	T.M.Bty.	CARIBOU.		PICADILLY.		11.0 a.m.
6.	5th.	Lan. Fus.	ROUSSEL.		(PORTSMOUTH (PITT. (PORTOBELLO.		11.15 a.m.
7.	5th.	Bde. H.Q.	CARIBOU.		PENGE.		11.40 a.m.

SECRET.　　　　　　　　　　　　　　　　　　　　　　　　　　　　　　　Copy No. 14

3/4th. Battn. Royal West Kent Regiment.

ORDERS NO. 12.

Ref. Maps,
Sheets 28, 27 & 19.
1/40,000.

1. The Battalion will move to-morrow by march route to Paddington Camp, PROOSBY Area, PROVEN.

2. Starting Point. Starting Point, junction of wooden road with DE WIPPE - POPERINGHE Road.

3. Route. International Corner - Road Junction F.11.b.6.8. Road Junction F.21.A.2.6. - to Paddington Camp.
Head of column will pass the Starting Point at 8.35 a.m.
Order of march, H.Q., "D", "C", "B", "A", First Line Transport.
An interval of 100 yards will be maintained between Coys., also between rear Coy. & Transport.
Dress :- Full Marching Order. Water-bottles to be filled. Orders will be issued later as to whether the Jerkin is to be worn or carried on the pack. All ranks must wear steel helmets.

4. Transport. (a) 2 lorries and 1 baggage wagon will report at H.Q. at 7.0 a.m. The 2 lorries will be for all blankets and Orderly Room Stores. The baggage wagon for Officers' valises.
Blankets must be tightly rolled in bundles of 10 and loaded on the 2 lorries at 7.0 a.m.
Officers' valises will be loaded on the baggage wagon by 8.0 a.m.
Captain H. G. Roberts is detailed as Loading Officer and will superintend the loading of the blankets and Officers' valises, and will not accept blankets from Coys. unless they are properly rolled and labelled.
(b) The Cookers and Mess Cart will proceed with the Battalion and be ready to move off by 8.30 a.m.
(c) Maltese Cart & Baggage wagon will remain in camp until called for by the Transport Officer at about 11.0 a.m.
Orders re Band will be issued later.

5. Lewis Guns. 2nd-Lieut. C.M.Helmes will arrange for the Lewis Guns to be collected and taken to Q.M. Stores, DUBLIN Camp, by 8.0 a.m. They will be collected by a limber at 10.30 a.m.
2nd-Lieut. Helmes will also instruct Corporal Westheuser to take charge of these guns and proceed to the new camp with the Lewis Gun Limber.
O.C. "D" Coy. will detail 2 Lewis Gunners to report to Corporal Westheuser to assist him.

6. Handing Over. 2nd-Lieut. G. M. Heaphy will remain behind to hand over the camp to the Camp Warden. All Coys. and H.Q. will detail 2 men each to remain behind and report to 2nd-Lieut. Heaphy at the Battalion Orderly Room at 8.45 a.m. to assist the handing over.

7. Dinners. Dinners are being served in new camp, except for men who are being left behind.
Os. C. Coys. will arrange for these men to carry their own rations.

8. Inspection. Os. C. Coys. will inspect their huts before leaving and make sure that the huts are left clean, and that no blankets, clothes, equipment, etc. are left behind.

9. ACKNOWLEDGE.

Lovett
Lieut. & Acting Adjutant,
3/4th. Battn. Royal West Kent Regiment.

Issued at 8.20 p.m.
Copies to :-

1. C. O.	7. M. O.	13. 2/Lt.G.M.Heaphy.
2. Actg. Adjt.	8. Q. M.	14. 2/Lt.C.M.Helmes.
3. O.C. "A" Coy.	9. T. O.	15. Capt.H.G.Roberts.
4. O.C. "B" Coy.	10. O/c Signals.	16. R. S. M.
5. O.C. "C" Coy.	11. T. O.	17. War Diary.
6. O.C. "D" Coy.	12. Lt.H.B.Lewis.	18. File.

"C" FORM.
MESSAGES AND SIGNALS.

Army Form C. 2123.
(In books of 100.)
No. of Message... C 576

Prefix... Code... Words...	Received.	Sent, or sent out.	Office Stamp.
£ s. d.	From... 2CB	At... m.	(R.W.K. 6/12/17)
Charges to Collect	By...	To...	
Service Instructions		By...	

Handed in at 2CB ... Office 1055p m. Received 110p m.

TO Royal West Kent

*Sender's Number.	Day of Month.	In reply to Number.	AAA
SCX433	6	—	

Ref my Q405/19 of today aaa your Battn will proceed to LA PANNE and **not** to NORTKERQUE as therein stated aaa Acknowledge ✓

FROM PLACE & TIME 52nd Inf Bde

This line should be erased if not required.
(19629) Wt528/M1970. 300,000 Pads. 4/17. McC. & Co., Ltd. (E1213).

SECRET.

ADMINISTRATIVE INSTRUCTIONS No.41.

G.405/19

The following instructions are issued relative to the move to NORDAUSQUES Area :-

1. **LOCATIONS :-**

Bde. H.Q.	-	NORDAUSQUES.
Lan.Fus.	-	NORDAUSQUES.
W.Rid.R.	-	ZOUAFQUES.
R.West Kent.	-	NORTKERQUE (Not TOURNEHEM).
Manch. R.	-	LOUCHES.
M.G.Coy.	-	AUTINQUES
T.M.Bty.	-	AUTINQUES.
93rd.Fd.Coy. R.E.)	-	LOUCHES.
No.4 Coy.Tn.	-	ZOUAFQUES.
52nd.Fd.Ambce.	-	LICQUES.

2. **FIRST LINE TRANSPORT :-**
   (a). All first line transport (less the animals and vehicles in attached Table A. to proceed by train) will proceed by road on 7th. and 8th. inst. under Lieut.H.T.DAWE B.T.O. All Transport Officers (except T.O. W.Rid.R) will proceed by road. Transport Sergeants (except W.Rid.R. and M.G.Coy.) will proceed by train. Attached Table B. gives the March Table of first line transport on 7th. and 8th. inst. Transport will halt night of 7th. inst. at WULVERDINGHE. Lieut. H.D.HYDE has to-day proceeded to take over billets at WULVERDINGHE from Area Commandant, LEDERZEELE.
   (b). Each unit will detail a mounted orderly to march with its first line transport. These orderlies will report to Lieut.H.D.HYDE at Church,WULVERDINGHE, at 2 p.m. 7th. inst., and will guide their unit's transport to billets in WULVERDINGHE.
   (c). Transport Officer W.Rid.R. will travel by omnibus train on 8th. inst., and will assist in supervising entraining and detraining of transport proceeding by train.

3. **BILLETING PARTIES :-**
   (a). Each unit of Brigade Group (except 52nd.Fd.Ambce) will detail billeting party of 1 officer and 3 other ranks, with bicycles, to proceed by 50th. Inf.Bde. omnibus train on 7th. inst. Party to report to entraining officer,50th.Inf.Bde., at PROVEN Station at <u>7.45 p.m. on 7th.</u> inst., rationed to night of 9th. inst. Detrain AUDRUICQ.
   (b). Billeting parties of units to be billeted in NORDAUSQUES, ZOUAFQUES, AUTINQUES and LOUCHES, will report to Lieut.S.G.TURNER, Asst.Bde.Major, at office of Commandant, NORDAUSQUES Area, which is at TOURNEHEM, at 9 a.m. on 8th. inst. As far as possible units at NORDAUSQUES, ZOUAFQUES and AUTINQUES, will occupy exactly the same billets as when last the Brigade was in the NORDAUSQUES Area. LOUCHES will be divided between Manch. R. and 93rd.Fd.Coy.R.E. under arrangements to be made by Lieut.S.G.TURNER with Area Commandant.
   (c). Billeting party of R.West Kent R. will report to Lieut.S.G.TURNER at office of RECQUES Area Commandant at RECQUES at 10.0 a.m. on 8th. inst. to take over billets at TOURNEHEM.
   (d). One man with bicycles from each billeting party will be at AUDRUICQ Station to meet personnel of his unit on detrainment, and conduct it to billets. Similarly one man from each billeting party must meet omnibus train at AUDRUICQ Station and conduct transport coming by train, to transport lines.

P.T.O.

(e). One man from each unit's billeting party (except R.West Kent R). will be at Eastern exit of NORDAUSQUES on NORDAUSQUES-ST.OMER Road at 12.30 p.m. on 8th. inst. to guide units transport coming by road, to destination. Guide from R.West Kent R. will meet his transport at Southern exit of NORTKERQUE on the NORTKERQUE - ZUTKERQUE Road at 2.0 p.m. on 8th. inst.

(f). 52nd.Fd.Ambce. will make billeting arrangements direct with 51st. Inf.Bde., in accordance with 17th.Div. R.A.M.C. Order No.52, para. 3 (b).

4. SUPPLIES :-

(a). For personnel and animals proceeding by road :- Rations and forage for consumption 7th. inst. and 8th. inst. will be carried on the man and animal. Rations and forage for consumption 9th. inst. will be delivered by the Train at WULVERDINGHE on night 7th. inst., and will be carried forward on the man and animal.

(b). For personnel and animals proceeding by train : - Rations for consumption 9th. inst. will be carried on the man, and will be delivered to units by lorries on the 7th. inst. Each unit (except 52nd. Fd.Ambce.) will send 1 N.C.O. to report to Supply Officer at PROVEN Railhead at 8.30 a.m. 7th. inst. to guide lorries to respective Camps.
Forage for consumption 9th. inst. will be delivered by the same lorries. This forage must be sent to PROVEN Station in the limber of each unit which is going by train on morning of 8th. inst. and left there in charge of a guard. The forage will be loaded on to the train and carried forward to AUDRUICQ. B.T.O. will detail 1 limber from each unit to meet omnibus train on its arrival at AUDRUICQ to pick up this forage for 9th. inst. and convey it to billets in NORDAUSQUES Area.

(c). Each unit must inform Bde. Supply Officer by 6.0 p.m. to-day exact number of men and animals proceeding by road and by train.

(d). Rations and forage for consumption 10th. and after will be delivered by Train to units in NORDAUSQUES Area.

5. LORRIES FOR THE MOVE :-

Lorries to assist in the move are allotted as follows :- To each Battn.- 2, To. M.G.Coy. & T.M.Bty - ½ each, to Bde. H.Q - 1. These lorries will be at junction of PROVEN - DUNKIRK and PROVEN - CROMBEKE Road, near PROVEN Station (F.1.c.3.0) at 8.0 a.m. on 8th. inst. Each unit must have a guide there to guide its lorries to its Q.M. Stores. Stores of T.M.Bty. which are to proceed by lorry must be sent to PUTNEY Camp by 8.30 a.m. 8th. inst.

6. ENTRAINING :-

(a). The attached Table A shows the exact composition of each train on 8th. inst. All trains start from PROVEN and unload at AUDRUICQ.

(b). Times given in Tables C & D are times at which trains depart. Troops travelling by personnel trains must arrive at PROVEN Station one hour before train starts. Transport must arrive 3 hours before train starts.

(c). Major E.F. TWISS, East Yorks Regt. attd. R.West Kent R. is detailed as entraining officer and will proceed by the last train. He will report to R.T.O. PROVEN 1½ hours before departure of first train.

(d). Major E.R. THOMPSON, Manch. R. is detailed as Detraining Officer. He will proceed on first train and report to R.T.O. AUDRUICQ on arrival.

(e). Units will forward to this office and to Entraining Officer by noon to-morrow, an accurate entraining strength, showing number of officers, other ranks, heavy draught animals, light draught animals, riders, and axles, proceeding on each train.

(f). Drivers and grooms will entrain with their animals. Water and feeds for 12 hours are to be taken in the train with animals. Petrol Tins from mobile reserve may be used, but must be replaced on vehicles at the end of the journey. Breast ropes must be taken. Floors of trucks are to be sprinkled with cinders or gravel. Animals are to be watered just before entraining.

(g). R.West Kent R. will detail one Company as loading and unloading Coy. to load the omnibus train. This Coy. will report to Entraining Officer 3½ hours before departure of omnibus train, and will proceed on the omnibus train. They will unload the omnibus train at AUDRUICQ and march straight to billets after unloading. O.C. R.West Kent. R. will ensure that a guide is available to guide this Coy. to billets.

(h). The following vehicles and animals will proceed by train :-

Each Battn. - All riders (less 1 for mounted orderly) 6 bicycles, 1 water cart, 4 field cookers, 1 mess cart, 1 limber = 12 axles per Battn.

93rd.Fd.Coy.R.E. - All riders and bicycles (less 1 for orderly), 1 water cart, 1 limber, 1 mess cart, = 4 axles.

52nd.M.G.Coy. - All riders (less 1 for orderly and 1 for Billeting Officer), 1 mess cart, 2 limbers, bicycles = 5 axles.

52nd.T.M.Bty. - All handcarts = 4 axles.

Bde. H.Q. - Riders, mess cart, limber, signal limber = 5 axles.

T O T A L 66 Axles.

All other first line transport will proceed by road in accordance with Table B.

7. STORES :-

No stores are to be left in the present area. If the baggage wagons and lorries allotted are insufficient to clear all stores the remainder must be carried on the man in the train, and units must arrange with their Transport Officer for transport to be at AUDRUICQ to clear these stores.

8. ACKNOWLEDGE.

Copies to :-
No.1	G.O.C.	16.	T.O. M.G.Coy.
2	Bde.Major.	17.	Q.M. Lan. Fus.
3.	Staff Captain.	18.	Q.M. W.Rid.R.
4.	Asst.Staff Captain.	19.	Q.M. R.West Kent
5.	B.T.O.	20.	Q.M. Manch. R.
6.	Lan. Fus.	21.	Signal Officer.
7.	W.Rid.R.	22.	52nd.Fd.Ambce.
8.	R.West Kent R.	23.	93rd.Fd.Coy.R.E.
9.	Manch. R.	24.	No.4 Coy.Train.
10.	52nd.M.G.Coy.	25.	Supply Officer.
11.	52nd.T.M.Bty.	26.	17th.Division Q. (for information.
12.	T.O. Lan. Fus.	27.	51st.Inf.Bde. (for information).
13.	T.O. W.Rid.R.		
14.	T.O. R.West Kent R.	28.	R.T.O. PROVEN.
15.	T.O. Manch. R.	29.	R.T.O. AUDRUICQ.
32.	Major.TWISS.R.West Kent.	30.	Area Cmdt. RECQUES.
33.	Major E.R.THOMPSON,Manch.R.	31.	Area Cmdt. TOURNEHEM.
34. 17.	Lieut.S.G.TURNER.		NORDAUSQUES.
35.	Q.M.S.MOISLEY.		

S. H. Smith
Captain,
Staff Captain,
52nd.Infantry Brigade.

TABLE A. (1).

Train.	Serial No.	Time of Start.	Unit.	ESTIMATED CONTENTS.					Time of Arrival.	Remarks.
				Offrs.	Men.	Animals.	Axles.	Bicycles.		
First Personnel	1.	2.0 p.m.	Bde.H.Q.	3	110				5.30 p.m.	
	2.	2.0 p.m.	Manch.R.	20	570					
	3.	2.0 p.m.	W.Rid.R.	31	710					
	4.	2.0 p.m.	Div.H.Q.	6	220					
			TOTAL	35	1610					
Second Personnel	5.	6.0 p.m.	Lan.Fus.	22	650				9.30 p.m.	
	6.	6.0 p.m.	R.W.Kent R (less loading Coy).	23	620					
	7.	6.0 p.m.	M.G.Coy.	7	130					
	8.	3.0 p.m.	93rd.Fd. Coy.R.E.	5	150					
			TOTAL	57	1550					

S. H. Smith

—— Captain,
Staff Captain,
52nd.Infantry Brigade.

TABLE A (2).

Train.	Serial No.	Time of Start.	Unit.	ESTIMATED CONTENTS.					Time of Arrival	REMARKS.
				Offrs.	Men.	Animals.	Axles.	Bicycles.		
First Omnibus.	9.	9.0 p.m.	Bde. H.Q.	1	22	22	5	17	1.0 a.m. 9th.inst.	
	10.	"	Lan.Fus.	1	35	24	12	6	"	
	11.	"	W.Rid.R.	1	35	24	12	6	"	
	12.	"	R.West Kents.	6	190*	24	12	6	"	* Includes loading party
	13.	"	Manch.R.	1	35	24	12	6	"	
	14.	"	52nd.M.G.Coy.	1	35	14	5	4	"	
	15.	"	52nd.T.M.Bty.	4	60	-	4	1	"	
	16.	"	93rd.Fd.Coy. R.E.	1	40	16	4	35	"	12 handcarts = 4 axles.
	17.	"	C.R.E.	1	4	6	-	1	"	
			TOTAL	12	456	154	66	80		

The times of start and arrival of all trains are subject to alteration.

S.H.Sm/t
Captain,
Staff Captain,
52nd. Infantry Brigade.

HQ R West Kids

TABLE B - TRANSPORT MARCH TABLE.

Serial No.	Date.	Unit.	From.	To.	To pass starting point.	Starting Point.	REMARKS.
1.	Dec.7.	Bde. H.Q.	PENGE Camp.	WULVERDINGHE	8.30 a.m.	Junction of PROVEN-DUNKIRK Road with PROVEN-CROMBEKE Road (near PROVEN railway station) F.1.c.3.0 Sheet 27.	(a). Interval of 200 yds. to be maintained between each unit, except Bde.H.Q. & M.G.Co who will march as one unit. (b). Route WORMHOUDT - LEGGERS-CAPPEL
2.	"	Lan. Fus.	PORTSMOUTH Camp.	"	8.30 a.m.		
3.	"	W.Rid.R.	PORTSDOWN	"	8.33 a.m.		
4.	"	R.West Kents.	PADDINGTON	"	8.43 a.m.		
5.	"	Manch. R.	PETWORTH	"	8.36 a.m.		
6.	"	M.G.Coy.	PUTNEY	"	8.40 a.m.		
7.	"	93rd.Fd. Coy.R.E.	PORTLAND	"	8.46 a.m.		
8.	"	No.4 Coy.Tn.	POPLAR	"	8.50 a.m.		
9.	Dec.8.	Bde. H.Q.	WULVERDINGHE	NORDAUSQUES.	9.9 a.m.	Cross roads 400 yds. North of the A in LE BERSTACKE (Map.HAZEBROUCK 5 a.)	(c) Intervals as in (v) above. (d). Route, WATT N - EAVENGHEM, To clear WATTEN by 11.45 a.m.
10.	"	Lan. Fus.		NORDAUSQUES.	9.0 a.m.		
11.	"	W.Rid.R.		ZOUAFQUES.	9.3 a.m.		
12.	"	R.West Kents		NORTKERQUES.	9.13 a.m.		
13.	"	Manch. R.		BOUCHES.	9.6 a.m.		
14.	"	M.G.Coy.		AUTINQUES.	9.10 a.m.		
15.	"	93rd.Fd. Coy.R.E.		LOUCHES.	9.16 a.m.		
16.	"	No.4 Coy.Tn.		ZOUAFQUES.	9.20 a.m.		

S. H. Smith
Captain,
Staff Captain,
52nd. Infantry Brigade.

"C" FORM.
MESSAGES AND SIGNALS.

Army Form C, 2¼
(In books of 100.)
No. of Message..........

Prefix... Code... Words...	Received.	Sent, or sent out.	Office Stamp.
£ s. d.	From............	At............m.	CWV
Charges to Collect	By.............		
Service Instructions		To.............	4·12·17
		By.............	

Handed in at ..XSY........ Office 11.6..m. Received 11.6..m.

TO	ROYAL WEST KENTS

*Sender's Number.	Day of Month.	In reply to Number.	AAA
SCX397	4th		

w/	Div	Admin	instns
to	47	para	4
aaa	supply	arrangement	aaa
for	57th	brigade	group
and	52nd	brigade	group
aaa	for	52nd	brigade
group	and	57th	brigade
group			

FROM	52nd Inf Brigade
PLACE & TIME	

*This line should be erased if not required.

SECRET.  17th Division.
A/1001.
3rd December 1917.

ADMINISTRATIVE INSTRUCTIONS.

NO: 47.

Reference 17th Division Order No.26.

1. LOCATION OF BILLETS.   RECQUES AREA.

UNIT.	LOCATION.	Area Commandant.
Divisional Headquarters.	Chateau COCOVE.)	
D.A.D.O.S.	ZUTKERQUE.)	
H.Q., 17th Divnl. Train.	NORDAUSQUES.)	RECQUES.
C.R.E.	WOLPHUS.)	
226th Machine Gun Coy.	GRASSE PAYELLE.)	
29th Mobile Vet. Section.	ZUTKERQUE.)	
50th Infantry Brigade Group.		
Brigade Headquarters.	NIELLES.)	
10th West Yorks.	RECQUES.)	
7th East Yorks.	LISTERGAUX.)	
7th Yorks. LA PANNE	)	
6th Dorsets.	NIELLES.)	RECQUES.
50th Machine Gun Coy.	DERTHAM.)	
50th Trench Mortar Bty.	NIELLES.)	
78th Field Company R.E.	LOSTRAT.)	
53rd Field Ambulance.	BLANC PIGNON.)	
No.2 Coy. Divnl. Train.	LA RECOUSSE.)	
51st Infantry Brigade Group.		
Brigade Headquarters.	LICQUES.)	
7th Lincolns.	AUDENFORT.)	
7th Borders.	BONNINGUES-LES-ARDRES)	
8th South Staffords.	LICQUES.)	
10th Sherwood Foresters.	SANGHEN.)	LICQUES.
51st Machine Gun Coy.	CLERQUES.)	
51st Trench Mortar Bty.	LICQUES.)	
52nd Field Ambulance.	LICQUES.)	
No. 3 Coy. Divnl. Train.	HERICAT.)	
52nd Infantry Brigade Group.		
Brigade Headquarters.	NORDAUSQUES.)	
10th Lancashire Fusiliers.	NORDAUSQUES.)	
9th West Ridings.	ZOUAFQUES.)	
12th Manchesters.	LOUCHES.)	
3/4th Royal West Kents.	TOURNEHEM. LAPANNE)	NORDAUSQUES.
52nd Machine Gun Coy.	AUTINQUES.)	
52nd Trench Mortar Bty.	AUTINQUES.)	
No. 4 Coy. Divnl Train.	ZOUAFQUES.)	
47th D.S.C.	RECQUES.)	

RAILHEAD.	SUPPLIES.	from 5th	PROVEN.
	Do.	from 8th	WATTEN.
RAILHEAD.	LEAVE.	from 5th	POPERINGHE.
	Do.	from 8th	AUDRUICQ.
CANTEEN.			LICQUES.
OFFICERS' CLUB.			LOUCHES.
CINEMA.			NORDAUSQUES.
DIVNL. CLOTHING STORE.			RECQUES.

LOCATION OF 51st and 52nd INFANTRY BRIGADE GROUPS in PROVEN AREA from 4th to 9th DECEMBER.

51st Infantry Brigade Group.	CANADA BRIGADE AREA
Brigade Headquarters.	POUNDON CAMP.
"A" Battalion.	POMPEY CAMP.
"B" Do.	PENTON CAMP.
"C" Do.	POODLE CAMP.
"D" Do.	PUTLOWES CAMP.
77th Field Company, R.E.	PARDO CAMP.
52nd Field Ambulance.	PRIORY CAMP.
51st Machine Gun Company.	PLAISTOW CAMP.
51st Trench Mortar Battery.	PRAED CAMP.
No. 3 Company, Divisional Train.	PASTURE CAMP.
52nd Infantry Brigade Group.	PROOSDY BRIGADE AREA.
Brigade Headquarters.	PENGE CAMP.
"A" Battalion.	PORTSMOUTH CAMP.
"B" Do.	PRIVET CAMP.
"C" Do.	PETWORTH CAMP.
"D" Do.	PADDINGTON CAMP.
93rd Field Company R.E.	PORTLAND CAMP.
51st Field Ambulance.	PROVEN.
52nd Machine Gun Company.	PUTNEY CAMP.
52nd Trench Mortar Battery.	PICADDILLY CAMP.
No. 4 Company, Divisional Train.	POPLAR CAMP.
AREA COMMANDANT for CANADA Area	Lieut-Col. HIGGINS BARNARD at PROVEN.
AREA COMMANDANT for PROOSDY Area.	Lieut-Col. LEDSIE at PROVEN.

2. HANDING OVER OF TRENCH AND AREA STORES.

25th Division will take over LANGEMARCK No. 1 & 11 areas and 58th Division will take over LANGEMARCK No. 111 area.

Formations will arrange to hand over all trench stores and dumps to incoming formations; receipts will invariably be obtained.

Area Stores such as tents, tarpaulins, trench shelters, Soyer stoves, washing bowls, beds, chairs, etc., will be handed over to incoming formations. In the event of no unit relieving, they will be handed over to the Area Commandants. Complete lists of all stores handed over will be made and receipts obtained and forwarded to D.H.Q.,

Divisional Notice Boards. Units or officers concerned will arrange to take all Divisional Notice Boards with them.

Extra Watercarts. Water-carts on charge of Divisional Canteen will be returned to D.A.D.O.S. store by noon, 6th inst.

That on charge of 52nd Brigade for HOUNSLOW Camp will be returned to O.C. XIX Corps Troops on 5th inst, and receipt taken.

Pack Saddles, Water Crates, etc., All pack-saddlery, water crates, water bottles, gum boots, hot food containers, ammunition belt boxes, etc., surplus to establishment, will be returned by 51st and 52nd Brigades forthwith and by 50th Brigade by noon (12 o'clock) 6th inst. All this equipment must be thoroughly cleaned before being returned.

3. SANITATION.

Particular care must be taken that all Camps are handed over to the relieving unit or to the Area Commandant concerned in a clean and sanitary condition.

4. SUPPLY ARRANGEMENTS :-

50th BRIGADE GROUP. Supply wagons will dump at Q.M.Stores on 5th inst., supplies for consumption 7th inst less those required for animals and personnel moving by road.

Supply wagons will then move by road and rejoin 1st line transport in HANDEKOT area.

Supplies for consumption 8th inst.will be delivered to HANDEKOT area by lorry on 6th inst.

Train wagons will refill and proceed to 2nd Staging area.

On arrival in final area on 7th inst., train wagons will deliver supplies to Q.M.Stores and continue to do so until further orders.

Supplies for consumption 9th inst. will be drawn from PROVEN and conveyed by lorry to new area.

51st BRIGADE GROUP. Supply wagons will dump at Q.M.Stores on 6th inst, rations for consumption 8th inst.

Train wagons will load at railhead on morning of 7th inst rations for consumption 9th inst, and then proceed by march route to staging area. On arrival in final area on 8th inst supplies will be delivered to Q.M.Stores.

52nd BRIGADE GROUP. Supply wagons will dump at Q.M.Stores on 7th inst supplies for consumption 9th inst.

P.T.O

Train wagons will move empty on 8th inst to Staging area and proceed to final area on the 9th. Immediately on arrival they will refill and deliver supplies for consumption,10th, to Q.M. Stores.

51st FIELD AMBULANCE will remain in PROVEN whilst the Division is in rest.

52nd FIELD AMBULANCE moves into PROOSDY with 52nd Brigade Group and thence to LICQUES with 51st Brigade Group.

53rd FIELD AMBULANCE moves from LANGEMARCK 11, to NIELLES area with 50th Brigade Group.

RAILHEAD for 5th December .... PROVEN.
RAILHEAD for 8th December .... WATTEN.

5. **AMMUNITION.**

   All mobile reserves of S.A.A., grenades, petrol tins, etc., must be completed before leaving the present areas.

6. **SALVAGE.**

   On no account must any Salvage be left behind in camps.

7. **BRIGADE SCHOOLS.**

   Brigade Schools will be broken up on dates to be notified later.
   Brigades will hand over camps occupied by schools to Area Commandant, LANGEMARCK 111, receipts being obtained and forwarded to D.H.Q.,

8. **EMPLOYED MEN.**

   Personnel temporarily detached on different employments will be relieved and rejoin their units in accordance with Appendix "A". Receipts will be obtained for all articles handed over by them and forwarded to D.H.Q., by 9 a.m., 9th December.

9. **TRANSPORT.**

   Brigade Transports will move complete.
   Strict March discipline will be kept by Brigade Transport Officer.
   Billeting parties will be sent on a few hours before transport moves.
   Area Commandants concerned have been warned.

10. **REINFORCEMENTS.**

    Reinforcements will continue to arrive at Corps Depot, MEROKEGHEM and will join under orders issued from time to time.

11. **LEAVE.**

    Leave parties will report to R.T.O. three quarters of an hour before train is timed to depart.

(5)

			To CALAIS	To BOULOGNE.
Leave Train	POPERINGHE		1.28 a.m.	10.51 a.m.
"	"	AUDRUICQ	10.29 a.m.	1.9 p.m.
"	"	"	1.78 p.m.	5.20 p.m.

Disbursing Officer will move from POPERINGHE to AUDRUICQ by train on 8th Dec.
Formations will ensure that all other ranks are paid on dates when the Disbursing Officer will not be present at either of the above stations during the move.

12. BATHS.

PROVEN area	....	COUTHOVE	60 men per hour.
"	....	TOURNHEM	
RECQUES area	....	RECQUES	
"	....	LICQUES	
"	....	NIELLES (under construction)	

Baths will be run under Divisional arrangements.

Clean Clothing Store.

Clean Clothes will be delivered to COUTHOVE baths as required by units.
RECQUES area ...... RECQUES.

13. EQUIPMENT.

All equipment must be completed as soon as possible.
All Lewis and Machine Guns will be sent to D.A.D.O.S. store for overhaul under arrangements to be made with D.A.D.O.S. by Brigades.

14. TRAIN ARRANGEMENTS.

As far as is known at present Brigade group personnel will move from ELVERDINGHE and PROVEN stations to AUDRUICQ station under orders which will be issued later.
Brigades will forward entraining strengths of Brigade groups as specified in D.O.864 by wire to D.H.Q., by 6 p.m., 4th December.
Particular attention is drawn to the necessity of rendering accurate returns.

15. FIELD CASHIER.

Field Cashier is at ST.SIXTE. Arrangements are being made for him to visit Brigade H.Q., in the RECQUES area.

16. CASUALTIES.

Formations will prepare and forward as early as possible accurate Casualty Lists from Novr.7th to the date Division leaves the line.

17. SOUP KITCHENS.

Soup Kitchens will not be taken over, but will be closed and personnel moved on morning 6th Decr.

(6)

18. **BURIAL PARTY.**

Personnel attached to the permanent Burial party will return to their units on 6th Decr. Permanent party will join D.H.Q. on 6th Decr.

19. **S.A.A.SECTION, INFANTRY PERSONNEL ATTACHED.**

Infantry personnel attached to S.A.A.Section, 50th D.A.C. will return to units on 5th Decr.

20. **MOBILE VETERINARY SECTION.**

29th Mob. Vet. Section will move with D.H.Q.Transport on 7th Decr. under orders to be issued by Camp Commandant.

                                          _____ Major,
                          D.A.A.G., 17th Division.

Distribution :-

"G"
  Camp Cdt.
  50th Inf. Bde.
  51st "   "
  52nd "   "
  Y.&Lancs.(Pioneers))
  17th Divl.Arty   ) for information
  50th "   "   )
  276 M. G. Coy.
  C. R. E.
  Signal Coy.
  A. D. M. S.
  Divl. Train.
  S. S. O.
  D. A. D. O. S.
  D. A. D. V. S. A.P.M., E.O.
  Salvage Coy.
  Divl. Burial Officer.
  Divl. Dumps Officer.
  Divl. Rlhd. Disbg. Officer.
  Area Comdts. Langemarckx 1, 11 & 111,
              Proosdy Area, Canada Bde area.
  R.T.Os. Poperinghe, Proven, Watten, Audruicq, Ilverdinghe.
  Area Comdts. Recques, Licques, Nordausque.
  75th Div "Q"
  38th Div "Q"
  XIX Corps,"Q".

LANGEMARCK AREAS.   APPENDIX "A".

NO: I to be relieved by 35th Division.

Burial Party.	CANAL BANK. Dug-Out No.5.	40 Other Ranks.
Divisional Bomb Store.	C.12.c.4.0.	1 Officer 2 N.C.Os 15 m
Baths.	CANAL BANK.	7 Other Ranks.
Sock Drying Room.	HUDDLESTONE CAMP.	6 Other Ranks.
Drying Tent.	Do.	3 Other Ranks.
Water Duty.	C.12.c.2.9.	2 Other Ranks.
45th Sanitary Section.	C.8.a.8.4.	2 Other Ranks.
Camp Wardens.	LANGEMARCK I.	2 Officers 2 N.C.Os 20 m
Gum Boot Drying Room.	ROSE CAMP.	1 N.C.O. 6 men.

LANGEMARCK NO: 2 Area.
To be relieved by 55th Division.

Church Army Hut.	DAWSONS CORNER.	1 Man.
Traffic Control.	BARDS CAUSEWAY.	1 Officer, 60 Other Ranks
Baths.	BRIDGE JUNCTION CAMP.	1 N.C.O., 10 men.
Sanitary Section.	45th Sanitary Section BARDS CAUSEWAY.	1 Sergt. 25 men.
Church Army Hut.	ELVERDINGHE.	1 Man.
Camp Wardens.	LANGEMARCK NO: 2 under Area Commandant.	1 N.C.O., 10 men.

LANGEMARCK NO: III Area.
To be relieved by 58th Division.

Guard.	SWISS COTTAGE.	2 N.C.Os, 12 men.
Baths.	INTERNATIONAL CORNER A.14.b.8.8.	9 men.
Camp Wardens.	In Area attached to Area Commandant ELVERDINGHE CHATEAU.	12 Men.

SECRET.   Copy No.

52ND INFANTRY BRIGADE O.O. NO. 209.

Ref. Maps
HAZEBROUCK
5.A.
1/100,000.

6th December 1917.

1. The 52nd Infantry Brigade Group (less 52nd Field Ambulance and surplus Transport) will entrain for RECQUES Area on the 8th December.

2. Surplus Transport will move by Road on the 7th December to LEDERZEELE Area and to RECQUES Area on 8th December.

3. Staff Captain will issue entraining Orders, Transport Orders and Administrative Instructions.

4. Brigade Headquarters will close in the PROODSY Area at 12.30 pm., 8th instant and reopen at NORDAUSQUES on arrival.

ACKNOWLEDGE.

Issued at 1.30 pm.

Copy No. 1 to Bde.H.Q.
2 to War Diary.
3 to Staff Captain.
4 to O.C., Sigs.
5 to E.T.O.
6 to Lan. Fus.
7 to W.Rid. Regt.
8 to R.W.Kent Regt.
9 to Manch. Regt.
10 to M.G.Coy.
11 to T.M.Bty.
12 to 93rd Fd.Coy.,R.E.
13 to 52nd F.Amboe.
14 to No.4 Coy.Train.
15 to Supply Offr., 52nd Inf.Bde.
16 to 17th Division.

Captain,
Brigade Major,
52nd Infantry Brigade.

SECRET.

G.405/20

CORRIGENDA TO ADMINISTRATIVE INSTRUCTIONS No.41.

1. **LOCATIONS AND BILLETING :-**
   Royal West Kent Regt. will be billeted at LA PANNE and not at NORTKERQUE. Billeting Party of Royal West Kent Regt. will report to Lieut. S.G. TURNER at office of Commandant, NORDAUSQUES Area at TOURNEHEM at 9.0 a.m. on 8th. inst., and not at RECQUES. Guide for transport moving by road for Royal West Kent Regt. is to meet transport at eastern exit of NORDAUSQUES on NORDAUSQUES - ST.OMER Road at 2 p.m. on 8th. inst., and not near NORTKERQUE.

2. **ENTRAINING :-**
   (a). Times of departure of personnel trains from PROVEN on 8th. inst. have been altered to the following :-

   First Personnel   departs 1.30 p.m.   (instead of 2 p.m.)
                      arrives AUDRUICQ 5 p.m.

   Second Personnel   departs 7 p.m.   (instead of 6 p.m.)
                      arrives AUDRUICQ 11 p.m.

   Entraining to commence 1 hour before time of departure of above trains. Billeting parties to be informed of changes in times.
   (b).   So far there is no change in time of Omnibus Train.

3. **ACKNOWLEDGE.**

Copies to all recipients of Admin. Instrons. No.41.

7.12.17

Captain,
Staff Captain,
52nd. Infantry Brigade.

Secret.   3/4th. Battn. Royal West Kent Regiment.   Copy No. ___

                                   Orders No. 13.

1. Move.   The Battalion will move to LA PANNE to-morrow by train
              from PROVEN Station, detraining at AUDRUICQ.

2. Details.   Starting Point, main road outside the Q.M. Stores.
              Head of column will pass starting point at 5.40 p.m.
              Order of March, Band, H.Q., "A", "B", "D".
              Dress :- Full Marching Order (water-bottles to be filled
              before starting), plus one blanket per man which will be
              rolled in the water-proof sheet and carried on the top of
              the pack.   In addition rations for the following day, less
              tea and sugar, (which is being carried on the cookers) will
              be carried on the man.

3. Loading   "C" Coy. is detailed as loading and unloading Coy. to load
   Company.   the omnibus train, and will report to the Entraining Officer
              at 5.45 p.m. at PROVEN Station.   This Coy. will proceed
              in the omnibus train which leaves PROVEN at 9.0 p.m.

4. Billets.   At LA PANNE H.Q. & Coys. will occupy the same billets as
              they occupied when the Battalion was last at LA PANNE.
              A Billeting Party, under Lieut. F.C.H. Compton, has proceeded
              to-day.

5. Transport. Lieut. D. B. Brook will be in charge of the Transport
              which is now with the Battalion, and will arrive with the
              Transport at PROVEN Station at 6.0 p.m.
              Lieut. D. B. Brook will report to the Adjutant at 10.0 a.m.
              to-morrow morning, 8th instant, for more detailed orders.

6. Blankets. Orders have already been issued in the warning order, which
              was issued this afternoon, with reference to the loading of
              the second blanket per man.   Also with reference to
              Officers' valises and mess-boxes.

7. Band.   Lieut. H. B. Lewis will arrange for the Band music, stands
              and instrument cases, and men's packs & rifles to be at the
              Q.M. Stores at 9.0 a.m.   It may not be possible to put the
              packs on the lorries, in which case they will have to be
              carried by the men.   In any case the band will have to
              carry one blanket each.

8.   ACKNOWLEDGE.

                                        Lieut. & Adjutant,
                                        3/4th. Battn. Royal West Kent Regiment.

Issued at 7.10 p.m.

        Copies to :-

        1. H.Q. Mess.   6. Q. M.
        2. O. C. "A" Coy.   7. Lieut. D.B. Brook.
        3. O. C. "B" Coy.   8. Lieut. H.B. Lewis.
        4. O. C. "C" Coy.   9. War Diary.
        5. O. C. "D" Coy.   10. File.

SECRET.

MOVE OF DIVISIONAL H.Q., 51ST & 52ND BRIGADES BY RAIL.
WITH REFERENCE TO D.O. 264.
SEPARATE INSTRUCTIONS HAVE BEEN ISSUED FOR MOVE OF 50th BRIGADE.

1. The 51st and 52nd Brigades Groups as specified in table attached to 17th Division Order No. 264 (less transport moving by road) will move by rail on 8th and 9th inst. from PROVEN to AUDRUICQ in two sets of tactical trains, composed as follows :-

   Two trains coaching stock each consisting of :-

   2 Brake Vans.
   2 First Class Coaches for officers.
   44 Third Class Coaches (to take 40 men each)
   2 Covered Goods Wagons.

   (Each of these trains will therefore accommodate 1760 O.R.)

   One train omnibus type consisting of :-

   1 Passenger Coach.
   70 Covered Wagons.
   17 Flats. (each to take 4 axles).
   2 Brake Vans.

2. Senior Officers will be detailed to act as entraining officers at PROVEN. They will report to R.T.O. half-an-hour before the arrival of the troops with full particulars as to entraining strength. They will travel on the last train.
   Detraining officers will be detailed to supervise detraining at AUDRUICQ - they will travel on the first train.

3. All transport and transport personnel to be entrained must arrive at the entraining Station 3 hours before the time of departure of the train.
   One company will be detailed for loading transport on the omnibus train, and will report to R.T.O. PROVEN 3¼ hours before the time of departure of the train. This company will travel on the train which they have loaded and off load at the detraining station.

4. All personnel (other than transport personnel and loading Coy) must arrive at the Station one hour before the time of departure of the train.

5. Routes to the Station and entraining facilities must be reconnoitred beforehand.

6. Horses will be watered shortly before entraining. Petrol Cans containing water must be placed in each horse box.
   The floors of horse boxes must be sprinkled with grit to prevent the horses slipping.

7. Units and animals of 52nd Bde will entrain with rations for consumption day following day of entrainment.

8. Amended orders re supply arrangements are attached hereto.

9. Personnel to travel on each train, wagons and horses to be sent by rail will be detailed by Brigades. Not more than 66 axles should be detailed for the omnibus trains.

P.T.O.

- 2 -

10.   Times of trains as follows :-

Dec.8th	Unit.	Commence entraining.	Depart.	Arrive AUDRUICQ.
Dec.8th	52nd Bde. ~~D.H.Q~~ 1st Personnel.	13 hours.	14 hours	17.30 hours.
"	~~D.H.Q.~~, 52nd Bde. 2nd Personnel.	17 "	18 "	21.30 "
"	52nd Bde., D.H.Q. Omnibus Train.	18 "	21 "	1.00 " 9th inst.
Dec 9th.	51st Bde. 1st Personnel.	13 hours.	14 hours	17.30 hours.
"	51st Bde. 2nd Personnel.	17 "	18 "	21.30 "
"	51st Bde. Omnibus Train.	18 "	21 "	1.00 10th inst.

These times are subject to alteration.

11.   52nd Brigade will arrange to accommodate 6 officers and 220 O.R. of D.H.Q. on the train leaving PROVEN at 14 hours, and 6 chargers of C.R.E. on omnibus train leaving PROVEN at 21 hours.

Mark Phillips Captain,

6/12/17.

D.A.Q.M.G., 17th Division.

G.
C.C.H.
Inf. Bdes.
CRE.
Signals.
ADMS.
Train
S.S.O.
DAWS
DAWVS.
47 D.S.C
R.T.Os. Proven - Audruicq

SUPPLY ARRANGEMENTS.

50th Brigade.

RATIONS FOR CONSUMPTION 8TH

Forage and Supplies for animals and personnel proceeding by road on 5th inst will be conveyed to WULVERDINGHE by lorry on 6th inst and issued to units.
Forage and Rations for personnel and animals will be loaded in detail at PROVEN Railhead on 6th inst and delivered to Units.
Brigade will arrange for representative from each battalion, Machine Gun Company, Trench Mortar Battery, Field Ambulance and Field Company to report Divisional H.Q., at 6.45.a.m. sharp on 6th inst, they will then be conveyed to Railhead by lorry and conduct lorries with Supplies to units.

Rations for consumption 9th and onwards will be delivered to units by Train Wagons.

51st Brigade.

RATIONS FOR CONSUMPTION 9th

will be carried on the man and animal. These will be delivered by Train Wagons on 7th inst.
Rations for consumption 10th, will be delivered to units billets in new area by afternoon 9th

Rations for consumption 11th inst will be delivered to units early on morning of 10th inst.

52nd Brigade.

RATIONS FOR CONSUMPTION 9th.

Forage and Supplies for animals and personnel proceeding by road on 7th inst will be conveyed to WULVERDINGHE by lorry on 7th inst and delivered to units.

Brigade will arrange for extra representatives from each battalion, Machine Gun Company, Trench Mortar Battery and Field Company to report S.S.O., 17th Division at PROVEN Railhead at 8.30.a.m. 7th inst to guide supplies which will be loaded on lorries to units.

Rations for consumption 10th will be delivered to units by Train Wagons on arrival in new area.

---------- " ----------

Small Coal Dumps have been formed in PASTURE and POPLAR CAMPS.
On and after 8th inst, Fuel dump will be at ZOUAFQUES.

Rank Phillips
Captain.
D.A.Q.M.G., 17th Division.

SECRET.  Copy No. ...

52ND INFANTRY BRIGADE ORDER NO.210.
❋❋❋❋❋❋❋❋❋❋❋❋❋❋❋❋❋❋❋❋❋❋❋❋❋❋❋❋❋

Ref Map
27 A.N.E.1/20,000.
27 A.S.E.1/20,000.
HAZEBROUCK 5.A.,
     1/10,000.
CALAIS 13.,
     1/100,000.

10th December 1917.

1.   The 52nd Infantry Brigade Group will move by March Route from the NORDAUSQUES AREA to the HOULLE AREA on the 12th instant.

2.   The move will be made in accordance with the attached "March Table".

3.   The exact locations of Units in the new Area are given in the Administrative Instructions (No. 42) issued today.

4.   TRANSPORT will accompany their respective Units on the march.

5.   The following distances will be maintained on the march :-
        100 yards between Companies.
        500   "   "   Units.
        100   "   "   Units and Transport.

6.   No.4 Company Train will move independently by any Route, but to be clear of NORDAUSQUES by 9 am.

7.   Strict march discipline will be maintained. The usual 10 minute halts will be observed.

8.   Brigade Headquarters will close at NORDAUSQUES at 10 am. and reopen at HOULLE at same hour.

9.   Arrival in Billets must be notified to Brigade Headquarters immediately.

10.   ACKNOWLEDGE.

Issued at 8.30 p.m.

Copy No 1 to Bde.H.Q.
          2 to War Diary.
          3 to Staff Captain.
          4 to O.C., Signals.
          5 to B.T.O.
          6 to Lan. Fus.
          7 to W.Rid. Regt.
          8 to R.W.Kent Regt.
          9 to Manch. Regt.
         10 to M.G.Coy.
         11 to T.M.Bty.
         12 to No.4 Coy.Train.
         13 to Supply Offr.,52nd Bde.
         14 to 93rd F.Coy.,R.E.
         15 to 51st Inf.Bde.
         16 to 17th Div.
         17 to 52nd Fd.Ambce.

H G Turner
Captain,
Brigade Major,
52nd Infantry Brigade.

C.D.D
CAB
D.CAB

MARCH TABLE to accompany B.O.219

Starting point: J.28.c.8.7. (Sheet 27.A.N.E.)

Ser.No.	Unit.	Date. DECR	From.	To.	Starting point.	Time of passing S.P.	Route.	Remarks.
1.	2do.H.Qrs.	12.	NORDASQUES.	HOULLE.		10.0 am.	CALAIS – ST.OMER RD. to Road Junct.C.9.c.6.9. – HOULLE.	
2.	Lan.Fus.	12.	do.	HOULLE.		10.7 am.	CALAIS – ST.OMER RD. Rd. Junct. C.8.b.6.3. BASSE BOULOGNE.	
3.	R.W.Kent R.	12.	LA PANNE.	MOULLE.		10.20am.	CALAIS – ST.OMER RD – CROSS RD. C.11.c.7.1. – LA HAUT MONT.	
4.	W.Rid.R.	12.	ZOUAFQUES.	do.		10.33am.	CALAIS – ST.OMER RD. LES MARNIERES.	
5.	Manch.R.	12.	LOUCHES.	HOULLE.		10.46am.	As for Ser. No. 1.	
6.	M.G.Coy.	12.	AUTINGUES.	LE COSTHOL.		11.9 am.	CALAIS – ST.OMER RDS. C.11.c.2.1. LE COSTHOL.	
7.	T.M.Bty.	12.	do.	do.		11.17 am.	As for Ser. No. 6.	
8.	93rd F.Coy.R.E.	12.	LOUCHES.	MOULLE.		11.22am.	CALAIS – ST.OMER RD. – C.11.c.7.1. – L'EGLISE.	
9.	52nd F.Amboe.	12.	LICQUES.	do.		11.33am.	As for Ser. No. 8.	
10.	No.4 Coy.Train.	12.	ZOUAFQUES.	do.			Move independently.	

"A" Form.
MESSAGES AND SIGNALS.

Army Form C. 2121.

TO { Lan Fus   Manch R
     W Rid R   52nd M G Coy
     R W Kent R how coy Train

Sender's Number: SCx462
Day of Month: 9
AAA

Ref 17 Div Administrative Instructions No 48 AAA Refilling point tomorrow 10th inst 2.0pm CALAIS road half mile west of LA RECOUSSE

From 52nd Inf Bde

ADMINISTRATIVE INSTRUCTIONS

No. 48   17th Division.

Reference 17th D. O. 266.   A/1001

                                             9th December, 1917.

1 LOCATION TABLE.

Unit.	Location	Area Commandant.
Divisional Headquarters	EPERLECQUES	}
D.A.D.O.S.	Do.	}
H.Q., Divl Train.	Do.	} EPERLECQUES.
C.R.E.	Do.	}
29th Mobile Vet. Scn.	HELLE BROUCQ.	
256th M.G.Coy.	HOLQUE.	
7th Yorks & Lancs (Pioneers)	EPERLECQUES.	
D. Q. R. F.		
50th INFANTRY BRIGADE GROUP.		
Brigade Headquarters.	SERQUES.	}
"A" Battalion.	Do.	}
"B" do.	LE BAS.	}
"C" do.	ZUDROVE.	}
"D" do.	BAYENGHEM.	} WATTEN.
50th M.G. Company.	OUEST MONT.	}
50th T.M. Battery.	WATTEN DAM.	}
78th Field Coy. R.E.	WESTROVE.	}
53rd Field Ambulance.	GRENOGE FARM.	}
No.2 Coy. Divnl. Train.	BLEUE MAISON.	}
51st INFANTRY BRIGADE GROUP.		
Brigade Headquarters.	NORDAUSQUES.	}
"A" Battalion.	Do.	}
"B" do.	LA COMMUNE.	}
"C" do.	NORTLEULINGHEM.	}
"D" do.	MENTQUE & LARONVILLE.	} TOURNEHEM.
51st M.G. Coy.	LA PANNE.	}
51st T.M. Battery.	Do.	}
77th Field Coy. R.E.	INGLINGHEM.	}
51st Field Ambulance.	MONNECOVE.	}
No.3 Coy. Divnl. Train.	WESTROVE.	}
52nd INFANTRY BRIGADE GROUP.		
Brigade Headquarters	HOULLE.	}
"A" Battalion.	Do.	}
"B" do.	Do.	}
"C" do.	MOULLE.	}
"D" do.	LE HAUT MONT.	} HOULLE.
52nd M. G. Coy.)	LE GOSTHOL.	}
52nd T. M. Bty.		}
93rd Field Coy. R.E.	HOULLE.	}
52nd Field Ambulance.	MOULLE.	}
No.4 Coy. Divnl. Train.	HOULLE.	}

RAILHEAD (Supplies and Leave.)		WATTEN.
CANTEEN.	EPERLECQUES.	
OFFICERS CLUB.	HOULLE.	
CINEMA.	HOULLE & NORDAUSQUES.	
DIVISIONAL CLOTHING STORE.	EPERLECQUES.	

2. SUPPLY ARRANGEMENTS.

    Railhead.   WATTEN.

10th December.

    50th Brigade will be drawn by Lorry and delivered by train wagons.
    51st Brigade will be drawn by Lorry and delivered by train wagons.
    52nd Brigade will be drawn by train wagons and delivered by 1st Line Transport.

11th December.

    50th Brigade will be drawn by train wagons and delivered by 1st Line Transport.
    51st Brigade will be drawn by Lorry and delivered by train wagons.
    52nd Brigade will be drawn by train wagons and remain loaded.

12th December.

    50th Brigade will be drawn and delivered by train wagons.
    51st Brigade will be drawn and delivered by train wagons.
    52nd Brigade will be drawn by Lorry and delivered by train wagons.

From the 13th December Train wagons will draw and deliver daily.

3. BAGGAGE WAGONS.

    Baggage wagons will be returned to the Train on arrival in EPERLECQUES Area.

4. 276th M.G.Coy will be attached to 52nd Brigade Group for supplies on arrival at HELLEBROUCQ.

5. BATHS.

    There are Baths at :-
        EPERLECQUES.   80 per hour.
        LE BAS.   50 per hour.
        TOURNEHEM.   80 per hour.

Baths will be run under Divisional arrangements.
Clean Clothing Store will be at EPERLECQUES and deliveries will be made to Baths as required.

6. LEAVE.

    Leave Train leaves WATTEN for CALAIS and BOULOGNE at 13.20 and arrives CALAIS 14.12, BOULOGNE 15.55.
    Return Train leaves BOULOGNE 0.54 and arrives WATTEN 3.30.
    Return Train leaves CALAIS 10.50, and arrives WATTEN 11.50.
Disbursing Officer will move to WATTEN on the 11th December by Train after attending to the 51st Brigade Leave Party.
    Arrangements are being made at WATTEN for Soup Kitchen and accomodation for Officers and Other Ranks proceeding and returning from Leave.
    Leave parties of the Brigades in NORDAUSQUES and HOULLE Areas will be conveyed to and from the Station by Lorry under arrangements to be issued separately.

7. IMPROVEMENTS TO BILLETS.

    Formations will requisition on the D.O.R.E., for material required for the improvements of Billets.

8. TRANSPORT.

    Strict march discipline will be kept on all transport during this move.

                                                         Major.
                                   D.A. .G., 17th Division.

SECRET.

ADMINISTRATIVE INSTRUCTIONS. NO. 42.

DECEMBER 10TH. 1917.

1. **LOCATIONS.** - Locations in the MOULLE Area are as follows :-

    1. Brigade. H.Q. - MOULLE.
    2. Lan. Fus. - MOULLE (BASSE BOULOGNE and WINOC).
    3. W. Rid. R. - MOULLE (LES MAFFIÈRES).
    4. R.W.Kent.R. - MOULLE (LE HAUT MOUT).
    5. Manch. R. - MOULLE (LA PLACE).
    6. 52nd. M.G.Coy. - LE COSTHOL.
    7. 52nd. T.M.Bty. - LE COSTHOL.
    8. 93rd. Fld. Coy.R.E. - MOULLE (L'ÉGLISE).
    9. 52nd. Fld. Ambce. - MOULLE (L'ÉGLISE).
    10. No.4.Coy.Train. - MOULLE (L'ÉGLISE).

2. Billeting parties of all the above units will report to Area Commandant at his office, near the Church, at MOULLE at 10.30 a.m. tomorrow 11th. inst. to take over billets. Billeting parties will return to their units tomorrow after completion of billeting.

3. *Compton* All Area Stores in the present area including paillasses are to be handed over and receipts obtained.

4. **ACKNOWLEDGE**

Copies to :-

1. Bde. Major.
2. Signal Offr.
3. Area Commandant MOULLE.
4. Supply Offr. No.4. Coy. Train.
5. Lan. Fus.
6. W.Rid.R.
7. R.W.Kent R.
8. Manch.R.
9. 52nd.M.G.Coy.
10. 52nd.T.M.Bty.
11. 93rd. Fld. Coy.R.E.
12. 52nd. Fld. Ambce.
13. No.4.Coy. Train.
14. 17th. Div. ... (for information).

S. H. Smith

Captain,
Staff Captain,
52nd. Infantry Brigade.

SECRET.   Copy No. 12

3/4th. Battn. Royal West Kent Regiment.

ORDERS NO. 14.

11-12-17.

Move. The Battalion will move by March Route to-morrow, 12th. instant, to MOULLE (LE HAUTMONT).

March Order. Starting Point, the cross roads past Transport Lines on LA PANNE-HORDA'SQUES Road (same as to-day).
Order of March :- Band, H.Q., "D", "C", "A", "B", Transport.
The Head of the Column will be at Starting Point at 10.0 a.m.
Intervals of 100 yards will be maintained between Coys. and 100 yards between rear Coy. and Transport.
Strict March Discipline will be maintained.
Dress :- Full Marching Order. Caps will be worn. Helmets will be carried under the supporting straps at back of pack.
Water-bottles will be filled.

Blankets. Officers' Valises. Blankets & Officers' Valises will be carried on two lorries, and will be dumped for loading by 8.0 a.m. as follows :-
H.Q., Band, "A", "C" & "D" Coys. at Battalion H.Q. "B" Coy. on road outside their billets. Sergt. Bilby will meet the lorries at Battalion H.Q. at 8.0 a.m., and will superintend the loading.
Loading parties will be detailed as follows :-
"C" Coy., 1 N.C.O. & 5 men, at Battalion H.Q. at 8.0 a.m.
"B" Coy., 1 N.C.O. & 3 men, at their own dump at 8.30 a.m.
These two parties will remain behind and proceed later under 2nd-Lieut. J. H. Heatley.

Billets. All billets must be left thoroughly clean, and each Coy. will leave a party of 1 N.C.O. & 3 other ranks to guard any stores which may not be able to be carried in the two lorries.
2nd-Lieut. J. H. Heatley will remain behind until everything is cleared from billets. He will then inspect billets to make sure nothing is left behind, and will then collect the rear parties of Coys. and proceed to new billets.
Lieut. F. C. H. Compton will also remain behind and hand over billets. He will obtain duplicate receipts, same to be forwarded to Battalion Orderly Room by noon, 13th. instant.

Mess Boxes. "A" & "B" Coys. Mess Boxes will be carried in the lorries, and dumped with their blankets. These Mess Boxes should be on the Coy. Dump by 8.30 a.m. H.Q., "C" & "D" Mess Boxes will be carried in the Mess Cart, and will be dumped at H.Q. by 9.0 a.m.

Rations. Os. C. Coys. will arrange a Haversack ration for all men who are being left behind.

ACKNOWLEDGE.

Lieut. & Acting Adjutant,
3/4th. Battn. Royal West Kent Regiment.

Issued at 6.30 p.m.

Copies to :-

1. H.Q. Mess.
2. O.C. "A" Coy.
3. O.C. "B" Coy.
4. O.C., "C" Coy.
5. O.C., "D" Coy.
6. Q. M.
7. T. O.
8. Lieut. H. B. Lewis.
9. Lieut. F.C.H. Compton.
10. 2nd-Lieut. J.H. Heatley.
11. R. S. M.
12. War Diary.
13. File.

S E C R E T.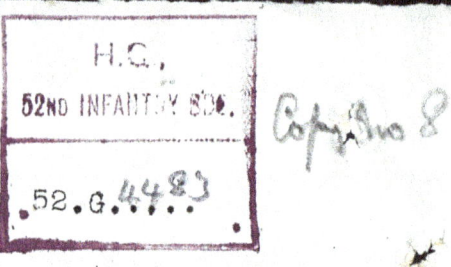

1. The following AMENDMENTS are made to Entraining Table issued with B.O.No.211, and Admin. Instrcns No.43.

2. ZERO hour is fixed at 12 Noon today.

3. TIMES to reach Entraining Station. TRANSPORT will arrive one hour earlier than the times laid down in the Table. PERSONNEL will arrive at times as fixed in the Table. For example:-
Lan. Fus. Personnel will reach the Station at Zero plus 13½ hours., Transport at Zero plus 11 hours.

ACKNOWLEDGE.

Captain,
Brigade Major,
52nd Infantry Brigade.

Issued to all Recipients
of B.O.211 and Admin. Instr.
No.43.

M O R E 1.

Lancashire Fusiliers,
West Riding Regt.
Royal West Kent Regt.
Manchester Regt.
53rd. Machine Gun Coy.
52nd. Trench Mortar Battery.
No.4.Coy.Train.
95rd. Fld. Coy. R.E.
52nd. Fld. Ambce.
236th. M.G.Coy.

    Reference Administrative Instructions No.45 para 5, billeting parties of Brigade Group will travel by first train from ARQUES station. Div. H.Q. will proceed by first train from ST.OMER.

L. W. Smith

Captain,
Staff Captain,
52nd. Infantry Brigade.

12/12/1917.

H.Q.,
52ND INFANTRY BDE.
52.G.442.

Copy No 8.

A.D.M.S.

1. Reference B.O.211.
    Zero hour will probably be 12 noon to-day. All ranks are to be confined within the vicinity of billets.

2. ACKNOWLEDGE.

S. H. Smith
Captain,
Staff Captain,
52nd. Infantry Brigade.

13/12/1917.

Copies to all recipients of B.O.211.

MOVE OF 17th DIVISION (less Artillery).

From Second Army.   To Third Army.

Entraining Stations.   Detraining Stations.

A. ARQUES.   A.
B. WIZERNES.   B.
C. ST. OMER.   C.

Train Number. From Stations.			Serial Numbers.	Date Dec.	Marche.	Time of depart.	Time of arr¹ at detraining Stations.		
A	B	C					A	B	C
1	2	3	4	5	6	7	8	9	10
1			1731	14th	H.T.54	3.27			
	2		1721	"	H.T.55	4.10			
		3	1711	"	H.T.56	5.20			
4			1730. 35. 36. 37.	"	H.T.58	7.27			
	5		1720. 25. 26. 27.	"	H.T.59	8.10			
		6	1701. 03. 05.	"	H.T.60	9.20			
7			1732.	"	H.T.62	11.27			
	8		1722.	"	H.T.63	12.10			
		9	1710. 15. 16. 17. 75.	"	H.T.64	13.20			
10			1778. 83.	"	H.T.66	15.27			
	11		1777. 81.	"	H.T.67	16.10			
		12	1712.	"	H.T.68	17.20			
13			1733.	"	H.T.70	19.27			
	14		1723.	"	H.T.71	20.10			
		15	1776. 82.	"	H.T.72	21.20			
16			1787. 08.	"	H.T.74	23.27			
	17		1724.	15th.	H.T.51	0.10			
		18	1708. 04a. 09.	"	H.T.52	1.20			
19			1734.	"	H.T.54	3.27			
	20		1786.	"	H.T.55	4.10			
		21	1704.	"	H.T.56	5.20			
22			1714.	"	H.T.59	7.27			
		23	1713.	"	H.T.60	9.20			

Trains to be consigned to ACHIET for regulation.

Traffic Office,
HAZEBROUCK AREA.
13.12.17.

Captain, for
A.D.R.T.

MOVE OF 17th DIVISION (Less Artillery).

TABLE "D".

UNIT.	Serial Numbers.	Description.
DIVISIONAL UNITS	1701.	Divisional Headquarters.
	1703	H.Q., Divisional R.E.
	1704	7th Batt. Yorks & Lancs. less 04a.
	1704a	1 Company, 1 Cooker and Teams of 7th Batt. Yorks & Lancs.
	1705	H.Q., and No: 1 Section Signals.
	1708	236th Machine Gun Company.
	1709	218th Divl. Employment Company.
50th INFANTRY BRIGADE.	1710	Brigade Headquarters.
	1711	10th Batt. West Yorks.
	1712	7th Batt. East Yorks.
	1713	7th Batt. Yorks Regt.
	1714	6th Batt. Dorset Regt.
	1715	Brigade Signal Section.
	1716	Brigade Machine Gun Company.
	1717	Brigade Trench Mortar Battery (Light).
51st INFANTRY BRIGADE.	1720	Brigade Headquarters.
	1721	7th Batt. Lincoln Regt.
	1722	7th Batt. Border Regt.
	1723	8th South Staff. Reft.
	1724	10th Notts. & Derby Regt.
	1725	Brigade Signal Section.
	1726	Brigade Machine Gun Company.
	1727	Brigade Trench Mortar Battery (Light).
52nd INFANTRY BRIGADE.	1730	Brigade Headquarters.
	1731	10th Batt. Lancs. Fusiliers.
	1732	9th Batt. West Riding Regt.
	1733	3/4th Batt. R.W.Kents Regt.
	1734	12th Batt. Manchester Regt.
	1735	Brigade Signal Section.
	1736	Brigade Machine Gun Company.
	1737	Brigade Trench Mortar Battery (Light).
DIVISIONAL TRAIN.	1775	H.Q., Divisional Train.
	1776	No: 2 Company, A.S.C.
	1777	No: 3 Company, A.S.C.
	1778	No: 4 Company, A.S.C.

UNIT.	Serial Numbers.	Description.
DIVISIONAL ENGINEERS.	1781	No: 77 Field Company, R.E.
	1782	No: 78 Field Company, R.E.
	1783	No: 93 Field Company, R.E.
MEDICAL UNITS.	1786	No: 51 Field Ambulance.
	1787	No: 52 Field Ambulance.
	1788	No: 53 Field Ambulance.
VETERINARY UNITS.	1790	No: 29 Mobile Veterinary Section.

C.516/6.

SECRET.

ADMINISTRATIVE INSTRUCTIONS NO.43.

The following Instructions are issued in connection with 52nd Infantry Brigade Order No.211 of today's date :-

1. ENTRAINING.:- (a). The Brigade Group will entrain in accordance with the attached Table "A".   ZERO hour and date will be notified by Wire to all Units when received. Entraining Station will be ARQUES in all cases.

    (b). The attached Table gives the times at which Units and Transport are to arrive at entraining Station, NOT times of start of Trains.

    (c). Instructions contained in 17th Div. Administrative Instructions No.49 of 11th inst& are to be carefully adhered to.

    (d). O.C., Lancashire Fusiliers will detail one strong Company to act as "Detraining Company". This Company will entrain on the First Train and will report to R.T.O. at Detraining Station on arrival.   It will unload all Trains and then rejoin its Unit.

    (e). O.C., Manchester Regiment will detail one strong Company to act as "Entraining Company". This Company will report to R.T.O., ARQUES at Zero plus 11½ hours, load all Trains and proceed on the last Train.

    (f). Major A.E. JONES, Royal West Kent Regiment is detailed as Entraining Officer.   He will report to R.T.O., ARQUES at Zero plus 11 hours, and will proceed on the last Train.

    (g). Major H. GARDINER, D.S.O., West Riding Regiment is detailed as Detraining Officer. He will proceed on first Train and will report to R.T.O. at Detraining Station on arrival.   He will rejoin his Unit on completion of unloading.

    (h). All Units must send Officers forthwith to reconnoitre Routes to and entraining facilities at ARQUES Station.   Entraining Officer will also reconnoitre entraining facilities at ARQUES Station forthwith.

    (i). Water and feeds for 12 hours are to be taken in Trucks with Animals.   Mobile Reserve of Petrol Tins may be used for this purpose, but must be replaced on Vehicles on detraining.

2. SUPPLIES.   Supply Wagons will rejoin Units today and will entrain full with their Unit.   The unconsumed portion of the Rations for consumption on Zero day, and Rations for consumption on Zero plus one day will be carried on the man. FORAGE for Zero plus one day will be carried on First Line Transport Vehicles, distributed amongst Vehicles as evenly as possible.   Rations and Forage for Zero plus 2 days will be carried on Supply Wagons.

3. BILLETING.   Each Unit of Brigade Group will hold in readiness 1 Officer, 6 Other Ranks and 3 Bicycles to proceed by Lorry under Orders which will be issued later.   2 days Rations must be taken.   Officers may only take what they can carry in a Pack as Kit.

4.   LORRIES.   Each Battalion will have 2 Lorries. Machine Gun Company ½ Lorry, Trench Mortar Battery ½ Lorry, Brigade Headquarters 1 Lorry, to assist in the move to entraining Station.   These will report at Units' Headquarters as soon after Zero hour as possible.   Lorry for Machine Gun Company and Trench Mortar Battery will report at Headquarters of Machine Gun Company.   NOT MORE than 4 men are to travel on each Lorry.   One Lorry for 236th Machine Gun Coy. has been applied for and if obtained will report at their Headquarters as for other Units.

5.   BAGGAGE WAGONS. will rejoin Units today and will entrain with them.

6.   STORES.   No Stores are to be left in the present Area.   Quarter Masters must take steps immediately to reduce these Stores to authorised amounts.

7.   TRENCH MORTAR BATTERY.   No Mules will be available to assist Trench Mortar Battery to move.

8.   BILLETING CERTIFICATES.   for the HOULLE Area must be made out in advance and must be held ready to hand in at short notice.

Lt Flemming

9.   ACKNOWLEDGE.

Copy No. 1 to G.O.C.
       2 to Bde. Major.
       3 to Staff Captain.
       4 to Asst. Staff Capt.
       5 to E.T.O.
       6 to Signal Officer.
     7-9 to Lan. Fus.
   10-12 to W. Rid. R.
   13-15 to R.W. Kent R.
   16-18 to Manch. R.
   19-20 to M.G. Coy.
      21 to T.M. Bty.
      22 to 236th M.G. Coy.
      23 to No. 4 Coy. Train.
      24 to Supply Offr., No. 4 Coy. Train.
   25-26 to 93rd F. Coy., R.E.
   27-28 to 52nd F. Ambce.
      29 to R.T.O., ARQUES.
      30 to Maj. H. GARDINER, D.S.O., W. Rid. R.
      31 to Maj. A.E. JONES, R.W. Kent R.
      32 to 17th Div. "G" (for information).

S. H. Smith
Captain,
Staff Captain,
52nd Infantry Brigade.

12/12/1917.

TABLE "A".

Train No.	Unit.	Date.	From.	entrain-ing Station.	TIME TO REACH DETRAINING STATION. Personnel.	Transport.
10.	Lon. Fus.	DATE OF ZERO hour of first of battle to all units by wire.	BOULL.	ARCUS.	Zero plus 13½ hours.	Zero plus 12 hours.
11.	Bde.Hq. & Sigs (less sect)		do.		Zero plus 17½ hours.	Zero plus 16 hours.
11.	L.G.Coy.		L. COSTROL.		Zero plus 17½ hours.	Zero plus 16 hours.
11.	T.M.Bty.		do.		Zero plus 17½ hours.	Zero plus 18 hours.
12.	W.Rid.R.		BOULL.		Zero plus 21½ hours.	Zero plus 20 hours.
13.	93rd F.Coy.R.E.		do.		Zero plus 25½ hours.	Zero plus 24 hours.
13.	Sig.A.Coy.train.		do.		Zero plus 25½ hours.	Zero plus 24 hours.
14.	E.W.Kent R.		do.		Zero plus 29½ hours.	Zero plus 28 hours.
15.	52nd F.Ambce.		do.		Zero plus 33½ hours.	Zero plus 32 hours.
15.	255th .G.C.		ALBROUCQ.		Zero plus 33½ hours.	Zero plus 32 hours.
16.	Mach.R.		BOULL.		Zero plus 39½ hours.	Zero plus 36 hours.

12/12/1917.

S. H. Smith
Staff Captain,
92nd Inf.Bde.Brigade.

SECRET.   Copy No....

52ND INFANTRY BRIGADE O.O. NO.211.
****

Ref Map
HAZEBROUCK,
5.A.
                                                    12th December 1917

1.   With reference to WARNING ORDER issued under
B.M.1. of 11th December, 52nd Infantry Brigade will be
prepared to commence entraining at ARQUES at 12 hours
notice, after Midnight 11/12th December.

2.   If movement is ordered a ZERO hour and DATE
will be notified by Brigade Headquarters and Units
must be ready to entrain 12 hours after the Zero hour
notified.
        Movement to the entraining Station will be
carried out in accordance with the attached Table.

3.   Detailed Instructions for entrainment will
be issued separately by Staff Captain.
        Extreme punctuality must be observed by Units
on the march to ensure arrival at Station at the
precise times ordered.
        Transport will NOT be marshalled on Roads
outside billets for more than half an hour before it is
due to march.

4.   In the event of movement taking place,
detailed Instruction for detrainment and locations
after detrainment will be issued later.

5.   Completion of move will be reported to Brigade
Headquarters immediately on arrival at billets.

6.   ACKNOWLEDGE.

Issued at 3.30 pm.

Copy No 1 to Bde.H.Q.
        2 to War Diary.
        3 to Staff Captain.
        4 to O.C.,Sigs.
        5 to B.T.O.
        6 to Lan. Fus.
        7 to W.Rid. Regt.
        8 to R.W.Kent Regt.
        9 to Manch. Regt.
        10 to M.G.Coy.
        11 to T.M.Bty.
        12 to 52nd F.Amb.
        13 to 93rd F.Coy.R.E.
        14 to No.4 Coy.Train.
        15 to 236th M.G.Coy.
        16 to Supply Officer.
        17 to 17th Division.

                                                    Captain,
                                                    Brigade Major,
                                                    52nd Infantry Brigade.

MARCH TABLE issued with B.O.O.O.211.

Train No.	Unit.	Date.	From.	Starting Point.	Route.	Entrain-ing Stn.	TIME TO REACH DETRAINING STATION. Personnel.	Transport.
10.	Lon. Fus.		HOULLE.	HOULLE.	TILLQUES – ST.MARTIN-au-LAERT, Southern outskirts of ST.OMER, ARQUES.	ARQUES.	Zero Plus 13½ hrs.	plus 12 hrs.
11.	Bde.H.Q. & Signal Sect.	DATE and ZERO hour will be notified by WIRE.	do.				17½ "	" 16 "
11.	M.G.Coy.		LE COSTHAL.				17½ "	" 16 "
11.	T.M.Bty.		do.				17½ "	" 16 "
12.	W.Rid.R.		HOULLE.				21½ "	" 20 "
13.	93rd F.Coy.R.E.		HOULLE.				25½ "	" 24 "
13.	No.4 Coy.Train.		HOULLE.				25½ "	" 24 "
14.	E.W.Kent R.		do.				29½ "	" 28 "
15.	52nd F.Amb.		do.				33½ "	" 32 "
15.	236th M.G.Coy.		HELLEBROUCQ.				33½ "	" 32 "
16.	Manch.R.		HOULLE.				37½ "	" 36 "

S E C R E T.      17th Division
A/1001.

ADMINISTRATIVE INSTRUCTIONS

NO: 49.   11th December 1917.

Reference 17th Division Order No.267.

1. **LOCATION OF BILLETS** will be issued later.

2. **BILLETING PARTIES.**

   Billeting parties not to exceed 1 Officer and 6 Other Ranks with 7 bicycles per unit, will proceed by lorry under orders to be issued later.

   O.C. Billeting parties will arrange guides to meet units and transport on arrival at detraining station and lead them to Camps.

   Formations will wire without delay to Divl H.Q. the total strength of billeting parties.

3. (a) The entrainment will be carried out in accordance with table in 'G' Order No. 267.
   (b) All transport and animals (with exception of Officers' Chargers) together with transport personnel will arrive at entraining station 3 hours before their train is timed to start.

   All personnel, except as above, will arrive at the entraining station 1½ hours before their train is timed to start.

   In all cases an Officer will report to the R.T.O 15 minutes before the troops arrive at the station.

   A complete marching-out state showing the number of men, horses, G.S., Limbered G.S. and two-wheeled vehicles, will be sent down with the transport of every unit so that accommodation in the train can be checked by the R.T.O. at the beginning of the entrainment.
   (c) Baggage and Supply Wagons will be entrained with their units
   (d) All ammunition echelons will be entrained full. Particular attention must be paid that all mobile reserves are complete
   (e) Water Carts will be entrained full. All water bottles must be full at the time of the entrainment.
   (f) Fires in Field Kitchens must be drawn before entrainment.
   (g) Horses will be watered shortly before entrainment. Salvaged four-gallon petrol tins should be thoroughly cleansed, filled with water and placed in horse vans.

   The floors of all trucks used for animals will be sprinkled with cinders or small shingle to prevent the horses slipping

   Breast ropes for horse trucks must be provided by units.
   (h) The composition of each train is as follows

   1 Passenger Coach..........30 Officers
   30 Covered Vans............40 men or 8 L.D.)
                               or 6 H.D. horses) per van
   17 Flats ....4 to 5 axles according to size of flat.

   No personnel or stores will be allowed in the brake vans at each end of the train

4. The following entraining parties will be detailed by Bdes
   (a) 50th Inf. Bde. 1 Company to report to R.T.O., St.OMER
                          3½ hours before the time of departure of first train. This company will be responsible for entraining all transport for the trains from St. OMER and will entrain on the last train.

P.T.O.

(4) Continued.

(b) **51st Inf. Bde.** 1 Company to report to R.T.O., WIZERNES, 2½ hours before the time of departure of first train. This Company will be responsible for entraining all transport for the trains from WIZERNES and will entrain on the last train.

(c) **52nd Inf. Bde.** One Company to report to R.T.O., ARQUES, 2½ hours before the time of departure of first train. This company will be responsible for entraining all transport for the trains from ARQUES and will entrain on the last train.

(d) These parties must work in conjunction with R.T.Os. St. OMER, WIZERNES and ARQUES. Entraining parties will work in reliefs. They will be billeted by R.T.Os and must be rationed by their units.

(e) Brigades will detail one Company to proceed with the first train for detraining under similar arrangements as for entraining.

(f) Brigades will detail Field Officers to superintend entraining and detraining.
Detraining Officers will proceed by the first train from each station. Names to be reported to this Office by 9 a.m. 12th inst.

(g) The A.P.M. will arrange for 6 Military Police to be on duty at each entraining station. They will proceed by the last train.

5 SUPPLIES.

(a) Units will carry the unexpended portion of the day's rations on the man and on the horse or in the First Line Transport.
(b) All units will entrain with rations for the day following the day of entrainment.
(c) Supply Wagons will be entrained full.

6 TRANSPORT.

(a) All Baggage and Supply wagons will be sent to their units by 12 noon 12th Decr.. The horses and personnel will remain with the units and move with the units' transport.
(b) Brigades will have 10 lorries to move supplies, kits and blankets to their entraining stations. They will notify this office by 10 a.m. 12th Decr. locations where lorries are required.

7 SOUP KITCHENS.

It is hoped to have Soup Kitchens running at the entraining stat

— Major.

11/12/17a   D.A.A.G., 17th Division.

S E C R E T.

17TH DIVISION,
A/1001.

12th December, 1917.

A D D E N D U M to ADMINISTRATIVE INSTRUCTIONS, No. 49.

1. INTRAINING.

The 6th Dorsets will be responsible for loading their own transport at ST.OMER or ARQUES. Loading party must arrive at Station 2½ hours before train is due to leave. Should they entrain by ARQUES, transport must arrive at the Station Z+40 and personnel at Z+41½.

2. INTRAINING STATIONS.

Intraining Officers must make themselves acquainted with entraining facilities at their stations, nearest watering points, etc.,

3. LORRIES TO CARRY BLANKETS, etc., to STATIONS.

Special attention must be paid that lorries are loaded and off-loaded with the least possible loss of time. If lorries arrive at the station and the train is not in, lorries must not be kept waiting but must be off-loaded at once. If these instructions are not carefully observed it will not be possible to move other units' blankets to the station as there are only a small number of lorries available.

The 47th Ammunition Sub Park situated at WATTEN will be responsible for the supply of lorries.

On receipt of Zero hour the 47th A.S.P. will detail the following lorries to report at once. -

No.	To	At.	To proceed to
Two.	H.Q. 10th W. Yorks.,	ZUDROVE.	ST. OMER.
Two.	H.Q. 10th Lancs.Fuslrs.	HOULLE.	ARQUES.
Two.	H.Q. 7th Lincolns.	NORDLEULIGHEM.	WIZERNES.
Two.	H.Q. 52nd Bde. H.Q.,	HOULLE.	ARQUES.
Two.	H.Q. 51st Bde. H.Q.,	NORDASQUES.	WIZERNES.

The following lorries will then report as follows :-

Time.	No.	To report to	At	To proceed to
Zero+12.	Two.	H.Q., 50th Bde.	SERQUES.	ST. OMER.
" 12.	Two.	H.Q., 9th W. Ridgs.	MOULLE.	ARQUES.
" 15.	Two.	H.Q., 7th Borders.	LACOMMUNI.	WIZERNES.
" 17.	Two.	H.Q., 7th E. Yorks.	Le BAS.	ST. OMER.
" 21½.	Two.	H.Q., 2/4 W. Kents.	MOULLE.	ARQUES.
" 23.	Two.	H.Q., 3th S. Staffs.	MENTQUE.	WIZERNES.
" 25½.	One.	H.Q., 52rd Fld.Amb.	WATTEN,	ST. OMER.

(2)

Time.	No.	To report to	At	To proceed to
Zero+25½	One.	H.Q., 52nd Fld.Amb.	MOULLE.	ARQUES.
" 25½	One.	H.Q., 226 M.G. Coy.	HILLEBRUCQ	ARQUES.
" 26½	Two.	H.Q., 10th Sherwoods.	N.PDASQUES.	WIZERNES.
" 27	Two.	H.Q., 7th York & Lancs.	HOLQUE.	ST. OMER.
" 29½	Two.	H.Q., 12th Manchesters.	HOULLE.	ARQUES.
" 29½	One.	H.Q., 51st Fld. Amb.	MOURCOVE.	WIZERNES.
" 31	One.	H.Q., 7th Yorks.	BAYINGHEM.	ST. OMER.
" 37	* Two.	H.Q., 6th Dorsets.	SERQUES.	ST. OMER. or ARQUES.

* If 6th Dorsets entrain at ARQUES, lorries will be required about 4 hours earlier.

Brigades will arrange for guides to pick up the one lorry for M.G. Coy. and T.M. Bty. at Brigade H. Q.,

O. C. 47th A.S.P. will issue instructions to each lorry driver as to whether he is to return to his park after completion of a duty or report to a unit for further detail.

Captain.
D.A.Q.M.G., 17th Division.

SECRET.   E   Copy No. 10

3/4th. Battn. Royal West Kent Regiment.

13-12-17.

March Orders No. 15.

1. **Move.** The Battalion will move by train from ARQUES to-morrow, the 14th instant.

2. **March Order.** Starting Point, Main road outside "C" Coy.'s Officers' Mess.
   Time of passing Starting Point, 2.0 p.m.
   Order of March :- H.Q., Band, "D", "C", "B", "A".
   Route :- TILQUES - ST. MARTIN-au-LAERT, southern outskirt of ST. OMER - ARQUES.
   Dress :- Full marching order and one blanket per N.C.O. and man. All water-bottles must be filled before starting. Steel helmets will be worn by all ranks.
   Officers' Chargers will be available on the march if required. If not required Coy. Commanders will notify T.O. by 9.0 a.m. to-morrow.

3. **Transport Arrangements.** The remaining blanket per man will be carried by lorry. Blankets must be tightly packed in bundles of ten, labelled and dumped at the Q.M. Stores by 8.45 a.m.
   Officers' valises to be at Q.M. Stores by 9.0 a.m.
   Mess boxes will be at Q.M. Stores at 9.0 a.m.

4. **Rations.** The unconsumed portion of to-morrow's ration will be carried on the man.

5. **Transport.** Orders have already been issued to Transport Officer and Quartermaster.

6. **ACKNOWLEDGE.**

                                       Lieut. & Acting Adjutant,
                                  3/4th. Battn. Royal West Kent Regiment.

Issued at 8.0 p.m.

1. H.Q. Mess.   7. T.O.
2. O.C. "A" Coy.   8. Lieut. H.B. Lewis,
3. O.C. "B" Coy.   9. R.S.M.
4. O.C. "C" Coy.   10. War Diary.
5. O.C. "D" Coy.   11. File.
6. Q.M.

"C" FORM.
MESSAGES AND SIGNALS.

Army Form C. 2123.
(In books of 100.)
No. of Message...

Prefix...... Code...... Words......

Received. From: ZEB
By: [illegible]

Sent, or sent out.
At.........m.
To.........
By.........

Office Stamp.
RWK
15/12/17

Charges to Collect

Service Instructions
4 Rcopies

Handed in at ZEB Office 9.54 a.m. Received 10.17 a.m.

TO Royal West Kents

*Sender's Number.	Day of Month.	In reply to Number.	AAA
52 X 525	15th	—	
Following	lorries	are	detailed
to	convey	blankets	and
store	to	new	area
aaa	Ecol	Batts	2
MG	Coy	and	T M
Bty	at	between	them
aaa	Units	will	detail
guide	to report	Bde	HQ
at	7 am	tomorrow	
16th	inst	to	conduct
lorries	to	their	respective
Hdqrs			

FROM PLACE & TIME   52nd Inf Bde

*This line should be erased if not required.

"C" FORM.
MESSAGES AND SIGNALS.

Army Form C. 2123.
(In books of 100.)

No. of Message............

Prefix......Code......Words......	Received.	Sent, or sent out.	Office Stamp.
£ s. d.	From.........	At............m.	RWK
Charges to Collect	By............	To............	15/12/17
Service Instructions		By............	

Handed in at............Office 9.30 p.m. Received............m.

TO — Royal West Kents

*Sender's Number.	Day of Month.	In reply to Number.	AAA
SCX 527	15		

units	will	detail	billeting
parties	as	under	to
report	these	HQ	at
9	am	tomorrow	16th
aaa	Battns	(each)	officers
1	NCOs	2	aaa
52nd	M—	Coy	1
officer	and	1	NCOS
aaa	52nd	TM	2/f
2	NCOS	aaa	93rd
field	Coy	RE	1
officer	and	1	NCO
aaa	52nd	field	Amb.
1	Officer	and	1
NCO	aaa	No	4
Coy	Train	1	officer

FROM
PLACE & TIME

*This line should be erased if not required.

"C" FORM.
MESSAGES AND SIGNALS.

Army Form C. 2123.
(In books of 100.)

and they will proceed by lorry to ROEAUINY NCO aaa

FROM PLACE & TIME: 52nd Infantry Bde

SECRET.

17th Division.
A/1001.
15th December, '17.

ADMINISTRATIVE INSTRUCTIONS.
No. 52.

1. LOCATION OF BILLETS.	PLACE.	Area Commandant.
Divisional Headquarters.	ACHIET-LE-PETIT.	
C.R.E.	-do-	
Divnl. Train Hd.Qrs.	-do-	ACHIET-LE-PETIT.
D.A.D.O.S.	-do-	
D.O.R.E.	-do-	
50th Infantry Brigade.H.Q.,	BEAULENCOURT.	Bde.H.Q., Camp.
50th T.M.Battery.	-do-	T.M.Camp.
50th M.G.Company.	-do-	M.G.Camp.
10th West Yorks.	-do-	"A" Camp.
7th East Yorks.	-do-	"B" Camp.
7th Yorks.	-do-	"C" Camp.
6th Dorsets.	-do-	"D" Camp.
7th York & Lancs(Pioneers)	-do-	"E" Camp.
53rd Field Ambulance.	-do-	Le Transloy Camp.
78th Field Coy. R.E.,	-do-	"F" Camp.
No.3 Coy.Train.		"F" Camp.
51st Infantry Brigade.		Bde. H.Q. Camp.
Brigade Headquarters.	BARASTRE	M.G.Camp.
51st T.M.Battery.	-do-	T.M.Camp.
51st M.G.Company.	-do-	"N" Camp.
7th Lincolns.	-do-	"M" Camp.
7th Borders.	-do-	"L" Camp.
8th South Staffords.	-do-	"K" Camp.
10th Sherwoods.	-do-	M.G.Camp.
51st Field Ambulance.	-do-	R.E.Camp.
77th Field Coy. R.E.	-do-	R.E.Camp.
No.3 Coy.Train.		
52nd Infantry Brigade.		
Brigade Headquarters.	ACHIET-LE-PETIT	Church St.
52nd T.M.Battery.	-do-	Kings St.
52nd M.G.Company.	-do-	New Camp.
10th Lanc.Fusiliers.	-do-	Bradford Camp.
9th Dcn.Fusrs.	-do-	Bedford Camp.
3/4th Royal West Kents.	-do-	HENLAM NORTH Cmp.
12th Manchesters.	-do-	HENLAM SOUTH Cmp.
52nd Field Ambulance.	-do-	BRICKFIELDS Camp.
93rd Field Coy. R.E.,	-do-	SAPPER Camp.
No.4 Coy.Train.	-do-	HALIFAX Camp.
236th M.G.Coy.	ACHIET-LE-GRAND.	
29th Mob.Vet.Section.	ACHIET-LE-PETIT.	
Cinema.	BARASTRE.	
Canteen.	BEAULENCOURT.	

Move on afternoon 16th, to ROCQUIGNY Brigade Area

2. RAILHEAD. Supplies. BAPAUNE.
3. LEAVE. Railhead for Leave. BAPAUNE.
   Leave Train departs.....10.p.m.,
4. FIELD CASHIER is at VILLERS-AU-FLOS.

Major,
D.A.A.G., 17th Division.

SECRET.  Copy No....

52nd INFANTRY BRIGADE O.O.NO.212.

Ref Map
57.c.Sd.2.   15th December 1917.

1. The 52nd Infantry Brigade Group will move from ACHIET-LE-PETIT to ROCQUIGNY tomorrow, 16th instant, in accordance with the attached "March Table".

2. Usual Intervals of 100 yards between Companies, 100 yards between Units and their Transport and 500 yards between Units will be maintained.

3. Billeting parties will report to B.T.O. at Office of Area Commandant at ROCQUIGNY at Noon tomorrow, 16th instant, to take over Billets in ROCQUIGNY Area. Units will make their own arrangements as to billeting parties meeting Units on arrival.

4. Lorries to assist in the move will report at Bde. H.Q. at 11.0 am. tomorrow, 16th instant. 2 will be allotted to each Battalion and ½ each to M.G.Coy. and T.M. Bty. Each Unit will send a Guide to Bde. H.Q. at 11.0 am., 16th instant, to guide Lorries to present C.T.Stores. Units will arrange for one of their billeting party to meet their Lorries at entrance to ROCQUIGNY and guide to C.T. Stores in new Area.

5. The usual hourly halts will be observed and allowance has been made for those halts in the "March Table".

6. Brigade Headquarters will close at ACHIET-LE-PETIT at 11.30 am. and reopen at ROCQUIGNY on arrival.

7. Arrival in new Area will be reported to Brigade H.Q. together with any "march" casualties.

8. ACKNOWLEDGE.

Issued at 11.45 pm.

Copy No 1 to Bde. H.Q.
2 to War Diary.
3 to Bde. Major.
4 to Staff Captain.
5 to O.C.,Sigs.
6 to B.T.O.
7 to Lan. Fus.
8 to W.Rid. Regt.
9 to R.W.Kent Regt.
10 to Manch. Regt.
11 to M.G.Coy.
12 to T.M.Bty.
13 to 52nd F.Ambce.
14 to 93rd F.Coy.R.E.
15 to O.C.,No.4 Coy.Train.
16 to Supply Officer.
17 to Area Commandant, ROCQUIGNY.(for information)
18 to 17th Division.

Captain,
Brigade Major,
52nd Infantry Brigade.

MARCH TABLE issued with Order No. 212.

Serial.	Date.	Unit.	To.	Starting point.	Time.	Route.	Remarks.
1.	Dec. 16th.	Bde. H.Q.	ROSCIGNY.	G.14.b.3.8. (Cross-roads.)	12.49 pm.	G.14.b.3.8. – GREVILLERS – TILLOY – H.33.b.5.3. – O.31.b.4.8.	
2.	16th.	Lan. Fus.			11.40 am.		
3.	16th.	W.Rid. R.			12.3 pm.		
4.	16th.	E.W.Kent R.			12.16 pm.		
5.	16th.	March. R.			12.29 pm.		
6.	16th.	M.G.Coy.			12.42 pm.		
7.	16th.	T.M.Bty.			12.49 pm.		
8.	16th.	93rd F.Coy.R.E.			1.3 pm.		Will march behind Bde. H.Q. Transport.
9.	16th.	52nd F.Ambce.			1.12 pm.		

"A" Form.
MESSAGES AND SIGNALS.

Army Form C. 2121.
(In pads of 100.)
No. of Message..........

Prefix	Code	Words.	Charge.			
Office of Origin and Service Instructions.		Sent At .... m. To .... By		This message is on a/c of : ..... Service. (Sig. of "Franking Officer.")		Recd. at .... m. Date .... From .... By ....

SECRET

TO { Lanc Fus W Rid Regt K R Kent Regt
Manch Regt M G Coy T M 15th
98th Fld Coy RE 52nd Fld Ambce }

Sender's Number	Day of Month	In reply to Number	
PMx 48	16		AAA

Warning order

Division is in Army Reserve and will be prepared to move at two hours notice

Acknowledge

From ....
Place ....
Time 3.15 a

To R.W.F.

SECRET

ADMINISTRATIVE INSTRUCTIONS NO. 46.

1. When the Brigade Group moves to-morrow, Transport Lines, Q.M. Stores, and B. Echelon will remain at the present Camps at ROCQUIGNY, as the 140th. Inf. Bde. are not moving out of BERTINCOURT till 22nd. inst.

2. Several units of 59th. Division are moving into ROCQUIGNY Camps to-morrow, and it will be necessary for nearly all units' Transport and Q.M. Stores to "double up". Units must give every assistance to 59th. Division.

3. Mess Carts, Water Carts, Cookers and Machine Gun Limbers will proceed with Units to-morrow, and will rejoin their First Line Transport on 22nd. inst. at BERTINCOURT. If units wish to take one or two other vehicles forward to-morrow they may do so, and any vehicles so taken forward can be accomodated to-morrow night at the Transport Lines of 140th. Inf. Bde. at BERTINCOURT, which were shown to Transport Officers by B.T.O. this morning. Units must ensure that men and animals detached from the Main Body of the Transport are given their rations and forage.

4. All First Line Transport and all Q.M. Stores which remain at ROCQUIGNY to-morrow will move on 22nd. inst. under orders of B.T.O. to Lines now occupied by 140th. Inf. Bde. at BERTINCOURT. B.T.O. has allotted Lines to units to-day.

5. Ten lorries will be at Road Junction O.27.d. at 10.0 a.m. on 22nd. inst. to convey blankets and other Q.M. Stores to new positions at BERTINCOURT. Two lorries are allotted to each Battalion, one to Brigade H.Q. and half each to M.G.Coy. and T.M.Bty. Each unit must have a guide at O.27.d. at 10.0 a.m. 22nd. inst. to guide its lorries to Q.M. Stores.

6. (a). Supplies for consumption 21st. will be carried on the man, and on animals which are going forward.
   (b). Supplies for consumption 22nd. inst. will be carried forward with units on 21st. inst. either on the man or on limbers.
   (c). Supplies for consumption 23rd. inst. will be drawn in Supply Wagons, and delivered at present Camps by 2.0 p.m. 21st. inst. Rations for consumption 23rd. inst. for men going to trenches will be conveyed in units First Line Transport from present Camps to the Headquarters to which units are moving on 21st. inst; these rations are to reach units by noon 22nd. inst. so that units may take them with them into the Line.

Copies to :-

All recipients of Admin. Instrons
No. 45 dated 20.12.17.

20.12.17

S.H. Smith
Captain,
Staff Captain,
52nd. Infantry Brigade.

SECRET.   COPY NO. 10

52ND INFANTRY BRIGADE C.O. NO.213.

Ref Map
57.C.,
1/40,000
                                                    20th December 1917.

1.   In continuation of 52nd Infantry Brigade "WARNING
ORDER" No. 52.G.4529, the 52nd Infantry Brigade will relieve
the 51st Infantry Brigade tomorrow in the OLD BRITISH FRONT
LINE and become the Support to the 59th Division.

2.   The Brigade will move in accordance with attached
"March" Table.

3.   Cookers M.G.Limbers and filled Water Carts will
move with Units. Remainder of Transport will be
Brigaded under B.T.O. and move on the 22nd instant.

4.   BILLETING PARTIES will be sent on ahead at 8.0 am.
and a meeting place between Billeting Parties and Units
will be arranged by Os. C. Units.

5.   Care will be taken on arrival that Water Cart and
Cookers are carefully CONCEALED.

6.   LORRIES will be available to assist in the move at
10.0 am.   at ROAD JUNCTION - 0.27.d.7.9.   Two
Lorries are allotted to each Battalion, ½ Machine Gun Coy.
and ½ Trench Mortar Battery, and one for Brigade H.Qrs.
        Each Unit will send a GUIDE to the rendezvous, to
guide Lorries to the Q.M.Stores.

7.   Units will move through HAVRINCOURT WOOD by Coys.
at 300 yards interval, on emerging from the WOOD movement
will be by Platoon at 200 yards interval. Usual Intervals
will be maintained as far as HAVRINCOURT WOOD.

8.   No. 4 Company Train and 52nd Field Ambulance will
move under Orders issued by the O.C., Train and A.D.M.S.
respectively

9.   COMPLETION OF RELIEF will be reported to Brigade H.Q.

10.   Brigade Headquarters will close at 12.30 pm. and
re-open on arrival at K.32.c.7.9.

11.   ACKNOWLEDGE.

Issued at 8.30 pm.

Copy No.   1 to Bde. H.Q.
           2 to War Diary.
           3 to G.O.C.
           4 to Bde. Major.
           5 to Staff Captain.
           6 to O.C., Signals.
           7 to B.T.O.
           8 to Lan. Fus.
           9 to W.Rid. Regt.
          10 to R.W.Kent Regt.
          11 to Manch. Regt.
          12 to M.G.Coy.
          13 to T.M.Bty.
          14 to 52nd F.Ambce.
          15 to Supply Officer.
          16 to No. 4 Coy.Train.
          17 to 17th Division.
          18 to 51st Inf. Bde.

                                            J.G. Turner
                                            /y. Captain,
                                            Brigade Major,
                                            52nd Infantry Brigade.

MARCH TABLE issued with O.O.No. 213.

Ser. No.	Date.	UNIT.	In relief of.	From.	Sector of line to take over.	TIME.	H.Qrs. at.	ROUTE.	REMARKS.
1.	DEC. 21.	Bde.H.Q.	51st Bde.H.Q.	ROCQUIGNY.		12.30 pm.	K.32.c.7.9.	BUS – YTRES – NEUVILLE – BOURSON VAL cross Roads at P.17.d., Plank Road to HAVRINCOURT. In HAVRINCOURT WOOD intervals of 300 yards will be maintained between Coys., on emerging from the WOOD movement will be by Platoons at 200 yards interval.
2.	21.	W.Rid.R.	7th Borders.		HINDENBURGH LINE from K.35.a.6.4. to K.34.a.9.6.	12.45 pm.	K.35.a.25.25.		
3.	21.	Lan.Fus.	7th Lincolns.		Q.3.b. & Q.4.a.	1.15 pm.	Q.4.c.55.60.		
4.	21.	March.R.	10th Sherwoods.		Q.3.a. & Q.3.c.	1.45 pm.	Q.3.b.2.2.		
5.	21.	E.W.Kent R.	9th S.Staffs.		HEDLEY AV.TRENCH – CHEETHAM SWITCH TRENCH as far as where it cuts Rd. at K.32.c.8.6.	2.15 pm.	K.31.b.2.2.		
6.	21.	M.G.Coy.	51st M.G.Coy.		Old British Front Line K.32.d.1.5. to K.32.d.7.0.	2.45 pm.	K.32.d.7.0.		
7.	21.	T.M.Bty.	51st T.M.Bty.		Billets in HAVRINCOURT.	3. 0 pm.	Cellars in HAVRINCOURT.		

RWKR

SECRET

ADMINISTRATIVE INSTRUCTIONS NO.46

1. When the Brigade Group moves to-morrow, Transport Lines, Q.M. Stores, and R. Echelon will remain at the present Camps at ROCQUIGNY, as the 140th.Inf.Bde. are not moving out of BERTINCOURT till 22nd.inst.

2. Several units of 59th.Division are moving into ROCQUIGNY Camps to-morrow, and it will be necessary for nearly all units' Transport and Q.M. Stores to " double up". Units must give every assistance to 59th.Division.

3. Mess Carts, Water Carts, Cookers and Machine Gun Limbers will proceed with Units to-morrow, and will rejoin their First Line Transport on 22nd. inst. at BERTINCOURT. If units wish to take one or two other vehicles forward to-morrow they may do so, and any vehicles so taken forward can be accomodated to-morrow night at the Transport Lines of 140th. Inf.Bde. at BERTINCOURT. which were shown to Transport Officers by B.T.O. this morning. Units must ensure that men and animals detached from the Main Body of the Transport are given their rations and forage.

4. All First Line Transport and all Q.M. Stores which remain at ROCQUIGNY to-morrow will move on 22nd.inst. under orders of B.T.O. to Lines now occupied by 140th.Inf.Bde. at BERTINCOURT. B.T.O. has allotted Lines to units to-day.

5. Ten lorries will be at Road junction O.27.d. at 10.0 a.m. on 22nd.inst. to convey blankets and other Q.M. Stores to new positions at BERTINCOURT. Two lorries are allotted to each Battalion, one to Brigade H.Q. and half each to M.G.Coy. and T.M.Bty. Each unit must have a guide at O.27.d. at 10.0 a.m. 22nd. inst. to guide its lorries to Q.M. Stores.

6. (a). Supplies for consumption 21st. will be carried on the man, and on animals which are going forward.
(b). Supplies for consumption 22nd. inst. will be carried forward with units on 21st. inst. either on the man or on limbers.
(c). Supplies for consumption 23rd. inst. will be drawn in Supply Wagons, and delivered at present Camps by 2.0 p.m. 21st. inst. Rations for consumption 23rd. inst. for men going to trenches will be conveyed in units First Line Transport from present Camps to the Headquarters to which units are moving on 21st. inst. these rations are to reach units by noon 22nd. inst. so that units may take them with them into the Line.

Copies to :-

All recipients of Admin.Instrons
No.45 dated 20.12.17.

S H Smith

20.12.17

Captain,
Staff Captain,
52nd. Infantry Brigade.

SECRET.
Not to be taken
beyond Bn. H.Q.

C.516/16.

[Stamp: HEADQUARTERS ... INFANTRY BRIGADE]

ADMINISTRATIVE INSTRUCTIONS NO: 45.

DECEMBER 20TH, 1917.

The following information and instructions are issued relative to the line shortly to be taken over by the Brigade :-

1. **LOCATIONS.** — Bde. H.Q. — C.3.d.7.4 (all officers except B.T.O).
   Front Line Bns. — Left - K.18.c.7.4
                    Right- K.24.b.3.8
   Support Bns. — Left - K.24.a.3.4
                 Right- K.24.a.8.2
   M.G.Coy. — K.20.d.2.5
   T.M.Bty. — K.24.d.5.8.

2. **DUMPS;-** S.A.A. & Grenades — Main Bde. Grenade Dump - K.23.d.4.9
                                Small Bde. Dump - K.24.b.6.4
                                Div. Grenade Dump - C.15.a.1.1

   R.E. Material — Main Bde. R.E. Dump - K.24.b.4.8
                       Small R.E. Dump - K.18.c.7.4
                       Div. R.E. Dump - METZ.

   There are also Battalion & Coy. Dumps for all Bns. Battalions will report by 6.0 p.m. on 23rd. inst. and daily thereafter what stores are on Bns. dumps. All units can draw direct on any Bde. Dump by merely presenting an indent to the N.C.O. i/c Dump and reporting to Bde. H.Q. what has been drawn. Dumps only contain the usual stores and any exceptional demands should be sent in to Bde. H.Q. at least 24 hours before the stores are required.

3. **SUPPLIES.;-** Rations and water are in all cases taken as far as Bn. H.Q. by limber, and in the case of the left front Bn. can be taken by pack animals as far as Coy. H.Q. Units will arrange direct with their transport officer where and when they wish rations delivered. 177th Bde. are only taking in on the man one days rations and water. The best time for delivering rations is reported to be immediately after dark.

4. **WATER.** — Water is taken in petrol tins to the front line. There are wells in FLESQUIERES near the A.D.M.S. and near the Church but they are shallow and unreliable, though quite fit for drinking.

5. **TRACKS.** — Transport proceeds by road either (a) METZ-TRESCAULT-HAVRINCOURT-FLESQUIERES; or (b) METZ-TRESCAULT-RIBECOURT-FLESQUIERES. (a) is reported to be the better way. No transport is allowed to proceed east of METZ between 6.0 a.m. and noon. Transport can go as far as TRESCAULT in daylight.

6. **RESERVE RATIONS.** — 5000 at CHATEAU, FLESQUIERES (K.24.a.5.7).

7. **PACK SADDLES & CRATES** — These will be taken over by B.T.O. from B.T.O. 177th Bde. on 22nd. inst. Units must indent on B.T.O. for any required.

8. **TRANSPORT LINES & Q.M. STORES** — Units will take over the Transport Lines and Q.M. Stores of 140th Inf. Bde. at BERTINCOURT, B.T.O. will allot lines to Transport Officers today.

(1).

9. SHELLED AREAS :- Churches at FLESQUIERES & RIBEMONT, cross roads at K.24.b.7.3 and Q.15.a.7.6, road between FLESQUIERES & RIBEMONT (Q.4.d. and Q.5.c.)

10. COOKERS & WATER-CARTS :- Cookers are not taken to FLESQUIERES but dixies are. Water-Carts may be taken to FLESQUIERES if desired, but must not remain there more than 2 hours.

11. S.O.S.-BOMBS and VERY LIGHTS will be handed over in the Line. There is a small reserve at Main Bde. Dump, but this cannot be drawn on without authority from Bde. H.Q.

12. GUM BOOTS :- There are about 500 pairs at the Drying Shed, which is at the CHATEAU, K.24.a.5.7. Units can draw these by arrangements with N.C.O. in charge of drying shed. Care must be taken to lose no Gum Boots.

13. DRYING SHEDS :- Supply Officer will arrange with B.T.O. for 3 cwt. coal to be delivered at Drying Shed K.24.a.5.7 on 23rd inst. Units can draw dry socks in exchange for an equivalent number of wet at the shed.

14. MEDICAL ARRANGEMENTS :-
   Collecting Post   - K.24.b.2.7.
   Bearers Post   - K.24.b.4.9.
   A.D.S.   - TRESCAULT.
   Main Dressing Stn. - RUYAULCOURT.
   Walking Wounded   - Q.10.a.0.1.

15. WATER POINTS :-
   TRESCAULT   - Q.10.a.5.5.
   METZ.
   METZ-NEUVILLE road, P.17.d.
   Q.15.a.7.6.

16. STROMBOS HORNS :- K.18.c.7.4, K.18.b.5.2, K.24.b.3.7.

17. RESERVE BOX RESPIRATORS :- About 1000 at house K.18.c.8.1.

18. BATHS :- BERTINCOURT & RUYAULCOURT.

19. CEMETERY :- K.24.a.8.7.

20. SALVAGE :- Ration Dumps at Battalion H.Q. are used as salvage dumps and salvage is sent down in empty ration limbers.

21. SOUP KITCHEN :- Soup Kitchen will be established at CHATEAU, FLESQUIERES, K.24.a.5.7. Supply Officer will arrange direct with B.T.O. for this kitchen to be supplied on alternate days, from 22nd. inst. inclusive, with necessary fuel and soup and tea etc.

22. HOT FOOD CONTAINERS :- B.T.O. will take over a certain number of these from B.T.O. 177th. Bde. on 22nd.inst., and will hand them over to units in the front line in the following proportions - Each Battn. 40 %, M.G.Coy. 15 %, T.M.Bty. 5 %. The utmost care must be taken to hand the full number over on each inter-battalion relief, and units will send to Bde. H.Q. receipts or copies each time they hand over or take over any hot food containers.

23. SANDBAGS - Each Battalion can draw from Div. R.E. Dump at METZ any time after 9.0 a.m. on 23rd. inst. 750 sandbags. M.G.Coy. can draw 250 and T.M.Bty. 250.

24. TRENCH FEET - At present no arrangements exist for the French powder treatment. Whale oil is to be used and can be obtained by indenting on Supply Officer.

25. PRISONERS CAGE - K.24.b.2.5.

26. TRENCH STORES - Lists of all stores taken over in trenches or at Transport lines or Q.M.Stores must be sent to Bde.H.Q. by 9.0 a.m. on 24th. inst.

27. EMPLOYED MEN :- Personnel shown in attached Table "A" are to report, with written instructions, to representatives of 177th Inf. Bde. outside the office of the Town Major TRESCAULT at noon on 22nd. inst. These men must take blankets and rations for 2 days. Their own units will continue to ration them.

Rates 5 days 24th

28. ACKNOWLEDGE. ✓

Copies to :-

1. G.O.C.
2. Bde. Major.
3. Staff Captain.
4. Asst. Staff Captain.
5. S.T.O.
6.7.8. Lan. Fus.
9.10.11. W.Rid. R.
12.13.14. R.W.Kent.R.
15.16.17. Manch. R.
18.19. M.G.Coy.
20. T.M.Bty.
21. O.C. Signals.
22. No.4.Coy. Train.
23. Supply Officer.
24. 93rd. Fld. Coy. R.E.
25. 52nd. Fld. Ambce.
26. 50th. Inf. Bde.)
27. 51st. " ") for information.
28. 17th. Div. G.)

S. H. Smith
Captain,
Staff Captain,
52nd. Infantry Brigade.

TABLE A.

Serial No.	Detail.	Unit providing.	Employ	REMARKS.
1.	1 N.C.O. & 2 men.	R.West Kent R.	Grenade Dump at K.24.b.6.4.	Must have knowledge of grenades.
2.	1 Sgt. & 4 men.	M.nch. R.	Main Grenade Dump, K.23.d.4.9.	" " "
3.	1 N.C.O.	L.N. Fus.	Box Respirator Reserve Dump at K.18.c.8.1.	" " "
4.	1 N.C.O. & 6 men.	W.Rid.Regt.	Bde. R.E. Dump at K.24.b.4.8.	
5.	1 N.C.O. & 4 men.	W.Rid.Regt.	Soup Kitchen at CHATEAU, K.24.b.5.7.	Some men to run kitchen at PILKEM to be sent if available.
6.	1 N.C.O. & 4 men.	R.West Kent R.	Gum Boot Stores & Drying Shed at CHATEAU, K.24.c.5.7.	

4 men R.West Kent Off. 7.00 17'Div April 3.00 AM 21 & APM 52'Div YPRES.

S.H. Sn H.
Staff Captain,
52nd. Infantry Brigade.

20th.December 1917.

Warning Order.

1. The Battalion will be leaving present camp at 3.30 p.m. to day.

2. (a) All blankets will be rolled and dumped at Batt. dump by ~~1pm~~ 1.30 p.m. ~~also~~

(b) Officers may take up a small bundle. These bundles will be dumped at Batt. dump by 1.30 p.m.

(c) Each Coy. & H.Q. may take up one mess box only. These will ~~also~~ be dumped by 2 p.m.

(d) Any spare stuff must be packed & dumped by 1.30 p.m.

(e) See over

(f) Each of Coy. & H.Q. will send an Officer & 6 men to ~~unpack the limbers~~ load. The Officers should make sure that everything is placed on the proper limbers as some of the limbers will be going to the Line & others to Echelon B.

(g) The R.S.M. will superintend the loading.

22/12/17.

James Wild
Lieut. 1/4 Roy. North Lancs.

(e) Lewis guns will be dumped at Battn dump at 1-30 PM and loaded under the supervision of 2n Lt C M Holmes. Each Coy will detail 2 men to accompany their Lewis guns.

SECRET.   Copy No...

52ND INFANTRY BRIGADE O.O.NO.214.

Ref Maps
Sheet 57.c.,
1/40,000.
                                                                            21st December 1917.

1.   The 52nd Infantry Brigade will relieve the 177th Infantry Brigade in the line on the night 22/23rd instant.

2.   Movements from the OLD BRITISH LINE and HINDENBURGH line will be carried out in accordance with attached Table.

3.   2 Guides per Battalion Headquarters, 1 per Company and 1 per Platoon will report at respective Headquarters of Units at 2.0 p.m. 22nd instant.

4.   1 Officer per Company, Nos. 1 of Lewis Guns and a proportion of N.C.Os. per Company will proceed into the line on the morning of the 22nd instant to learn the situation and take over Stores etc., and will remain there until arrival of respective Companys.
      Intelligence Officers will also take over all details during daylight on the 22nd instant.

5.   Battalion Commanders will take over Defence Schemes, the Work in hand and the general policy of work.

6.   The formation of a Brigade School will be notified later.

7.   Battalions will be prepared to supply 25 men each to the 93rd Field Company, R.E. on Dec. 23rd for work. (for tomo)

8.   Brigade Headquarters will close at K.32.c.7.9. at 3.0 pm. 22nd instant and reopen at same time at G.3.d.3.2.

9.   Machine Gun Company will take over from 177th Machine Gun Company on the night 23rd/24th under Instructions to be issued later by D.M.G.O., 17th Divn.

10.   Completion of Relief will be reported to Brigade Headquarters in B.A.B. Code.

11.   ACKNOWLEDGE. ✓

Issued at 8.30 a.m.

Copy No 1 to Bde.H.Q.   15 to Supply Officer.
        2 to War Diary.   16 to No.4 Coy.Train.
        3 to G.O.C.   17 to 17th Division.
        4 to Bde.Major.   18 to 177th Inf.Bde.
        5 to Staff Captain.
        6 to O.C., Signals.
        7 to B.T.O.
        8 to Lan. Fus.
        9 to W.Rid. Regt.
     ✓ 10 to R.W.Kent Regt.
       11 to March. Regt.
       12 to M.G.Coy.
       13 to T.M.Bty.
       14 to 52nd F.Ambce.

                                        M.C.Morgan
                                        Captain,
                                        Brigade Major,
                                        52nd Infantry Brigade.

MOVEMENT TABLE issued with O.O.NO.214.

Ser. No.	Date.	UNIT.	In relief of.	SECTOR.	Time of start.	ROUTE.	REMARKS.
1.	22/23.	Lan.Fus.	4th Lincolns.	Left front sub-sector.	3.30 pm.	Platoon guides will lead Battalion Headquarters and Platoons by the usual Tracks.	Intervals of 1.. yards will be maintained between Platoons. Machine Gun Company will send Nos. 1 of each Section and a proportion of Officers into the line on 22nd inst. to learn situation and remain until arrival of guns.
2.	22/23.	W.Rid.R.	4th Leciesters.	Right front sub-sector.	3.45 pm.		
3.	22/23.	K.W.Kent R.	5th Lincolns.	Left support.	3.30 pm.		
4.	22/23.	march.R.	5th Leciesters.	Right "	3.45 pm.		
5.	23/24.	M.G.Coy.		As for 177th Brigade.	Notified later.		
6.	22/23.	T.M.Bty.		do.	3. 0 pm.		
7.	22/23.	Bde.H.Q.	177th Bde.H.Q.	H.Q. at Q.3.d.3.2.	2. 0 pm.		

SECRET.   Copy No. 8

3/4th. Battn. Royal West Kent Regiment.

ORDERS NO. 18.

30-12-17.

1. General Relief.	The Battalion will relieve the 7th. Battn. Border Regt. in Front line of Right Sub-Sector to-night.
2. Detailed Relief.	"A" Company will relieve "B" Coy., Border Regt., on Right front Company Sector. "D" Company will relieve "C" Coy., Border Regt., in Left front Company Sector. "B" Coy. relieves R.S. Coy., Border Regt., A. "C" Coy. relieves L.S. Coy., do. do., D.
3. March Details.	Leading Company will pass starting point, F.8.A.5.8., at 1.15 p.m.(Corps Signals). Order of March :- "D", "A", "B", "C" Intervals of 100 yards to be maintained between platoons. Route :- Bertincourt, Ruyantcourt, Plank Road, from F.17.D., continued through Havrincourt Wood. Guides :- One Guide per Coy.H.Q., one guide per platoon and 1 guide for H.Q., will meet Battalion on the Square, Havrincourt at 3.30 p.m. Dress :- Fighting Order with overcoat en bandoliere round haversack. Leather Coats will be worn. Transport :- 2 Limbers with Coy. Stores, Lewis Guns, etc. will march behind Coy. 1 Limber and Mess Cart behind H.Q. Transport will report to H.Q. & Coys. at 11.30 a.m. for loading. Officers' Valises :- Mess Cart for Valises 11.30 a.m. sharp, at Battn. H.Q.
4. Relief Complete.	Relief Complete notified by Code as follows :- "A" - Alright. "B" - Bon. "C" - Compy. "D" - Duty.
5. Details of Work.	Details of work in hand to be taken over from opposite number and continued to-night. Work report daily with Situation.
6. Rations.	Unexpended portion to be carried on the man.
7. Positions.	R. A. P. K. 16. d. 9. 1. B. H. Q. K. 15. d. 9. 1.
8.	ACKNOWLEDGE.

2nd-Lieut. & Assistant Adjutant,
3/4th.Battn.Royal West Kent Regiment.

Issued at 12.10 p.m.

Copies to :-
1. O. C. "A" Coy.   6. Q. M.
2. O. C. "B" Coy.   7. C. O.
3. O. C. "C" Coy.   8. W. D.
4. O. C. "D" Coy.   9. File.
5. T. O.

On His Majesty's Service.

WAR DIARY

JANUARY - 1918.

4'6TH. BRIGADE R.F.A. Volume XXXlll.

47TH. BRIGADE R.F.A. Volume XXXlll

14TH. DIV'L. AMMUN. COLUMN. Volume XXXlll.

X/14, Y/14, Z/14 & V/14 TRENCH MORTAR BATTERIES.

3/c R W Kent R!
Vol 8
Jan 1916

Army Form C. 2118.

WAR DIARY
or
INTELLIGENCE SUMMARY

(Erase heading not required.)

Army Form C. 2118.

Month: January 1918

Unit: 3/4th Batt. Royal West Kent Regt.

Place	Date	Hour	Summary of Events and Information	Remarks and references to Appendices
	3/1/18		a/Major N.T. MONCKTON proceeded to Senior Officers Course Aldershot. No march. Hg Strength.	
GRAINCOURT	4/1/18		Coys & Hds attended 2nd in Command of Battalion returned. Hg Strength. Officers 41 O.R. 847. Left PLESQUERES at 12 noon to take over line of Right Sub Section front Grainville trenches. Relief as per schedule two K.33.a.c.D	ORDERS ATTACHED MARKED A
	8/1/18		Battalion relieved the forward battalion in Right Sub Sect Grainville front line. 1 Guards O.R. killed. M.G. tornado (104th R.I.R.) 9 wounds taken by A Coy.	ORDERS ATTACHED MARKED B
	11/1/18			
	13/1/18		52nd Infantry Brigade relieved the 50 Infantry Brigade Battalion relieved by 1/4 Dorset in Right front sub section. The Battalion proceeded by March route to GRODI CAMP VELU.	ORDERS ATTACHED MARKED C

E. James LIEUT.
Comdg. 3/4th Batt. R.W. Kent Regt.

WAR DIARY
or
INTELLIGENCE SUMMARY

(Erase heading not required.) 1st Battn Royal West Kent Regt

January 1918. Army Form C. 2118.

Place	Date	Hour	Summary of Events and Information	Remarks and references to Appendices
N.E. of HERMIES	19/20/1/18		52nd Infantry Brigade relieves the 57th Infantry Bde in Left Sector Divisional Front. The Battalion relieved 7 Lincolns Right in Support.	ORDERS MARKED D.
	23/24/1/18		The Battalion relieved the Lancashire Fus in Left Sector. A & D Companies in Lancashire Front line. B & C Coy support. At Hermies American Army attached for Instruction to Battalion from 14th Jany to 26th Jany 1918. Major Warren joins the Battalion.	ORDERS ATTACHED MARKED E.
SPOIL HEAD J.35.D.	27/28/1/18		The Battalion relieved by the Lancashire Fusiliers & moves to Reserve and Spoil Heap at J.35.D.	ORDERS ATTACHED MARKED F.
	31/1/1/18		The 52nd Infantry Brigade relieved on the left sector of the Divisional Front & moves into Divisional Res. The Battalion relieved by 6th Dorset Regiment. Proceeds by March Route to PHIPPS CAMP.	ORDERS ATTACHED MARKED G.
PHIPPS CAMP			Battalion Strength Officers 35 O.R. 729. Killed 2 Wounded 5	

ORDERS
A

Secret. 3rd Bn Royal Berkshire Regt. Copy N° 8
                                      4.1.18

             Operation Orders
                  N° 18
             ─────

Relief 1 The Battn will be relieved
          to-night by the Lancashire Fusiliers.

Details 1 "A" Coy will be relieved by "B" Coy
Relief   Lancashire Fus
          "B" Coy by "A" Coy Lancs Fus
          "C" "   " "C" "   "   "
          "D" "   " "D" "   "   "
          Battn will then proceed to OLD
          BRITISH FRONT LINE

Guides 2 Guides for the incoming Battn will
          be required as follows:—
          1 NCO & 3 men from each Coy &
          1 NCO from BHQ, & will report at
          Bn HQ at 1.30 pm today. These
          guides will then be taken by
          our MONCKTON to present location
          of Lancs Fus. OC Coys will
          insure that all their guides are
          quite certain of their routes from
          HAVRINCOURT to their Coys.

SHEET 2.

Lewis Guns   3. Lewis Gun limbers will meet
                 Companies at cross roads K.27.d.4.7
                 just south of HAVRINCOURT town
                 Square. Lewis Guns & ammunition
                 will be carried as far as this.
                 Lieut FLEMING will detail a
                 NCO to superintend loading of
                 Battn Lewis Guns.

Maxonocin Packs
Mess Boxes   4. Maxonocin Packs & Mess Boxes for
                 A & D Coys will be sent to B.H.Q
                 by 3.45pm via GEORGE ST.
                 B & C Coys will be sent to
                 same rendezvous as for Lewis
                 Guns limbers by 5.0pm. O.C "C" Coy
                 will detail a NCO to take charge
                 of Mess Boxes which must not be
                 sent away from front line till
                 after 4.0pm.

Relief   5. Before leaving the line each
complete   Coy will report relief complete
                  as follows:-
                        A Coy   PUSH
                        B "   ICE
                        C "   WATTY
                        D "   STREAK
                  & will then march back

SHEET 3.

(Cont) 5. independently to new positions in BRIGADE RESERVE

Guides for new Location
6. Each Company & HQ will detail 1 NCO & 1 Runner to report to BHQ 9.30am this morning. Lieut FLEMING will take this party to present location of 1st/1st Ins. & will take over from & quote number. He will then leave 1 NCO & runner to remain in new location to meet companies on arrival, & return to Battn. with remainder of party, who will act as guides to their Coys to new location on completion of relief.

Petrol Tins
7. All empty water tins will be carried by Companies to their new location.

Trench Stores
8. OC Coys will obtain duplicate receipts for all Trench Stores handed over & send in to the Adjutant by 9.0 am the following morning.

Rations
9. Rations for 5th not at new positions. Coys will arrange to draw on arrival. Companies will also

SHEET 4

Coy HQ : detail parties to unload L.G. +
            hiraonm Packs.

Lewis Guns. Companies will arrange to mount
             Lewis Guns for AA defence by
             dawn 5th inst.

It is hoped that cookers will be at new
location with hot food for Coys on their
arrival.
Arrival in new position to be notified
to Bn H Q at K.32 c 7.7.

ACKNOWLEDGE

                                        [signature]
                                        2/Lieut
Issued a: Asst Adjt
                                        HUGE

Copies to :-
    1   C.O
    2-5 Rifle Coys.
    6   2/ Lt MONCKTON
    7   2/ Lt FLEMING
    8   W D

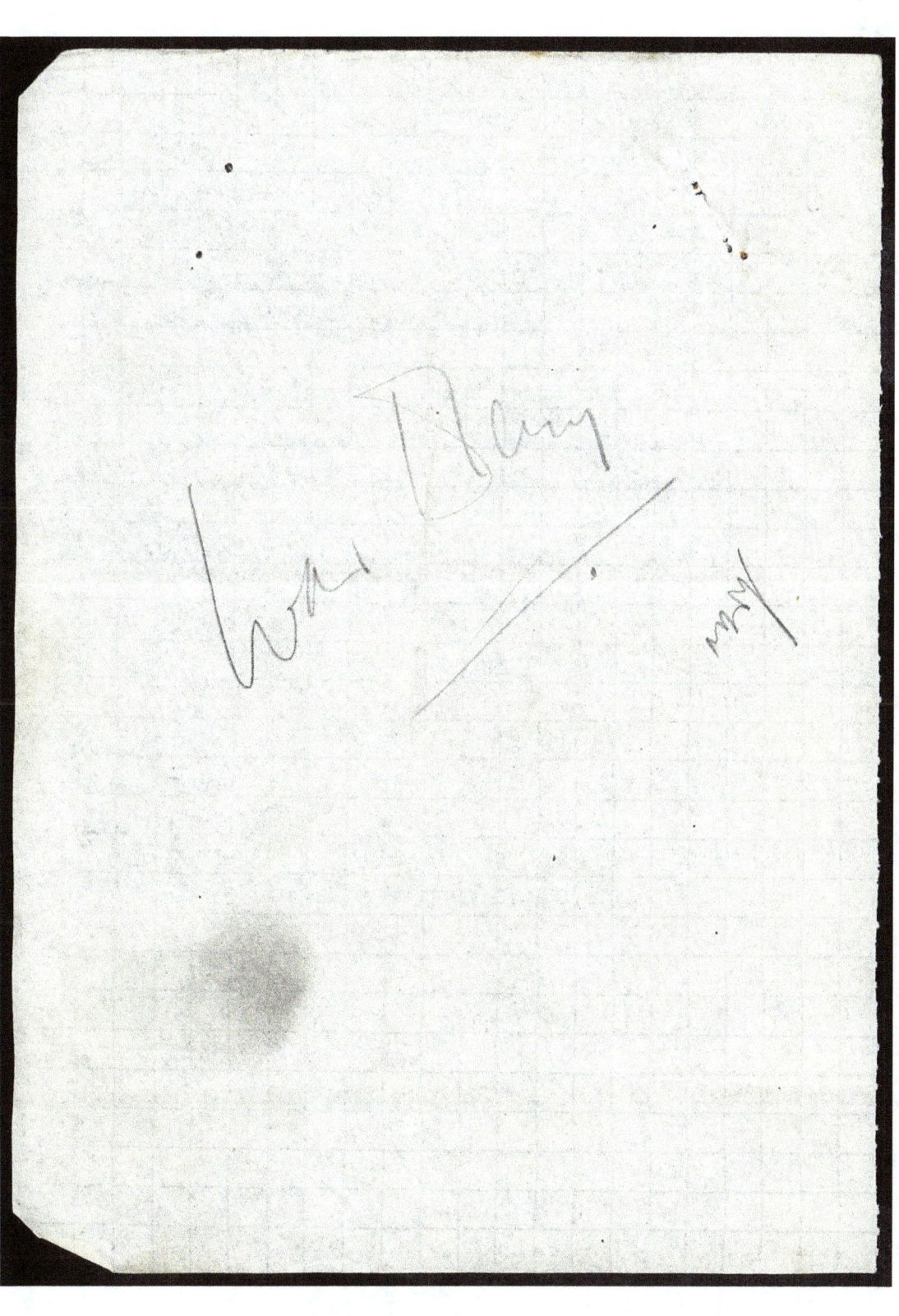

SECRET.   Copy No. 8

52ND INFANTRY BRIGADE O.O. NO. 217.

Ref Map
17th Div.T.1.,
1/10,000.
                                         2nd January 1918.

1. The following inter-Battalion Reliefs will take place on the Night, 4/5th January :-

2. The 10th Lancashire Fusiliers will relieve the 3/4th Royal West Kent Regiment in the RIGHT Front Sub-Sector (Headquarters at K.15.d.5.1.)
The 9th West Riding Regiment will relieve the 12th Manchester Regiment in the LEFT Front Sub-Sector. (Headquarters at K.15.d.8.3.)

3. Details of Relief will be made direct between Os. C. concerned.

4. On Relief, the 12th Manchester Regiment will move back into Brigade Support in TANK TRENCH and TANK SUPPORT and occupy accommodation vacated by 9th West Riding Regiment.
The 3/4th Royal West Kent Regiment will move back into Brigade Reserve in OLD BRITISH FRONT LINE., K.32.a.,c. and d., and occupy accommodation vacated by 10th Lancashire Fusiliers.

5. All DEFENCE SCHEMES, SPECIAL MAPS, AIR PHOTOS and TRENCH STORES will be handed over on Relief.
Duplicate RECEIPTS will be taken and a copy forwarded to Brigade Headquarters by 12.0 Noon, 5th instant.

6. All details of WORK in progress, and contemplated and all WORKING PARTIES supplied will be carefully handed over to relieving Units.

7. On completion of Reliefs, the 9th West Riding Regiment will extend the LEFT Boundary Northwards and take over the Front held by the 10th Sherwood Foresters as far as K.10.a.80.25.
This extension will be completed by Midnight, 4/5th.

8. Details will be arranged direct between O.C., 9th West Riding Regiment and O.C., 10th Sherwood Foresters. (Headquarters, K.9.c.30.15.)

9. Completion of Reliefs will be reported to Brigade Headquarters by the Code words "ONCE AGAIN".
Completion of extension by 9th West Riding Regiment will be reported by the Code word "EXTEND".

10. ACKNOWLEDGE.

Issued at 8.30 pm.

Copy No. 1 to Bde.H.Q.   No.9 to Manch. R.
       2 to War Diary.   10 to M.G.Coy.
       3 to Staff Capt.   11 to T.M.Bty.
       4 to O.C., Sigs.   12 to 50th Inf.Bde.
       5 to B.T.O.   13 to 51st Inf.Bde.
       6 to Lan. Fus.   14 to 17th Div.
       7 to W.Rid. Regt. 15 to 77th F.Coy.R.E.
       8 to R.W.Kent Regt. 16 to 78th F.Coy.R.E.
                                   17 to 93rd F.Coy.R.E.

J.R. Lindley
Capt.,
A/Bde. Major,
52nd Inf.Bde.

Guide for Transport arrange

unloading party

Instruction to QM Guides for T. [illegible]

Off & NCO [illegible] take

over OBL from L.T.

Gen Reif

Detailed Reif

All Patrol Comm 1 per Coy HQ

Guides for L.T. & HQ 1 per Platoon. metal?

Blankets

March

Salvage Coy

Returns of Stores

Coys to arrange for Mess Stores

Report H.Q. by letter A.B.C.D

Sigs. to take over

SgtBett — [illegible] Lemon!

Carthew

ORDERS
B

Secret   Copy N. 1

3/4 Royal West Kent Regt
Operation Orders No 19
                                          7/1/18

Relief   1   The Battn will relieve the 15th
              Bn Lancs Fus in the Right Front
              Sub-Sector Divisional Area
              on the night 8/9th inst.
              The Divisional Front is now
              being held by 2 Brigades with
              1 Brigade in Divisional Reserve
              at HAPLINCOURT.
              The Manchester Regt will be on
              our left & 1st Brigade on our
              Right Boundary.

Detailed 2. Battn dispositions on completion
Relief   of relief will be as follows:-
                  Left Front   A Company
                  Right "   D   "
                  Left Support   B   "
                  Right "   C   "
              The Battn will move from present
              position in following order of march
              with 100 yards intervals between
              Platoons & companies
                      A Company
                   D   "
                      B   "
                      C Headquarters

SHEET. 2.

Cont'd 2. Head of column to move off at 4.0 p.m.

Guides 3. Guides from Lancs Fus will be at starting point (on road by Batt'n cookers) before companies move off. 1 per platoon & 1 per Batt Headquarters.

Dress 4 Fighting Order, overcoats & leathern jerkins

Reconnaissance 5. Each Coy will send 1 Officer at 2.0 p.m. to take over and reconnoitre dispositions in Company sectors. These Officers will make sketches of dispositions & hand them over to their Company Commanders on arrival.

Transport 6 1 Limber per Company & 1 per Batt'n H.Q, which will bring up rations & water from "B" Echelon, will be available for companies to carry Lewis Guns, Mayoun Packs, Dixies & Mess Boxes.
Each Company will detail

SHEET 3

Cont'd 6. 2 guides to conduct limbers to respective Company Dumps. T.O. will also arrange Transport to take Officers Valises & Blankets back to B Echelon. Also horses to take back Cookers & Water cart.

Trench Stores 7. O.C. Coys will obtain receipts of all stores taken over & send copies in duplicate with morning papers to B.H.Q. on the 9th inst.

Work Programme 8. Work for first night in the line will be handed over to O.C. coys by the outgoing Coy commanders of the Lancs Fus.

Cooking Hot Food 9. Each Coy will take 2 Cooks into the line to carry on cooking arrangements as before.

Location of B.H.Q. 10. K15 d.9.2 (100 yards north of position occupied by B.H.Q. last time.
R.A.P. will be as before.

SHEET 4

Completion of Relief 11. By code word to BHQ as follows:-

A Coy	PUSH	
B "	SIXPENCE	
C "	LORNE	
D "	~~LORNE~~ FIJI	

11 ACKNOWLEDGE

Issued at   pm

J.H.Burnham
2/Lieut
Actg Adjt
HUGE

Copies to :-
1. C O
2. 10th Bn Lancs Fus
3-6. All Coys
7. I O
8. W D

These orders must not be taken into Front line

"C" Form.
MESSAGES AND SIGNALS.

Army Form C. 2123.
(In books of 100.)
No. of Message _____

Prefix ____ Code ____ Words ____
£   s.   d.
Charges to Collect
Service Instructions

Received. From ____ By ____

Sent, or sent out. At ____ m. To ____ By ____

Office Stamp.

Handed in at NSY   Office 8.0? m.   Received 8/?P m.

TO Huge

Sender's Number	Day of Month	In reply to Number	A A A
DHX 44	7		
Return	B0215	AA	for night
8/9th	jam	road	night
9/10th	AM	ends	ack
		ok	
		6104	

FROM PLACE & TIME NusR

* This line should be erased if not required.

S.E.C.R.E.T.   Copy No....

52ND INFANTRY BRIGADE O.O. NO. 218.

Ref Maps
1 7th Div.T.2.,
1/10,000
57.C. N.E.,
1/20,000.
                                                    7th January 1916.

1.   The following Inter-battalion Reliefs will take place on the night - 8/9th January.

2.   (a)   The ROYAL WEST KENT REGIMENT will relieve the LANCASHIRE FUSILIERS in the Right Front Sub-sector. The LANCASHIRE FUSILIERS, on Relief, will come back into Brigade SUPPORT, occupying positions vacated by the MANCHESTER REGIMENT.

  (b)   The MANCHESTER REGIMENT will relieve the WEST RIDING REGIMENT in the Left Front Sub-sector. The WEST RIDING REGIMENT will move back into Brigade RESERVE on Relief, occupying positions vacated by the ROYAL WEST KENT REGIMENT.

3.   All details of Relief will be arranged direct between Os. C. concerned.

4.   PATROLLING will not be interfered with.

5.   SECTOR MAPS, DEFENCE SCHEMES, all AIR PHOTOS., ANTI-GAS and Trench STORES will be handed over and duplicate RECEIPTS taken, one copy of which will be forwarded to Brigade Headquarters by Noon - 9th instant.

6.   All details of WORK in progress, and contemplated, and all WORKING PARTIES supplied will be carefully handed over to opposite numbers.

7.   Completion of Relief will be reported to Brigade Headquarters by the Code words - "NIL RETURN".

8.   ACKNOWLEDGE.

Issued at 7.0 am.

Copy No 1 to Bde.H.Q.
        2 to War Diary.
        3 to Staff Captain.
        4 to O.C. Sigs.
        5 to B.T.O.
        6 to Lan. Fus.
        7 to W.Rid. Regt.
        8 to R.W.Kent Regt.
        9 to Manch. Regt.
        10 to M.G.Coy.
        11 to T.M.Bty.
        12 to 50th Inf.Bde.
        13 to 51st Inf.Bde.
        14 to 17th Division.
        15 to 77th F.Coy.,R.E.
        16 to 78th F.Coy.,R.E.
        17 to 93rd F.Coy.,R.E.

F.M.Rindley Captain,
A/Brigade Major,
52nd Infantry Brigade.

ORDERS
Cº

Secret   7th Royal West Kent Regt   Copy No 8
            Operation Orders No 20
                                               13/7/18

Relief 1. The 50th INFANTRY BRIGADE will relieve the 57nd Inf Bde in the Right Sub Sector Divisional Area tonight 13/14th Augt. The Battn will be relieved by the 6th Battn DORSET REGT & Companies as follows:-

    "C" Coy by A Coy 6th Dorset Regt
     B   -"-   D   -"-
     D   -"-   B   -"-
     A   -"-   C   -"-

Guides 2. Two Guides per BHQ, 1 per Coy HQ & 1 per Platoon will report to Battn HQ by 2.30pm with full instructions.
One Guide per Company also to be detailed to guide transport of incoming Battn to respective Coy Dumps. These will report with other guides to BHQ at 2.30pm.
2/Lt BROADBENT will report to BHQ at 2.0pm & march guides down to J 36 b 9 2 & appoint them to their respective Companies of incoming Unit.

SHEET 2

No 1 Lewis Gun Teams

3. No 1's of Lewis Gun Teams of incoming Unit will report to Companies during the afternoon to get familiar with Lewis Gun posts during the hours of daylight.

Trench Stores

4. OC Coys will obtain receipts for all stores handed over & send copies in duplicate to B.H.Q in new area by 9.0am 14th inst.

Transport

5. (a) PETROL TINS. All Petrol Tins will be carried by Companies until met by limbers at point on HAVRINCOURT — HERMIES Road, 300 yards from road junction at K 27 d 3-7

(b) MARSOUIN PACKS will be carried by Companies to same rendezvous.

(c) Box Mess Boxes will be sent to Bn H Q by 3.30pm

(d) Gum Boots. Every man will wear his Gum Boots & carry ankle boots. These will be changed at the rendezvous 300 yards from road junction

SHEET 3

Cont' 5 (d) at K 27 d 3 7 where OC Coys
& Lieut L.R.S. MONCKTON for HQ
will hand over all Gum Boots
to Cpl Gray, who will carefully
examine to see that ankle
straps are securely fastened
to all boots, & give receipts
to O C Coys for Total received.
Cpl Gray will see to loading
of Gum Boots on G S Wagon
waiting there & return with
them to Gum Boot store
HAVRINCOURT & obtain receipt
for total handed in. He will
then return with G S Wagon
to Transport Lines.

Coy Commanders must take
great care to return every pair
issued to them. An explanatory
note will be required for G O C
in the case of any shortage.

(e) LEWIS GUNS will be carried by
Companies to rendezvous, 300
yards from road junction at
K 27 d 3-7 where limbers will
be waiting.

Relief 6. Completion of relief will be
Complete notified to H Q as follows:-

Cont'd 6.
SHEET 4
A   PUSH
B   SIXPENCE
C   LOTTIE
D   FIJI

March 7. (a) On completion of relief, Coys will march back independently to GROP1 Camp at I.29.d.8.3 – 500 yds SW of LEBUCQUIÈRE

(b) Route HAVRINCOURT, PLANK ROAD, through HAVRINCOURT WOOD, RUYAULCOURT & cross roads at P.2.d.0.3. 100 yards interval will be maintained between platoons to the cross roads at P.17.d.

(c) Guides from B Echelon will meet Companies at cross roads EAST of BERTINCOURT at P.2.d.0.3

Arrival in new camp will be notified to Battn H.Q.

Cookers 8. Cookers with hot tea rum & food will meet Companies at cross roads P.17.d.

SHEET 5

Advance 9. Each Company may send
Party.   advance party of 1 N.C.O
          + 2 men. These to report
          to B.H.Q by 10.0 am

       10 ACKNOWLEDGE

13-1-18   J. Moulton
                                      2/Lieut
Issued at   am   Acty Adjt
                                       HUGE
Copies to:-
       1 C.O
    2-5 All Coys
       6 Q.M
       7 2/Lieut BROADBENT
       8 W.D.

S E C R E T.   Copy No.

52ND INFANTRY BRIGADE O.O. NO. 220.

Ref Map
DEMICOURT,
1/10,000.
57 C.,
1/40,000.

11th January 1918.

1. The 52nd Infantry Brigade will be relieved in the Right Sector, by the 50th Infantry Brigade, on the night - 13/14th.

2. The Relief will take place in accordance with attached Table.
On Relief, the 52nd Infantry Brigade will take over the accommodation vacated by the 50th Infantry Brigade, and will be in Divisional Reserve.

3. 2 Guides per Battalion Headquarters, 1 per Company Headquarters, and 1 Guide for each Platoon will be detailed for relieving Units.

4. Advance Parties for Units of 52nd Infantry Brigade will proceed to their respective destinations on the morning of the 13th instant.

5. All DEFENCE SCHEMES, WORK in hand, GENERAL POLICY, AIR PHOTOS and Trench STORES will be handed over.

6. Details of Relief will be arranged direct between Os.C. concerned.

7. Completion of Reliefs will be notified by PRIORITY wire to Brigade Headquarters in B.A.B. Code.

8. Command of the RIGHT Sector will pass from G.O.C., 52nd Infantry Brigade to G.O.C., 50th Infantry Brigade at 10.0 am. on 14th instant.

9. On Relief, the MANCHESTER REGIMENT will be accommodated at the SPOIL HEAP - J.34 c.9.1., and will be employed on work in the "Battle Zone" - under the C.E., 5th Corps. Work to commence from the 14th instant. This Battalion will be at the tactical disposal of G.O.C., LEFT Brigade, and will, in case of urgency, receive Orders from him direct.

10. ACKNOWLEDGE.

Issued at 9.30 pm.

Copy No. 1 to Bde.H.Q.
         2 to War Diary.
         3 to Staff Capt.
         4 to O.C.,Sigs.
         5 to B.T.O.
         6 to Lan. Fus.
         7 to W.Rid. Regt.
         8 to R.W.Kent Regt.
         9 to Man.h. Regt.
        10 to M.G.Coy.
        11 to T.M.Bty.
        12 to 50th Inf.Bde.
        13 to 51st Inf.Bde.
        14 to 56th Inf.Bde.
        15 to 93rd F.Coy.,R.E.
        16 to O.C.,Supplies.
        17 to No. 4 Coy. Train.
        18 to 17th Division.

J.R. Lindley Captain,
A/Brigade Major,
52nd Infantry Brigade.

P. T. O.

MARCH TABLE issued with 52ND INFANTRY BRIGADE O.O. NO. 220.

Ser. No.	UNIT	DATE	FROM	TO	Relieved by.	ROUTE	REMARKS
1.	March.	JAN. 13/14th.	Left Front Line.	SLAG HEAP. J.35.a.4.	E.Yorks.	Via South side of CANAL. Crossing at J.34.d.	Guides to be at J.36.b.9.2. on Road S. of CANAL - 4 pm.
2.	E.W.Kent R.	13/14th.	Right Front Line.	GROA/CAMP. I.29.d.8.3.	Dorsets.	Via South side of CANAL, RUYAULCOURT. - BERTINCOURT.	Guides to be at J.36.b.9.2. on Road S.side of CANAL - 5pm.
3.	Lan.Fus.	13/14th.	Support.	SAUNDERS CP., 0.4.c.8.8.	W.Yorks.	As for Ser. No. 2.	Guides to be at J.36.b.9.2. on Road S. side of CANAL - 6 pm.
4.	W.Rid.R.	13/14th.	Reserve.	PHIPPS CAMP. 0.6.c.8.4.	Yorks.	Via PLANK ROAD, RUYAULCOURT - BERTINCOURT.	Guides on arrival at destination.
5.	M.G. Coy.	13/14th.	Line.	SAUNDERS CP. 0.4.c.8.8.	50th M.G.C.	As for Ser. No. 4.	Relief to be complete as far as possible by daylight.
6.	T. M.Bty.	13/14th.	Line.	-do-	50th T.M.B.	As for Serials Nos. 2 & 3.	Relief to be complete as far as possible by daylight. Pieces will be exchanged.
7.	Bde. H.Q.	14th.	J.36.b7.4.	0.4.d.8.7.	50th Bde.H.Q.	CANAL to CROSSROADS, J.34.d.6.6. BERTINCOURT - 0.4.d.8.7.	

THE USUAL INTERVALS WILL BE MAINTAINED&

11/1/1918.

P.T.O.

ANNEXE to 17 Div. Summary No. 20.

Report on preliminary examination of prisoner of 104 R.I.R. 24 Res. Div. captured near FLESQUIERES (K.11.d.) this morning, 11th. January.

※※※※※※※※※

Prisoner, a Saxon native of CHEMNITZ, lost his way while going for coffee and wandered into our lines. The 24 Res. Div. is still holding its normal Sector of the line, and its order of Battle remains the same, viz :-   133)
                                                      104) R.I.R., 24 Res. Div.
                                                     107)

There is no talk of a Divisional relief.

Prisoner has heard nothing of any impending German attack on our front. His Battalion, the 3rd., had been in the line 8 days, companies alternating their positions every few days. The resting Bn. (2nd.) was in CAMBRAI. Prisoner could not give the position of the Battalions in Support.

His own Company was disposed in depth between the Sunken Radd (GRAINCOURT - LA JUSTICE) and the outpost line, which was stated to be approx. 500 yards from our line and 1,000 yards from the Sunken Road. The outpost line consists of small groups of the enemy disposed in shellholes, and is held both by day and by night.

Prisoner's Coy., had 6 Light M.Gs.

When in the Sunken Road, prisoner lived in cubby holes dug into the bank. There are 3 dugouts in the road, each capable of holding about 20 men and the Pioneers are constructing two more at the present moment.

Prisoner states that trenches are to be dug West of the Sunken Road and that the Pioneers (18th. Bn.) have already erected wire along the line of the trenches. (Confirmed by aeroplane photos.)

The Sunken Road is used by horse transport as far as the dugouts which are stated to be a short distance from the CROSS ROADS (LA JUS-TICE).

The route to the trenches from CAMBRAI was along the main road as far as FONTAINE, and thence across country by by-roads.

A direct hit on a cellar in ANNEUX a few weeks ago, when prisoner's company was there, had caused many casualties.

Prisoner "spent Christmas Day joyfully in CAMBRAI."

※※※※※※

- 2 -

12. OTHER UNITS SEEN.
Elements of the II/12th and of the 18th Pioneer Battalions have been seen by prisoner in FONTAINE AND CAMBRAI respectively. The 3rd and 4th Reserve Pioneer Coys. of the II/12th Pioneer Battn. belong to the 24th Reserve Division. One Coy. of the 18th Pioneer Battn. belongs to the 9th Reserve Division, believed to be resting in the CAMBRAI area.

Before Christmas, prisoner had seen a party of 50 men of the 52nd R.I.R., 107th Division in CAMBRAI.

13. GAS
Prisoner stated he had never experienced gas in any form either on the Russian or Western front. His Division was not afraid of gas and knew very little about it. There was no gas training and no special orders about wearing the mask in the ready position (Hoohste Bereitschaft). Although it was supposed to take the German soldier 2 seconds to adjust his mask from the ready position, he could not do it himself under 2 minutes. It took him 5 minutes to put on his mask from the slung position. He did not think that the others in his Battalion were any quicker than he was.

(From G.H.Q. Summary).

DISTRIBUTION OF THE ENEMY'S FORCES.
21st Res. Div.
According to a report, the 21st Res. Div., from South-West of CAMBRAI, was resting in the GHENT area on the 3rd January. Confirmation is required.

German Contingent in PALESTINE.
The first contingent of German troops which has reinforced the PALESTINE front appears to be organised as a mixed formation of all arms, known as Pascha 2, commanded by Colonel von Frankenberg, and consisting of three composite columns numbered 701, 702, and 703.
Each of these three columns consists of the following units :-
Infantry Battalion.   Close-range gun detachment.
Machine Gun Company.   Field artillery detachment.
Cavalry Troops.   Pioneer detachment.
Trench Mortar detachment.

Artillery Reinforcements for the Western Front.
(a) During the last fortnight of December, a certain number of trains containing artillery units are known to have entered Belgium from Germany. (See Summary No.898).
(b) It is reported that Austrian heavy batteries with tractors passed through DUISBURG towards CREFELD on the 30th December.
(c) It is estimated that, at the beginning of December, the German heavy artillery was distributed as follows :-
       Western Theatre .. .. .. 1,300 batteries.
       Eastern Theatre .. .. .. 470 batteries.
Since the middle of October, a number of artillery units are known to have arrived on the Western front, but it cannot yet be estimated how many batteries have actually been transferred.

The 1919 Class.
According to reliable information, a company of the 89th Grenadier Regiment (17th Div) received a draft of forty recruits of the 1919 Class at the beginning of December.
This is the first definite evidence which has been received of the drafting of the 1919 class in any considerable numbers, to infantry units on the Western front.

(ANNEXE TO V CORPS SUMMARY OF INTELLIGENCE 11/1/18)

EXAMINATION OF ONE PRIVATE OF THE 12th COY., 3rd BATTALION,
104th R.I.R., 24th RES. DIVISION.

1. METHOD OF CAPTURE.
Prisoner lost his way while carrying food from one post to another in the outpost line and wandered into our line in K.11.d.

2. ORDER OF BATTLE.
East to West .. .. 107th R.I.R.
104th R.I.R.
133rd R.I.R.

3. DISPOSITIONS.
The 104th R.I.R. has one Battalion in line, one Battalion in support, probably in dugouts in the CANTAING LINE and one Battalion resting in the Northern suburbs of CAMBRAI.
The Battalion in line has one Coy. in the outpost line holding the entire Battalion frontage. This appears to extend approx. 350 yards North Westwards from the bank at K.12.d.9.3. Two Coys. of the Battalion are in the Sunken Road in K.6.b. and L.1.c. One Coy. is in cellars in ANNEUX. The outpost line consists purely of rifle pits and organised shell-holes.

4. RELIEFS.
The 3rd Battalion has been in line 8 days and the 2nd Battn. is now in rest. Prisoner knew of no impending Divisional relief. There had been no rumours of this in the Regiment lately.

5. ROUTES TO TRENCHES.
The 3rd Battn. marched to the line through CAMBRAI and FONTAINE and then across country through F.20. - F.26.- L.1. (air photos show tracks here).

6. FIELD KITCHENS.
The Field Kitchens of the 3rd Bn. come to the Western end of FONTAINE F.15.c.85.15 at about 3.a.m. every morning.

7. STRENGTHS AND LOSSES.
12th Coy. 3rd Battn. Ration strength 150 - Trench strength about 100.
The 12th Coy. lost 13 men in a cellar in ANNEUX through a direct hit by a 6" shell. Apart from this losses since coming into the line on the 3rd January have been light.

8. DRAFTS.
The 3rd Bn. received a draft of 32 men from the 243rd R.I.R. 53rd Res. Division on the Eastern front just after Christmas.

9. MACHINE GUNS.
12th Coy. has 6 Light Machine Guns. The three extra guns were issued during the last period of rest.

10. DEFENCES.
The line along the GRAINCOURT - LA JUSTICE Road is known as the main line of resistance. At present owing to weather conditions more attention is being paid to wiring than to digging. All wiring is being carried out by the R.E. Three deep dugouts are under construction in the Sunken Road in L.1.c. (This is confirmed by aeroplane photos).

11. TRAFFIC ON ROADS.
Wagons carrying R.E. material come into ANNEUX nightly - they are unloaded at about F.25.a.3.5. There is very little traffic forward of ANNEUX.

P.T.

ORDERS
D

SECRET.   Copy No. 13.

3/4th. Battn. Royal West Kent Regiment.

OPERATION ORDERS 21.   18-1-18.

Relief. The 52nd. Infantry Brigade will relieve the 51st. Infantry Brigade in Left Brigade front on the night 19/20 January.
The Battalion will relieve the 7th. Lincoln Regt. in Left Support. Companies relieve opposite numbers.

March detail. Battalion will move from present Camp in following order of march :-

        "B" Company.
        "A"   "
        "C"   "
        "D"   "
        H.Q. "

Leading company to move off at 2.15 p.m., 200 yards being maintained between companies to entraining point VELU LOOP. J.25.d., where Battalion will entrain on small gauge Railway.

Entraining.

Detraining. Battalion will detrain at J.29.b.1.1.

Guides. 2 per Battn.H.Q., & 1 per Coy.H.Q., 1 per platoon will meet the Battn. at R.E. Dump, 29.b.3.0., at 4.30 p.m. 200 yards will be maintained between platoons from this point.

Dress. Fighting Order, Great Coats, Jerkins and water-proof sheets. Water Bottles full.
Gum Boots will be worn and Ankle Boots carried slung round the neck.

Transport. The Transport Officer will detail the following transport to report B.O.R. :-
11.30 a.m. limber to be loaded with Officers' Valises & blankets to be taken to "B" Echelon.
1. 0 p.m. limber to collect Marsouin Packs, Mess & Medical Comforts Boxes to be conveyed to the Line by rations limbers.
1.30 p.m. limber to transport Battn. Lewis Guns & Ammunition from present Camp to entraining point.
He will also arrange for removal of Orderly Room to "B" Echelon.

Trench Stores. 1 Officer, 1 N.C.O. per Coy., & Sergt. Belsey for H.Q. will report H.Q., 7th. Lincoln Regt. at 3.0 p.m. to take over Trench Stores from opposite Coy.

Work & Stores. Duplicate of Stores taken over will be sent in with morning papers on 20th instant.
Os.C. Coys. will take over work on hand.

Completion of Relief. Will be notified to Battn.H.Q. by the following Code :-
    "A" Coy.   Push.
    "B" " . Bill.
    "C" " . Lottie.
    "D" " . Dad.

OFFICERS' Valises, Blankets & Pack. To be ready for loading 11.30 a.m. Blankets will be rolled in bundles of 10, tied and labelled.

Marsouin Pack & Mess Boxes. To be ready for loading at 12.30 p.m.

Rations. Will be conveyed direct by Transport to respective dumps.

Entraining Officer. Major Waite will report to entraining point 40 minutes before train starts.
No. 2 Train,
6.30 p.m.

(See Sheet 2).

- 2 -

Camp. Os. C. Coys. will ensure that the present Camp is left scrupulously clean.

Runners.
1 H.Q. Runner will report to Os. C. Coys. before they move off.
2 Coy. Runners will return with this Runner to H.Q.

ACKNOWLEDGE.

J.K. Wenham
2nd-Lieut. & Acting Adjutant,
3/4th. Battn. Royal West Kent Regiment.

Issued at ____ p.m.

Copies to :-

1. C.O.
2. Major C.E. Waite.
3. M.O.
4. H.Q. Mess.
5. O.C. "A" Coy.
6. O.C. "B" Coy.
7. O.C. "C" Coy.
8. O.C. "D" Coy.
9. O.C. 7th. Lincoln Regt.
10. Q. M.
11. T. O.
12. R. S. M.
13. W. D.
14. File.

ORDERS
E

SECRET.   COPY No. 2

52ND INFANTRY BRIGADE O.O. NO. 221.

Ref Maps
MOEUVRES &
17th Div.T.S.
1/10,000.
                                                              17th January 1918.

1. The 52nd Infantry Brigade will relieve the 51st Infantry Brigade in the Line on the night - 19/20th January.
    Details of Relief will be arranged direct between Os. C. concerned.

2. 2 Guides per Battalion Headquarters, 1 per Company and 1 per Platoon will be detailed for the *relieving Unit*.

3. 1 Officer per Company, Nos. 1 of Lewis Guns, and a proportion of N.C.Os. per Company, will proceed into the Line on the morning of the 19th instant to learn the Situation and take over Stores, etc., and will remain there until arrival of respective Companys.
    Intelligence Officers will also take over all details during daylight on the 19th instant.

4. Battalion Commanders will take over Defence Schemes, the work in hand, and the general policy of work, also all Sector Maps and Air-photos.

5. Command of the Left Sector of the Divisional Front will pass from G.O.C., 51st Infantry Brigade to G.O.C., 52nd Infantry Brigade at 10.0 a.m. - January 20th.

6. Completion of Relief will be reported to Brigade Headquarters by the Code words "SETTLED IN MUD".

7. The 52nd Machine Gun Company will relieve the 51st Machine Gun Company on the night - 20/21st.
    Details of Relief to be arranged direct between Os. C. concerned.
    Nos. 1 of each Section and a proportion of Officers will proceed into the Line on the 19th instant to learn the Situation and remain until arrival of Guns.

8. The 12th Manchester Regiment will find the working party of 200 for C.E., Vth Corps on the 19th instant, and on completion of work will be accommodated at the SPOIL HEAP J.35.d.

9. The 52nd Brigade Sapping Platoon will relieve the 51st Brigade Sapping Platoon on the night - 19/20th.
    Details of Relief to be arranged direct between Os. C., Platoons.

10. ACKNOWLEDGE.

Issued at 5.0 am.

Copy No 1 to Bde.H.Q.   No. 9 to Manch. Regt.
       2 to War Diary.   10 to M.G.Coy.
       3 to Staff Capt.   11 to T.M.Bty.
       4 to D.C., Siege.   12 to 51st Inf.Bde.
       5 to S.T.O.   13 to 50th Inf.Bde.
       6 to Lan. Fus.   14 to Supply Officer.
       7 to W.Rid. Regt.   15 to No.4 Coy.Train.
       8 to R/W.Kent Regt.   16 to 17th Division.

                                                    Captain,
                                                    A/Brigade Major,
                                                    52nd Infantry Brigade.

                                                    P.T.O.

MOVEMENT TABLE issued with O.O.No.221.

Ser. No.	Date.	UNIT.	In relief of	Sector.	Time of start.	REMARKS.
1.	19/20. Jan.	Lan.Fus.	8th S.Staffords.	Left Front Sub-sector.	3.0 pm. from PHIPPS CAMP Siding.	By Light Railway to HERMIES. Guide to meet Unit at de-training Point – J.29.b.1.1. (approx) – 4.0 pm.
2.	do.	W.Rid.R.	10th Sherwood Foresters.	Right Front Sub-sector.	As Ser.No.1.	As for Serial No. 1.
3.	do.	R.W.Kent R.	6th Lincoln Regt.	Support.	3.30 pm. from PHIPPS CAMP Siding.	By Light Railway to HERMIES. Guides to meet Units at de-training Point Junction J.29.b.1.1. (approx) – 4.30pm.
4.	do.	March.R.	"	Reserve.	"	After completion of work, move into camp J.35.d. and be in Brigade Reserve.
5.	do.	T.M.Bty.	51st T.M.B.	Line.	3.30 pm. from PHIPPS CAMP Siding.	By Light Railway to HERMIES. Guide to meet Unit at de-training Point – 4.30 pm.
6.	20/21.	L.T.M.Coy.	51st M.G.C.	Line.	3.0 pm. from PHIPPS CAMP Siding.	If possible – by Light Railway to Loop 407 (F.14.b.central) Guide to meet Unit at de-training Point – 4.30pm. If Railway cannot be arranged – by March Route via HERMIES.

Units will move out of HERMIES with intervals of 200 yards between Platoons.

14/1/1918.

SECRET   3rd ROYAL WEST KENT REGT   Copy No 7
OPERATION ORDERS
No 22   23-1-18

1 Relief   The Battn will relieve the 15th Bn LAN FUS in LEFT BRIGADE SUB SECTOR tonight 23/24th inst.

2 Dispositions will be as ordered in WARNING ORDER issued on 21st inst.

3 Guides   From LAN FUS will report to OC Coys & Bn HQ at present HQ as follows:- 1 per Coy HQ, 1 for each platoon to report to B.HQ & Coy HQ at 5.0pm. Coys must be ready to move off at 5.15pm. These guides will conduct Coys to the respective Coy HQs of LAN FUS where they will be met by additional guides in the case of FRONT LINE Coys to guide platoons to their posts.
1 Guide for BHQ from LAN FUS will report at present BHQ at 5.30pm. Personnel from will be ready to move off at this hour.

4 Dumps   The RSM & ORs will proceed at 2.0pm to LAN FUS HQ to take over stores. Each Coy will send 1 Officer & 1 OR to the Coy of the LAN FUS whom they are relieving to take over TRENCH STORES by daylight.

SHEET 2

4 Coys. Duplicate receipts for all TRENCH STORES taken over will be forwarded to Bttlj[?]n[?] in morning papers of 24th inst.

5 H.Q RUNNERS. Lt MONCKTON will detail 4 H.Q runners to report to LAN FUS H.Q at 10.0am with a note to the O.C. of LAN Fus requesting that these runners be guided to Coy H.Qs of LAN FUS. These runners will return to present B.H.Q after having ascertained the whereabouts of Coy H.Q of LAN FUS.

6 RATION DUMPS For all Coys & B.H.Q will be at KILBIE[?]

7 RATIONS B & C Coys will supply Ration carrying parties as follows:-
B Coy 1 NCO + 15 men for A Coy
C "   1 NCO + 15   "   D "
In addition B & C Coys will supply their own Ration carrying parties. These parties will proceed to Ration Dump immediately on completion of relief. Ration parties of D & A Coys will also proceed to Dump to draw their rations & guide their parties back to their Coy H.Q.

SHEET 3.

8. PETROL TINS. All Coys will dump their empty tins in the new dump K14b1.5 before moving from present locations i.e. before 5.15pm

9. DEFENCE SCHEME. Coys will take over Defence Schemes from Companies whom they relieve.

10. PATROL & WORK orders will be issued later.

11. RELIEF. The W.Riding R⁺ will relieve Barton as present garrison. Representatives will be reporting to Bn H.Q. to take over Trench Stores. Duplicate receipts must be obtained.

12. SIGNALS. B. C. & D Coys will take Fullerphones up with them, & on no account will they be handed over. A Coy will take over Fullerphone from D Coy A & Q Bns in the line.

13. RELIEF COMPLETE will be reported as follows -
    A Coy   PUSH
    B   SIXPENCE
    C   LOTTIE.
    D   FIJI.

14. ACKNOWLEDGE

Arty Major

"wired at 11am
Requests:-
 1-4 All Coys
 5 10th Bn LANCASHIRE Fus
 6 H Q
 7 W I
 8 FILE

SECRET.   Copy No. 8

52ND INFANTRY BRIGADE O.O. NO. 222.

Ref Maps
17th Div.Maps
T.3., 1/10,000
MOEUVRES,
1/20,000.   22nd Jany. 1918.

1. The following Inter-battalion Reliefs will take place on the night - 23/24th January. :-
    (a) The Royal West Kent Regiment will relieve the Lancashire Fusiliers in the LEFT Sub-sector of the Brigade Front. The Lancashire Fusiliers, after Relief, will move back to Brigade Reserve, occupying Camp vacated by Manchester Regiment in J.35.d.
    (b) The Manchester Regiment will relieve the West Riding Regiment in the RIGHT Sub-sector of the Brigade Front. The West Riding Regiment, on Relief, will move back into position vacated by Royal West Kent Regiment and become Support Battalion.

2. Details of Relief and Arrangements for Guides will be mutually arranged between Os. C. concerned.

3. Patrolling will not be interfered with.

4. Sector Maps, "Defence Schemes", all Air Photos, Patrol Maps, Patrol Report Forms; also, anti-gas Appliances and Trench Stores will be handed over and Receipts obtained.

5. All Details of Work in Progress, and contemplated; also Working Parties, will be carefully handed over.

6. Disposition Maps will be submitted to Brigade Headquarters by 6.0 pm., 24th.

7. Completion of Reliefs will be reported to Brigade Headquarters by the Code words - "3.70. received".

8. ACKNOWLEDGE.

Issued at 9.0 pm.

Copy No 1 to Bde.H.Q.
        2 to War Diary.
        3 to Staff Captain.
        4 to O.C., Signals.
        5 to B.I.O.
        6 to Lan. Fus.
        7 to W.Rid. Regt.
        8 to R.W.Kent Regt.
        9 to Manch. Regt.
       10 to M.G.Coy.
       11 to T.M.Bty.
       12 to 50th Inf.Bde.
       13 to 71st Inf.Bde.
       14 to 17th Division.
       15 to 79th F.A.Bde.
       16 to A.F.A.Bde. (93rd)

J.R. Kindley Captain,
A/Brigade Major,
52nd Infantry Brigade.

ORDERS
F

Secret   Copy No 6
                    Hargl.
                    Operation Orders 23
                                    27/1/18

1. **Relief.** The Battalion will be
   relieved to night 27/28th inst
   in the left Sub Sector
   by 10th Btn LANCASHIRE FUS.
   and will move into
   Brigade Res at the
   Stagg Sheap I.35.d.15.60.

2. **Dispositions.** As follows:-
   L FRONT B Coy relieved by C Coy L.F.
   L SUPPORT A   "   "   D   "   "
   R FRONT   C   "   "   B   "   "
   R SUPPORT D   "   "   A   "   "

3. **Guides**
   Front Companies will detail
   1 Guide per post to meet
   incoming Companies at
   Company HQ at 5.30 pm.
   No other Guides will be
   required.

4. **Trench Stores**
   Will be handed over &
   duplicate receipts obtained
   one copy to be sent to
   Batt HQ by 9.0 am the
   following morning.

Sheet II

5. Gum Boots

Ankle boots will be worn & Gum Boots carried to point on road 50 yards SW of Support Bn HQ where Transport will be waiting. O.C. Companies must ensure that all Gum Boots on Charge are brought out of the line & handed over to Corporal in charge of loading & a receipt obtained.

6. Lewis Guns

will be carried by Companies to Cooks road. K 14 C 35.95 300 yards E of SUPPORT Bn HQ where Transport will meet Coys.

7. Maudslam Packs
PETROL
TINS

Will be loaded on same limber as Lewis Guns. Every Petrol Tin must be brought out of the line also Coy Stretchers will be loaded

Sheet III

8. Advance
   Party

   1/R Supt, 1 NCO per Coy
   + 1 NCO from H.Q
   will report to Bn.
   H.Q at 2.30 pm. They
   will proceed to the
   Slagg Heap & take
   over from Opposite Numbers
   of Lancashire Fus.
   The NCO will then
   return to Support
   BN HQ at 7.0 pm and
   act as Guides to
   Companies for new location

Cookers
   With hot meal will
   meet Coys on arrival
   at Slagg Heap.

Blankets
   1 Blanket per man will
   be at the Slagg Heap

Completion of
   Relief
   To be notified to HQ
   as follows:-

A	AERIAL
B	BAT
C	CALTHORPE
D	DOUGLAS

Issued at
Copies to C.O.
         Companies
         File
         WD.

A.Wenham 2/L
adjt
No 5

SECRET   3/4 R.W. KENT Regt   180
D.O. N° 23

1. An inter Company relief will take place tonight
    "B" Coy relieves "A" Coy
    "C" "   " "   " "D" "

2. Arrangements for relief will be arranged mutually between O.C Companies.

3. Relief will take place as soon as possible after dark, so as not to interfere with the night's work.

4. All work orders are being issued seperately by Major WAITE

5. Patrols will be found tonight by FRONT LINE Coys. Intelligence Officer will arrange with OC B & C Coys as to the time the Patrols will go out & what special information is required.

6. Completion of relief will be reported by Fullerphone as follows:-
     A - ABDULLA
     B - BEESWING
     C - CAPSTAN
     D - DERESZKE

7. <u>Rations</u> The two Front Line Companies will draw their rations the relief takes place, & take them up to the Front Line

8. ACKNOWLEDGE

Issued at 1-0 pm

Copies to
    OC Coys
    FILE
    W.D.

JH Wynyham
Actg Adjt
HUGE

Secret   Copy No 8

52ND INFANTRY BRIGADE O.O.223.

Ref Maps
17th Div. Map
T.3., 1/10,000
MOEUVRES,
1/20,000.

26th January 1918.

1. The following Inter-Battalion Reliefs will take place on the night - 27/28th January:-

    (a) The Lancashire Fusiliers will relieve the Royal West Kent Regiment in the LEFT Sub-sector of the Brigade Front. The Royal West Kent Regiment, after Relief, moving back into Brigade Reserve, occupying Camp vacated by Lancashire Fusiliers in J.35.d.

    (b) The West Riding Regiment will relieve Manchester Regiment in the RIGHT Sub-sector of the Brigade Front. On Relief, the Manchester Regiment will occupy positions vacated by West Riding Regiment and become Support Battalion.

2. Details of Reliefs and arrangements for Guides will be arranged between Os. C. concerned.

3. Patrolling will not be interfered with.

4. Sector Maps, "Defence Schemes", all Air Photos, Patrol Maps, Patrol Report Forms; also Anti-gas Appliances and Trench Stores will be handed over and Receipts obtained.

5. All Details of work in Progress, and contemplated; also Working Parties, will be carefully handed over.

6. Disposition Maps will be submitted to Brigade Headquarters by 6.0 pm., 28th instant.

7. Completion of Reliefs to be reported to Brigade Headquarters in "D.A.E." - Lancashire Fusiliers wiring 12 figures - West Riding Regiment 24 figures - Royal West Kent Regiment and Manchester Regiment 36 figures.

8. ACKNOWLEDGE.

Issued at 9.0 pm.

Copy No 1 to Bde. H.Q.
       2 to War Diary.
       3 to Staff Captain.
       4 to O.C., Signals.
       5 to B.T.O.
       6 to Lan. Fus.
       7 to W.Rid. Regt.
       8 to R.W.Kent Regt.
       9 to Manch. Regt.
      10 to M.G.Coy.
      11 to T.L.Bty.
      12 to 51st Inf.Bde.
      13 to 16th Inf.Bde.
      14 to 17th Division.
      15 to 79th F.A.Bde.
      16 to 93rd A.F.A.Bde.

F.R. Lindley Captain,
A/Brigade Major,
52nd Infantry Brigade.

ORDERS
G

SECRET   7/4 ROYAL WEST KENT REGT   COPY N° 5
OPERATION ORDERS 24

30-1-18

RELIEF 1. The 52nd Inf Bde will be relieved by the 50th Inf Bde on the night 31st Jan/1st Feb in the Left Sub Sector of the Div Front, & on relief will move into Divisional Reserve.
     The Battn will be relieved in the present location by 6th DORSET REGT, companies by opposite numbers, & on relief will move into camp at J34.D.

DETAILED RELIEF 2. Companies on completion of relief will march back independently to camp at J34.D & occupy accommodation of opposite numbers of 7th YORKS REGT.

ADVANCE PARTY 3. OC Coys & RSM for HQ will detail 1 NCO + 4 men to proceed to camp J34.D & take over from opposite numbers of 7th YORKS. This party will parade under Lt FLEMING at 2.0pm outside B.H.Q. The NCOs detailed for this party will meet companies at entrance to new camp & guide them to respective quarters.
   pr Coy A NCO & of 6th DORSET REGT will report to OC Coys during the morning of 31st inst to take over accommodation in present location. They will act as guides to incoming Coys of 6th DORSET REGT.

LEWIS GUNS 4. Lewis Guns on AA duty will remain mounted until relieved by guns of 6th DORSET REGT & will be re-mounted in new location. The two AA mountings will also be taken to new camp

SHEET 2

TRANSPORT 5. Transport Officer will arrange for transport to report to present camp after delivering rations to J34 D. Officers valises, mess Boxes Lewis Guns, except guns on duty, will be ready for loading at 3.30 p.m. Maltese cart with M.O. stores will also be ready for loading at this hour.

DRESS & BLANKETS 6. Fighting Order, overcoats, jerkins. Blankets to be rolled & carried on top of haversack.

TEAS 7. Will be under Coy arrangements.

RELIEF COMPLETE 8. Will be notified to H.Q by runners.

9. ACKNOWLEDGE.

Actg Adjt
3/4 ROYAL WEST KENT REGT

Issued at
Copies to
1-4 O.C Coys
5 H.Q
6 W.D.

O C Coy

Amendment to O O N° 24

ROUTE — On relief Companies will march back independently to PHIPPS CAMP via SLAGG HEAP at J.34.D thence to BERTINCOURT, thence via BERTINCOURT – HAPLINCOURT ROAD to PHIPPS CAMP.

BLANKETS will be rolled in bundles of 10 by Coys & be ready for loading at 3.30pm.

LEWIS GUNS Lewis Guns, Stores etc will be ready for loading at 3.30pm.

GUIDES N C O or men sent forward as advance party will meet Companies at Rd junction J.2.D.0.4 where HAPLINCOURT Road joins BERTINCOURT, & guide Coys to accommodation allotted to them in PHIPPS CAMP.

COOKERS will move off with the Transport. Estimated time of departure 5.30pm.

Lieut
Actg Adjt
HUGE

31/1/18

"C" Form.
MESSAGES AND SIGNALS.

Army Form C. 2123
(In books of 100.)

No. of Message ....

Prefix....Code....Words....	Received. From ..N5Y... By...............	Sent, or sent out. At............m. To............ By............	Office Stamp
£ s d			
Charges to Collect			
Service Instructions.			

Handed in at .... Office .... m. Received .... m.

TO Hoge

*Sender's Number	Day of Month	In reply to Number	A A A
MX 61	27		
4	BO 224	g 30th	aaa
Table	attached	Serial	1 HORBY
units	to	1 34 D	serial
4	HOGE	move	4
PHIPPS	camp	aaa	HORBY
HUSK	and	BTo	HUSK
to	acknowledge	aaa	Added
All recipients BO 224			

FROM HUSK
TIME & PLACE

*This line should be erased if not required.

SECRET   52nd Infantry Brigade Order No. 224.   Copy No. 8

Ref: Maps.
17th Divisional
Map 1:5 40,000,
and 57c 1:20,000

30th January 1918.

1. The 52nd Infantry Brigade (less M.G. Coy) will be relieved by the 50th Infantry Brigade (less M.G. Coy) on the night 31st Jan/1st Feb. in the Left Subsector of the Divisional Front.

2. The relief will take place in accordance with the attached table.
   On relief the 52nd Inf. Bde. will take over the accommodation vacated by the 50th Inf. Bde. and will be in Divisional Reserve.

3. The usual proportion of guides will be detailed for the incoming units.

4. Advance parties of the 52nd Inf. Bde. will proceed to their respective destinations on the morning of the 31st inst.

5. All Defence Schemes - Work in hand - General policy and Trench Stores will be handed over.
   Only maps as detailed in S.S.99 will be handed over.

6. Details of relief and guides will be arranged direct between O's. C. concerned.

7. Completion of reliefs will be notified to Bde. H.Q. by the code sentence "NIL DESPERANDUM".

8. Command of the Left Sector will pass from G.O.C. 52nd Inf. Bde. to G.O.C. 50th Inf. Bde. at 10am on 1st Feb.

9. The 52nd M.G. Coy. will be relieved by 50th M.G. Coy. on the night 2nd February.
   Details of relief to be arranged direct between O's.C concerned.
   Completion of relief will be reported to Bde. H.Q. in B.A.B. code and repeated to 50th Inf. Bde.

10. Acknowledge.
    Issued at 7.30 pm.

Copy No. 1 to Bde. H.Q.
       2 to W.R. Regt.
       3 to Staff Captain
       4 to Cable Section
       5 to B.T.O.
       6 to Lancs Fus.
       7 to W. Rid. R.
       8 to R. W. Kent R.
       9 to March R.
      10 to M.G. Coy
      11 to T.M. Bty
      12 to 51st Bde.
      13 to 16th Bde.
      14 to 50th Bde.
      15 to 79th F.A. Bde.
      16 to 83rd A.F.A. Bde.
      17 to 116 Coy R.E.
      18 to Supply Officer
      19 to No. 1 Coy Train
      20 to 17th Division

J.R. Ruxley
a/Brigade Major
52nd Infantry Brigade

Table issued with 52nd Infantry Brigade Order No. 224.

Serial No.	Unit	Date	From	To	Relieved By.	Remarks.
1.	West Riding Regt	night of 9/10th	Right Front Line	PHIPPS CAMP	Yorkshire Regt	By train from HERMIES
2.	Lancashire Fus.	-do-	Left Front Line	HERMIES	West Yorkshire Regt	
3.	Manchester Regt	-do-	Support	SAUNDERS CAMP	East Yorkshire Regt	By train from HERMIES
4.	Kings Own Yorks Regt	-do-	Reserve	CAMP J.34.B	Dorset Regt	
5.	52nd T.M. Bty.	-do-	Line	HERRICK CAMP	50th T.M. Bty.	
6.	52nd Bde. HQ.	1st Oct.	J.26.B.7.3.	Q.4.D.8.7.	50th Bde. HQ.	By march route
7.	52nd M.G. Coy.	night of 9/10th	Line	SAUNDERS CAMP	50th M.G. Coy.	By train from HERMIES

An interval of 200 yards between Platoons will be maintained East of SLAG HEAP J.35.D.

Censored
Vol 9

52/17

War Diary

of

3/4th Bn. Royal West Kent Regt

From 1st February — To 28th February

Scouts & 7" Ent. Bn.

WAR DIARY
or
INTELLIGENCE SUMMARY

Army Form C. 2118.

(Erase heading not required.)

February 1918

Place	Date	Hour	Summary of Events and Information	Remarks and references to Appendices
PHIPPS CAMP	1/2/18		Instructions received for the entraining & entrainment.	
	5/2/18		Draft left for the 8th Battalion Royal Warwickshire Regt. consisting of the following officers. 2/Lt W.J. Kay & 56 O.R's and one newly commissioned officer. The remaining officers were also posted to the R.W. Regt as follows:— 2/Lt Burham, 2/Lt Jackson, 2/Lt C.D. Pullinger, 2/Lt Tibby, 2/Lt Shepley, 2/Lt Camp at 11.30am & started 24 March Rte & remained for ROISEL.	ORDERS attached Marked A
	6/2/18		Draft left for England, under Sgt Major Kimball, consisting of the following officers & captains J.A. Vanner & J. Peake & 58 O.R's. 2/Lt A.C. Marshall and other ranks 26 of 2 returning to details of their Companies.	ORDERS attached marked B

WAR DIARY
or
INTELLIGENCE SUMMARY

Army Form C. 2118.

February 1918 of The 3/4 Bn. Royal West Regiment

Place	Date	Hour	Summary of Events and Information	Remarks and references to Appendices
Shelter Camp	6/2/18		Continued. The following Officers were also posted to the 6th K.R.R. Regt. returning from leave.— Lieut A.C. Clifford & 2/Lt C.C. Bunge MC. The party embarked at Shepp Camp at 6.30 am and were conveyed to entraining point FREMICOURT.	
	6/2/18		Major K.C.N. Nairn retired by 7th K.Div. to take over from to O.C. Reinforcement Camp Lieut J.E. Moneilton proceeds to 19 K Division 1 March probation as signalling officer.	
	10/2/18		Draft of two 7th Battalion Royal West Kent Regiment comprising of the following	Other Ranks marked noted C.

WAR DIARY
or
INTELLIGENCE SUMMARY

Army Form C. 2118.

February 1916

Place	Date	Hour	Summary of Events and Information	Remarks and references to Appendices
Huppy Camp	10/7/16		Soon turned Captain Shatto. Captain T. Agnett 17th R. Warrington, of Ein Murphy of all ranks and on this Knuth of 6:70 Companies. The following Officers rec'd also first to the 7th Battalion were few rested on returning from leave. Lt. McNeally, & Cpl. Steer. A draft under command of 2nd Lieut. Camp at 9.30am proceeded to MONDESCOURT on the NOYON - CHAUNY Road. The remainder of the Battalion including the following officers Lt. Col. E. Jones Major C Stopher, Lt. Fleming, 2nd Lt. Newnham marched to the other Ranks of Head-quarters Huppa Camp to Volu Wood.	
	11/7/16			

Army Form C. 2118.

WAR DIARY
or
INTELLIGENCE SUMMARY

(Erase heading not required.) The 3/4th R. West Kent Regt.

February 1918

Place	Date	Hour	Summary of Events and Information	Remarks and references to Appendices
VEL-U WOOD	11/2/18		No 5016 R.S.M. Martin. F. awarded Croix de Guerre (Belgian)	
	13/2/18		2/Lt J.R. Henham proceeded to England for six months. Lt J.S. Fleming resumed duties of adjutant.	
	16/2/18		(?)/Lt J.B. Kennedy struck off strength and 17th Div'n wire a. 503. of 13/2/18	
	18/2/18		3 candidates for commissions to England (Sergts Batt, Anthony & L/Cpl Potter)	
	19/2/18		Major A.S. Grover reported from base to help in settling up accounts of unit. 1 candidate for commission to England - Sergt Wood	
	20/2/18		1 candidate for commission to England - Cpl Scott	
	22/2/18		Capt A.L. Walker R.A.M.C. orders to join 7/Batt Yorks + Lancs.	
	27/2/18		Lt J.S. Fleming, Lt F. Fairhurst, 2/Lt H.A. Southgate + 2/Lt P.O.R. Kempson to 7/Lt Suffolk ching Batt: under authority of 17th Div: Letter O.F. 374/5/58 of 20/2/18	
	28/2/18		Major K.C. Kramer reported on completion of duty as O.E. Reinforcements, V Corps	
	29/2/18		Major A.E. Jones returned to Base	

K.C.Kramer Major
3/4th R.West Kent Regt.

SECRET.   Copy No. _____

3/4th. Battn. Royal West Kent Regiment.

4-2-18

ORDERS No. 25.

1. Reference the absorbing of the Battalion into other Battalions of the Royal West Kent Regiment, the party already detailed for the 8th Battalion will move to-morrow, the 5th instant ; this party will consist of "A" Coy. and details of other Companies.

2. The following Officers have also been posted to this Battalion :-
   ~~Major K. C. H. Warner,~~   Captain F. C. Needham,
   Lieut. J. H. Selfe,   2nd-Lieut. C. D. Whitbourn,
   2nd-Lieut. E. G. Quested.
   Lieut. J. H. Selfe & 2nd-Lieut. E. G. Quested will proceed with the party. ~~Major Warner will proceed at a later date.~~
   Captain Needham and 2nd-Lieut. C. D. Whitbourn will join the Battalion on returning from leave.

3. A. Details.
   This party will parade at 9.0 a.m., rolls will be checked by Sergt. Ward, and their packs will be taken off and the men will fall out until 10.30 a.m. when the party will march to YTRES Station where it will entrain and proceed to ROISEL.

   B. Dress.
   Full Marching Order. 1 blanket per man. Water Bottles must be full.

   C. RATIONS.
   "A" Coy. Cooker will proceed with this party to the station. Dinners will be served there - the remainder of the day's rations will be carried on the man. Rations for the 6th instant will be carried in bulk.

4. Transport.
   The Transport Officer will arrange for transport as follows :-
   Two limbers to take Officers(Valises, Coy. Mess Box, and Rations for the 6th instant. He will also detail 1 Riding Horse, to report to 2nd-Lieut. E. G. Quested at 10.25 a.m.
   Transport will proceed at the rear of the party.

5. Band.
   Those who are proceeding with the party will parade at 10.25 a.m. and the Band will play the party to the station. Instruments will be carried back from the station in one of the limbers.

6. Train Arrangements.
   Lieut. J. S. Fleming and 2 O.R. of H.Q. will report to R. T. O., YTRES, at 12.0 noon. He will send one of these men back to meet the party on the Bertincourt-Ytres Road to guide the party to the station.

7. Any men wishing to see this party off will parade in Church Parade Order at 9.30 a.m. - under 2nd-Lieut. H. R. Rimington - on same parade ground.

8. ACKNOWLEDGE.

                                          [signature]
                                    2nd-Lieut. & Acting Adjutant,
                                    3/4th. Battn. Royal West Kent Regiment.

Issued at _____ p.m.

   Copies to :-

   1. C. O.   6. Lieut. J. S. Fleming.
   2. O.C. "A" Coy.   7. Actg. Q. M.
   3. O.C. "B" Coy.   8. T. O.
   4. O.C. "C" Coy.   9. R. S. M.
   5. O.C. "D" Coy.   10. Sergt. Underdown, H. J.

SECRET.

Copy No. 8

3/4th. Battn. Royal West Kent Regiment.

5-2-18.

ORDERS No. 26.

1. Reference the absorbing of the Battalion into other Battalions of the Royal West Kent Regiment, the party already detailed for the 6th. Battalion, will move to-morrow, the 6th. instant ; this party will consist of "B" Coy. and details of other Companies.

2. The following Officers have also been posted to the Battalion :-
   Captain T. L. Tanner.
   Lieut. V. A. Weeks.
   Lieut. D. B. Brook.
   Lieut. W. C. Clifford.
   2nd-Lieut. C. C. Berger, M.C.
   2nd-Lieut. A. C. Broadbent.

   Captain Tanner, Lieut. Weeks, Lieut. Brooks & 2nd-Lieut. Broadbent will proceed with the party. Lieut. Clifford & 2nd-Lieut. Berger will join the Battalion on returning from leave.

3. Details.
   A. This party will parade at 6.0 a.m. ; the rolls will be checked, after which the party will enbus at Phipps Camp at 6.30 a.m. and conveyed to Entraining Point, FREMICOURT.
   B. Dress :- Full Marching Order, 1 Blanket per man. Water Bottles must be full.
   C. Rations :- Party will have breakfast before it moves off. The unconsumed portion of the day's ration will be carried on the man. Rations for the 7th. and 8th instant will be taken in bulk.
   D. Mess Boxes & Officers' Valises, including those belonging to Officers on leave, will be taken with the party.

4. ACKNOWLEDGE.

2nd-Lieut. & Acting Adjutant,
3/4th. Battn. Royal West Kent Regiment.

Issued at 8.20. p.m.

Copies to :-

1. C. O.
2. O.C. "B" Coy.
3. O.C. "C" Coy.
4. O.C. "D" Coy.
5. Actg. Q. M.
6. T. O.
7. R. S. M.
8. War Diary.
9. File.

SECRET. No. 4

3/4th. Battn. Royal West Kent Regiment.

ORDERS No. 27.   9-2-18.

(1) The draft detailed to join the 7th. Battalion, Royal West Kent Regiment, will move to-morrow, the 10th instant. This draft will consist of all Other Ranks remaining with the Battalion with the exception of those detailed to remain behind with Battalion Headquarters, ~~and~~ the following Officers *will proceed*
        Captain E. Watts.
        Lieut. F. C. Levett.
        2nd-Lieut. H. R. Rimington.
        2nd-Lieut. G. M. Heaphy.
        2nd-Lieut. C. M. Holmes.
2nd-Lieuts. K. Blew and J. H. Heatley will join the 7th. Battalion on returning from leave, and 2nd-Lieut. S. H. Webb on leaving Rest Station.

(2) Details.
  (a) This party will parade at 8.45 a.m., and the rolls will be checked by Sergt. Ward, after which the party will enbus outside the Camp at 9.30 a.m., and proceed to MONDESCOURT on the NOYON-CHAUMAY Road.
  (b) Dress :- Full marching order, ~~one~~ blankets per man. Water bottles must be full.
  (c) Rations :- The party will have breakfast before it moves off. The unexpended portion of the day's ration will be carried on the man. Rations for the 11th. & 12th. instant will be carried in bulk.
  (d) Mess Boxes and Officers' Valises, including those belonging to Officers on leave, will be taken with the party, *also 1 extra blanket per man*

(3) ACKNOWLEDGE.

                2nd-Lieut. & Acting Adjutant,
                3/4th. Battn. Royal West Kent Regiment.

Issued at 6.40 p.m.

Copies to :-

1. O.C. "C" Coy.   5. R. S. M.
2. O.C. "D" Coy.   6. H. Q. Mess.
3. Q. M.   7. War Diary.
4. T. O.   8. File.

(C O P Y).   To be communicated verbally.

The Officer Commanding,

    3/4th. Royal West Kents.

       In bidding farewell to the 3/4th. Royal West Kents the G.O.C. wishes to express his appreciation of their service while they have been with the Division under his Command.

       In everything they have been called upon to do they have shown the same fine spirit; and he has been fully confident that whatever the task, the officers and men would have carried it through.

       The G.O.C. desires you to convey his thanks to all ranks and regrets that he cannot do so personally.

He wishes you and all officers and men under your command the best of luck in the future.

                      (Signed)   W. N. NICHOLSON, Lieut.-Colonel,

                               A.A. & Q.M.G., 17th. Division.

3/2/18.

www.ingramcontent.com/pod-product-compliance
Lightning Source LLC
Chambersburg PA
CBHW081427300426
44108CB00016BA/2317